CHILDREN, FAMILIES
& COMMUNITIES
CONTEXTS AND CONSEQUENCES

Second Edition   Edited by Jennifer M. Bowes

OXFORD
UNIVERSITY PRESS

OXFORD

UNIVERSITY PRESS

253 Normanby Road, South Melbourne, Victoria 3205, Australia

Oxford University Press is a department of the University of Oxford.
It furthers the University's objective of excellence in research, scholarship,
and education by publishing worldwide in

Oxford New York

Auckland Bangkok Buenos Aires Cape Town Chennai
Dar es Salaam Delhi Hong Kong Istanbul Karachi Kolkata
Kuala Lumpur Madrid Melbourne Mexico City Mumbai Nairobi
São Paulo Shanghai Taipei Tokyo Toronto

OXFORD is a trade mark of Oxford University Press
in the UK and in certain other countries

Copyright © Jennifer Bowes 1999, 2004
First published 1999
Reprinted 2000, 2001, 2002, 2003
Second edition published 2004

National Library of Australia
Cataloguing-in-Publication data:

Children, families and communities: contexts and consequences.

2nd ed.
Bibliography.
Includes Index.
For undergraduate students.
ISBN 0 19 551735 0.

1. Socialization—Australia. 2. Environment and children—Australia.
3. Parent and child—Australia. 4. Family—Australia—Psychological aspects.
5. Children and adults—Australia—Psychological aspects. I. Bowes, Jennifer.

303.320994

Typeset by OUPANZS
Printed through Bookpac Production Services, Singapore

Contents

Figures and Table

Preface

This book is about the ways in which children, families and communities influence one another, and how different contexts can affect them all. Our interest stems from a concern with the well-being of children and their development into confident and competent members of society. Most contributors to the book come from a background of developmental psychology and wish to extend the growing focus in that field on development in context, moving away from past consideration of children as isolated individuals whose development proceeds regardless of context. In particular, we are concerned with exploring aspects of context for children growing up in Australia.

Our engagement with consideration of children, families and communities has led to a wider concern: a concern for the well-being of children, families and communities, and for their development.

Development implies a process and some kind of desirable outcome. We see outcomes in a contextual way. Rather than focus on competently functioning individual children and individual families, we want to put the emphasis on successful interconnections among children, families and communities. An optimum outcome for individuals is to operate well and to contribute within their families and communities. A family's participation in the life of the wider community is seen as a goal for family development as well as an index of the conditions for development of children. Ultimately this can lead to a stronger social unit, one in which individuals provide support for one another and work well together. We hold a view of individuals as interdependent rather than entirely independent, a view contrary to prevailing views in developmental psychology that may take contextual influences into account but see them in terms of their influence on independently functioning individuals.

In examining the role of context in children's development, we are not claiming that context is all that needs to be considered in human development or in the functioning of families and communities. We are not concerned with exploring in this book the important question of the relative influence of environment and genetics on development—a growing focus in developmental science as we learn more about genetic codes.

Our claim is rather that children, families and communities cannot be considered apart from one another. Any attempt to analyse children's development or to consider policy that might enhance the well-being of children in our society must take into account the families of those children and the communities to which they belong. It is important to remember, however, that the effect is not one-way, with context affecting children only. Children are active participants in the daily lives of families and communities and influence and change their families and communities through their involvement. In doing so, they are part of the construction of the contexts that surround them. Sometimes the influence of children on their families and communities can be linked to individual characteristics. Children with disabilities, for instance, affect family dynamics and, either directly or through their special needs and the intervention of parents, adults with disabilities and other community figures, they can also influence community attitudes, resources and services.

The book attempts to lay down some theoretical groundwork for exploring these mutual influences. Such analysis is important for understanding and promoting through effective social change the development and well-being of children and the strengthening of families and communities. We felt that this kind of analysis has not been readily available to students or practitioners who work with children and families in the fields of health, education or welfare, particularly in Australia.

In many ways the Australian contexts in which children and families live are different from those elsewhere. As Robyn Hartley has written, 'Australia has a unique history, important elements of which are an indigenous population, a British colonial past and recent extensive immigration of people from many different countries and cultures'.[1]

There is also great diversity in this country within individuals, families and communities. For example, although Australia is a relatively prosperous country with one of the world's leading health systems, the Indigenous population suffers from health problems that are more characteristic of the Third World. Children whose parents are employed have different lives and different opportunities from those whose parents are unemployed. Families living in the isolation of outback Australia have different lives from those of families in big cities. Many children, families and communities suffer from social exclusion[2] due to the widening gap in financial, social and educational resources between rich and poor in this country.[3] There are multiple differences in contexts, and multiple pathways by which contexts can affect children, families and communities. Such diversity suggests that our discussions concerning contexts, their interconnections and their consequences are relevant also beyond Australia.

Our aim in this book is not to catalogue differences in context, but to analyse the ways in which those contexts affect the lives of children and families. However, to explain why or how children, families and communities develop as they do, a concern with context is not sufficient. Individual characteristics also need to be discussed because people react in different ways to what appears to be the same context. For example, some children thrive at school whereas others struggle and are miserable. In fact, children in the same family generally differ more than they resemble one another and this holds true even when genetic effects have been taken into account.[4] Differences between siblings can be explained by a combination of personal characteristics and the different contextual influences they encounter inside and outside their families.

The book examines contextual differences on several levels, beginning with the individual, exploring the contexts in which children and families are involved, and ending with issues of social policy. The introductory chapter in Part A explores the central concepts of context and consequences, and acquaints the reader with the theoretical framework used throughout the book. Part B presents three examples of individual characteristics that can affect well-being and development in children, families and communities. The characteristics—disability, ethnicity and gender—were chosen to exemplify ways in which individual characteristics interact with contexts to produce a range of outcomes. This does not imply that other child characteristics such as age or temperament are less important. A range of individual characteristics could have been chosen for this kind of analysis. Equally, the characteristics of family and community members other than children also interact with contexts, resulting in consequences for children, families and communities. Depression or substance abuse in mothers, for example, has consequences for their children, families and local communities,[5] and the quality of teaching staff in child care can affect children[6] as well as their families and communities.

Part C examines the effects of three contexts that directly involve most children: families, schools and other educational settings, and the local community. Community influences are highlighted by an examination of the consequences of isolation or diminished community connectedness for families and children. The final chapters in Part D look beyond face-to-face contexts to issues of social policy that are more distant from individual children and families but nevertheless exert a strong influence on their lives. The three areas explored—child protection policies in response to child neglect and abuse, the removal of Indigenous children from their families as a result of government policy, and the changes in provision of child care in Australia in relation to changes in social policy—illustrate the ways in which the wider society can intervene directly in the lives of children, families and communities.

Notes

1   R. Hartley, 'Families, Values and Change: Setting the Scene', in *Families and Cultural Diversity in Australia*, ed, R. Hartley, Allen & Unwin, Sydney, 1995, p. 1.

2   J. Kahn & S.B. Kamerman, *Beyond Child Poverty: The Social Exclusion of Children*, Institute for Child and Family Policy, Columbia University, New York, 2003.

3   B. Birrell, J. Dibden & J. Wainer, *Regional Victoria: Why the Bush is Hurting*, Centre for Population and Urban Research, Monash University, Melbourne, 2000; A. Taylor & B. Birrell, 'Communities on the Metropolitan Periphery: The Sunshine Coast and Cranbourne Compared', paper presented at the People, Places, Partnerships Conference, University of New South Wales, Sydney, April 2003.

4   R. Plomin & D. Daniels, 'Why are Children in the Same Family so Different from Each Other?', *Behavioral and Brain Sciences*, 10, 1994, pp. 1–16.

5   M.H. Bornstein, 'Parenting Infants', in *Handbook of Parenting*, vol. 1, ed, M.H. Bornstein, Lawrence Erlbaum, Mahwah, NJ, 2002, pp. 3–43.

6   R. Roupp, J. Travers, F. Glantz & C. Coelen, *Children at the Centre: Final Report of the National Day Care Study*, Abt Associates, Cambridge, MA, 1979.

Acknowledgments

This book is a result of the active collaboration of all its contributors. As the idea developed for the first edition and the theoretical structure of the book was elaborated, lively meetings of the contributors took place, which produced much of its intellectual content. We are grateful to all of the authors for their involvement in this process and for their careful revision of chapters for the second edition, but owe a special debt to two contributors. Jacqueline Goodnow and Ailsa Burns provided inspiration for the book with their *Children and Families in Australia* (published in 1985), and both encouraged its development, contributing generously with their ideas and experience. Alan Hayes co-edited the first edition, taking a great interest in the book from its initial planning to its rewriting for the second edition.

I wish to acknowledge also the excellent work done by Sandra Wong and Margaret Bowes in preparation and checking of the manuscript and thank Tim Fullerton for his careful editing of the book. Thanks are due to Brown & Benchmark for permission to reproduce a figure in this book. Table 1 on page 167 from the ABS *National Survey of Indigenous People*, 1994, cited in HREOC, p. 14, is copyright of the Commonwealth of Australia, reproduced with permission. All contributors to the book have had great support from children, families, and academic or other professional communities. I particularly wish to thank Nigel Stapledon and our children for their encouragement and assistance in bringing this second edition to completion.

Jennifer Bowes

Contributors

Jennifer Bowes is Associate Professor and Head of the Institute of Early Childhood, Macquarie University. She has a research background in educational and developmental psychology. Her teaching and research have been in the area of child development, parenting and the interconnections between children, families and communities. She is director of Child, Family and Community Education @ Macquarie, a professional development program, and team leader of the Child Care Choices research project, a longitudinal investigation of the effects of multiple and changeable child care in the first three years of life on the development of young children. She is also involved in the Longitudinal Study of Australian Children, and the Health for Life project, which investigates links between parents' work and children's health and well-being.

Deborah Brennan is an Associate Professor and Head of the Department of Government and International Relations at the University of Sydney. She specialises in Australian politics, gender and politics and the comparative study of welfare states. She was a founding member of the National Association of Community Based Children's Services and is currently the ACOSS policy adviser on child care. Her publications include *The Politics of Australian Child Care: Philanthropy to Feminism and Beyond* (2nd edn, Cambridge University Press, 1998).

Ailsa Burns is a Research Associate in the Department of Psychology, Macquarie University. Her longstanding research interest in the changing nature of families in Australia has led to the publication of many articles and books, including *Children and Families in Australia* (with J.J. Goodnow, Allen & Unwin, 1985), *Australian Women: Contemporary Feminist Thought* (with N. Grieve, Oxford University Press, 1994), and *Mother-headed Families and Why They Have Increased* (Erlbaum, 1994). Her current interests include family aspects of aging.

Kate Burns is a lawyer with a background in anti-discrimination, human rights and international law. From 1991 until 1997 she worked with the Human Rights and Equal Opportunity Commission. While there, she was the senior researcher and writer with the Commission's National Inquiry into the Separation of Aboriginal and Torres Strait Islander Children from their Families. Since then she has taught and practised in the area of anti-discrimination law in the university sector and worked as an in-house lawyer at the University of Sydney.

Judy Cashmore is an Associate Professor in the Faculty of Law, University of Sydney and an Honorary Research Associate at the Social Policy Research Centre, University of New South Wales. Her research has focused on children's involvement with and perceptions of legal and child welfare processes. This includes investigating children's role as child witnesses; research into their participation in decisions concerning residence and contact following parental separation; reports on systems abuse (harm caused by the very systems that are set up to protect children) and on physical punishment; and a longitudinal study of wards leaving out-of-home care. She is involved in a number of government and non-government committees, including the New South Wales Child Death Review Team, the Ministerial Advisory Council, and heads the Board of the Association of Childrens Welfare Agencies in New South Wales and Defence for Children International (Australia).

Pamela Coutts is an Associate Professor and Head of Department in the School of Education, Macquarie University. Her research interests are in the area of social cognition as it applies to educational issues and include children's ideas about responsibility, student decision-making about subject choice in secondary school and perceptions about homework. Professor Coutts is responsible for both undergraduate and postgraduate courses in educational psychology within the School of Education.

Monica Cuskelly is a Senior Lecturer in Special Education at the Fred and Eleanor Schonell Special Education Centre at the University of Queensland. Her research interests include the development of people with Down syndrome, the impact on families of having a child with a disability, and the development of self-regulation in normally developing children and those with an intellectual disability. Dr Cuskelly is Co-director of the Schonell Centre Down Syndrome Project.

Maureen Fegan is Director of the Early Childhood Road Safety Education Program at the Institute of Early Childhood, Macquarie University. She has a longstanding involvement with community groups, including those in rural and remote areas of Australia, with particular emphasis on facilitating provision of innovative and flexible early childhood services that support families.

Jacqueline J. Goodnow is a Professorial Research Fellow in the School of Behavioural Sciences, Macquarie University. She has a long-term interest in cross-generational relationships and the ways in which individuals and their social or cultural contexts influence one another. Recent books include *Development According to Parents* (with W.A. Collins, Lawrence Erlbaum, 1990), *Men, Women and Household Work* (with J.M. Bowes, Oxford University Press, 1994) and *Cultural Practices as Contexts for Development* (edited with P. Miller & F. Kessel, Jossey-Bass, 1995). In recognition of her work she has been made a Companion of the Order of Australia (AC) and, in the USA, received the G. Stanley Hall Award for Distinguished Contributions to Developmental Psychology.

Norma Grieve is a Senior Associate, and formerly Reader, in the Department of Psychology, University of Melbourne. She is the co-editor of *Australian Women: Feminist Perspectives* (Oxford University Press, 1981), *Australian Women: New Feminist Perspectives* (Oxford University Press, 1986) and *Australian Women: Contemporary Feminist Thought* (Oxford University Press, 1994). With Patricia Grimshaw, she introduced Women's Studies at the University of Melbourne.

Alan Hayes is Professor of Early Childhood Studies at the Institute of Early Childhood and Dean of the Australian Centre for Educational Studies at Macquarie University. He was foundation President of the Australasian Human Development Association, a Fellow of the Australian Psychological Society and the American Psychological Association, and an Alexander von Humboldt Research Fellow. His research on families and child development includes analysis of families in which one child has special needs, and such families' links to the community. He is extending this interest further to explore the influence of social networks on children and their families. Currently he is a member of the Board of Management of the Australian Institute of Family Studies, Chair of the Interim Committee for a New South Wales Institute of Teachers and Chair of the Australian Council for Children and Parenting.

Karen Menzies is an Aboriginal woman from the Wonnarua people of the Hunter Valley, New South Wales. She spent two years at the Human Rights and Equal Opportunity Commission with the National Inquiry Team that conducted the Stolen Generations Inquiry and produced the *Bringing Them Home* Report. She is a member of the National Social Policy Committee of the Australian Association of Social Workers and currently Chair of its Reconciliation and Indigenous Issues Working Party. She has extensive teaching and advisory experience in child protection, human rights, and Indigenous and cross-cultural issues.

Cathrine Neilsen-Hewett is a Lecturer at the Institute of Early Childhood, Macquarie University. Her research interests include links between children's in-school and out-of-school peer relationships and school adjustment and bullying in early childhood. Dr Neilsen-Hewett has lectured in courses on child and adolescent development at the University of Sydney and Macquarie University and is currently responsible for a third-year course, Families and Communities in a Culturally Diverse Society, and jointly responsible for a Masters course, Child Development in Context.

Johanna Watson is Principal Research Officer at the NSW Parenting and Research Centre, Department of Community Services. Her research and teaching interests in developmental psychopathology, in particular the influence of the social context on children's life chances, reflect her initial background as a clinical child psychologist. Her current research interests focus on child temperament, parenting and the quality of child care and other community services in relation to social and emotional development.

PART (A)

Contexts and Consequences

Contexts and Consequences:

Impacts on Children, Families and Communities

Jennifer Bowes and Alan Hayes

This chapter outlines the rise of interest in the interconnecting contexts of children, families and communities and the consequences of those interconnections. Families and communities can offer both opportunities and constraints for children's participation in the world and their general development, and the impact of context varies with the child's age and other characteristics such as disability, ethnicity and gender. The interest in context has led to descriptions of 'the ecology of childhood', and explorations of 'the cultural nature' of children's development.[1] It has led also to the recognition that—for the analysis of child development, family life or social policy—we need studies on the ways in which children, families and communities are interconnected. The pathways that lead to negative and positive consequences for individual children, families and communities also need close examination as do the best opportunities for intervention to enable a turning point in life trajectories.

The chapter begins with the assumptions made in this book about the meaning of context, and discusses the ways in which contexts need to be described to allow a greater understanding of their consequences for children and families. It goes on to provide an account of some of the approaches to context in the lives of children and families, looking particularly at the ecological model put forward by Urie Bronfenbrenner and the cultural development model proposed by Barbara Rogoff.[2]

We then introduce the broad model of contexts and consequences that has been used here as a framework for child–family–community interconnections. Two key features of this model are the bidirectionality of influence among the three elements (for example, families affect children and children affect families) and the ways that influence can 'bubble up' from the individual level to influence broader social policy or 'trickle down' from policy level to affect individual children, families or communities. In the discussion of consequences for children, families and communities, the challenges facing each of these three elements are examined in relation to the resources available for them from themselves, and each other element, to deal with challenges. In doing so, the concepts of risk, vulnerability, protective factors, resilience and developmental pathways are introduced and discussed in the context of the strengths-based approach to working with individuals, families and communities. The importance of these concepts in understanding the consequences of different person–context interactions, and in planning policy and prevention programs, is explored in relation to issues raised in later chapters of the book.

The meaning of context

This first section of the chapter is concerned with what we mean by context, how context has been described, and the aspects of context that need to be considered when we talk about the interconnections among children, families and communities. It is useful to consider some concrete examples, such as the hypothetical case of Nathan.

> Nathan is three and a half years old, and is a healthy, active and engaging child. He lives with his parents in the outer suburbs of an Australian city. Both parents have paid jobs, have a happy marital relationship and have completed high school education. Nathan's two older sisters, aged eight and ten, attend the local primary school and include Nathan in their games at home whether they are playing school or practising soccer. Nathan attends a long day care centre for two days per week, and his grandmother looks after him for one day, while his mother goes to work part-time. When at home with his mother on the other two week days and with both parents on the weekend, Nathan plays computer games, helps his mother cook, is read to by his parents and is taken to visit friends. Sometimes his father takes him to his workplace when he needs to collect paperwork to be completed at home.

What can we say about context from this example? The first point is that context is a *multiple* rather than a unitary term. It is misleading to assume that children below school age have only one context, namely the home. Young children like Nathan experience many contexts, inside and outside the home.

They are cared for by a range of different people (see Chapter 6 for the current situation in Australia). Within the one setting they have many different kinds of interactions, such as playing with siblings and being read to by parents, effectively experiencing multiple contexts.

Even at such an early age, children's lives include contexts in which they themselves are not directly involved, contexts such as Nathan's father's workplace and his sisters' school. We can see that context does not have to involve face-to-face contact. Nathan is learning about the workplace through going there with his father and watching his father work at home. He is learning about schoolwork from copying his sisters as they do their homework. The decision of the local council to put aside land for a park and to provide safe playground equipment for young children is also influencing Nathan's life. Context, then, can be experienced indirectly and still have considerable impact on the developing child.

These multiple contexts affect children's development through the opportunities they open up or the constraints they impose. Nathan is a fortunate child who is growing up in a context of high human and social capital (see Chapters 5 and 7 for more detail about these terms). He is offered many opportunities for learning. He knows a variety of contexts and his relationships with the people there are secure and non-threatening. He is a healthy and well-adjusted child—the kind of child that other people enjoy—so that his development is likely to be enhanced by the opportunity to interact with a wide variety of people.

What are the features of context that might constrain rather than open up opportunities for children? First, there are personal characteristics such as a difficult temperament. Aggressive children, for example, may experience fewer opportunities for successful and pleasurable interaction with other children and with adults than do their more amiable peers. As discussed in Chapter 5, family factors can also introduce constraints. Because of their characteristics or circumstances, some families restrict the opportunities available to their children through a lack of resources, psychological as well as financial, or through limited dealings with the world outside the family. Some communities, too, can be restrictive. Those that provide few resources to families and have impoverished social networks restrict the opportunities for children and families within them. (See Chapter 7 for an analysis of the role of communities and the effects of isolation.)

Descriptions of context

What is the best way to describe contexts? Let us look now at an example of context, a long day care centre set up especially to include disadvantaged children,[3] and consider its features.

The centre is located in an inner city street in the middle of public housing. It has two large indoor spaces, one used as a play space for children, the other used for sessions in which parents are taught how to play with their children and strategies to deal with the challenges of their own lives and with parenting. There is a small outside area with play equipment. Five staff and twenty-five children are present at any one time. Families are recruited to the centre by an outreach worker. Children are offered free child care so that parents can attend parent education and support sessions on site. Parents and children are required to attend a minimum number of sessions per week.

This description is plainly incomplete. It gives only an objective outline of the physical features of the context and some hints on the interactions that take place at the centre. It is also apparent from the description that this early childhood centre has been set up as part of a larger context in which society takes responsibility for the well-being of its children. In matters of child protection, the state intervenes in the family in a variety of ways (see Chapter 8). This centre is a clear representation of a set of wider social values and laws.

The other hidden aspect of this context, but one that is true of all contexts, is that it is always changing. From one day to the next, with different staff and different children and parents, and with different interactions occurring, the centre changes and keeps changing. Through their participation, the people involved are creating the context they also experience. For the people involved in the centre, it is not simply one context but multiple contexts. Staff, children and parents experience the centre in different ways: as a context for work, for social contact, for play, for learning or for multiple purposes. Each individual has a different emotional response to the centre, and this too is subject to change. One child, for example, may find it frightening; another may be fascinated by the new experiences. One parent may welcome the assistance and support available at the centre; another may find it threatening or humiliating. In this sense, contexts need to be seen subjectively in addition to being described objectively.

Our brief description of the centre did not contain many aspects of the context that might assist us in predicting consequences for children and families. We need to ask more questions. How do people interact in the centre, for example; how are values communicated; and how in this context are the families' strengths taken into account? We might ask what the participants expect to happen, what they think they are learning, and whether they believe that the skills learnt can be transferred to another context.

Contexts can be described in terms of the practices, activities or events that take place within them.[4] Each context also carries with it a type of 'social contract', a set of obligations and beliefs about responsibilities and the actions that should take place.[5] Contexts also have an emotional element. The responses of individuals to the setting and the relationships between individuals in the setting are of great importance when it comes to linking contexts with consequences.[6] Once these elements are included in descriptions of context, we can begin to make those connections.

In summary, contexts are more complex than they at first seem. Contexts are multiple, changing over time, as individuals themselves change. Perceptions of contexts are important, as are the expectations we hold about the opportunities and obligations associated with contexts. In addition, contexts come with a history and can be described in objective and subjective ways. Their influence on people is linked to emotional responses. These ideas about context come from a variety of theoretical models and research projects, and a brief review follows.

Models of context

Within studies of child development there are now widespread attempts to address the kind of criticism made by Oakley in 1994: 'the emphasis on childhood as an individual process unfolded from within has tended to neglect the impact on children and childhood of social and cultural contexts'.[7] Although there has always been interest in context in the past, increasing attention is now given to the contexts of development and how development and context interrelate.

A superficial view of context, which is less frequent in current psychological research, is seen in the 'social address' approach. This simplifies context by referring to an individual's membership of a broad social category such as socio-economic status or a particular ethnic group. Diversity within groups is not considered in this approach, nor is the possibility that people brought together under the same label may perceive their social group membership in a different way. In the discussion on ethnicity in Chapter 3, for example, we see that having an 'Aboriginal' or 'Chinese' identity is not a simple matter of social address. It involves people's perceptions of the meaning of the social group, their reasons for membership, and the constraints imposed by others on using the term.

Studies of context in child development have moved beyond this 'social address' model to consider the multiple influences of the social contexts in which most children are involved: family, school and the peer group. Early research studies documented the physical aspects of these contexts, and later studies looked at psychological aspects such as the nature of the interactions that occurred in these settings.[8]

While such studies are relevant and important, they do not account for all of the contextual influences on children's lives. It was the social ecological model put forward by Bronfenbrenner that moved thinking beyond the contexts in which children are immediately involved to consider also the effects of more distant contexts such as social policy and culture. In addition, Bronfenbrenner's model, influenced by Kurt Lewin's theory of dynamic psychology, extended Lewin's psychological 'life space' in order to 'confront the real world of interactions, relationships and contexts. Actions then lie at the adaptive interaction between the person and the environment'.[9]

Bronfenbrenner's Social Ecology Model

Figure 1 is a diagrammatic representation of Bronfenbrenner's model. Presented as an expanding set of contextual structures, his model has the developing child at its centre along with that child's particular characteristics such as age and gender. Each surrounding contextual layer is seen as nestled within the other 'like a set of Russian dolls',[10] and the relationship between child and setting is seen as a dynamic one. Bronfenbrenner explained it thus: 'The ecology of human development involves the scientific study of the progressive mutual accommodation between an active, growing human being and the changing properties of the immediate settings in which the developing person lives, as this process is affected by relations between these settings, and by the larger contexts in which the settings are embedded.'[11]

The system of contextual influences closest to the child is called the *microsystem*. The microsystem consists of the face-to-face settings with which children are involved such as the immediate family, the school or child care centre, the doctor or the church. Settings are seen to influence children not only through their physical features but through the personality and belief systems of people in those settings, and the effect of the settings is modified by children's perception of the context and the people within them.

In addition, Bronfenbrenner included in his model the importance of emotion in the effect of context on the developing child. His definition of development includes the importance of emotional attachment with other people as a powerful element in the process by which the microsystem wields its influence: 'Learning and development are facilitated by the participation of the developing person in progressively more complex patterns of reciprocal activity with someone with whom the person has developed a strong and enduring emotional attachment, and when the balance of power gradually shifts in favour of the developing person.'[12]

The next layer of the model is called the *mesosystem*. The mesosystem refers to the interrelationships between settings in which the child actively participates. It refers to the degree of congruence or match between two settings in the microsystem. An example is the match between home and child care centre. If the styles, expectations and values of people working in a child

Figure 1   Bronfenbrenner's social ecology model

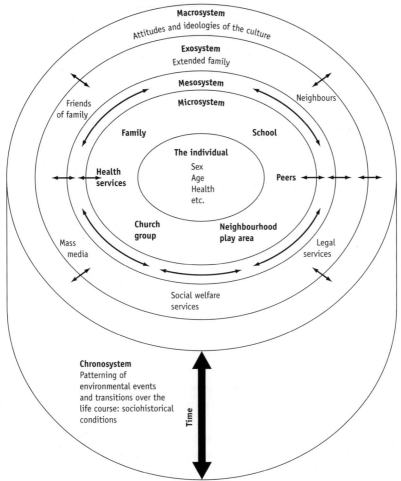

Source: Adapted from Figure 2.6 in J.W. Santrock, *Adolescence*, Brown & Benchmark,
Dubuque, IA, 1996, p. 54.

care centre are similar to those that children have experienced at home, they
and their parents will settle more readily into the routines of the centre. If, to
take another example, children are not prepared for school by their experiences in another setting such as home, child care centre or pre-school, skills
such as holding a pencil, cutting with scissors or tying shoelaces, can make
transition very difficult and delay development in the new context.

Bronfenbrenner's model contains a further system, the *exosystem*, which
refers to the linkages between two or more settings. It is represented as a step

further removed from the child than the microsystem and mesosystem because in the exosystem the child is not directly involved in all settings but is nevertheless directly affected by them. The three exosystems most likely to influence children, through their influence on family members, are the parents' workplaces, parents' social networks, and community influences. These are all discussed in more detail later in the book (see Chapters 5 and 7).

The outermost system shown in Figure 1, the *macrosystem*, refers to broad societal or cultural contexts. The macrosystem incorporates the sets of values or cultural belief systems around which life in a society is organised, and which are passed on through families, schools, churches and other social and government institutions. In Australia, as in the USA, one such value might be the relative importance of the individual (as opposed to the group).[13] Such values, of course, vary among the subgroups within a country.

The influence of the outer layers of the model on the developing child are illustrated by the 'trickle down' effect of changing societal attitudes and practices over the last twenty years in Australia concerning women's increasing involvement in the paid workforce. Many of these women are also the mothers of young children, and their working outside the home has altered parenting practices and the patterns of child care that characterised the previous generation of families.[14]

In response to the needs of mothers in the workforce, out-of-family child care has become part of the life of many families. While parents are at work, children below school age may be cared for in one or several of a range of formal and informal settings. Formal child care, as well as enriching children's knowledge of many school-like activities, presents a new setting of group care involving larger groups of children than would be present in a family. This kind of setting demands social skills of sharing, learning to play cooperatively with other children and forming relationships with adult carers—skills that children have been found to develop in child care centres.[15] This example shows how wider social influences such as changes in the patterns of work can affect families and children. The effects of social policies are particularly demonstrated in Part D of this book.

Two additions made to his model by Bronfenbrenner are important in that they affect the way we think of context and how it influences individuals.[16] The first addition was the inclusion of the idea of individuals seeking their *developmental niche* or actively seeking contexts to match their own characteristics. Children in a child care centre, for example, who enjoy construction or who see other children building with blocks and think that those children are like them, may choose the 'block corner' over the 'book corner', finding for themselves a developmental niche—a setting that, in turn, will influence their future choices and behaviour.

This idea is a valuable one, not least because it takes us away from the notion that the paths of influence between context and individual are one-way, that individuals are passive victims of the contexts that they encounter or are subject to at a distance. With the intense interest in context that his model inspired, Bronfenbrenner himself acknowledged that the role of the developing individual in seeking and constructing contexts had been neglected: 'For some years, I harangued my colleagues for avoiding the study of development in real-life settings. No longer able to complain on that score, I have found a new *bête noir* [*sic*]. In place of too much research on development "out of context", we now have a surfeit of studies on "context without development".'[17]

The second addition to Bronfenbrenner's model has been a time dimension, the *chronosystem*, as shown in Figure 1. This is important because it acknowledges that, just as individuals change over time, so too do contexts. Developmental and historical change need to be taken into account in any model of the interrelationships between people and their context. An example of the effects of an individual's development on context can be seen in differing approaches to behaviour management in the education system according to the age of the student. Teachers use different methods of discipline with kindergarten children, for example, from those they use with high school students.

Historical time also changes the nature of contexts that affect children and families. An example is the changing attitudes towards immunisation of young children in Australia. The poliomyelitis epidemics during the late 1930s had an enormous impact on children and families of that time, with parents and children living in fear of the disease, obliged to deal with prolonged hospitalisation of children, and having education disrupted by the closure of schools. When immunisation against major infectious diseases became available, families who had witnessed the polio epidemic were more than anxious to have their children immunised. The impact of such historical events, however, weakens when several generations, protected by widespread immunisation from major infectious diseases, have not personally experienced the diseases or their social impact. This appears to have happened in Australia, which during the early 1990s had one of the lowest immunisation rates among developed countries.[18] The emergence of new diseases that threaten the health of children such as meningoccocal septicaemia, and of whole societies such as SARS, as well as a concerted national government campaign to encourage immunisation, have led to a close to universal childhood immunisation rate in Australia in recent years.[19] Such historical changes in attitude have clear implications for the health of children and for the well-being of families and communities.

Bronfenbrenner's model of social ecology has had a great impact on thinking about the interaction between people and contexts. His model is being actively discussed, criticised and explored as researchers come to grips with its implications for research into child development.[20] In addition, his model has provided a useful foundation for the exploration of issues such as the provision of social services to families,[21] and the development of a national agenda for early childhood in Australia.[22] It has also guided the design of many recent major research studies of children[23] and has influenced the structure of this book with its progression from individual through proximal to more distal contextual influences.

Rogoff's analysis of the cultural nature of development

Another major influence on our thinking about context has been the work of Barbara Rogoff, who was critical of some features of the model of contextual influences proposed by Bronfenbrenner. One criticism was that in many parts of his writing (but not all) people are 'treated as products of their immediate settings and "larger" contexts'.[24] The diagrammatic representation of nested contexts presented in Bronfenbrenner's model is seen by Rogoff as unduly and even inadvertently separating 'person and culture into stand-alone entities'. Her analysis places more emphasis both on the active nature of the developing child and on their lack of separation from context. She sees individuals not as responding to contexts or seeking contexts that fit their characteristics and interests but as participants in contexts who by their participation help create and change those contexts. For example, Rogoff explains how this happens in relation to learning cultural norms through cultural participation:

> Some of the most dramatic issues of autonomy and interdependence have to do with social relations across generations, between adults and children. Through participation in those relationships and those with peers, the next generation learns about its community's models of how individuals and communities relate. In the process, each generation may question and revise the practices of its predecessors, particularly when distinct practices of different communities are juxtaposed in their lives.[25]

Rogoff's analysis is valuable in that it makes clear the changing nature of contexts. Families, for instance, are constantly changing contexts for children's development due to the changing family membership (for example, the birth of a new baby or parental separation) and their own individual courses of development (parenting changes as parents gain more skills and confidence as parents) as well as the involvement of that child in the family (see Chapter 5). Schools change constantly with different personnel and different cohorts of children (see Chapter 6) and even government policy comes from a changing context according to the party in power and the people who occupy key positions in the ministry and public service departments.

Another contribution Rogoff has made to our understanding of context in development is her close attention to the processes of learning that take place in cultural contexts. Rogoff has built on the work of Lev Vygotsky,[26] taking his idea that children learn though the assistance of more experienced members of their community, adult or child, operating with their assistance at a level of thinking that they would not be capable of alone at that stage (operating in what Vygotsky termed their 'zone of proximal development').[27] Her elaboration of the processes of 'guided participation' beyond the educational settings that were Vygotsky's focus, to everyday cultural contexts, is also a valuable contribution. It extends her earlier work on cognitive development in cultural context through the use of cultural tools and through an 'apprenticeship' with other cultural members,[28] and Lave and Wenger's model of how we develop through our participation in numerous communities of practice, moving from initial peripheral to central participation.[29]

Rogoff's cultural analysis is also important in reminding us that a range of practices and beliefs are found in different countries of the world and in different groups within our own communities. The danger of much research on child development deriving from European-American samples is that these research findings can be misinterpreted as representing developmental patterns and processes for all groups. The examples of different approaches to child rearing presented by Rogoff are a timely reminder of this danger and offer a critical lens for reassessment of our views about the norms of child development.

Interconnections

Our concern in this book with the interconnections among children, families and communities, despite Rogoff's concerns about the dangers of diagrammatic simplification, is shown in Figure 2.

The first observation to make is that the arrows linking the three elements are bidirectional, indicating that each element influences and is influenced by the other. Children, for example, are affected by the family context, but equally they themselves contribute to it. In this model, children are also seen as having an influence directly on their community as well as being influenced by it, either directly or indirectly. Government policy, for example, may affect a family's ability to afford child care (as seen in Chapter 10), and children may be removed from a child care centre as a consequence. In this case, the effect on the child trickles down from the community to the individual family.

On the right-hand side of Figure 2 is a summary of the objective and subjective features of context, as discussed earlier in this chapter. To explore the further implications of Figure 2, we turn now from our examination of context to discuss the *consequences* for children, families and communities of contextual influences, and the processes by which those consequences come to pass.

Figure 2   Framework for the book: interconnections among children, families and communities

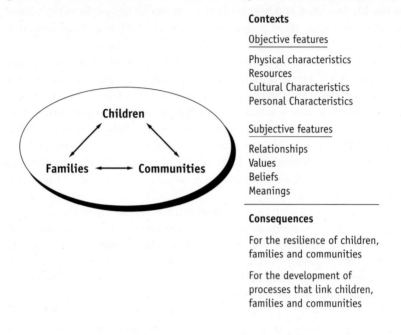

Contexts

Objective features

Physical characteristics
Resources
Cultural Characteristics
Personal Characteristics

Subjective features

Relationships
Values
Beliefs
Meanings

Consequences

For the resilience of children, families and communities

For the development of processes that link children, families and communities

⟵──⟶   = The set of processes that link elements in the framework

Consequences for children, families and communities

Until recently, outcomes from or consequences of the interaction between individual characteristics and contexts have been considered mainly for individuals. Cowan, Cowan and Schulz[30] suggest that this reflects a research approach that sought to show, mainly with reference to individual characteristics, which people might be at risk of particular psychological disorders or undesirable behaviours such as depression or aggression.

These authors argue for an additional level of analysis of consequences, namely outcomes for families. Desirable outcomes for families might be demonstrated by the psychological and physical health of the individual members, by their capacity to fulfil their roles, and by the ability of the family to continue as a well-functioning unit.[31] There is, of course, no single outcome, but an ever-changing series of outcomes that either go on to become part of the demands on families or a component of their resources.

We wish to argue that consequences for the community also need to be taken into account. The community level of analysis is particularly important for policy analysis and for the planning of prevention or intervention programs to circumvent or reduce negative consequences for individuals and families. Factors such as community connectedness and the availability of community resources and support have been shown to be linked with lower levels of child abuse and other measures of family well-being (see Chapter 7). Policy changes and intervention programs need to be designed with a view to the 'social capital' they bring at a community level as well as the cultural and psychological capital they bring to the children and families that they target.

Our working models of the ways in which children, families and communities are interconnected affect the decisions we make, particularly at policy level, and in the outcomes we predict.[32] One type of interconnection that is relevant for predicting outcomes relates to the processes by which the impact of an event, decision or policy affects children, families and communities. In a keynote address, Goodnow explained how effects can 'bubble up' through the different levels: 'When people decide, for example, to delay having children, or to have only one or two children, the effects do not stop at the family level. The smaller number of children makes a difference at the level of schools and neighbourhoods, alters the extent to which women return to the paid workforce and, in the longer term, affects the nature of a country's tax base.'[33]

In her address, Goodnow gave a good example of how effects can also 'trickle down':

> Changes in the employment market provide an example of effects that 'trickle down'. The most widely known studies would be those from the United States which document the effects of a depressed economy on family life. Some of those studies look at the short- and long-term consequences of the Depression in the 1930s, extending in some cases over generations (e.g., Elder, 1974, 1995). Others are currently examining the effects of a depressed rural economy on patterns of authority within families and on the way adolescents with their unpaid labour needed on a farm that may not survive, feel about their own future (e.g., Conger & Elder, 1994).[34]

The question remains as to how individual characteristics and contexts interact to produce a range of consequences at an individual, family and community level. As mentioned earlier, the concern with context in this book does not mean that circumstances alone are what make the difference. The picture is more complex. The response of individuals and families to life-challenges results from the resources they have available to them from a combination of factors within individuals as well as within the contexts that surround them. Most attention, however, has focused on context in terms of key developmental settings such as home, school and community to the exclusion of interest in the nexus between people and context.

A key study that addressed the way in which characteristics of people and circumstances work together to produce positive or negative outcomes was conducted over three decades in Hawaii by Werner and Smith.[35] These researchers studied children who had experienced high risk in their first two years of life, due to low birthweight, complications during birth and living in families that through poverty, family conflict or parental psychopathology made them poor child-rearing contexts. Children growing up with such characteristics and in such circumstances might be expected to have poor outcomes.

While this was true of many in the group, for a third of the children the consequences were the opposite of those expected. This subgroup of the 'at risk' children became well-functioning responsible adults who were caring, confident and competent in their adult activities. These children had several features in common. They came from families that were not too large (no more than four children), and they had at least one positive attachment to an adult who gave them a lot of attention. In addition to this difference in context, these children showed distinctive personal characteristics such as a personality that made other people respond to them in a positive way, high self-esteem, a sense of personal control over their lives and a tendency to plan. They had also had opportunities through school, work, the church or the military to have experiences that boosted self-esteem and competence. It is readily apparent that such distinctive features of context and personal characteristics are interrelated. High self-esteem may have roots in personality, but may also be influenced by the personal attention from adults received by these 'resilient' children.

In the light of such studies, it has proven very difficult to predict the outcomes for many children considered at risk in infancy. In addition, the search for predictors of positive and negative outcomes has led many researchers to ignore or underestimate the role of chance events in making the outcomes of development uncertain. Nevertheless, studies such as that of Werner and Smith point to the importance of looking not only at risk factors but also at factors that are linked to resilience in difficult circumstances. A developing research emphasis on factors likely to boost resilience in children, families and communities mirrors a shift in focus by practitioners from working from the deficiencies or 'at risk' status of individuals, families and communities to taking a strengths-based approach.[36] A strengths-based approach involves identifying and working with the strengths that people bring with them. For example, an otherwise chaotic family may show concern for the health of their children. This concern can form the basis for support provided by community agencies. Underlying the strengths-based approach is research on its effectiveness in boosting the self-esteem, parenting confidence and self-efficacy of parents—all factors that have been identified as associated with resilience.[37]

Terms and factors associated with resilience

Various studies, notably those by Werner,[38] Rutter[39] and Garmezy,[40] have led to consideration not only of the factors associated with resilience but of how protective factors can buffer children, families and communities from risk and vulnerability.[41] The concepts of risk, vulnerability, protective factors, and resilience are worth examining in more detail, keeping in mind that risk is currently seen as a less useful concept than resilience. The more useful policy question at present is how might a balance be achieved in matching the challenges inevitably experienced in life with the resources to enable people to deal with those challenges in a way that has benefits rather than negative consequences for individuals, families and communities.

Risk

It is common to see risk factors listed under the headings of child, family and community characteristics.[42] Some examples of risks associated with child characteristics are low birth weight, prenatal exposure to toxins or infections, chronic illness, difficult temperament and poor self-esteem. Family factors that have been shown to pose risks for children include poverty, violence, parents who use drugs or alcohol, and abuse and neglect. Some community risk factors are neighbourhood violence and crime, lack of support services for families, poor housing and social and cultural discrimination. Listing possible sources of risk for children, however, does not indicate the complexity of the way risk operates to affect people's lives.

Risk is really a probability statement about negative outcomes. We might say, for example, that a child born of drug-addicted parents or with a disability is at risk in terms of development. However, as Cowan, Cowan and Schulz[43] pointed out, not all individuals at risk develop the same negative outcomes, and some individuals at risk never develop a disorder. Equally, some individuals with no risk factors do go on to develop disorders. It is interesting, for example, to note that at the age of four, more children with disabilities actually come from the group considered normal at birth than from those considered 'at risk'.[44]

Risk factors are not clear-cut. Is poverty always a risk for children, for example? Think of the successful business people, motivated to succeed, who have emerged from childhood poverty. Is shyness always a risk for later development? Children who spend a lot of time on their own can develop into creative artists or writers. It depends on the person and his or her circumstances, what is seen as a positive or negative outcome, and the number of risks present at the same time. It may be that some experience of risk is necessary to develop resilience. There is little evidence that positive experiences by themselves are sufficient to develop resilience.[45]

The concept of risk is complex in other ways, as Cowan, Cowan and Schulz explain: 'In real life, people move in and out of risk status. Psychological risks may fluctuate as life circumstances change. As time goes on, individ-

uals are increasingly likely to be faced with new risks, to develop new vulner-
abilities, and to have new opportunities to develop resilience.'[46]

This dynamic view of risk is a useful one compared with the static category
view of psychological pathology. It allows us to see development as a moving in
and out of adaptation to the inevitable changes and challenges in life.[47] The
extent to which people are susceptible to negative consequences depends on
their vulnerability and resilience in those circumstances and at that time.

Despite these qualifications, it is unusual for risks to occur one at a time. It
is far more common for children to experience multiple stressors or for
adverse experiences to accumulate in life. The risk of child psychiatric disorder increases markedly with each new additional adverse or stressful experience. Rutter and Quinton, for example, found that whereas children who
experienced one of the family factors associated with psychiatric disorder
were no more likely than children without that experience to develop
pathology, two stressors occurring together multiplied the risk by four and
more than two raised the risk of pathology still higher.[48] As Michael Rutter
explained: 'The clear implication is that the main risk lies in the experience
of many adversities, the increased risk being quite low in relation to any single adverse experience. It immediately follows that one of the major factors
(probably the major factor) accounting for individual differences in responses
to adversity is the extent of adversity experienced.'[49]

Vulnerability

Vulnerability is characterised by a reduction in flexibility and capacity to
cope. Resilience, by contrast, is the capacity to adapt and mobilise the personal and social resources to cope in the face of life challenges.[50] Both
responses may arise in response to adverse experiences. If a similar stress has
been managed successfully in the past, the result is likely to be resilience. On
the other hand, vulnerability may stem from a genetic disposition or from
characteristics that have developed through experience—low self-esteem or
depression, for example. It is a term used only when risk is present. At other
times, that characteristic may not make a difference to general functioning.
Cowan, Cowan and Schulz explain this interaction of risk and vulnerability
with the following analogy:

> A sailboat is returned to the water after a brief time in dry dock, dur-
> ing which a crack in the hull has been hurriedly patched. As long as the
> weather is reasonably good and the waves are moderate, the boat is fine
> and will probably remain so indefinitely. If a violent storm springs up,
> all sailboats in the vicinity are at risk for damage, but this sailboat is par-
> ticularly vulnerable to severe damage as soon as the storm begins.[51]

In this way the prior characteristics of children, their families or their communities can make them vulnerable to risks. In a study of aggression in children, for example, Miller et al.[52] found that while parental depression was not associated in a direct way with children's aggression, the presence of depression in parents was a factor in making children more likely to be aggressive when there was conflict within the family. In this example, conflict was like a storm threatening all the children concerned. But those children who were vulnerable as a result of parental depression were more prone to aggressive reactions.

Protective factors

When risk is present, some children, some families and some communities are more resilient than others. There are factors operating to protect or buffer them in part or completely from the negative consequences that might be predicted in risk situations. Werner and Smith[53] suggest that risk and protective factors work together to achieve a balance between an individual's power and the power of the social or physical environment. For example, drug use by their peers poses a risk of drug use for teenagers. But a protective factor such as a strong social group sanction against drug use can serve to balance the relationship between individual and peer group use.[54] Other examples of factors that increase resilience in the face of risk are the protective effects for children with divorced parents of a warm relationship with at least one of them (see Chapter 5), and the buffer provided by social networks in families at risk of child abuse through poverty or unemployment. Several protective factors consistently linked to resilience in the face of multiple risk factors have been identified by Rutter: the person's overall level of cognitive functioning, a sense that it is possible to cope with challenges, the opportunity to make decisions and to learn from mistakes as well as successes, and warm, supportive relationships.

Resilience

In a reconsideration of the concept of resilience, Michael Rutter has cautioned against the tendency to view resilience as a characteristic of an individual, 'fireproofing' them against adversity. The same individual, for example, may show resilience in the face of one set of stressors but be vulnerable to another. Although resilience refers to 'relative success despite the experience of stress and adversity', it is dependent on the events concerned and involves 'a process or range of processes' rather than a 'magic formula'.[55]

Research has shown some of the different routes to resilience associated with various adverse events or stressful experiences. Children who have spent a lot of time in an institution, for example, and have developed antisocial behaviour as children, sometimes function well as adults when they marry or live in a supportive relationship.[56] As another example, the Christchurch longitudinal project in New Zealand showed that children found to have relatively good outcomes as adults despite multiple family adversity as children were more likely to have had personal resources to help them cope (higher intelligence as children and lower rates of novelty-seeking as adolescents) and were less likely to have had delinquent friends when they grew up.[57] In a third example, which studied families of children with a disability, resilience seems to be related to the communication skills of family members, their capacity to be flexible, their degree of commitment to maintaining the family unit, their problem-solving abilities, and the extent to which they maintain their social networks and develop sound working relationships with professionals.[58]

According to Rutter, paths to resilience relate to overall level of risk and sensitivity to risk as well as to opportunities to reduce the impact of stress or adversity, to reduce negative chain reactions and increase positive chain reactions, and to open up new opportunities. All of these mechanisms are potentially open to efforts of intervention and prevention.

Community resilience in the face of risk is a less researched area. As may be seen in Chapter 7, however, the notion of social capital is useful in the prediction of factors that might buffer communities in times of risk or that might lead to community resilience. Just as in families, the level of physical, psychological and cultural resources of a community can either weaken its resilience or strengthen it in times of external threat such as high unemployment.

Balance between vulnerability and resilience

The balance between vulnerability and resilience depends on the demands being placed on individuals, their resources to cope, the supports available to meet the demands, and appraisal of the balance of challenges versus resources. In turn, the resources available within any family are also dependent upon the extent of other, competing pressures. Access to support outside the family, for example, appears to be very important in ameliorating the stress experienced by parents.[59]

Patterson[60] suggests that families facing a recurring problem such as chronic illness or disability in a child could either be more resilient or more vulnerable than other families in the face of stress. Some families could be more resilient because they have developed, over time, the resources to cope. Other families may be made more vulnerable by the constant demand on their capacity to cope. Patterson suggests that there is evidence for both of these outcomes. Hetherington[61] reported that there is greater variance on most outcome measures among families living with chronic stress than in other families.

Appraisal is an important element of most current models of stress and coping, and accounts in part for individual differences in response to stress. As well as contributing to variation, appraisal is also important in explaining variability. Appraisal is ongoing so that one's response to an event may change over time. Reappraisal may even change the evaluation of events, such that a personal 'disaster' at one time may be reframed to become 'a growth point of my life' with the passage of time.

Consequences in terms of outcomes, processes and pathways

The concepts of risk, vulnerability, protective factors and resilience provide the building blocks for a dynamic model of the consequences for children, families and communities of the interplay between individual characteristics and contextual factors. Just as there is no single steady balance of vulnerability and resilience for individuals, it is misleading to search for a single developmental process to a particular outcome. It is often assumed that a single developmental process can be identified to explain the behaviour and development of all people irrespective of their specific characteristics or circumstances.[62] Instead, a framework is needed to incorporate the range of developmental routes.

The concept of developmental pathways or trajectories[63] has been used for this purpose, as Cairns and Cairns have explained, referring to the results of a ten-year longitudinal study of adolescent development:

> There is considerably more regularity in individual lives than we thought we would find. Lives seem not to be predestined so much as they are kept on course by correlated forces from within and without. Yet there are instances of remarkable and durable shifts in trajectory. In those cases of enduring and productive change, there is engagement of internal forces—Norman Garmezy has called them 'concealed competencies'—coupled with changes in the familial, peer, school, or broader social system.[64]

In sum, pathways to the same end can be multiple, and within what may appear to be predictable pathways there can be dramatic changes in direction.

The consequences of different pathways are often presented in terms of probability. In his discussion of pathways to crime, for example, Kazdin[65] concluded that: 'influences can place a child on a trajectory or path. The trajectory or path is not a fixed or a determined course. Some outcomes become more probable (e.g., being arrested, bonding with delinquent peers) and other outcomes become less probable (e.g., graduating from high school, entering a monastery) [p. 257].'

The challenge is to identify the pathways generally followed on the road to crime or drug dependence, for example, and then to identify points along the pathway where intervention might have the greatest chance of success.

Studies of resilience have indicated that there is often a distinct turning point that changes a life trajectory, whether that is joining the armed forces or forming a partnership with a supportive partner. It has been suggested that commonly experienced transition points in life, such as starting school or high school, or the birth of a first child, could be the optimal times for intervention and support programs to succeed in diverting trajectories in the direction of resilience rather than vulnerability in the face of stressful events.

The model outlined in this chapter of the influence of personal and contextual factors on consequences for children, families and communities has implications for understanding development, predicting policy outcomes, and designing prevention and intervention programs. It is the model used throughout this book to analyse contexts and consequences of a range of issues for children, families and communities in Australia.

The concepts of risk and resilience and of different developmental pathways are central to any consideration of intervention in the lives of children, families or communities. They assist in identifying groups 'at risk', the protective factors that can be introduced or augmented by changes to context, and the opportune times for intervention during developmental pathways.[66] Various models of intervention are examined in Chapter 7 in relation to isolated families, and the implications for future social policy challenges of the theoretical framework presented in this chapter are explored in more detail in Chapter 11.

Notes

1   U. Bronfenbrenner, 'The Biological Model from a Life Course Perspective: Reflections of a Participant Observer', in *Examining Lives in Context*, eds, P. Moen, G.H. Elder Jr & K. Lüscher, American Psychological Association, Washington, DC, 1995, pp. 599–618; B. Rogoff, *The Cultural Nature of Human Development*, Oxford University Press, New York, 2003, p. 45.

2   Bronfenbrenner, 1995; Rogoff, 2003.

3   The description is based partly on a parenting program operated by SDN Children's Services.

4   M. Cole, 'The Supra-individual Envelope of Development: Activity and Practice, Situation and Context', in *New Directions for Child Development*, no. 67, eds, J.J. Goodnow, P.J. Miller & F. Kessel, Jossey-Bass, San Francisco, 1995, pp. 105–18; P.J. Miller & J.J. Goodnow, 'Cultural Practices: Toward an Integration of Culture and Development', in Goodnow, Miller & Kessel, 1995, pp. 5–16.

5   J.J. Goodnow, 'Differentiating Among Social Contexts: By Spatial Features, Forms of Participation, and Social Contracts', in *Examining Lives in Context*, eds, P. Moen, G.H. Elder Jr & K. Lüscher, American Psychological Association, Washington, DC, 1995, pp. 269–301.

6   Bronfenbrenner, 1997.

7   A. Oakley, 'Women and Children First and Last: Parallels and Differences Between Children's and Women's Studies', in *Children's Childhoods: Observed and Experienced*, ed, B. Mayall, Falmer Press, London, 1994, p. 22.

8   See A.W. Wicker, *An Introduction to Ecological Psychology*, Cambridge University Press, Cambridge, 1979, and M. Bonnes & G. Secchaiaroli, *Environmental Psychology*, Sage, London, 1995, for historical accounts of ecological and environmental psychology.

9   R.B. Cairns & B.D. Cairns, 'Social Ecology Over Time and Space', in Moen, Elder & Lüscher, 1995, p. 403.

10   U. Bronfenbrenner, *The Ecology of Human Development*, Harvard University Press, Cambridge, MA, 1979, p. 3.

11   Bronfenbrenner, 1979, p. 21.

12   Bronfenbrenner, 1979, p. 60.

13   S. Harkness, C.M. Super, C.H. Keefer, C.S. Raghavan & E.K. Kipp, 'Ask the Doctor: The Negotiation of Cultural Models in American Parent–Pediatrician Discourse', in *Parents' Cultural Belief Systems*, eds, S. Harkness & C.M. Super, The Guilford Press, New York, 1996, pp. 289–310.

14   From 1986 to 2002, the percentage of couples with dependants who were both employed rose from 48.5 per cent to 57 per cent. P. McDonald, 'Families and Welfare Services', in *Australia's Welfare 1997*, eds, H. Moyle & D. Gibson, Australian Institute of Health and Welfare, Canberra, 1997, pp. 55–95; Australian Bureau of Statistics, *Australian Social Trends 2003*, catalogue no. 4102.0, Australian Government Publishing Service, Canberra, 2003.

15   K.A. Clark-Stewart, C.P. Gruber & L.M. Fitzgerald, *Children at Home and in Day Care*, Lawrence Erlbaum, Hillsdale, NJ, 1994.

16   U. Bronfenbrenner, 'Developmental Ecology Through Space and Time', in *Examining Lives in Context*, eds, Moen, Elder & Lüscher, 1995, pp. 619–48.

17   U. Bronfenbrenner, 'Recent Advances in the Research on Human Development', in *Development as Action in Context*, eds, R.K. Silbereisen, K. Eyforth & G. Rudinger, Springer-Verlag, Heidelberg, Germany, 1986, p. 288.

18   P. Boss, S. Edwards & S. Pitman, *Profile of Young Australians: Facts, Figures and Issues*, Churchill Livingstone, Melbourne, 1995.

19   Australian Bureau of Statistics, 2003.

20   Cairns & Cairns, 1997; J.C. Sontag, 'Toward a Comprehensive Theoretical Framework for Disability Research: Bronfenbrenner Revisited', *Journal of Special Education*, 30, 3, 1996, pp. 319–44.

21   J. Garbarino, *Children and Families in the Social Environment*, Aldine de Gruyter, New York, 1992.

22   Australian Government Task Force on Child Development, Health and Wellbeing, *Towards a National Agenda for Early Childhood*, Australian Government Department of Family and Community Services, Canberra, 2003.

23   National Institute of Child Health and Human Development Early Child Care Research Network, 'Does Quality of Child Care Affect Child Outcomes at Age 4½?', *Developmental Psychology*, 39, 2003, pp. 451–69; A. Sanson, *Introducing the Longitudinal Study of Australian Children*, Australian Institute of Family Studies, Melbourne, 2002.

24   Rogoff, 2003.

25   Rogoff, 2003.

26   L. Vygotsky, *Mind in Society: The Development of Higher Psychological Processes*, Harvard University Press, Cambridge, MA, 1978.

27   Rogoff, 2003, p. 282 for Rogoff's account of her debt to Vygotsky's ideas.

28   B. Rogoff, *Apprenticeship in Thinking: Cognitive Development in a Social Context*, Oxford University Press, New York, 1990.

29   J. Lave & E. Wenger, *Situated Learning: Legitimate Peripheral Participation*, Cambridge University Press, Cambridge, 1999; E. Wenger, *Communities of Practice: Learning Meaning and Identity*, Cambridge University Press, New York, 1998.

30   P.A. Cowan, C.P. Cowan & M.S. Schulz, 'Thinking about Risk and Resilience in Families', in *Stress, Coping and Resiliency in Children and Families*, eds, E.M. Hetherington & E.A. Blechman, Lawrence Erlbaum, Mahwah, NJ, 1996.

31   J.M. Patterson, 'Chronic Illness in Children and the Impact on Families', in *Chronic Illness and Disability*, eds, C.S. Chilman, E.W. Nunally & F.M. Cox, Sage, London, 1988, pp. 69–107.

32   J.J. Goodnow, 'Meeting the Needs of Children, Families and Communities', in *Shaping the Future for Young Children, Their Families and Communities*, Centenary Conference Monograph, eds, A. Fleet & A. Hayes, Institute of Early Childhood, Macquarie University, Sydney, 1997, pp. 13–26.

33   Goodnow, 1997, p. 17.

34   Goodnow, 1997, p. 18.

35   E.E. Werner & R.S. Smith, *Kauai's Children Come of Age*, University of Hawaii Press, Honolulu, HI, 1977.

36   C. Dunst, C. Trivette & A. Deal, *Supporting and Strengthening Families: Methods, Strategies and Practices*, Cambridge, MA, Brookline Books, 1994.

37   Dunst, Trivette & Deal, 1994.

38   E.E. Werner, 'Risk, Resilience and Recovery: Perspectives from the Kauai Longitudinal Study', *Development and Psychopathology*, 5, 1993, pp. 503–15; Werner & Smith, 1977; E.E. Werner & R.S. Smith, *Vulnerable but Invincible: A Longitudinal Study of Resilient Children and Youth*, Adams-Bannister-Cox, New York, 1989; E.E. Werner & R.S. Smith, *Overcoming the Odds: High Risk Children from Birth to Adulthood*, Cornell University Press, Ithaca, NY, 1992.

39   M. Rutter, 'Resilience in the Face of Adversity: Protective Factors and Resistance to Psychiatric Disorder', *British Journal of Psychiatry*, 147, 1985, pp. 598–611; M. Rutter, 'Psychosocial Resilience and Protective Mechanisms', *American Journal of Orthopsychiatry*, 57, 1987, pp. 316–31.

40   N. Garmezy, 'Resilience and Vulnerability to Adverse Developmental Outcomes Associated with Poverty', *American Behavioral Scientist*, 34, 1991, pp. 416–30; N. Garmezy, 'Children in Poverty: Resilience Despite Risk', *Psychiatry*, 56, 1993, pp. 127–36.

41   M.A. Zimmerman & R. Arunkumar, 'Resiliency Research: Implications for Schools and Policy', *Social Policy Report*, VIII, no. 4, Society for Research in Child Development, Ann Arbor, MI, 1994.

42   See, for example: Australian National Crime Prevention National Anti-Crime Strategy (Australia), *Pathways to Prevention: Developmental and Early Intervention Approaches to Crime in Australia*, Attorney General's Department, Barton, ACT, 1999; Australian Government Task Force on Child Development, Health and Wellbeing, *Towards the Development of a National Agenda for Early Childhood: Consultation Paper*, Commonwealth of Australia, Canberra, 2003.

43   Cowan, Cowan & Schulz, 1996.

44   G.P. Aylward, N. Gustafson, S.J. Verhulst & J.A. Colliver, 'Consistency in the Diagnosis of Cognitive, Motor and Neurologic Function over the First Three Years', *Journal of Pediatric Psychology*, 12, 1987, pp. 77–98.

45   M. Rutter, 'Resilience Reconsidered: Conceptual Considerations, Empirical Findings, and Policy Considerations', in *Handbook of Early Childhood Intervention*, eds, J.A. Shonkoff & S.J. Meisels, Cambridge University Press, Cambridge, 2000, pp. 651–82.

46   Cowan, Cowan & Schulz, 1996, p. 7.

47   Cowan, Cowan & Schulz, 1996.

48   Rutter & Quinton, 1977, cited in Rutter, 2000, p. 657.

49   Rutter, 2000, p. 258.

50   A. Hayes, 'Developmental Psychology, Education and the Need to Move Beyond Typological Thinking', *Australian Journal of Education*, 34, 1990, pp. 235–41.

51   Cowan, Cowan & Schulz, 1996, pp. 10–11.

52   N.B. Miller, P.A. Cowan, C.P. Cowan, E.M. Hetherington & G. Clingempeel, 'Externalising in Preschoolers and Early Adolescents: A Cross-study Replication of a Family Model', *Developmental Psychology*, 29, 1993, pp. 3–18.

53   Werner & Smith, 1992.

54   M.D. Newcomb & M. Felix-Ortiz, 'Multiple Protective and Risk Factors for Drug Use and Abuse: Cross-sectional and Prospective Findings', *Journal of Personality and Social Psychology*, 63, 1992, pp. 280–96.

55   Rutter, 2000, pp. 661–2.

56   Rutter, 2000.

57   Fergusson & Lynsky, 1996, and Stattin et al., 1997, cited in M. Rutter, 2000, pp. 660–1.

58   G. Singer & L. Powers, 'Contributing to Resilience in Families: An Overview', in *Families, Disability and Empowerment: Active Coping Skills and Strategies for Family Interventions*, eds, G. Singer & L. Powers, Brookes, Baltimore, 1993, pp. 1–25.

59   G. Hornby & M. Seligman, 'Disability and the Family: Current Status and Future Developments', *Counselling Psychology Quarterly*, 4, 1991, pp. 267–71; J. Shapiro, 'Stress, Depression and Support Group Participation in Mothers of Developmentally Delayed Children', *Family Relations*, 38, 1989, pp. 169–73.

60   Patterson, 1988.

61   M. Hetherington, 'Stress and Coping in Children and Families', in *Children in Families Under Stress*, eds, A. Doyle, D. Gold & D. Moscowitz, Jossey-Bass, San Francisco, 1984, pp. 7–33.

62   M. Cherkes-Julkowski & N. Gertner, *Spontaneous Cognitive Processes in Handicapped Children*, Springer-Verlag, New York, 1989.

63   The terms 'pathway' and 'trajectory' are often used interchangeably in the literature. In this chapter, 'pathway' is the preferred term and is used in a generic way. A distinction between the two terms has been made by Elder in a conference discussion (XVth Biennial Meeting of the International Society for the Study of Behavioral Development, Berne, July 1998). Elder suggests that 'trajectory' be used to refer to an individual lifecourse whereas 'pathway' should be used to refer to well-worn, standard routes of development; a similar distinction has been made in J.J. Goodnow, 'Contexts, Diversity, Pathways: Linking and Extending', in *Hills of Gold: Rethinking Diversity and Contexts as Resources for Children's Developmental Pathways*, eds, C.R. Cooper, G. Coll, T. Bartko, H. Davis & C. Chatman, Lawrence Erlbaum, Mahwah, NJ, in press.

64   R.B. Cairns & B.D. Cairns, 'Risks and Lifelines in Adolescence', paper presented at the Biennial Meeting of the Society for Research in Child Development, Kansas City, April 1989.

65   A.E. Kazdin, 'Conduct Disorder Across the Life-span', in *Developmental Psychopathology: Perspectives on Adjustment, Risk and Disorder*, eds, S.S. Luthar, J.A. Burack, D. Cicchetti & J.R. Weisz, Cambridge University Press, Cambridge, 1997, pp. 248–72.

66   Goodnow, 1997.

PART B

Characteristics of Children:
Effects of Disability,
Ethnicity and Gender

In Part B we focus on personal characteristics by considering the impact of three particular features on individuals, their families and their communities. For each of the three characteristics—disability, ethnicity and gender—we also consider how community attitudes and policies influence the perceptions and self-definitions of the people concerned, how people choose to act on the basis of these characteristics, and the family and community response to those characteristics and actions.

The three topics are chosen as major characteristics influencing daily lives and the pathways people follow in life. We might have chosen other characteristics such as age or temperament, characteristics that exercise as much influence as disability, ethnicity or gender. The characteristics under discussion, however, are illustrative of some general processes by which individual characteristics affect the context in which children and families develop and function, and each brings out different aspects of the interconnections among children, families and communities.

We begin with an exploration of individual characteristics because research in this area first challenged the assumption that contexts affected all children uniformly. Recent research in child development has focused much more on diversity among individuals and their pathways through life.

Children's personal characteristics were also the focus for early discussion of the bidirectional effects of context. Bidirectional processes are illustrated in the parenting of children with a disability (Chapter 2), in accommodation of society to ethnic differences such as language (Chapter 3), and in processes by which children learn gender roles (Chapter 4).

The three chapters illustrate also how people or contexts 'define' or 'construct' one another. Categories such as 'disabled' or 'ethnic' have a meaning that depends on context. Part of that meaning can derive from individuals themselves who construct their own identities, seeing themselves, for example, as part of the deaf community or as 'Koori'.

Personal characteristics can also be used to identify people as part of an in-group or an out-group, and we see this in the ethnically defined divisions described in Chapter 3 and in peer groups of boys and girls discussed in Chapter 4. The ways in which personal characteristics of children and adults affect the social contexts of children, families and communities, are the concern of all three chapters in Part B.

Disability:

Characteristics, Contexts and Consequences

Monica Cuskelly and Alan Hayes

Disability affects a large number of individual Australians, their families and their communities. In 1998 there were 278,100 individuals with 'severe or profound core activity restriction' living in households who had acquired the disability before the age of 18.[1] Severe and profound core activity restrictions are labels used by the Australian Bureau of Statistics to refer to those individuals who sometimes (severe) or always (profound) need help with a core activity (self-care, mobility and communication).[2] Consistent with the focus of this book, this chapter examines aspects of the development of people with disabilities in the context of their families and communities.

The rapid movement away from institutional care to life within their families and communities has been one of the most important factors in improving the quality of life for people with disabilities in Australia and other Western countries. The changes that have occurred in their opportunities have been little short of revolutionary. Access to the wide range of experiences offered by life with their families and communities has enabled their individuality to emerge in ways that were not possible in many institutions.[3] In turn, cleaner, safer living conditions and better health care and nutrition have resulted in increased longevity and improved health.[4]

Life away from institutions, for all the many benefits it gives to the person with a disability, may have nevertheless a range of consequences, including those related to the increased burden of care that falls on families and communities. Consistent with the ecological framework described in Chapter 1, this illustrates the way in which changes in one part of a system may have unanticipated consequences for other parts. Before considering the consequences for children, families and communities, it is important to examine the nature of disability and how context affects perceptions of disability.

This chapter, then, addresses three questions:

- What kind of characteristic is disability and what impact does context have on its expression?
- Does context influence beliefs about and attitudes to disability?
- What are the consequences for children, families and communities?

Contexts

What kind of characteristic is disability?

Some definitions

The World Health Organization has recently modified the framework it proposes for understanding disability.[5] Disability is understood as an umbrella term that incorporates the three components of impairments, activity limitations and participation restrictions. The framework reflects a biopsychosocial model of disability. It combines the medical model that views disability purely as a personal characteristic and the social model that views disability as a product of socially constructed barriers. The biopsychosocial model recognises that disability is an interaction between attributes of the person and aspects of the context in which the person is operating. The World Health Organization provides the following definitions:

- *Impairments* are problems in body functions (for example, mental, sensory neuromusculoskeletal functions) or structures (for example, structure of the nervous, metabolic or endocrine systems) such as a significant deviation or loss. The degree of impairment may be mild, moderate, severe, or complete.
- *Activity limitations* are difficulties an individual may have in executing activities such as learning and applying knowledge, mobility, or self-care.
- *Participation restrictions* are problems an individual may experience in participating in life situations such as engaging in the life of their community and in interpersonal relationships.

There are substantial numbers of individuals who have more than one impairment, a situation likely to lead to increased activity limitations and restrictions on participation.[6] In addition, secondary conditions—that is, sequelae of the original disabling condition (for example obesity resulting from the inobility restrictions that follow from some physical disabilities)—

may also bring additional limitations and contribute to the individuals' exclusion from society.[7]

These definitions make it clear that disability as a characteristic is inseparable from the context(s) in which the individual lives. The remainder of this section expands on this interconnectedness. There are some important distinctions between the terms. Impairment is a personal attribute. The extent of the activity and participation restrictions that results from impairment can be reduced or increased by context. An impairment such as blindness may be less disabling in an appropriately supportive environment. The restrictions that may flow from disability are, at least in part, socially constructed. Mobility aids (such as wheelchairs and walking frames), building access (such as ramps or lifts) and communication systems (such as Braille and sign language) all reduce the extent of restrictions experienced by people with a physical or sensory impairment. Societies vary, however, in the importance they place on ensuring that such measures are available to reduce the handicapping effects of impairment and disabilities.

The example of Martha's Vineyard aptly illustrates this point. Martha's Vineyard is a small community in which those with hearing and those who are deaf both use sign language. In this context, deafness does not impede participation in community life and, as a result, is less of a handicap than it is in other communities.[8] Importantly, those in this community who are hearing-impaired are regarded as unique individuals in their own right. They are not defined by their disability as 'the deaf'.

The Martha's Vineyard community tends to be a notable exception to the pattern of behaviour towards people with hearing impairment, although it is possible that individuals with other impairments do not find the community as accommodating. In most other communities disability is viewed negatively, and often those affected are inappropriately seen as members of a homogeneous group. In reality, 'the disabled' (or, as we prefer, persons or people with disabilities) are notable for their heterogeneity—as with all groups of human beings. There are numerous types, levels, causes and consequences of disability. Even within the various disabling conditions there is considerable variation in the characteristics associated with each.[9]

Does context influence beliefs about and attitudes to disability?

Disability provides an important insight into the ways in which the beliefs, perceptions and attitudes of any community or society alter the context for children and their families. Today the terms 'disability' and 'disabled' generally carry negative connotations. This has not always been the case. Across history, societies have varied considerably in the ways in which they defined disability and the value they placed upon people with disabilities.[10]

As Stratford[11] relates, children with Down syndrome were regarded by the Olmecs of Ancient Mexico (1500 BC to 300 AD) as hybrids of humans and the gods. They appear to have been given this special status because they were often the children of older, more important members of the tribe; relatively few survived, and so those who did were regarded as rare and special; and they were visibly striking in their facial and physical characteristics.

By contrast, the concept of democracy, developed in ancient Greece, actually formalised discrimination against people with disabilities, and against women and slaves (labelled the 'private people'). Unlike the 'public people'— a minority of 40,000 male citizens of Athens who were entitled to exercise their democratic rights—these 'private people' (or 'idiots' from the Greek language) were excluded because they were viewed as ignorant. Over time the term 'idiot' has taken on wider, even more negative connotations, beyond its original political meaning. In a similar fashion, other terms such as 'imbecile', 'dumb' and 'spastic' have become pejorative.

Not only the terminology has changed. The incidence and the prevalence of disabilities have shown changes across history. Incidence refers to the rate of births of children with a particular condition.[12] Prevalence refers to the number of people with a disability living in the community at any given time.[13] One of the most noticeable changes to occur is the increased survival rate of infants born with disabilities; and, at least for some conditions, life span has also increased.[14] In Australia at the turn of the century, for example, the survival age of children with Down syndrome was around seven years. Life expectancy for those born today is approaching that of the general population, largely as a result of better medical care and living conditions, although specific medical problems such as the presence of congenital heart disease still significantly influence survival.[15]

Improvements in the care provided have flowed from changes in attitude towards those with a disability. As one example, children with Down syndrome were denied access to heart surgery for a number of years although the technology was available. Now that these children are given the necessary medical care, their survival rate has improved significantly.[16] These improvements may be related to economic factors, level of service and cultural beliefs and attitudes. In some parts of the world, infanticide is still practised when children are born with marked impairments or congenital defects, and this results in greatly reduced prevalence of children with disabilities in these societies. In addition, our capacity to identify the genetic bases of conditions has increased, following the improvements in gene technology. This means that conditions that once would have been regarded as of unknown aetiology are now labelled and understood. As a further consequence, appropriate and timely medical care is more available, leading to the possibility of better outcomes. This knowledge may also be used to prevent the births of children with certain characteristics, another example of the multiple outcomes that may result from any change. Not all parents, and not all individuals with a disability, see this change as a useful one for our society but feel it reflects a basic lack of acceptance of those with disabilities.[17]

Ways of seeing: from types to variants

Seeing individuals as a unitary group that is regarded as distinctly different, irrespective of context, and 'other than us' or an 'out-group', is the first step in dehumanisation, a process too often suffered by those with a disability and by their families.[18] Valsiner identified this process as an example of typological thinking, which he defined as 'thinking in static categories that are...context free'.[19]

Societies define disability in different ways. The definition of disability, and the community reaction to those labelled as 'disabled', says as much about the people who define the out-group as it does about its members. In particular, it highlights the tendency to overlook the wide individual differences among people with any disability, and to overgeneralise the core characteristics. For example, the communication difficulties of people with cerebral palsy may be mistakenly regarded as evidence of intellectual impairment. There may also be a tendency to focus only on the disability and overlook characteristics that are common both to those who are disabled and to the rest of the population.

This tendency highlights some important characteristics of human perception, cognition and communication. There would appear to be a restricted 'zone of difference' in which variation is permissible. Those whose characteristics place them outside this zone are in danger of rejection. This way of thinking can, however, lead to erroneous classifications, inaccurate typologies and distorted social evaluation. These in turn are the bases for creating out-groups. Disability is an especially salient case given the extent of its negative evaluation.

Stigma and disability

People who are seen as different, such as those with disabilities, may be subjected to stigmatisation.[20] The term 'stigma' is used to refer to any characteristic of a person that is 'deeply discrediting'.[21] Stigmatisation is the negative social reaction to the person who possesses such a 'stigma' (or visible sign). The person who is stigmatised is given a negative social identity by others, the consequence of which is often social isolation, and possibly even hostile interactions. As Fullwood and Cronin observed,[22] the task for persons with disabilities is frequently one of managing the insensitivity of others. Parents of children with disabilities often have to develop skills for handling negative reactions and impart these skills to their children.

When considering concepts such as stigma it is important to recognise the central role of context. In societies that did not place a premium on formal education, those individuals whose only difficulty is in acquiring reading and/or writing would be less likely to be seen as different from the mainstream. As Mercer observed,[23] some children are regarded as disabled only in the context of formal schooling, operating as 'normal' children in the world beyond the classroom. In this case a particular context highlights differences that in others may not be of note.

Those who are members of groups that are negatively evaluated (or stigmatised) may attempt to change their status and join more acceptable groups. Tajfel labelled this process as 'passing'.[24] Children with a disability usually have limited options for passing as a member of the in-group. Their out-group status is clearly apparent, even to strangers. To this extent, some people with disabilities have fewer options for passing than members of other out-groups.[25] Across cultures and historical eras, those with a disability have tended to be seen as a clear out-group.[26] As well as being the characteristic that is most difficult to pass, disability may be seen as one of the least 'claimed' characteristics.

In Western societies, some disabilities are more acceptable than others.[27] Acceptability is likely to be influenced by the age of the affected person (with younger children being more acceptable than adolescents or adults), by behaviour (with less troublesome children being more acceptable than those who are disruptive), and by developmental difference (with those who show average intellectual ability being more acceptable than those who are cognitively impaired).[28] Cultures may differ in the types of condition that are regarded as acceptable, and these judgments may be influenced by gender, religious affiliation or social status. Those whose conditions take frightening forms (for example those with epilepsy or schizophrenia) may be more likely to be seen as unacceptable and to be avoided.

In summary, disability is part of the range of human variation. How people perceive those with disabilities has varied historically and culturally, and continues to change. The ways in which impairments are viewed reflect the influence of culture and context. In turn, views of disability affect the extent to which an impairment results in restrictions to full engagement in life's opportunities.

Consequences

What are the consequences for children, families and communities?

Consequences for children with disabilities

There has been an overwhelming concentration on the negative aspects and consequences of disability in the research literature, with virtually no consideration given to the other side of the balance sheet, although the recent emphasis on quality of life begins to deal with this aspect. In an effort to bring some balance, Allen Crocker edited a special issue of the *American Journal on Mental Retardation* devoted to the topic of happiness in individuals with intellectual disability.[29] This group appears to have relatively good self-perceptions, at least during childhood and adolescence.[30] Self-esteem, of course, is not a product solely of an individual, or their impairment; it is the product of the interaction the individual has with his or her environment. As an example, Mrug and Wallander found that young people with physical disabilities had higher self-concepts when they attended an integrated school rather than being educated in a segregated setting.[31]

Despite the negative view of disability in our society, there is evidence that some individuals with an impairment accept this aspect of themselves and do not wish to change and become one of the out-group from the 'normal' mainstream. This can be seen in the rejection by some deaf people of cochlea implants to improve their hearing. Deaf people have a distinct culture with a separate language, and many have no inclination to leave that culture. Parents of deaf children have spoken of having to 'let go' of their children so that they can more completely move into the mainstream of deaf society, even though this means that contact with their child is substantially reduced. In addition, there are reports available that make it clear that some individuals, at least, accept their impairment as integral to their understanding of self: 'For those of us with congenital conditions, disability shapes all we are. Those disabled later in life adapt. We take constraints no-one would choose and build rich and satisfying lives with them. We enjoy pleasures other people enjoy, and pleasures peculiarly our own. We have something the world needs.'[32]

Individuals with a disability have many of the same experiences as those without disability. Some of these are joyful and some are distressing, and they differ across types of impairment as well as across individuals.[33]

Some individuals with disabilities adopt the negative views of disability held by those around them, thus undermining their capacity to develop a view of themselves that incorporates and accepts their impairment.[34] Low self-esteem may also flow from lack of opportunities for educational advancement, productive work, creative expression, or social fulfilment.

As one example of the negative outcomes of disability, children with a disability are more likely to be victims of crime and subject to abuse than are those who are developing normally and this is another indicator of their marginal status in society.[35] The causes of their vulnerability to maltreatment are complex, and may be associated with the increased caregiving demands in a family with few resources (material or personal) to meet their needs, but may also be associated with their perceived status in our society so that predators may feel there will be no retribution for ill-treating them. Cooke and Standen also raised the issue of service providers failing to 'see' the abuse of children with a disability.[36]

The following sections deal with just some of the areas in which having an impairment is likely to have consequences for the individual.

Opportunities for and constraints on education and employment

In Australia and other developed countries there has been a significant improvement in educational opportunities and access to public life and spaces. Nevertheless limitations of access to experience and opportunity remain a defining feature of the participation restrictions that flow from impairment and disability. Increased opportunities and improvements in quality of life have occurred, largely as a function of recognition of the importance of context. Those involved with children who have a disability have come to understand that education and experience can have a substantial impact on the capacities of people who previously had been left in unstimulating environments because little was expected of them. Policies of inclusion, intended to increase access of children with disabilities to the life of their communities, may be difficult to implement in the face of prejudice and lack of acceptance.

Not all social and historical factors have resulted in an increase of opportunities for such children. Some changes have acted to limit their choices and access to involvement in community life. For example, changes in the urbanisation of the society, the more sophisticated tools that have become available through technological changes, and changes to employment opportunities affect the society as a whole, including those with a disability.

These changes can have positive and negative consequences. An example of positive consequences is the enhanced educational and employment prospects for those with sensory or physical impairments as a result of new technologies that aid sensory acuity and communication. An example of negative consequences is the shift in employment opportunities for those with intellectual disabilities that has resulted from the reduction in rural and unskilled work. Increases in educational standards, expectations, and the minimum qualifications needed to enter many occupations may also act to exclude persons with disability from the usual life of communities. There is a need, however, to highlight differences across cultures. For example, in the USA many people with disabilities work because there is no regulation of wages but, as a result, there is also considerable opportunity for exploitation. In this case, the consequences are a complex mix of the positive and the negative.

Ability to form relationships and to obtain emotional support and opportunities for self-expression and development may also be reduced. Marital opportunities may be particularly restricted. In addition, while policies of de institutionalisation may have been intended to enhance opportunities for contact with the community at large, in practice they may lead to 'ghettos' with restrictions similar to those that apply to recently arrived ethnic minority members. In fact, it may be worse for those with a disability, because the size of the community is restricted and their capacity to act for themselves may be limited.

Opportunities for and constraints on peer relationships

Social engagement and companionship are basic human needs. One of the most important requirements for the development of social relationships is access, and another is an openness by possible partners.[37] Friendships require reciprocity and for some children, despite the desire and the competence required to form relationships, personal intent may be frustrated by social rejection. The problem may be that children with a disability simply cannot find a peer with whom to form a friendship.

The health problems associated with many disabling conditions may also have social consequences. In addition to the direct impact of illness on the quality of life, increased social isolation may ensue as periods of hospitalisation interfere with the maintenance of friendships.[38]

Social isolation may be the usual experience for individuals with a disability, particularly after they have completed schooling. Although many remain living in the community, often residing within the family home, they are usually dependent on family members for their social networks and have little contact with others.[39] As Carr concluded, it is still the case for many children with a disability that their families *are* their social networks, with restricted friendship and peer contact outside of home.[40]

Consequences for families and their members

Although the birth of a child with a disability heralds many fundamental changes for families, it is usually overlooked in discussions of the family in general. Many influential books on family life completely neglect this subset of families, which is another example of the view of these individuals and their families as not of the mainstream.[41] This is despite the fact that there are more similarities than differences, with families of children with disabilities having similar roles, responsibilities and relationships to those of families, in general.[42] Nevertheless, it is obvious that disability in a child has an impact on the family as a unit and on its individual members. For many years the aphorism 'a disabled child means a disabled family' had great currency in the research and professional literature: an attitude that probably did much to harm such families.

Disability is an example of areas of potential stress, strain and/or life problems over which individuals have limited control. There are, however, many aspects over which family members can have control, and individuals will vary in their openness to exploring these possibilities. The work of Gallimore and colleagues has provided a framework for examining family life when there is a child with a disability.[43] They underscore the need to focus on the key issue confronting families of creating 'a sustainable and meaningful daily routine of family life', and label this process 'family accommodation'. Among the areas of accommodation they list are child care, domestic tasks and household jobs, social support, financial resources and parental roles. They also highlight the importance of a model of family accommodation that 'takes account of *all* family members, not just the child with delays'. Families vary in the extent to which they can achieve this. Education, material resources, personality, prior experience, available social supports and general coping skills may all facilitate accommodation.

Parental response to disability

The personal response of parents to having a child with a disability will also vary. One important consideration is time: early responses may differ markedly from those experienced later in the family's life. It is likely that the initial response to the birth of a child with an impairment is more uniform than at any other time. Almost all parents go through a process of grieving, a process that for some may never be entirely resolved.[44] While grief is a normal, if complex, human response, denial generally impedes the process of acceptance.[45]

The search for cures through the use of unconventional therapies is an example of the attempt to control a situation that threatens many aspects of family equilibrium. It is easy to understand the appeal of alternative, unconventional treatments. When people are confronted by a disease or disorder that cannot be cured, it is understandable that they should grasp any option, even if of unproven efficacy and not without risk. For some families, involvement in alternative programs unites the parents and gives a sense of hope. The balance, however, is a sensitive one as the search for a 'cure' may also perpetuate denial.[46]

Parents of children with disabilities may be at greater risk of stress-related illnesses and psychological problems such as chronic anxiety.[47] There can also be physical sequelae, such as developing back problems as a consequence of lifting an immobile child or constant tiredness due to the sleep disturbance of the child.[48] Personal characteristics,[49] family characteristics[50] and community characteristics[51] will all play a part in assisting or undermining parental capacities to cope. Social support has been shown to be very important in assisting parents to cope with having a child with a disability.[52] The availability of such support will depend upon the acceptance by the community of the individual with a disability, the acknowledgment of the increased difficulties associated with parenting a child with a disability, and an acceptance of some community responsibility to support the family—all of which are clearly contextual issues. A cross-cultural study comparing Korean and United States mothers of a child with a disability found that Korean mothers received less informal and professional support and experienced higher levels of stress than the United States mothers.[53] Not all families will be vulnerable, and many will prove to be remarkably resilient.[54] Singer et al concluded from their review of the literature on stress and coping that most parents of children with disabilities do not show demoralisation.[55] This echoes Byrne and Cunningham's conclusion that 'stress is not an inevitable consequence for families'.[56] Even in families who experience stress, many also report positive aspects of parenting a child with a disability.[57] In a longitudinal investigation of families of children with autism, Gray found that the majority of parents reported that their family was coping better than they had been a decade previously.[58] This improvement was attributed to a number of changes including a decrease in the difficult behaviour of the child with autism, an improvement in services, and there was also an indication that parents' coping strategies had improved over time. There is a danger in focusing only on the family as a unit as this overlooks the fact that the system is composed of individuals, of whom all have unique experiences and perspectives. Most research investigating family and parental response to disability is based on maternal reports, which may limit our understanding of the range of experiences. Those studies that have investigated differences in parental experiences and perceptions usually report some differences between fathers' and mothers' responses. Mothers and fathers respond differently to the disability of their child,[59] use services differently,[60] and also use different strategies for coping.[61] Siblings also show a variety of responses.[62]

Consequences for siblings of children with a disability
Much of the literature that examines the issue of care provision across the life span for those with a disability focuses on the role of parents. However, many individuals with a disability will outlive their parents, and care will therefore need to be provided by other family members or through government or non-government agencies. Griffiths and Unger found that 44 per cent of siblings were prepared to take on responsibility for their brother or sister if it became necessary.[63] Krauss et al[64] found that a large proportion of siblings of individuals with an intellectual disability intended that their brother or sister would live with them when their parents were no longer able to provide care.

The literature on the adjustment of siblings to having a brother or sister with a disability is generally quite pessimistic about the consequences. Few studies have been open to the possibility that the experience might have positive outcomes for the non-disabled siblings. It seems clear that the siblings of children with more severe disabilities such as autism are more likely to suffer negative consequences, as children, than are the siblings of children who have disorders that make a less dramatic impact on the individual (Down syndrome, for example).[65] Historical changes are evident, however, and there appears to be a general improvement in the outlook for brothers and sisters of a child with a disability.[66] This change may be due to a number of factors including parental awareness of the possibility of negative outcomes for their other children and greater societal acceptance of children with disabilities.

Family characteristics and response to disability

In any family, size and structure (nuclear, one-parent or blended) may have an influence on the impact of life events. One-parent families may experience more stress[67] and have greater difficulty in coping than intact families.[68] Gallagher and Bristol,[69] however, caution that there has been little systematic research to support this conclusion. Again, it is most likely that there will be considerable variation across one-parent families, both in the type and number of problems encountered and in their coping resources.

Ethnicity and cultural background influence a family's daily life and value systems and are reflected in the beliefs parents hold about their role in the development of their children. One study has found that African-American mothers of children with moderate intellectual disability reported less stress than their Anglo-American peers.[70] It may be that cultural values related to children, achievement and parenting act to affect the appraisal of the situation. This can be clearly seen in the study reported by Farber and Ryckman,[71] who highlighted the fact that families of upper socio-economic status (SES) with a strong orientation to achievement may suffer what they labelled a 'tragic crisis' when their aspirations for their child are dashed by the news of the child's disability. More recently it has been found that parents from higher socio-economic groups were more likely to reject a child with Down syndrome than those from less advantaged groups.[72] At the other end of the spectrum, low SES families may be so beset with problems and have such limited resources to overcome their difficulties that it becomes extremely hard to cope with the additional demands of a child with a disability.[73]

The personal, social and financial resources of a family are often stretched by the presence of a child with a disability. There is incontrovertible evidence that a child with a disability imposes increased financial burdens on families.[74] Society generally accepts that there are increased costs, as evidenced through the provision of benefits and other specialised resources to such families, but families still have to shoulder much of the financial burden and almost all of the caregiving burden. Fujuira[75] reported that in the USA 61 per cent of individuals with an intellectual disability were living with their families, and Carr[76] reported a similar finding for Britain. In Queensland, 86 per cent of individuals with a disability live at home and family members are the primary providers of support.[77]

Having a child with a disability brings with it extra costs for the family. However, many of the families with a child with a disability are already at an economic disadvantage; indeed, their poverty may be one of the factors con- tributing to their child's condition.[78] Park, Turnbull and Turnbull[79] report that almost one-third of children with a disability living in the USA live in families whose income is below the poverty line. Poverty then brings addi- tional limitations for the family and the child across at least five dimensions of family quality of life identified by Turnbull and her colleagues: health, pro- ductivity, physical environment, emotional well-being and family interaction.

It is important that families' experiences of living with a child with a dis- ability are not characterised as always burdensome. A small number of researchers have begun the attempt to understand the positive experiences of living with a family member with a disability. There is evidence, for example, that the brothers and sisters of a child with a disability have very positive rela- tionships with their siblings with a disability, with a number of reports finding more positive relationships in these families than in comparison families where all children are developing normally.[80] Muirhead[81] and Stainton and Besser[82] interviewed parents of children with a disability and discovered that parents believed there had been a number of personal and family benefits in having a child with a disability. Hastings and Taunt[83] provide a review of pos- itive perceptions and experiences of family members.

The interactive cycle between the functioning of individuals and that of the family as a system needs to be considered. There is a great deal of research examining the impact of the individual with a disability on family life. Adap- tive behaviour, rather than overall level of severity of the disability, may bear a stronger relationship than degree of severity of intellectual disability to the stress experienced, particularly by mothers of young children.[84] Tempera- mental characteristics and the level of behavioural problems also seem to have a stronger influence on family stress levels than the degree of severity of the intellectual disability per se.[85]

Characteristics of other family members are also important in determin- ing the coping strategies adopted by families, and therefore their effectiveness, and these characteristics themselves will vary between and within families across time. Barbarin, Hughes and Chesler[86] investigated the effectiveness of coping strategies used by parents whose child has cancer. They found that parents reported better marital functioning when the coping styles they adopted were complementary. In addition, individual resources related to parental educational levels,[87] as well as factors related to the number of chil- dren in the family[88] and the health of family members,[89] influence family functioning and developmental outcomes.

Stage of family life may be an important aspect to consider, with elevated potential for stress at transition points such as the initial diagnosis, or when par- ents recognise the faster developmental rate of younger siblings of the child with a developmental disability, or on entry to school, or at puberty, or when residential or other adult life issues become central.[90] Many of the problems encountered by families may also reflect the mismatch between the life cycle in such families and the community norms. The gap may become particularly marked when in adulthood the person with a disability continues to behave in ways that are usually associated with childhood, such as tantrums or aggressive outbursts. In later life, elderly parents may find that they lack the personal and physical resources to cope with these problems. Their situation may be exacerbated by the lack of residential placement options. We are in the midst of a period of substantial demographic change, with increased longevity for both individuals with disabilities and the members of their families.

Community perceptions of families of children with a disability

We have mentioned several times the part that community perceptions and acceptance of individuals with disabilities can play in assisting families in their multiple roles in regard to their child with a disability. In addition, there is the question of how much recognition is given by the wider community to the need for families to invest extra effort. The community may perpetuate distorted perceptions of the need for superhuman, almost saintly characteristics to care for a child with a disability. Alternatively, it may minimise the level of care required (they get benefits and services, so what are they complaining about?). The reality will lie somewhere between these extremes and vary according to child, family and community. For those who want a more adequate picture of family life, and who wish to develop a deeper understanding of the lives of mothers of a child with a disability, we strongly recommend the book *Public Policy, Private Lives*, by Bowman and Virtue,[91] which includes the stories in their own words of ten women in this situation.

Links to the community for families of children with a disability

Parents of a child with a disability are more likely to report social isolation than are parents whose children are developing normally, as can be seen in this mother's words: 'I miss my friends. I miss my family . It is the camaraderie of people outside disabilities that I miss'.[92] The problem of limited friendships for families following the birth of a child with a disability may have several causes. It may not only be a matter of isolation or ostracism, but withdrawal of families from their previous social networks. It can also be a matter of preoccupation with the demands of caring and maintaining other aspects of family life. Mothers of a child with a disability are less likely to be involved in work outside the home, and this may have serious consequences for their capacity to form friendships.[93]

Employment can be a protective mechanism for mothers in particular.[94] This protective effect may be due to release of tension, the sense of competence that may be associated with accomplishment, or to the social opportunities that work provides.[95] Unfortunately, employment opportunities are often not available, at least to the same extent, for the mothers of a child with a disability,[96] with fathers' work also being affected in some families.[97] Finding a solution to the lack of opportunities in this domain is clearly not within the capacities of families with a child with a disability but requires a concerted commitment from their community.

Consequences for families depend, on the one hand, upon the interplay of the specific characteristics of both the children with the disability and their families. On the other hand, families are affected by the beliefs, attitudes, values and actions of the members of their communities and the wider society. Just as people with disabilities vary greatly in their characteristics, attainments and life outcomes, so too do families.

Before viewing disability as the cause of the particular patterns of functioning observed in such families, there is a need to consider the extent to which these patterns of functioning are similar to those that are the norm for the community to which a family belongs. In order to gain a balanced perspective on the impact of having a child with a disability, the key issue is to determine those patterns of functioning that relate to disability as opposed to those that do not. Such a perspective places the emphasis first on the person, rather than the disability, and next on the family, rather than only one of its members. As such, it moves away from the view that the child with the disability is central to all major family decisions, characteristics and outcomes.

Consequences for communities

Earlier in this chapter the historical and cultural differences in societal attitudes to people with disabilities were discussed. The emphasis was on the impact of beliefs, attitudes and values on those affected. But beliefs, attitudes and values also have an effect on those who hold them. For example, tolerance and acceptance, as opposed to prejudice and rejection, are features of open societies. Openness to diversity can be seen as part of the 'adaptive fitness' of societies and an index of advancement of the moral, intellectual and social capital of societies. Cultural differences lead to diversity of moral, intellectual and social norms, and economic factors may further constrain the extent to which openness is possible.

Family and community responsibilities
We have recently seen more major changes to government policies for the disability sector.[98] Some have been positive while others may act to increase the burden on individual families; for example, recent changes to residential service provision for children with severe behavioural disturbances may make the situation for some parents even worse.[99]

De-institutionalisation and the pressure for family care may result in an inadequate redistribution of resources. It may be unclear what the responsibilities of families are, and what their communities should be expected to provide. After an era of government assumption of increasing responsibility, with a growing negativity towards charitable non-government agencies, economically straitened times have brought a reversal, with governments increasingly withdrawing from direct service delivery. Unfortunately, this is occurring before the re-establishment of appropriate community services and in a climate where it is increasingly difficult to raise funds from non-governmental sources. The rhetoric is that the community cares, but the reality is an entrenched resistance by the community to taking on the role that governments have played, and a consequent lack of funds moving from the private sector (businesses and individuals) to charities. Ironically, governments still want to regulate and set policy constraints, but are not willing to provide adequate funding for the implementation of new standards and models, let alone maintenance of existing services and supports. Despite the reduced funding by governments, there is also evidence that, at least in Britain, many families, particularly those from ethnic minorities, are likely to miss out on their remaining entitlements.[100]

In Australia, services are not equally available to all our citizens. Where one lives makes a big difference to one's daily experiences. People who live in rural and remote communities have very different experiences from those in metropolitan areas. For families with a child with a disability this context can have a profound impact on the level of services, and many families have made the decision to leave their homes and move to communities where they see more opportunities for their child with a disability.

While family characteristics and resources will impact on family response to having a member with a disability, it is important to recognise the role society plays in supporting or increasing the burden on families, as well the direct impact on the individual with the disability. These influences come from both informal and formal aspects of society. We have already discussed some of the informal ways in which acceptance or rejection of the individual can impact on families. Governmental policy embodies the formal ways in which our society responds to disability in its citizens.

Bowman and Virtue wrote about experiences with their own daughters:

Our experience was personal but it was also political. Nothing could have changed the disability but the circumstances of our lives and the lives of our children were shaped by social and economic policies. Caring for our daughters was hard but it was made so much harder by lack of support, lack of information, lack of child care, inadequate housing, living on a low income and struggling through the medical maze—all issues of public policy.[101]

While disability has increasingly become visible to the community through events such as the Special Olympics and disability-focused advertising campaigns, there is still quite a way to go before tolerance and acceptance are widespread. Until that is achieved, prejudice and rejection will continue to set the context for too many people with disabilities and their families. Such attitudes have the consequence of increasing the level of handicap that flows from impairment and disability. As one slogan puts it: *'Your attitude; my handicap'*. Such attitudes, of course, handicap us all.

Student exercises

1   What do you associate with the word 'disability'? Write down the thoughts that immediately come to mind and discuss these with a fellow student.

2   Take a tour of your community. Make a list of all the aspects that could increase the difficulty of living and access for people with disabilities (such as buildings that are difficult to enter in a wheelchair). Analyse your list to identify those features that could easily be modified and those that are more difficult to change.

3   In what ways can contexts alter the experiences and developmental opportunities for children with disabilities? How can professionals such as teachers, therapists or social workers change contexts to make children with disabilities and their families less vulnerable?

4   Consider how the various types of disability might exacerbate normative life stressors such as changing schools or having a seriously ill parent.

5   What factors may contribute to the increased vulnerability of children with a disability to abuse and how might these be addressed? Consider individual, community and policy changes that might contribute to an improvement in this area.

Notes

1   Australian Institute of Health and Welfare, 'People with an Intellectual or Early Onset Disability in Australia', *Journal of Intellectual & Developmental Disability*, 28, 2003, pp. 79–83.

2   Australian Bureau of Statistics, *Disability, Ageing and Carers: Summary of Findings*, catalogue no. 4430.0, Australian Bureau of Statistics, Canberra, 1999.

3   M. Crombie, P. Gunn & A. Hayes, 'A Longitudinal Study of Two Cohorts of Children with Down Syndrome', in *Adolescents with Down Syndrome: International Perspectives on Research and Programme Development*, ed, C. Denholm, University of Victoria, Victoria, BC, 1991, pp. 3–13.

4   J. Steele, 'Epidemiology: Incidence, Prevalence and Size of the Down's Syndrome Population', in *New Approaches to Down Syndrome*, eds, B. Stratford & P. Gunn, Cassell, London, 1996, pp. 46–72.

5   World Health Organization, 'International Classification of Functioning, Disability and Health', WHO, Geneva, 2001.

6   See, for example, M.A. Traci, T. Seekins, A. Szalda-Petree & C. Ravesloot, 'Assessing Secondary Conditioning Among Adults with Developmental Disabilities: A Preliminary Study', *Mental Retardation*, 40, 2002, pp. 119–31.

7   R.J. Simeonsson, J.S. McMillen & G.S. Huntington, 'Secondary Conditions in Children with Disabilities: Spina Bifida as a Case Example', *Mental Retardation and Developmental Disabilities Research Reviews*, 8, 2002, pp. 198–205.

8   N.E. Groce, *Everybody Here Spoke Sign Language: Hereditary Deafness on Martha's Vineyard*, Harvard University Press, Cambridge, MA, 1985.

9   See, for example, A. Hayes & P. Gunn, 'Developmental Assumptions about Down Syndrome and the Myth of Uniformity', in *Adolescents with Down Syndrome: International Perspectives on Research and Programme Development*, eds, C. Denholm & J. Ward, University of Victoria, Victoria, BC, 1990, pp. 73–80; D. Power, 'Deaf and Hard of Hearing Students', in *Educating Children with Special Needs* (3rd edn), eds, A. Ashman & J. Elkins, Prentice Hall, New York, 1998, pp. 345–81.

10   A.B.D. Clarke & A.M. Clarke, 'The Historical Context', in Stratford & Gunn, 1996, pp. 12–22.

11   B. Stratford, 'In the Beginning', in Stratford & Gunn, 1996, pp. 3–11.

12   Steele, 1996.

13   Steele, 1996.

14   See for example, A.H. Bittles, B.A. Petterson, S.G. Sullivan, R. Hussain, E.J. Glasson & P.D. Montgomery, 'The Influence of Intellectual Disability on Life Expectancy', *Journal of Gerontology*: Series A: Biological Sciences and Medical Sciences, 57A, M470–M472, 2002; L.Y. Wong & L.J. Paulozzi, 'International Classifications of Functioning, Disability and Health', WHO, Geneva, 2001.

15   Steele, 1996.

16   K.A. Hallidie-Smith, 'The Heart', in Stratford & Gunn, 1996, pp. 85–99.

17   E. Parens & A. Ach, 'Disability Rights Critique of Parental Genetic Testing: Reflections and Recommendations', *Mental Retardation and Developmental Disabilities Research Reviews*, 9, 2003, pp. 40–7.

18   D. Thomas, *The Social Psychology of Childhood Disability*, Methuen, London, 1978.

19   J. Valsiner, 'Two Alternative Epistemological Frameworks in Psychology: The Typological and Variational Modes of Thinking', *Journal of Mind and Behavior*, 5, 1984, p. 450.

20   E. Goffman, *Stigma*, Penguin, Harmondsworth, 1963.

21   Goffman, 1963, p. 13.

22   D. Fullwood & P. Cronin, *Facing the Crowd: Managing Other People's Insensitivities to Your Disabled Child*, Royal Victorian Institute for the Blind, Melbourne, 1986.

23   J. Mercer, *Labelling the Mentally Retarded*, University of California Press, Berkeley, 1973.

24   H. Tajfel, *Human Groups and Social Categories*, Cambridge University Press, Cambridge, 1981.

25   See Chapter 3 for examples of 'passing' in ethnic minority groups.

26   M. Rosen, G. Clark & M. Kivitz, *The History of Mental Retardation: Collected Papers*, vols 1 & 2, University Park Press, Baltimore, 1976; Clarke & Clarke, 1996.

27   M. Nakamura, 'Acceptance or Refusal of Disability in a Tolerant Society: Reexamination of the History of People with Disabilities in America', *Japanese Journal of Special Education*, 39, 6, 2002, pp. 15–29.

28   A. Hayes, 'Families and Disabilities: Another Facet of Inclusion', in Ashman & Elkins, 1998, pp. 39–66.

29   A.C. Croker, 'Introduction: The Happiness in All Our Lives', *American Journal on Mental Retardation*, 105, 2002, pp. 319–25.

30   M. Cuskelly & I. de Jong, 'Self-Concept in Children with Down Syndrome', *Down Syndrome Research and Practice*, 4, 1996, pp. 59–64.

31   S. Mrug & J.L. Wallander, 'Self-Concept of Young People with Physical Disabilities: Does Integration Play a Role?' *International Journal of Disability, Development and Education*, 49, 2002, pp. 267–80.

32   H.McB. Johnson, 'My Right to Life', *Weekend Australian Magazine*, 3–4 May, 2003, p. 21. Also see N. Watson, 'Well, I Know This is Going to Sound Very Strange to You, But I Don't See Myself as a Disabled Person: Identity and Disability', *Disability and Society*, 17, 2003, pp. 509–27.

33   P. Bramston & C. Mioche, 'Disability and Stress: A Study in Perspective', *Journal of Intellectual & Developmental Disability*, 26, 2001, pp. 233–42.

34   S. Stieler, 'Students with Physical Disabilities', in Ashman & Elkins, 1998, pp. 463–519.

35   S. Vig & R. Kaminer, 'Maltreatment and Developmental Disabilities in Children', *Journal of Developmental and Physical Disabilities*, 14, 2002, pp. 371–86.

36   P. Cooke & P.J. Standen, 'Abuse and Disabled Children: Hidden Need...?', *Child Abuse Review*, 11, 2002, pp. 1–18.

37   T. Heiman, 'Friendship Quality Among Children in Three Educational Settings', *Journal of Intellectual & Developmental Disability*, 25, 2000, pp. 1–12.

38   C. Hughes, M.S. Rodi, S.W., Lorden, S.E. Pitkin, K.R. Derere, B. Hwang & X. Cai, 'Social Interactions of High School Students with Mental Retardation and Their General Education Peers', *American Journal on Mental Retardation*, 104, 1999, pp. 533–44; E.A. Nowicki & R. Sandieson, 'A Meta-analysis of School-age Children's Attitudes Towards Persons with Physical and Intellectual Disabilities', *International Journal of Disability, Development and Education*, 49, 2002, pp. 241–65.

39   A. Jobling & M. Cuskelly, 'Life Styles of Adults with Down Syndrome Living at Home', in *Down Syndrome Across the Life Span*, eds, M. Cuskelly, A. Jobling & S. Buckley, Whurr Publishers, London, 2002, pp. 109–20.

40   J. Carr, 'Long-term Outcomes for People with Down's Syndrome', *Journal of Child Psychology and Psychiatry*, 35, 3, 1994, pp. 425–39.

41   See, for example, K. Funder, ed, *Images of Australian Families*, Longman Cheshire, Melbourne, 1991; D. Gittins, *The Family Question* (2nd edn), Macmillan, London, 1993; B. Gottlieb, *The Family in the Western World from the Black Death to the Industrial Age*, Oxford University Press, Oxford, 1993; H. Mackay, *Reinventing Australia: The Mind and Mood of Australia in the 90s*, Angus & Robertson, Sydney, 1993.

42   A. Bower & A. Hayes, 'Mothering in Families With and Without a Child with a Disability', *International Journal of Disability, Development and Education*, 45, 1998, pp. 313–22.

43   See, for example, R.G. Gallimore, L.P. Bernheimer & T.S. Weisner, 'Family Life is More Than Managing a Crisis: Broadening the Agenda of Research on Families Adapting to Childhood Disability', in *Developmental Perspectives on Children with High Incidence Disabilities*, eds, R. Gallimore, L.P. Bernheimer, D. MacMillan, D. Spence & S. Vaughn, Lawrence Erlbaum, Mahwah, NJ, 1999, pp. 40–80; R.G. Gallimore, J.J. Coots, T.S. Weisner, H. Garnier & D. Guthrie, 'Family Responses to Children with Early Developmental

Delays II: Accommodation Intensity and Activity in Early and Middle Childhood', *American Journal on Mental Retardation*, 101, 1996, pp. 215–32.

44   M. Seligman & R.B. Darling, *Ordinary Families, Special Children*, The Guilford Press, New York, 1989.

45   L. Powers, 'Disability and Grief: From Tragedy to Challenge', in *Families, Disability, and Empowerment: Active Coping Skills and Strategies for Family Interventions*, eds, G. Singer & L. Powers, Paul H. Brookes, Baltimore, 1993, pp. 119–49.

46   G. Eden-Piercy, J. Blacher & R. Eyman, 'Exploring Parents' Reactions to their Young Child with Severe Handicaps', *Mental Retardation*, 24, 5, 1986, pp. 285–91.

47   R. Cummins, 'The Subjective Well-Being of People Caring for a Family Member with a Severe Disability at Home: A Review', *Journal of Intellectual & Developmental Disability*, 26, 2001, pp. 83–100.

48   G. Stores & L. Wiggs, *Sleep Disorders in Children and Adolescents with Developmental Disorders*, Mac Keith Press, London, 2001.

49   See, for example, G. Hedov, G. Anneren & K. Wikblad, 'Swedish Parents of Children with Down's Syndrome', *Scandinavian Journal of Caring Sciences*, 16, 2002, pp. 424–30.

50   S. Button, R.C. Pianta & R.S. Marvin, 'Partner Support and Maternal Stress in Families Raising Children with Cerebral Palsy', *Journal of Developmental and Physical Disabilities*, 13, 2001, pp. 61–81; D.C. Lustig, 'Family Coping in Families with a Child with a Disability', *Education and Training in Mental Retardation and Developmental Disabilities*, 37, 2002, pp. 14–22.

51   D.E. Gray, 'Ten Years On: A Longitudinal Study of Families of Children with Autism', *Journal of Intellectual & Developmental Disability*, 27, 2000, pp. 215–22.

52   See, for example, J.S. Greenberg, M.M. Seltzer, M.W. Krauss & H.W. Kim, 'The Differential Effects of Social Support on the Psychological Well-being of Aging Mothers of Adults with Mental Illness or Mental Retardation, *Family Relations*, 46, 1997, pp. 383–94; A. Taanila, L. Syjälä, J. Kokkonen & M.R. Järvelin, 'Coping of Parents with Physically and/or Mentally Disabled Children', *Child: Care, Health & Development*, 28, 2002, pp. 73–86.

53   J.Y. Shin, 'Social Support for Families of Children with Mental Retardation: Comparison Between Korea and the United States', *Mental Retardation*, 40, 2002, pp. 103–18.

54   C. Cunningham & S. Glenn, 'Parent Involvement and Early Intervention', in *Current Approaches to Down's Syndrome*, eds, D. Lane & B. Stratford, Cassell, London, 1985, pp. 521–9.

55   G. Singer, L. Irvine, B. Irvine, N. Hawkins, J. Hegreness & R. Jackson, 'Helping Families Adapt Positively to Disability: Overcoming Demoralization through Community Supports', in Singer & Powers, 1993, pp. 67–83.

56   E. Byrne & C. Cunningham, 'The Effects of Mentally Handicapped Children on Families— A Conceptual Review', *Journal of Child Psychology and Psychiatry*, 26, 6, 1984, p. 852.

57   R.P. Hastings & H.M. Taunt, 'Positive Perception in Families of Children with Developmental Disabilities', *American Journal on Mental Retardation*, 107, 2002, pp. 116–27.

58   Gray, 2000.

59   M.A. Roach, G.I. Orsmond & M.S. Barratt, 'Mothers and Fathers of Children with Down Syndrome: Parental Stress and Involvement in Childcare', *American Journal on Mental Retardation*, 104, 1999, pp. 422–36.

60   L. Little, 'Differences in Stress and Coping for Mothers and Fathers of Children with Asperger's Syndrome and Nonverbal Learning Disorders', *Pediatric Nursing*, 28, 2002, pp. 565–70.

61   E.L. Essex, M.M. Seltzer & M.W. Krauss, 'Differences in Coping Effectiveness and Well-being Among Aging Mothers and Fathers of Adults with Mental Retardation', *American Journal on Mental Retardation*, 104, 1999, pp. 545–63.

62   M. Cuskelly, D. Chant & A. Hayes, 'Behaviour Problems in Siblings of Children with Down Syndrome: Associations with Family Responsibilities and Parental Stress', *International Journal of Disability, Development and Education*, 45, 1998, pp. 295–311.

63   D.L. Griffiths & D.G. Unger, 'Views about Planning for the Future among Parents and Siblings of Adults with Mental Retardation', *Family Relations*, 43, 1994, pp. 1–8.

64   M.W. Krauss, M.M. Seltzer, R. Gordon & D.H. Friedman, 'Binding Ties: The Roles of Adult Siblings of Persons with Mental Retardation', *Mental Retardation*, 96, 1996, pp. 83–93.

65   A. Gath & D. Gumley, 'Family Background of Children with Down's Syndrome and of Children with a Similar Degree of Mental Retardation', *British Journal of Psychiatry*, 149, 1986, pp. 161–71; A. Bågenholm & C. Gillberg, 'Psychosocial Effects on Siblings of Children with Autism and Mental Retardation: A Population-based Study', *Journal of Mental Deficiency Research*, 35, 1991, pp. 291–307.

66   M. Cuskelly, 'Adjustment of Siblings of Children with a Disability: Methodological Issues', *International Journal for the Advancement of Counselling*, 21, 1999, pp. 111–24.

67   M.B. Olsson & C.P. Hwang, 'Depression in Mothers and Fathers of Children with Intellectual Disability', *Journal of Intellectual Disability Research*, 45, 2001, pp. 535–43.

68   Beckman, 1983.

69   J.J. Gallagher & M. Bristol, 'Families of Young Handicapped Children', in *Handbook of Special Education: Research and Practice: Low Incidence Conditions*, eds, M.C. Wang, M.C. Reynolds & H.J. Walberg, Pergamon, Oxford, 1989, pp. 295–317.

70   S. Flynt & T. Wood, 'Stress and Coping of Mothers of Children with Moderate Mental Retardation', *American Journal of Mental Deficiency*, 94, 3, 1989, pp. 278–83; C. Salisbury, 'Stressors of Parents with Young Handicapped and Nonhandicapped Children', *Journal of the Division of Early Childhood*, 11, 2, 1987, pp. 154–60.

71   B. Farber & D.B. Ryckman, 'Effects of Severely Mentally Retarded Children on Family Relationships', *Mental Retardation*, 2, 1965, pp. 1–17.

72   B. Shepperdson, 'Changes in the Characteristics of Families with Down's Syndrome Children', *Journal of Epidemiology and Community Health*, 39, 1985, pp. 320–4.

73   B. Meyer-Probst, H.D. Rosler & H. Teichmann, 'Biological and Psychosocial Risk Factors and Development During Childhood', in *Human Development: An Interactional Perspective*, eds, D. Magnusson & V.L. Allen, Academic Press, New York, 1983, pp. 225–46; A. Sameroff & R. Seifer, 'Familial Risk and Child Competence', *Child Development*, 54, 1983, pp. 1254–68; E.E. Werner & R.S. Smith, *Vulnerable but Invincible*, Wiley, New York, 1982.

74   E. Emerson, 'Mothers of Children and Adolescents with Intellectual Disability: Social and Economic Situation, Mental Health Status, and the Self-assessed Social and Psychological Impact of the Child's Difficulties', *Journal of Intellectual Disability Research*, 47, 2003, pp. 385–99.

75   G.T. Fujuira, 'Demography of Family Households', *American Journal on Mental Retardation*, 104, 1998, pp. 545–63.

76   Carr, 1994.

77   Queensland Government, 'Disability: A Queensland Profile', Queensland Government, Brisbane, 1999.

78   A. Birenbaum, 'Poverty, Welfare Reform, and Disproportionate Rates of Disability Among Children', *Mental Retardation*, 40, 2002, pp. 212–18.

79   J. Park, A.P. Turnbull & H.R. Turnbull III, 'Impact of Poverty on Quality of Life in Families of Children with Disabilities', *Exceptional Children*, 68, 2002, pp. 151–71.

80   See, for example, M. Cuskelly & P. Gunn, 'Sibling Relationships of Children with Down Syndrome: Perspectives of Mothers, Fathers and Siblings', *American Journal on Mental Retardation*, 108, 2002, pp. 234–44.

81   S. Muirhead, 'An Appreciative Inquiry About Adults with Down Syndrome', in *Down Syndrome Across the Life Span*, eds, M. Cuskelly, A. Jobling & S. Buckley, Whurr Publishers, London, 2002, pp. 149–58.

82   T. Stainton & H. Besser, 'The Positive Impact of Children with an Intellectual Disability on the Family', *Journal of Intellectual & Developmental Disability*, 23, 1998, pp. 57–70.

83   Hastings & Taunt, 2002.

84   M. Hanson & M. Hanline, 'Parenting a Child with a Disability: A Longitudinal Study of Parental Stress and Adaptation', *Journal of Early Intervention*, 14, 3, 1990, pp. 234–48.

85   P.J. Beckman, 'Influence of Selected Child Characteristics on Stress in Families of Handicapped Infants', *American Journal of Mental Deficiency*, 88, 1983, pp. 150–6. It is important to note that the disabilities affecting individuals vary greatly in their impact on health, longevity, functioning and well-being. These variables influence the response of the person with a disability and are also important in the reactions of their families. For example, a comparison of stress levels in families where there is a child with Down syndrome or autism found significantly higher stress levels for the autistic group. A. Donovan, 'Family Stress and Ways of Coping with Adolescents Who Have Handicaps: Maternal Perceptions', *American Journal on Mental Deficiency*, 92, 6, 1998, pp. 502–9.

86   O.A. Barbarin, D. Hughes & M.A. Chesler, 'Stress, Coping and Marital Functioning among Parents of Children with Cancer', *Journal of Marriage and the Family*, 47, 1985, pp. 473–80.

87   H. Coon, G. Carey & D.W. Fulker, 'Community Influences on Cognitive Ability', *Intelligence*, 16, 2, 1992, pp. 169–88.

88   S. Fisman & L. Wolf, 'The Handicapped Child: Psychological Effects of Parental, Marital and Sibling Relationships', *Psychiatric Clinics of North America*, 14, 1991, pp. 199–217.

89   W.A. Horwitz & A.E. Kazak, 'Family Adaptation to Childhood Cancer: Sibling and Family Systems Variables', *Journal of Clinical Child Psychology*, 19, 1990, pp. 221–8.

90   Cunningham & Glenn, 1985.

91   D. Bowman & M. Virtue, *Public Policy, Private Lives*, Australian Institute of Intellectual Disability, Canberra, 1993, p. i.

92   'Peg', in Bowman and Virtue, 1993, p. 127.

93   M. Cuskelly, L. Pulman & A. Hayes, 'Parenting and Employment Decisions of Parents with a Preschool Child with a Disability', *Journal of Intellectual & Development Disability*, 23, 1998, pp. 319–33.

94   M.E. Warfield, 'Employment, Parenting, and Well-being Among Mothers of Children with Disabilities', *Mental Retardation*, 39, 2001, pp. 297–309.

95   Cuskelly, Pulman & Hayes, 1998.

96   M. Einam & M. Cuskelly, 'Paid Employment of Mothers and Fathers of an Adult Child with Multiple Disabilities', *Journal of Intellectual Disability Research*, 46, 2002, pp. 158–67; Cuskelly, Pulman & Hayes, 1998.

97   Einam & Cuskelly, 2002.

98   See for a discussion C. Bigby & E. Ozanne, 'Shifts in the Model of Service Delivery in Intellectual Disability in Victoria', *Journal of Intellectual & Developmental Disability*, 26, 2001, pp. 177–90.

99   Gray, 2002.

100 K. Atkins & J. Rollings, 'Informal Care in Asian and Afro/Caribbean Communities: A Literature Review', *British Journal of Social Work*, 22, 1992, pp. 405–18; N. Murray, 'Listening to the Silent Minority', *Community Care*, 20, 1992, pp. 12–13; P. Russell, 'Handicapped Children', in *Childcare Research, Policy and Practice*, ed, B. Kahan, Hodder & Stoughton, London, 1989.

101 Bowman & Virtue, 1993.

(3)

Ethnicity:

Spotlight on
Person–context Interactions

Jacqueline J. Goodnow

'Ethnicity' is a characteristic often defined—when a shorthand definition is needed—in terms of differences in people's country of origin. For example, consider this conversation overheard at a wedding between Tony Mulcahy and Angela Petradopoulos (names fictional, family backgrounds unchanged). His great-great-grandfather came from Ireland; her parents arrived in Australia from Athens shortly before she was born. The people speaking are an uncle (A) and an aunt (B) of the groom:

A: You know, this is the family's first ethnic wedding.
B: What do you mean? Two have married Americans; one's married a Dubliner; and two have married Maoris.
A: You know what I mean. It's our first ethnic wedding.
B: Mmm. I gather her father's not too happy. He would have preferred her to marry a Greek. Probably feels Mulcahy's a strange name, too hard to pronounce.

People clearly do not always agree in the way they use the term 'ethnic'. The uses of social categories or 'boxes' into which people are grouped are not always the same. One set of interesting questions then has to do with the kinds of groupings that people make, either for themselves or for others. Why do people make some groupings rather than others? Do these groupings matter? What consequences do they have? How do they come to change?

To explore such questions, we need to look beyond the surface labels and their uses. We need, to be more specific, to look at the nature of:

- social categories—the boxes in which we place others or ourselves
- social contexts—our social worlds rather than the geographic areas we live in
- processes—the ways in which people and their contexts influence one another.

Why these areas? We need an understanding of *social categories* because grouping by ethnicity is just one example of what we do all the time. We always group people in some way or another: as short or tall, as male or female, child or adult, fair or dark. We may add a rider ('not your usual Scandinavian type', for example), but grouping is still there. We usually describe ourselves for others by way of boxes they will easily understand. 'I'm average in height' or 'I'm a bit on the skinny side', for example, are statements about boxes, as are the references we often see in newspapers to 'Mediterranean in appearance'.

We need a closer look at *social contexts* in order to specify the difference between one and another. We make little progress as long as we describe contexts in gross terms: describing some, for example, as more stimulating, more tolerant, more diverse or more rigid than another. Nor do we get far if the way we describe one context is of little use when we come to describe another. We need descriptions that are transferable. And, because all contexts change, we need descriptions that help us explain how they change.

And how can we describe the *processes* that link the characteristics of contexts with the characteristics of individuals? The challenge has to do with ways of specifying the processes that link the characteristics of contexts with the characteristics of individuals. It is one thing to establish correlations: to determine, for example, that people of Type X have trouble or do well in places that are Type Y. But that is only part of the story. The next step is to locate the processes that account for these interconnections. In doing so, we need to give more than lip-service to the argument that processes need to be thought of as bidirectional. It is easy to say that people influence contexts and contexts influence people. Being more specific about those mutual influences is a more difficult matter.

The emphasis in this chapter on understanding categories, contexts and processes means that I shall give relatively little space to reports noting that people from some countries of origin do especially well at school, are over-represented among the unemployed, tend to live in particular neighbourhoods, display more signs of family stress, have lower rates of divorce, or are more caring of their ageing parents than are people from other groups. Reports of this kind are valuable and there are now several available.[1] To help us generalise across groups and across chapters, however, we need to look at general issues.

I shall also use examples that may not at first sight fit a focus on ethnic groupings in Australia. Sometimes these examples refer to the position of Indigenous Australians, at other times to events or groupings in other countries.

The reasons for using Indigenous examples are twofold. One is to bring out the variable meanings of ethnicity: from an Indigenous perspective, everyone who arrived after 1788 might be regarded as 'ethnic'. The other is to remind us that the points being made about person–context interconnections in relation to ethnicity apply also to other social categories. Whenever one group regards another as 'other', as 'different', many of the same processes swing into action. 'Ethnicity' and 'ethnic' grouping, then, are not issues that matter only to 'ethnics'. In fact, what we learn from considering ethnicity helps to illuminate the nature of all our lives.

The reason for occasionally looking outside Australia is that doing so often sharpens our understanding of the Australian scene. We become aware, for example, that Australian distinctions among ethnic groups often reflect recency of arrival. To use Gillian Bottomley's expression, the meaning is often that 'ethnics' have recently come 'from another place'.[2]

Distinctions based on country of origin, however, are often made in places where recent immigration is not the case. Examples are the distinctions between Serbs and Croats in what was Yugoslavia, between 'Afrikaners', 'blacks', and 'English' in South Africa, or within the USA between African-Americans and 'Caucasians' (a strange term, which in general means 'white' or, in some states, 'non-Hispanic white'). In effect, we are reminded that describing people in terms of their country or region of origin is not always a response to who came first or later. Country of origin is instead often a shorthand way of referring to perceived differences in lifestyle and social identity.[3]

Contexts

Social groupings as social categories

One old way of thinking about ethnicity sees it as a fixed characteristic, an unchangeable grouping: people either 'are' or 'are not' African, Chinese, German, Greek, Russian and so on. All that contexts then do is to respond to this 'essence' or fixed characteristic. Children merely need to notice the given differences among people and learn the names that go with the visible ones.

The wedding vignette, however, highlights the fact that the terms 'ethnicity' and 'ethnic' often vary in their meaning. One person's use of the term 'ethnic' is not the same as another's. One country's use of the term is also often not the same as another's. One person's self-identification is often not the same as the identity officially assigned. And all the meanings may vary from time to time.

These variations provide a base for an alternative to the usual assumption of fixed characteristics or 'natural kinds'. This is that *ethnicity is a social category.* It is a box in which we place people, or in which people place themselves.[4]

Does this change of framing matter? We shall concentrate on how it helps us to describe contexts and specify processes. It will also become clear that the change in framing has more than academic consequences. It helps us to understand the ways in which, in the course of everyday life, we make judgments, identify ourselves, share meanings, and communicate with one another.

Categories and their qualities

Categories may vary in how broad or narrow they are ('Asian' is a broad category; Cantonese is narrower). Categories differ also in the labels and the meanings attached, and in the extent to which people see membership in one group as incompatible with belonging to another. Angela's father, for example, may not have been happy about the marriage. He did not, however, refuse to come to the wedding or declare that from this moment on Angela was no longer a member of the family.

To bring out the nature and impact of category qualities in relation to ethnic groupings, we highlight three features:
- the extent to which categories and their meanings are shared
- the functions that social categories serve
- the ways in which categories change.

The extent to which categories and their meanings are shared
Anthropologists often describe the difference between one social context and another in terms of the extent to which people share meanings—the extent to which they take the same world view, interpret events in the same way, and work from the same 'cultural models'.[5]

Does this feature of categories matter? One impact, the argument runs, is on the extent to which we understand one another and have the sense that we are understood. Another impact is on the extent to which we feel that here is a person or a place with values possibly similar to our own, rather than awkwardly 'different' or 'foreign'.

When people emigrate or travel from one place to another, the likelihood increases that their sense of who they are will not be fully shared by those they encounter. Even identifying oneself by country of origin may not produce much in the way of shared meaning. It is difficult, for example, to convey the significance of identifying oneself as Macedonian to people who are unaware of a possible difference between Macedonian and Greek, or as Hakka to people for whom 'Chinese' is a category with no further distinctions within it.

Ethnic groupings also bring out the particular lack of agreement that may exist between an officially assigned category and the one in which we place ourselves. Take, for example, the demographer's or the statistician's grouping on the basis of 'country of origin'. The easiest way for bureaucracy to make ethnic groupings is by birthplace. But that grouping may not coincide with the way an individual or a family sees itself. I may regard myself, for example, as a Pole, a Ukrainian or an Assyrian even if political circumstances have meant that neither I nor my parents were born in Poland, the Ukraine or Assyria. I may be classed in Australia as 'Vietnamese', in the sense that this is where I and my parents were born, but regard myself as ethnically Chinese on the grounds that our earlier ancestors were from China, we speak a Chinese dialect at home, and no Vietnamese would ever think of us as 'Vietnamese' (that is, we maintain the distinction and so do the people around us).

This is not to say that the experience of unshared meanings is unique to immigrants. Think, for example, of what it is like trying to describe to someone else a time you have spent in another place, even on a holiday. Being an immigrant, an expatriate or a 'returnee' to one's own country simply heightens the likelihood that experiences and meanings will not be shared.

The functions that social categories serve
Dividing people into groups can serve several functions. Some of these functions are regarded, especially by psychologists, as 'cognitive'. Once we group people, once we decide that they belong to this or that type, we can make quick judgments about them. The judgments may be 'quick-and-dirty', but they will be quick. We also do not need to carry around with us a large number of possible types. The 'cognitive load' is lightened.

Categories may also provide a quickly available explanation for what we see. 'Ah', we say to ourselves, 'you do that because you are young, old, a student, an American'. Or: 'These people are having difficulty because they are Turks, Lebanese or "whingeing Poms"'. Our explanation for the problem is their ethnicity rather than that they are poor, hemmed in by local restrictions, or know that there is another way to live. We may then feel no further need to think about the matter.

Psychologists who are more socially oriented remind us that we also create new categories, or shuffle around old ones, to meet our changing social needs. We create new names, for example, in order to express a sense of change or difference, hence the emergence in the 1950s of a variety of names designed to capture what was different about the newcomers: 'New Australians', 'reffos', 'Balts'. Some of those names seem strange to us now, but they were attempts to create a feeling of order within variety and to put a finger on what the differences were. They were also, to note another social need or social function, groupings designed to keep at a distance people who were felt to be not exactly like 'us'.[6]

That last function—'distancing' other people—is especially well illustrated by the labels often used to place some people outside our usual concerns. Think, for example, about groupings such as the 'deserving' and the 'undeserving poor', or 'dole bludgers' and 'welfare cheats'. Consider also the debate over refugee detention centres. Here the use of distancing terms has been accompanied by moves to avoid having the distanced group appear as individuals (no photographs, official visiting only). The labels by themselves, however, carry some major messages. Different types of treatment seem warranted when we talk about 'illegal refugees', 'economic refugees', 'boat people' and 'queue jumpers' as against 'refugees' or 'asylum seekers'. Give some thought especially to the debate over children in refugee detention centres. In some descriptions, they are the children of 'boat people', of parents who care so little about their children that they 'throw them overboard'. They are held in detention because their parents are 'illegals' and the responsibility for what happens to them rests with their parents. In contrasting descriptions, these are first of all 'children' and they should be treated with the care we normally extend to the young, regardless of what their parents have done. Their placement 'behind barbed wire', without schooling and without protection from various types of threat for periods that can extend to years, is 'inhumane'. It undermines the sense we have of ourselves as 'Australian', with its implication of commitment to 'decency' and 'a fair go'. It is also, in a reverse use of legal categorisations, in itself 'illegal', in violation of both national and international agreements about the treatment of children.

In effect, we can see all around us the way social categories are a standard part of debates and decisions about action. We cannot simply say 'no categories'. Nor can we avoid distinctions having moral overtones. What we can do, however, is to think about the distinctions that are important to us and the grounds for their being important. What we can avoid also is being persuaded without thought by labels that seem to justify giving up principles that are important to us.

Self descriptions as categories

It is easy to think of social categories as terms that are tacked on by others. What about the other side of the picture? Where do we place ourselves? Why in some boxes rather than others?

As with our descriptions of others, self-descriptions can vary from one situation to another. How, for example, would you describe yourself to someone you have not yet met? Would that vary depending on the person and the place? Saying 'I'm Chinese', for example, would not be helpful if you were a resident of Hong Kong.

The wish not to be placed in other people's boxes provides a further basis for particular kinds of self-description. The name 'Anglo-Celtic', for example, is proposed from time to time as a way to describe a particular group. The proposal usually comes from members of that group. Its main function appears to be one of claiming a distinctive identity rather than accepting the lumping together that a term such as 'Anglo' or 'English-speaking' implies.

The ways in which categories change

We have already noted that categories can change from time to time. Now we need to ask: what gives rise to change?

We have already partly answered this question. The groupings change as our needs to make particular distinctions change. In the early days of post–1945 immigration, for example, the main concern was to distinguish between European groups: to separate, for example, the northern Europeans (for example the 'Balts' or the 'Poles') from people who came from further south (the 'Mediterranean' group). Since that time, Australia has taken in more immigrants from countries known as 'Asian'. The contrasts that now seem to stand out for the people who are 'already in place' are between 'Asian' and 'non-Asian', and between various subgroups within that very broad category, 'Asian'.

For an example of the changing functions that distinctions serve, consider the distinctions we make between restaurants. Few Australians would speak of going to eat at an 'ethnic' restaurant. They would feel the need for a more specific description. Especially in urban areas, few would refer to eating at an 'Asian' restaurant. They would feel the need to specify whether the food was Cambodian, Chinese, Japanese, Korean, Thai or Vietnamese. They may even differentiate within the 'Chinese' group, specifying the region. In effect, the groupings shift to meet our changing purposes and our changing awareness of differences.

The example of restaurants, however, leaves out two important components of change. One of these is the extent to which a social category is officially assigned or is open to self-description. On Australian census forms, for example, people can decide whether they identify themselves as Indigenous or not. When it comes to issuing passports, however, most societies are not willing to accept an individual's own description of a place of birth or of a particular ancestry. Now the category is one that is officially determined.

Self-description clearly allows for change more easily than does official assignment. With Aboriginality emerging now as a point of pride, the incidence of self-categorisation as Indigenous is increasing, making the Australian context now seem demographically different from what it was even a short while ago.

The other ingredient of change is the wish or capacity of people to resist being grouped or named in particular ways. That ingredient we shall expand on in the course of looking at the processes highlighted by regarding ethnic groupings as social categories.

Specifying processes

What processes are highlighted by framing ethnicity and ethnic groupings as social categories rather than as 'essences' or fixed characteristics? We single out two:

- the way in which categories tend to wipe out attention to individual differences
- the extent to which people accept, resist, transform or question a category and its basis.

Categories and the nature of attention

The moment we place people in a category by virtue of one characteristic, the way in which we perceive other characteristics shifts. I place you in a particular ethnic group, for example, by virtue of your name, and immediately become more likely to assume that you will have some other characteristics: that you will be, for example, more rather than less industrious, bookish, frugal, interested in sport, easy to understand.

The effect on attention that is especially highlighted by considering ethnic groupings is one that is called 'the outgroup homogeneity effect'.[7] One of the effects of any social grouping is that we quickly lose sight of differences among the people within the group. The members of any group that we see as 'them' tend to be seen as like one another. In contrast, we see 'us' as made up of obviously diverse individuals. We may, in fact, have difficulty perceiving even physical differences among other groups. 'All Chinese look alike' is an old saying, but to the Chinese the differences among themselves are obvious. To them, perhaps, it is the 'Europeans' who all look alike.

The end result is not only galling to the person whose individuality has just been wiped out. We also lose sight of dimensions that cut across groups. There may, for example, be more similarity in values between a middle-class Lebanese from Beirut and a middle-class locally born Australian than there is between the Beirut-born and a Lebanese who grew up in a small village. Between the latter two can be a shared knowledge of place, of history and of language that is greater than what is to be found in the former pair. Their views with regard to education or parenting, however, may be far apart.

Once again, the tendency to overlook differences within a group is not restricted to the lives of immigrants. We all become alert to out-group homogeneity effects, for example, when we are overseas. 'I know some Australians', say some of the people we meet. They then expect that we will be like these other Australians, often to our dismay.

Acceptance, resistance, transformation and questioning

In one-way descriptions of contextual effects, social contexts may be regarded as simply imposing categories. These groupings are seen as already present in the culture. People, as they become socialised or acculturated, are then seen as simply taking over the established or pre-packaged categories.

The reality highlighted by ethnic groupings is more dynamic. People may publicly object to a label such as 'New Australian'. They may invent or propose new categories: 'Anglo-Celtic', for example. They may, in a second or third generation, relabel themselves and reidentify with a parent's or grandparent's country of origin.

How far are such transformations or resistances possible? Or is this emphasis on resistance and transformation a somewhat romantic notion, simply softening the limited extent to which we have choice or raise questions about the boxes in which we are placed?

Clearly there are circumstances under which we raise no questions. At other times, however, even officially assigned categories may come to be questioned. An example is the recent and continuing debate over 'the stolen generation' of Indigenous children (see Chapter 9). Until recently, few people questioned the right of various welfare agencies or government departments to make decisions as to whether children were of 'mixed blood' and, on that basis, could legitimately be removed from their families. Now the motives, legalities and consequences of those categorisation policies are being broadly questioned.

There are also limits, other than legal limits, to the freedom with which people may happily change their category descriptions of themselves. During 1996, for example, heated debate took place in Australia over the legitimacy of an author presenting herself as Ukrainian and her book as written 'from the inside' of a history of persecution (the 'Demidenko debate'). In the same year there were also arguments about the ethics of a non-Aboriginal artist (Elizabeth Durack) representing her paintings as being by an Aboriginal (under the name of Eddie Durrup). In neither case was the law broken. There was, however, strong social disapproval and a sense of inappropriateness, making us aware that there is still a great deal to be understood about the way we respond to what we see as 'wrongful' claims to membership of a particular group.[8]

Variations in context

Our overheard conversation at the beginning of this chapter introduced the ways in which we group people by country or region of origin. It pointed to differences between contexts in terms of the kinds of groupings that are made. It also introduced the need to understand the process of grouping in itself. To demonstrate some further ways of delineating contexts and processes, I start again with a concrete example.

On the current or recent Australian scene, some of the most 'visible' people have a variety of surnames, for example (in alphabetical order): Peter Abeles, Victor Chang, Ernie Dingo, Cathy Freeman, Yasmine Gooneratne, Mary Kostakides, Indira Naidoo, Emily Kngwarreye, Mark Phillippoussis, Aiden Ridgway, Richard Tognetti, John Yu. Who are these people? What are they known for? Can you pronounce these names? Can you identify the countries where these names originate? What names would you add to illustrate the diverse images of 'Australians'? What areas of visibility or achievement do these names involve? Are there some groups that tend to be 'invisible', or for which the popular image seems especially inaccurate? Do people passively accept the images that others have of them?

The nature of contexts: pathways and opportunities

One of the reasons for examining that list of names is to highlight the need to think about the areas in which people achieve success or become visible. It is not simply that people from various groups differ in their overall levels of achievement. Instead, they tend to become visible in specific fields and to be thought of as associated with those fields, for example the arts, media, medicine, politics, sport and so on.

Anthropologists and sociologists use those differences to point out one useful way to describe the difference between one social context and another—in terms of 'structure and opportunity'. Psychologists more often use terms such as 'pathways' or 'lifelines'.[9] In both cases the general notion is that people follow a variety of paths and that societies make it harder or easier for people from various groups to make a sound initial choice, to recover from an error, or to shift from one path to another. People from various ethnic groups, then, may differ not only in the kinds of achievement they value. They may differ also in the information they have about what is possible, and in the extent to which they encounter doors that are open or closed, and people who are able and willing to provide the information they need.

The nature of contexts: Images and multiple group memberships

It is easy to see that contexts differ in their demographics, for example in the number of people who are locally born or born overseas. That list of names helps us see that they differ as well in the visibility of people from various social groups and in the images (positive or negative, accurate or inaccurate) that go with the distinctions.

Do these images matter? Suppose we anchor that question in comments on a phrase often used in discussions about ethnic groupings. This is the phrase 'multicultural context' or 'multicultural society'. Australia, it is often said, is a 'multicultural society'. What does the phrase mean?

At one level, the term simply refers to the presence of people who were born in different countries and who possibly follow lifestyles different from those of the mainstream culture.

Most anthropologists would add another level. All societies, they propose, are made up of several groups and contain more than one lifestyle. Even among 'Anglo' groups, for example, there is formal medicine and 'alternative' medicine. There is also conventional schooling and 'alternative' schooling. What matters, anthropologists propose, is not the simple presence of these alternatives but the ways in which the community perceives them and the people who endorse them. People may, for example, regard formal approaches and alternative approaches as being impossible to combine. They may consider the people who endorse one approach rather than the other to be narrow-minded or gullible. Between the two groups there may be various degrees of tolerance, scorn, competition, or attempts at suppression.

This general line of argument is often summarised by the phrase 'multiplicity and contest'. No society, the proposal runs, operates with a single, neatly organised set of rules or values. Instead, to take a 1992 comment from the anthropologist Claudia Strauss, we need to recognise 'conflict, contradiction, ambiguity, and change in cultural understandings—the way cultural understandings are "contested" or "negotiated" in current jargon'.[10]

From this point of view, a truly multicultural or 'pluralist' society is one where people from different cultural groups can negotiate, maintain or change lifestyles from positions of equal power, visibility and respect. Australia has not reached that ideal state, although it could be described as moving towards it.

Is the definition of multiculturalism purely an academic matter? The answer is no, for reasons that are best brought out by taking a look at the term 'bicultural identity'. It used to be said that the immigrant child in Australia was inevitably 'torn between two worlds'. Being 'torn', however, occurs only in contexts where membership in one social group (for example, being a properly Australian schoolchild) is seen as being incompatible with another (for example, being of the Spanish-speaking community, or being a Muslim and following an Islamic dress code). The perceived incompatibility, it should be noted, may exist on both sides. That is, either group may see a child, an adolescent or an adult as having ceased to be 'one of us' by virtue of having become 'one of them'.

In most lives, however, as Parke and Buriel have especially demonstrated, we manage to be members of several groups, involving family, schools, friendships, leisure or religion, for example.[11] Most of the time we are also able to combine those memberships, altering our ways of acting and speaking as we shift groups. The difficulties start only when we are short on navigating skills, when the shifts violate our own sense of what we are or of what is right, or when the shifts are seen not as adjustments to necessity but as signs of insincerity, disloyalty or betrayal. Those conditions are not unique to immigrant experience, as many a person who has changed 'class' or religion would point out. They may, however, be more likely to occur as families emigrate and come to terms with a new country.

A particular process: Social reflection or image-making?

A frequent proposal within analyses of contexts is that contexts exert their effects by a process of 'mirroring' or 'social reflection'. The general argument is that we tend to see ourselves as others see us, to develop in some respects a 'looking-glass self'.[12]

Obviously we do not always see ourselves in simple mirror-like fashion. Nor are we totally dependent on others agreeing with what we say or finding it at least meaningful. Nonetheless we have to work a little harder or find new ways of establishing who we are and what we mean in situations where, to use the mirror metaphor, we are invisible or the reflected picture is superficial, a caricature or a negative image. To be an immigrant, or to be classed as 'an ethnic', carries all those hazards.

To speak only of hazards, however, is to ignore the extent to which people make an active effort to control the images that others have of them, to make or transform the image rather than simply to accept it or try to come to terms with it. The general argument here comes especially from the work of Henri Tajfel on ways of responding to prejudice.[13]

All of us, Tajfel pointed out, wish to maintain a positive self-image. When we are members of a group that has a poor image in the eyes of a more established or prestigious group, we may make several strategic moves. We may attempt to 'pass': to become accepted as members of the more privileged group, to be seen as 'just like them'. We may also seek to change the image that others have of us, or to take control of that image and turn it into one of our own making.

Taking control of the name applied to us provides an example. You, the established group, may originally construct the category and the label 'wog'. I may object to it. Later, when you have learnt not to use it, I may then claim it as my own and use it deliberately (as is the case for members of the Australian comedy team who describe themselves as 'wogs'). Terms such as 'black' and 'queer' may show a similar pattern. The preference of some Indigenous groups for the application to them of terms such as 'Koori' (terms of their choosing) is part of a similar pattern. It is also an example that invites an interesting contrast with the situation in New Zealand, where the names used for the main ethnic groupings ('Māori' and 'Pākehā', with the latter referring to 'whites') are Māori terms, used by both Māori and Pākehā. In all such cases we need to ask who has the power to give a name or to change one. And when do people seek to do so?[14]

Consequences

Preparing for life outside the family

A father had this advice for his children as they began school in an area where they were likely to encounter misunderstanding and prejudice: 'Just think of yourself as like a tennis ball. The harder they throw you down, the higher you bounce back.'

The father's advice prompts some initial thinking both about the position of newcomers to a country and about changes in anyone's life. What kinds of anticipatory advice come to mind when you think about changes in our own life? Who offered advice? Were there people whom you could ask and who would also be well informed? What conditions influence the kind of advice or preparation that is offered, and its usefulness?

The comments offered will again deal with possible ways of delineating contexts and processes. In essence, contexts now emerge as differing in the extent to which an individual is likely to find 'like-minded' people. When that occurs, children are likely to hear the same message from several sources (for example, from parents, from neighbours and from their peers). Parents will also find it easier to establish support networks: people to whom they can turn for advice and information, or for reassurance when everything seems too mysterious or difficult.

In essence also, all families offer some forms of preparation for life outside the family. Family members may, for example, point to differences between people and supply names and images for various categories. They may provide information about opportunities and about what to expect when a transition is made (the transition to school or to paid work, for example). They may also indicate the extent to which they would find acceptable or unacceptable a child's adopting new ways of speaking, dressing, achieving or spending time.

What particular aspects of family preparation are highlighted by considering the nature and impact of ethnicity? The first that we single out has to do with the way we view differences across generations. Differences are most easily thought of in terms of 'disagreement' or 'conflict'. Immigrant families, however, remind us that some generational differences may be quite acceptable to parents (differences in educational level, for example).[15]

Considering immigrant or ethnic families also highlights the need to ask what members of the family we are talking about. 'The family' suggests that here is a group that functions like a single, solid unit. The reality is that each parent, or each older sibling, is likely to play a different role in the introduction of a child to the world outside the family.

One prompt towards this rethinking comes from the evidence of an increase, within Australia, of marriage across ethnic groupings.[16] Within marriages of this kind it is all the more likely that each parent will play a different part, varying with their knowledge of the world outside the family and with what they value.

A second prompt towards the notion of differential input comes from the special role of older siblings within immigrant families. They are, for instance, the more likely sources of information about the way that Australian schools and Australian peer groups work than the parents may be. Nguyen and Ho add the insightful comment that this situation may not hold when an older child comes into the country after a younger child does, a phenomenon not unknown among refugee Vietnamese families, where members of the family may leave the country of origin at different times or be admitted to Australia at different times. The older child may then be in the awkward situation of having the younger one offering to be the guide or map-maker.[17]

Those comments about what happens within the family, however, may make it sound as if everything depends on who is in the family. *What difference does the nature of the outside world make?* Research on ethnicity and on minority groups highlights two needs.

One of these is the need to be careful about regarding neighbourhoods as monolithic, as containing people who are all of one type or all of like minds. Analyses of ethnic groupings often contain the term 'ethnic communities'. It is a term, however, that has come to be used with caution. It is possible to speak of 'ethnic concentrations', as Birrell does in describing the extent to which Vietnamese are currently to be found in areas such as Sydney's Cabramatta or Melbourne's Springvale.[18] These concentrations, however, may be temporary, being most marked when the arrivals from a particular country are relatively recent and need the networks that can be provided by people who are similar in background, language and current problems. Later generations are likely to be more dispersed, highlighting the need for us to ask about the functions that are served by being in an area where there are others from a similar background, and how those functions change from time to time.

The other need is to ask what specific kinds of preparation occur under what circumstances. We now know, for example, that parents are more likely to talk to their children about racial differences in neighbourhoods that are 'mixed' rather than 'all-of-one-kind'.[19] We also know that parents use more than one strategy in their training of children. They may, for instance, teach children the history of their own group. They may teach children what to do or say when they experience prejudice. They may also promote distrust of the out-group. The strategies they use are often related to the age of the child and to the parents' own experiences of racial bias.[20] Both conclusions derive from studies of African–American families. This type of research, however, and the kinds of findings reported, are clearly relevant also to person–context interconnections in Australia with its diversity of family backgrounds.

One-way assimilation or mutual accommodation?

On the outside wall of a central hospital in Melbourne is a sign that says the equivalent of 'casualty/emergency' in English, Greek and Italian. This is not a painted sign. The letters are large and plastered onto the wall as part of the building.

When did this signposting occur? What prompted it? The sign and these questions highlight an aspect of person–context interconnections that is often referred to by the term 'accommodation'.[21] In effect, people or groups, when they need to interact with one another, engage in some forms of accommodation to the other's status, competence, needs or values. Accommodation, the argument runs, is almost always mutual, although it may be asymmetrical (that is, one person accommodates more than the other does). Accommodation is also usually selective: that is, a change is more readily made in some situations and some areas than in others. To take an Australian example, English speakers are more likely to make some language accommodations in emergency hospital situations than they are in schools. They are also more likely to make changes in the food they eat than they are in the kinds of law that they feel should prevail.

Contexts may now be seen as varying from one another in the extent to which accommodation is asymmetrical and in the areas where accommodation occurs or is pushed for with strong feeling. Australia is quite different from Quebec, for example, where the language used in official documents and street signs has swung from all-English to a mixture of French and English, and then to French alone, with bitter and public fighting over each change.

Varying also are *the forms of pressure or persuasion* that people see as appropriate to use in the course of seeking change on the part of another group. Australia has a history of distinguishing among people with English, Irish and Scots backgrounds (weaker distinctions than they once were, but still present). Towards each other, these groups would often engage in tactics of exclusion from prized positions or resources, but shooting, bombing, or setting places on fire were not widely regarded as reasonable forms of contest. To use a phrase that is more often heard in discussions of police actions or domestic violence, negative actions were expected to stay within a 'reasonable use of force'.

In contrast, the record between 'black' and 'white' was often one of dealing with differences by physical removal: by direct wiping out in earlier times, and later by formally restricting where Indigenous people could live, excluding them from participation as citizens (by denying them the right to vote, for instance), or by removing children from their parents. One suspects that part of the fear that some immigrant groups inspire derives from the apprehension that they will use forms of pressure and persuasion no longer regarded as acceptable between 'civilised' groups.

Those examples highlight the *selectivity of accommodation*. Food, for example, is an area where accommodations often occur. Within Australia there have been changes in food habits on the part of both the 'Anglos', who were the majority in the 1950s, and the immigrants themselves. By contrast, accommodations in an area such as law—in deference to Aboriginal law or Islamic law, for instance—have been minimal.

What distinguishes such areas? One difference proposed has to do with the extent to which there is already a 'niche' in the existing social context. Australians, for example, already had the habit of eating either 'Chinese' or 'Italian' in restaurants. All they needed to do was to expand their definition of 'something different'.

In contrast there is no available 'niche' that would allow a different legal system to take precedence. There is instead a tradition of 'one law', and a sense that this is the way things should be. A sense of 'the way things should be' is probably the important condition. There appears to be the least accommodation when a particular way of doing things is regarded as part of a moral or a natural order. When people see an issue as part of a 'basic' social contract, as part of some 'natural' pattern of rights and obligations, as what God or nature surely intended, then accommodation seems least likely to occur. The greater the number of areas then that are felt to be part of the moral or natural order (for example when the moral order unexpectedly covers not only aspects of religion but also touches on food, drink or clothing), the more there will be a sense of a 'different' group.

Implications for the lives of all people

You do not need to be a 'foreigner' or an 'ethnic' or to belong to any special group in order to benefit from considering how life is influenced by differences in social contexts in combination with differences among individuals. The ideas are transferable to the nature of everyone's life.

All of us, as children or adults, need to learn how to participate in social groups. All of us encounter labels, expectations and assigned identities that we may welcome, resist, modify or transform. All of us move into some areas of activity rather than others—sometimes based on tradition or stereotypes, sometimes on active choice, sometimes because of what is available. And all of us can benefit from the help of others who know how things are done, who can act as guides or mentors.

Those several aspects of participation in a social context become clearer, and take some special forms, whenever we try to create or modify a path rather than follow one that is already established. In this situation it is more likely that we will encounter other people's labels, with their distinctions between 'us' and 'them' and their ideas about what we are like or what we should do. There is likely to be a mixture of open and closed doors in front of us, of willingness and unwillingness to meet our particular needs or interests. The path will also call for navigating skills, for a more active search for information on how to proceed, and for people who can act as guides. All those aspects of living become clearer when we consider the implications of being placed, or of placing oneself, in a group with an 'ethnic' label.

Student exercises

1 How does it help our understanding of what ethnicity means for children, families and communities to regard ethnic groups as social categories rather than as having fixed characteristics?

2 Discuss the strategic moves presented by Tajfel that members of a group with a poor public image might make to improve their image and acceptance by the majority groups. How can these strategies be used by children to counter taunts and bullying based on their ethnic group membership?

3 Without looking, how many languages do you think are used at the beginning of the phone book, or in advice sheets on how to vote? What languages might be added next? What other indications can you think of that suggest some recognition on the part of English speakers that more than one language is now spoken in Australia? How does this illustrate 'accommodation'? Are accommodations made in areas other than language?

4 When and why might people describe themselves in terms such as 'moderate Muslim', 'cultural Catholic' or 'not an orthodox Jew'? Are there other terms that might serve similar functions?

5 You have gone shopping in a large department store with a young child, who has wandered off. How would you describe her to others? How do you think she might describe you, or herself?

Notes

1 R. Hartley, ed, *Families and Cultural Diversity in Australia*, Australian Institute of Family Studies, Melbourne, 1995. Each chapter describes a particular group of immigrants (since 1945) to Australia, and is written by a member of that group.

2 G. Bottomley, ed, *From Another Place: Migration and the Politics of Culture*, Cambridge University Press, Cambridge, 1992.

3 Hartley, 1995, p. 3, makes a similar point in commenting on self-identification as belonging to a particular group: 'The focus for a sense of belonging may be on common physical characteristics, the possession of a distinct language or dialect, a particular religion, a sense of geographical and historical continuity...or a distinct lifestyle...Country of birth is significant because it often coincides with some or all of the factors mentioned but this clearly need not be the case'.

4 Jean Martin, in an early and influential analysis of immigration in Australia, called ethnic groupings a 'social construction': J.I. Martin, *The Migrant Presence*, Allen & Unwin, Sydney, 1979.

This chapter takes the term 'social category' from the work of several social psychologists who have been concerned with the nature of social grouping in general, without specific reference to immigration or ethnicity. Their research has concentrated, for example, on the ease with which people move into distinctions between 'us' and 'them' and on the effects of social categorisation on later judgments about people. See, for example, the work of Penelope Oakes, Peter Robinson, Henri Tajfel and John Turner, with a first introduction to these to be found in a useful general text. K. Durkin, *Developmental Social Psychology*, Blackwell, Oxford, 1995.

Useful also is a book by Hirschfield that is especially concerned with the ways in which some social categories come to feel like 'natural kinds' rather than 'cultural artefacts'; L.A. Hirschfield, *Race in the Making: The Child's Construction of Human Kinds*, MIT Press, Cambridge, MA, 1996.

5   R.G. D'Andrade & C. Strauss, eds, *Human Motivation and Cultural Models*, Cambridge University Press, New York, 1992.

6   For a summary account of some of the labels that arose, see the chapter on inequality and disadvantage in A. Burns & J.J. Goodnow, *Children and Families in Australia*, Allen & Unwin, Sydney, 1985.

7   For a general review of studies on in-group and out-group perceptions, see P.W. Linville, P. Salovey & G.W. Fischer, 'Stereotyping and Perceived Distributions of Social Characteristics: An Application of Ingroup—outgroup Perception', in *Prejudice, Discrimination, and Racism*, eds, J.F. Davidio & S.L. Gaertner, Academic Press, San Diego, CA, 1986, pp. 165—208.

8   See also the autobiographical account of a change in self-identification by the artist and writer Sally Morgan: S. Morgan, *My Place*, Fremantle Arts Centre Press, Fremantle, 1987.

9   See R.B. Cairns & B.D. Cairns, *Lifelines and Risks: Pathways of Youth in Our Time*, Cambridge University Press, New York, 1994.

10   C. Strauss, 'Motives and Models', in *Human Motivation and Cultural Models'*, eds, R.G. D'Andrade & C. Strauss, Cambridge University Press, New York, 1992. See also J.J. Goodnow, 'Parenting and the "Transmission" and "Internalization" of Values: From Social-cultural Perspectives to Within-family Analyses', in *Parenting Strategies and Children's Internalization of Values*, eds, J. Grusec & L. Kuczynski, Wiley, New York, 1997, pp. 333—61.

11   R.D. Parke & R. Buriel, 'Socialization in the Family: Ethnic and Ecological Perspectives', in *Handbook of Child Psychology*, ed, W. Damon, Wiley, New York, 1997, pp. 463—552.

12   The term 'looking-glass self' is from C.H. Cooley, *Human Nature and the Social Order*, Scribners, New York, 1902. For a careful analysis of this concept, see F.E. Aboud, *Children and Prejudice*, Blackwell, Oxford, 1988.

13   H. Tajfel, *Human Groups and Social Categories*, Cambridge University Press, Cambridge, 1981.

14   Exerting control over the language spoken provides another example. Within New Zealand most official functions now start with some statements in the Māori language, regardless of whether the speaker is 'Māori' or 'Pākehā'. That use of language undoubt-edly has several bases. There is, for example, one language rather than the multiple set to be found within Australia. The political representation of Māoris is also very different from what exists for, say, Aboriginal Australians. For one discussion, see G.M. Vaughan, 'A Social Psychological Model of Ethnic Identity and Development', in *Children's Ethnic Socialization: Pluralism and Development*, eds, J.S. Phinney & M.J. Rotheran, Sage, Newbury Park, CA, 1987, pp. 73—91.

15   For a discussion of this way of framing cross-generation differences, see J.J. Goodnow, 'Acceptable Disagreement Across Generations', in *Beliefs About Parenting*, ed, J.G. Smetana, Jossey-Bass, San Francisco, 1994, pp. 51—64. For a broad discussion of 'ethnic families' in relation to the contexts they encounter, see Parke & Buriel, 1997, or A.O. Harrison, M.N. Wilson, C.J. Pine, S.Q. Chan & R. Buriel, 'Family Ecologies of Ethnic Minority Children', *Child Development*, 61, 1990, pp. 347—62.

16   See V. Carrington, 'The Interethnic Family in 1990's Australia', paper presented at the Australian Family Research Conference, Brisbane, 1996. See also C. Price, 'Ethnic Intermixture in Australia', *People and Place*, 2, 1993, pp. 8–10.

17   V. Nguyen & M. Ho, 'Vietnamese–Australian Families', in Hartley, 1995, pp. 216–40.

18   R. Birrell, 'Ethnic Concentrations: The Vietnamese Experience', *People and Place*, 1, 1993, pp. 26–32.

19   M.C. Thornton, L.M. Chatters, R.J. Taylor & W.R. Allen, 'Sociodemographic and Environmental Correlates of Racial Socialization by Black Parents', *Child Development*, 61, 1990, pp. 401–9.

20   D. Hughes & L. Chen, 'When and What Parents Tell Their Children About Race: An Examination of Race-related Socialization in African–American Families', *Applied Developmental Science,* 1, 1997, pp. 200–14.

21   H. Giles, N. Coupland & J. Coupland, 'Accommodation Theory: Communication, Context, and Consequence', in *Contexts of Accommodation*, eds, H. Giles, N. Coupland & J. Coupland, Cambridge University Press, Cambridge, 1991, pp. 1–68.

Sex and Gender:

Impact on Children, Families and Peer Groups

Ailsa Burns and Norma Grieve

The culture is almost entirely male still: the way issues are discussed, the way they're presented, the things you have to do to develop support for yourself. Women don't have the kind of tutelage, they don't have the mentoring, particularly they don't have the sort of implicit understanding of what it is to be a mate. That all makes it more difficult.[1]

While some [discrimination against girls in education] still exists, many parents, teachers, academics and community workers have expressed concern that...boys are not coping with the changes as well as girls. The evidence seems to support these concerns. It is imperative that this is addressed, for the sake of the boys themselves and for society more broadly.[2]

In the preceding chapter it was argued that ethnicity is essentially a social category. The situation with gender is more complex: it is both a biological and a social category. The borderline between the biological and the social is notoriously difficult to chart. By now a great deal of research has explored the issue, revealing much complexity and no simple answers. In this chapter we consider this research in the context of changing relations between males and females in Australian society. In doing so we follow the convention of using the term 'sex' to denote biological sex, and 'gender' to denote male–female differences that appear to be partly or wholly social in origin.

The similarities between men and women are of course much greater than the differences: they share the same cultures, the same abilities and the same needs. Nevertheless, in all societies there are very large differences between the lives that men and women lead: men dominate public life, while women do most of the domestic and lower-status work. Why? Are the biological differences indeed so great that these social differences follow by a law of nature? Or do social forces largely cause the differences in lifestyle? And if so, what are the relevant social forces, and how do they operate?

Contexts

Sex differences in behaviour and attitudes

One approach to these questions has been through attempts to pinpoint difference by comparing males and females on a wide range of abilities and traits. It is said that this approach owes much to the policy of several major United States psychology journals, which required published articles to include a breakdown of results by sex. Multitudinous reports of statistically significant sex differences followed, some of them paralleling popular beliefs, others not. Much of this material was brought together in Maccoby and Jacklin's classic *Psychology of Sex Differences* (1974),[3] which reviewed two thousand such studies and concluded that the differences reported between the sexes were relatively few, and modest. They noted that most sex differences that did emerge were group averages, which occurred in the context of substantial overlap between male and female behaviour. In some cases the differences were apparent only under particular circumstances, or among particular subgroups. Maccoby and Jacklin considered that, where differences were found, both nature (in the form of biology) and nurture (in the form of differential socialisation of boys and girls) had a part to play. They also believed that 'self-socialisation' was of great importance. This latter term refers to the process whereby each child, having realised at an early age that it is either a boy or a girl, and that this is important, sets about acquiring the behaviours that its social group deems to be sex-appropriate: usually through observation and imitation.

Maccoby and Jacklin argued against the view, which was current at the time, that since males and females did differ in some ways (for example in aggression, nurturance, and some verbal, spatial and mathematical abilities) they should be channelled into their 'areas of strength'; that is, men into higher education and leadership, and women into domesticity. But their book did not include any other suggestions for social change. At the time of its publication, however, another strand of gender research was introducing a much more radical proposition: that Western (and other) societal arrangements constituted a massive male-constructed system for oppressing women.[4]

This research pointed to sex-based differences in (among other things) access to educational and career opportunities, rates of pay, expectations about who would do the unpaid domestic labour, sexual freedom, and a raft of moral expectations and demands. At a still more radical level, it indicted language (in particular the English language) as a kind of primal soup within which every form of male-favouring attitude flourished. Feminist researchers pointed out, for example, that the use of the ubiquitous 'he' and 'him' to denote a person of either sex automatically excluded women from the world of real action. Even a short quotation from an influential psychologist illustrates the point, and reads strangely to modern ears: 'Every society consists of men in the process of developing from children into parents. Man's childhood learning, which develops his highly specialised brain–eye–hand coordination and all the intrinsic mechanisms of reflection and language is contingent on prolonged dependence. Only thus does man develop conscience and dependence on himself which will make him, in turn, dependable...'[5]

Social changes over recent decades have brought considerable differences to the gendering of social arrangements. For example, until the late 1960s in Australia around 27 per cent of boys and less than 20 per cent of girls had completed Year 12, and there was a widespread view that education was less important for girls. But after 1977 the gender difference reversed, and by the early 1990s some 80 per cent of girls but only 70 per cent of boys completed secondary school. The girls were also achieving higher grades in the majority of subjects and overall—up to 19 per cent higher in some states in some years—and by 2001, of those proceeding to higher education 56 per cent were females.[6]

These trends have raised some community concern that a system that previously discriminated in favour of boys is now discriminating against them. The real situation, however, is a good deal more complex. More girls are doing well because many of the old biases against them—for example inadequate science teaching, low expectations and sexist textbooks—have been overcome. But many more boys and girls now stay on at school because there are few jobs for those who leave early, and this enlarged group includes 'non-academic' students who have trouble with, or who are not interested in, the school curriculum. One consequence is that the gender differences in cognitive abilities described by Macklin and Jacklin now occur in a changed form.

Mathematical abilities are a case in point. Mathematics used to be a subject more commonly taken by boys, and boys' performance was clearly superior. But in recent years girls have tended to do better than boys in maths subjects at all but the very highest levels.[7] What has happened? Maths can be studied at higher or lower levels, and the figures show that mathematically more able girls are likely to take intermediate level units, although many would be able to handle the advanced level. At the same time, large numbers of boys of varying ability enrol in intermediate level units, where they are competing with girls from a narrower more advanced ability range. In consequence many of the boys do less well, while many of the girls fail to do justice to their abilities. Thus a continuing gender bias in subject choice underlies this change in outcome.

By contrast, English has always been a popular school subject for girls, and more of them now enrol in higher level courses—but they nevertheless outperform the boys, being almost twice as likely to be placed in the top quarter of students and half as likely to be in the bottom quarter. The increased proportion of students undertaking Year 12 seems to be a factor here too, with many boys having poorer language skills that become increasingly apparent in the senior school years. Poorer language skills may also underlie the boys' lesser achievement in a number of other subjects, where learning and assessment procedures now require students to be good readers and communicators. These higher demands for language skills derive from knowledge advances and from labour market requirements, so they are unlikely to go away.

This is an issue common to many countries today. In Australia, increasing community anxiety about boys' educational problems resulted in 2002 in a Commonwealth Parliamentary inquiry[8] that concluded, in the words quoted at the beginning of this chapter, that boys are not coping with the changes in educational demands as well as girls. It went on to discuss possible causes, and intervention programs that could reduce educational under-achievement.

If time has altered educational outcomes, it has not, however, altered the sex differences found in personality and social attributes. Boys in all cultures continue to be described (on average) as being more aggressive than girls, playing more roughly than girls, and being more assertive. Females at all ages are (on average) more involved in relationships, more ready to seek, offer and receive help, more likely to self-disclose, better at understanding others' emotions, more likely to use care-based reasoning and, in conversation, more likely to collaborate and self-deprecate. From adolescence onwards, boys (on average) have more self-confidence and a greater sense of entitlement, and are less willing to admit to negative emotions; girls (on average) report more depression, sadness, shame and guilt.[9] However, there is a large amount of overlap between the behaviour of girls and boys in these respects, and great variety within each sex. Interestingly, self-ratings on scales of 'masculinity' can be more predictive of self-concept and well-being than is biological sex.[10]

Male and female lifestyles also demonstrate both changes and continuities since the 1970s. While many more women are in the Australian labour force, and more have made it to senior positions, the majority continue to be in lower level jobs. Corporate business, politics, administration, industry and the professions continue to be dominated by men. (At the same time, men are finding it harder to find and keep a job.[11]) Only 0.6 per cent of men take more than six months off work following the birth of a child, whereas 57 per cent of women do so; 96 per cent of men are back at work within six weeks.[12] At home, Australian women continue to do most of the housework, although they are spending less time on it. Both men and women have increased the amount of time they spend caring for children, especially young children, but the increase has been greater among women.[13] However, there are fewer of these young children. The birth rate fell steadily from the 1970s to reach 1.70 in 2000 (below population replacement rate). Of these fewer children, many more were born out of wedlock (29.2 per cent by 2000).[14] Most of these births were to de facto couples rather than to lone women, but breakdown rates among these couples were high.

This and a high rate of divorce brought a marked increase in the number of one-parent families, which are mostly headed by women. The number of these one-parent families jumped by almost 20 per cent over the five years to 1996, and by 2001 had reached 21.6 per cent of all families with dependent children. These families now make up close to half (43 per cent in 1996) of all households living in poverty.[15] Overall, then, the roles of men and women have changed considerably from the 'traditional' father/provider and mother/homemaker model, but it cannot be said unequivocally that the status of women has improved.

Over the last decades, then, gender roles have shown some unpredicted changes, and some tenacious inequities. What do we know about the development of males and females that can help us to understand these changes and continuities? In the rest of this chapter we look at present thinking on the issue.

Consequences

Gender role socialisation

It is a commonly accepted view that children are 'socialised' into the gender roles that are considered appropriate in their particular culture, and that parents play a critical role in this process. In its simplest version,[16] the socialisation model refers to the ways in which parents project their ideas of what is appropriate onto their child. They can do this in many ways. They can choose sex-differentiated clothing, toys, books and room furnishings for their daughters and sons. They can pass on what they consider to be gender-appropriate behaviours (for example neatness, dependence, self-reliance) by praise, disapproval, teasing and punishment. They can provide gendered learning opportunities (football for boys, ballet for girls). And, in particular, the different behaviours of mothers and fathers provide children with gender role models.

In this explanation the child's primary gender role is learnt at home. Later experiences and maturation build on and perhaps modify the primary learning, but the basic structure is laid down in early childhood.

This explanation puts great power into the hands of parents as shapers of their children's behaviour. Those who espouse it point in evidence to the fact that most parents do provide children with sex-differentiated toys and clothes; that fathers do report treating boys and girls somewhat differently;[17] that mothers do tend to discuss emotions more with toddler daughters than with sons[18] and to be more accepting of anger in boys and fear in girls; and that adults in general do react differently to a baby that they believe to be a girl or a boy.[19] Further support for the influence of parents comes from the fact that gender roles differ between social classes and ethnic groups, with Australian society providing a particularly rich mix of ethnic group differences.

However, apart from the family's social class and cultural values, family influences are typically quite small. Maccoby and Jacklin's literature review[20] found no evidence that boys closely resemble their own fathers and girls their own mothers, as same-sex imitation theory would predict. And when parents deviate from gender-typical norms, their children do not appear to follow them. Parents who have tried to rear children in an androgynous fashion do not have much success in reducing their gender-typed behaviour or attitudes, and the children of lesbian and gay couples are no less gender-typed than those of heterosexual parents.[21] Common observation tells us that children do not simply imitate the behaviour of their same-sex parent: fathers do not generally play with trains, nor do mothers skip.

Furthermore, where sons and daughters *are* treated differently, causality is usually difficult to establish. Logically, it is just as likely that the parents are reacting to the child's behaviour as shaping it.[22] And while social class and cultural effects are clear, they appear to be *group* effects rather than due to the influence of individual parents. For these reasons, there is now growing agreement that parental effects have probably been over-emphasised, and that in modern Western societies, at least, the power of individual parents over the gender socialisation of their children may be quite modest. Rather than being the authors and producers of their children's gender roles, parents are seen more as stage hands, responsible for delivering the costumes and props called for by the script. The script is written elsewhere.

A number of other factors have contributed to this downplaying of the role of parents. One is the finding from behaviour genetics that family environment has rather little effect on a range of children's personality traits and abilities. There are of course similarities between parents and children in characteristics such as aggression, sociability, emotionality and learning ability, but twin and adoptive studies suggest that these similarities stem mostly from shared genetic inheritance. When this is allowed for, the similarities largely disappear. Children reared in the same home by the same parents do not, on average, turn out to be similar unless they share genes; for example, the personalities of adoptive siblings brought up in the same home bear (on average) little resemblance to each other. Conversely, children who share genes do not become much more similar by being raised together; identical twins reared together are not noticeably more alike than identical twins reared apart.[23] This is not to say that some characteristics are not highly influenced by parental behaviour; undoubtedly, some characteristics, such as communication patterns, are.[24] But there is no evidence as yet that gender role development is among them.

A second contribution to parental role minimisation comes from the perception that, in modern societies, parents have lost much of their power over children. The parents cannot generally expect their children to follow in their footsteps, to work with or for them, to learn the skills they consider desirable, or to accept the friends, the activities, the clothes, the religion and/or the marriage partners that parents select. The schools, the labour market, the peer group, the youth culture, the electronic media and the consumer economy have appropriated much of their authority. From this viewpoint the role of today's Western parents is to provide as much support as they can while their children try to find an acceptable place in a changing world. This involves fitting in with this world's gender prescriptions, whatever these may be.[25] An example told to the authors tells of a mother trying to do her best in this respect. Faced with a boy who insisted on wearing his sister's dress to kindergarten, the anxious mother waited for his return. He arrived home in his underpants: 'It was too hot so I took it off,' he said.

A third contribution comes from development of the concept of self-socialisation: the notion that the child contributes to its own socialisation once it has developed a concept of personal gender identity. It is then in a position to recruit and select from the culture those aspects that can be assimilated into this internal cognitive structure. This model was developed by Kohlberg[26] and focused on the development of gender identity (I am a boy/girl, always was, always will be, and I do boy/girl things), a process normally completed by about six years of age. Other writers,[27] more convinced of the two- to three-year-old's capacity for social learning in the gender domain, have dated the child's selective modelling and identification of gender-stereotyped activities as occurring some years before the full acquisition of gender identity. These early gender constructs are naturally rudimentary and typically concerned with establishing some differences between males and females as categories—as, for example, when young children draw female stick figures with skirts, even though their own mothers mostly wear jeans.

A fourth and related contribution comes from studies of children's peer groups. Maccoby,[28] for example, considers that in Western societies today the ways in which small boys and girls are treated by their parents are remarkably similar. It is when children become part of a peer group, and especially around the age of five to twelve years, that 'the social experience of the two sexes truly diverge'.[29] This is especially the case where numbers of same-age children spend time together (as in city and suburban schools) and are allowed a fair amount of freedom from adult control. Under these circumstances the children tend to segregate themselves by sex, and it is these same-sex peer groups that pressure their members towards conformity. A similar point is made by Thorne,[30] who spent a year in the classrooms and playgrounds of two primary schools in the USA and described the 'different cultures' of the boys' and girls' groups.

These various influences, then, have contributed to the view that parents play only a modest role in gender development, and that the real power lies elsewhere, in some combination of self-socialisation and peer group socialisation. We now consider these latter two effects in more detail.

Group socialisation and self socialisation

If it is children themselves, rather than parents, who promote gender roles, how and why do they do it? One answer is offered by Harris's group socialisation theory of development. Harris sees it as part of our nature, as a social species, to form into groups. From an early age we are drawn to others whom we perceive as being like us, as indeed are the young of other primates, who seek each other out as playmates. An important aspect of group membership is the fact that the group has limits: some are in, and some are out. To categorise oneself as belonging to a certain group, then, one needs to be able to make distinctions between those who belong and those who do not.

Age and sex are the most fundamental category differences between humans, and the evidence is that human infants can make these distinctions from an early age, before they are one year old. By the age of two, they are beginning to show a preference for children of their own sex, and they become distressed if teased by adults who ask them if they belong to the opposite sex, just as they do when accused of being a baby.[31]

These category distinctions become more sophisticated as children move through the pre-school years. How does this occur? The evidence is that children observe the behaviours of a variety of old and young males and females, and abstract some principles that they then use as a guide for their own behaviour. For example, Perry and Bussey[32] asked children to observe four men and four women (the 'models') choosing between pairs of objects (an apple and a banana, for example). They then asked the children which items they themselves preferred. When all four male models chose one item, and all four females chose the other, the children were more likely to select for themselves the item chosen by the same-sex model. But when the male and female models split on their choices, the children's choices were also more mixed. In a follow-up study one male and one female model were set up as 'deviant', in that they always chose the opposite objects to that chosen by their three same-sex peers. When asked to choose for themselves, the children favoured the choices made by the three same-sex models over those made by the deviant same-sex model, indicating that they were modelling themselves on the 'reliable' models.

Other studies[33] have introduced variations on this procedure, with similar findings: the more clearly sex-typed the behaviour of the models, the more it is likely to be imitated by same-sex child observers. A further sex effect also emerges from this research, in that girls are more willing than boys to attend to and imitate cross-sex models and cross-sex-typed behaviours, and girls know more about male activities than boys do about female activities.[34] Perceived power as well as categorical sex is involved here, as the boys' resistance to a female model is reduced when she is presented as powerful.[35] For example, television's *Xena: Warrior Princess* does not lack young male imitators.

All in all, we can see that from a very early age children are engaged in a complex gender calculus, not usually of course at a very conscious level. Bussey and Bandura[36] emphasise that emotions are important guides to gendered behaviour, and become more so with age. They found that two- to three-year-old children claimed that other children would feel good after playing with sex-typed toys, and bad after playing with cross-sex ones; but only the older children reported this about themselves. Furthermore, those who said they would feel good or bad after sex-appropriate or inappropriate play actually spent more time playing with sex-typed toys. The authors interpret this to mean that as children get older they internalise a kind of gender-superego, which directs their behaviour by rewarding them for same-sex behaviour and punishes them for straying from this.

With gender self-categorisation well established, group socialisation theory sees the child, by the age of three to four years, as mature enough to move into a playgroup. The playgroup asserts a powerful attraction. Child-rearing patterns vary from culture to culture, but the children's playgroup is universal because it meets the human need for affiliation. If not many children are available, the playgroup will include both sexes and a range of ages; but, if there are sufficient numbers, they will split up into age- and sex-segregated groups. These groups themselves comprise subgroups of special friends and best friends, because the group also meets the human need for special attachments. And, meeting a further inbuilt drive among social species, the group establishes a rough hierarchy (especially among the boys), and allots its members a status within this hierarchy.[37] The playgroup is by no means a fixed entity. Members come and go, and a good deal of squabbling and jockeying for status is the norm. However, when faced with another group seen as such (another class, another school, another team), group solidarity stiffens: members focus on their similarities and downplay the differences.[38]

Through middle childhood the effects of self-segregation into boys' and girls' groups are especially strong. The two groups develop somewhat different cultures, and pressure their members to conform to these cultures. They have some success in this, including long-term success. One longitudinal study, for example, found that children who as pre-schoolers displayed qualities of temperament that were at odds with gender-typed expectations—such as timidity and anxiety in boys—modified these behaviours during the school years. Behaviour considered more gender-appropriate—such as timidity in girls—did not undergo the same change.[39]

Group membership has another effect. In line with the fact that each in-group is the other group's out-group, conformity is enhanced in the presence of the other sex. More precisely, it is enhanced when the other sex is categorised as 'the other' (as when certain games are categorised as 'boys' games' or 'girls' games'). When this categorisation is absent or minimal, individuals collaborate perfectly well, for example in out-of-school friendships with neighbours, or in school activities requiring a high level of cooperation.[40]

Ethnographic studies of children's playgroups have turned out to be a rich source of information regarding boys' and girls' learning of gendered social skills. Four main differences between the two have been noted: the size of the group, the content of interactions, the style of play, and the modes of influence practised. Boys tend to play in larger and more hierarchical groups in larger public spaces ('the oval'). Whereas boys are friends on the basis of shared activities, girls' close friendships are with a few girls, and marked by shared confidences ('You can tell them your secrets').

As to style of play, girls' groups do not show the rough and tumble play of the boys' groups: the mock fighting and wrestling, the throwing of bodies on one another that stops short of physical hostility and aggression. Verbally boys appear to try to establish dominance by insults, threats, teasing, and capping each other's stories. Among Australian boys there is a great deal of talk about 'bashing up'. A grade 2 boy explained to one of the authors that at school playtime each day he and his classmates had to defend their cubby against raids by the grade 3 boys (the out-group) who wanted to 'bash it up. So we have to stop them and we have to bash them up or they would bash us up and then they would bash our cubby down'.[41]

All these physical and verbal assaults are meant to be taken in good part. A poignant example of the competition and dominance struggles in boys' groups was reported by a man who remembered the two 'sissies' of the class fighting over who would not be at the bottom of the hierarchy, while the other boys watched the spectacle as 'a bit of a joke'.

Girls appear to be less competitive and more facilitative of their friends. They disclose more to each other, tend to express more agreement with one another, and try to ensure that all have a turn in conversation.[42] This facilitation comes at a price. Tannen[43] noted that girls who were immodest or self-promoting were considered unlikable. The life of those who violate the implicit egalitarian ethic can be a misery, with no one speaking to them except to deliver hurtful remarks ('You're a pain'). Shifting alliances and betrayals are common, and painful, with past disclosures used as weapons ('They worm your secrets out of you and then whisper behind your back'). At the same time, there are 'gestures of intimacy that one rarely sees among boys…girls stroke and comb their friends' hair'.[44]

Finally, girls and boys differ in the ways they try to influence others. Boys issue direct demands and engage in verbal and power assertion, giving orders and pushing and shoving their way in. They learn an important lesson in the process: that competition and tough talking do not necessarily cut across cooperative relations in groups, teams or couples. Girls' methods of influence tend to be less assertive, making suggestions ('Why don't we…?') and using other ways of toning down blatant domination. They use verbal reasoning when other girls violate the rules, and exert social control in various indirect ways including gossip and 'talking behind their backs' about those who have infringed the implicit rules (regarding the taking of turns, for example). In line with the notion that in-group membership and conformity become most salient in the presence of the out-group, it becomes increasingly difficult through primary school for children to play with members of the opposite sex group (although they may play together individually at home, or elsewhere). Neither the 'toughest and roughest' girl, nor a gentle or 'sissy' boy, can be a member of the cross-sex group. Any sign of interest can provoke intense teasing—usually expressed in sexual/romantic terms ('she's your girlfriend', 'you love him')—augmented by chasing and threats of kissing, contamination and pollution. Both boys and girls are active in this so-called 'border-work' (a term borrowed from anthropology), which has the effect of strengthening the boundaries between the groups. However, in some schools, ten- to twelve-year-old boys can be antagonistic to the girls to the point of serious harassment.[45]

The boys' groups are generally more gender-differentiating than those of the girls. They strongly reject girls and girlish things, and difference and dominance are themes in their discourses: girls are boring, dumb, weak, cry when teased, aren't as strong as boys, can't run fast enough to play with them, and so on. Clark comments that these judgments can be manifestly absurd. For example, in one primary school where the boys described girls as weak things there was a girl who was the world under-eight BMX champion.[46]

Rough-and-tumble play has an acknowledged biological basis, mediated through the degree of exposure in the womb to the predominantly 'male' hormone, testosterone; thus it is predictably more characteristic of the play of males. However, the boys' exaggerated enactment of their developing masculinity appears to be performed in the hope of validation by male peers. Thorne[47] observed that one of the few boys who felt free to join the girls' group on occasions could do so because of his 'unquestioned masculinity as one of the best athletes and the most popular boys in the school'. Some children made perceptive comments about these performances. A girl interviewed by Clark remarked that 'they have to be mean to us otherwise they will turn into girls or something', echoing Nancy Chodorow's[48] view that a boy 'often comes to define masculinity largely in negative terms, as that which is not feminine'. Another girl commented that 'boys are really nice at home; when they're with their boyfriends they get really mean', and a boy noted that 'you have to be really brave to treat girls nicely'.

Beyond middle childhood

Adolescence and cognitive maturity bring an increasing understanding of the multidimensional nature of gender attributes, and an increasing involvement with opposite-sex peers. At the same time, the physical and emotional changes of puberty heighten awareness of difference, a process that has been referred to as 'gender intensification'.[49] This can have adverse effects for girls, who may perceive their roles as less important and less valued than those of boys, lose confidence relative to boys, and settle for a narrower, more traditionally 'feminine' set of occupational goals.[50]

Differences in 'gender schematisation' also become more marked at adolescence. The term 'gender schema' is used to refer to the fact that some individuals pay a great deal of attention to information relevant to gender and organise their mental world in terms of gender-appropriate and gender-inappropriate categories, whereas others do not see gender as such an important category for understanding the world. Where these differences in gender schematisation come from is not understood, but they emerge quite early, and greater schematisation is associated with greater rigidity in gender-related behaviour.[51] In adolescence, differences in gender schematisation become greater as individuals construct their own way of being in the world.

At the social level the influence of same-sex groups remains strong, but there is a more marked differentiation into subgroups with similar interests and goals: the surfies, the swots, and so on. Constructions of femininity and masculinity differ from one subgroup to another. The girls' groups almost always accept their members' forming romantic attachments to boys, but the male groups are more diverse in their attitudes to girls, with some subcultures continuing to see them as weak and inferior, and valuable only for sexual self-assertion.[52]

Maccoby makes the interesting observation that in many societies childhood and adolescent groups are controlled by the adults (for example as 'youth groups' organised by the political authorities—the Red Guards, Hitler Youth—and in the segregated male living quarters in some traditional cultures). However, modern Western societies 'have cut [these] youthful peer groups free from adult involvement and influence to an extraordinary degree'.[53] Thus they enjoy a certain freedom to make up their own rules and activities, and to develop a greater diversity of gender roles. This does not mean, of course, that they are unaffected by adult interests; indeed some pop stars catering to youth audiences have cultivated unusual gender roles as part of their public appeal.

Beyond adolescence

We started our discussion of gender socialisation by asking how research on this topic can help us to understand recent change in the roles of men and women, and also how it is that some hoped-for changes—notably greater equity in public life—have not eventuated. What insights can we offer?

One source of insight concerns the correlates of different gender role variants. For example, Antill[54] and his associates found that Australian men and women were more egalitarian in their gender roles if they were younger, had been married a shorter time, had fewer children, were better educated, had less male income but more female income, had lower (but not very low) male occupational status, and voted for the ALP. Men with more 'feminine' traits (as measured by the Sex Role Inventory scale) were more egalitarian, shared more household tasks, did more female-typed household jobs and carried out more tasks overall than their traditional counterparts. The happiest couples were those where both partners scored high on 'femininity', but the happiest individuals (men and women) were those high on 'masculinity'.

This line of research suggests that gender egalitarianism in adulthood is associated with a constellation of environmental conditions, and also with personal traits that are measured by 'masculinity–femininity' scales. Interestingly, recent thinking on these scales suggests that they are misnamed, and that rather than measuring masculinity and femininity per se, they measure two major human tendencies: towards agency (a focus on autonomy and the self) and towards communion (a focus on connecting with others). Most cultures encourage the development of agency in males and communion in females, but everybody has a degree of both, with the degree being influenced by socialisation experience. This suggests that any practice that encourages the two tendencies in both boys and girls—including practices that influence childhood and adolescent peer groups—is likely to promote gender equity and harmony.

A second insight comes from Maccoby's[55] observation that cross-culturally there is much more variation in the roles of fathers than of mothers. Women are primary caregivers in every known society, but the degree of parenting responsibility undertaken by men varies greatly. Recent increases in the time spent by Australian fathers with their children, and in particular with very young children,[56] and the fact that some 98 per cent now attend the birth of their children, indicate an impressive shift towards the normalisation of behaviours and feelings previously widely regarded as outside the masculine range. In this respect, it is of interest that physical play with fathers is reported to develop sons' sensitivity to the feelings and motivations of others, a skill normally considered a female speciality.[57]

A third insight concerns the continuing dominance of men in the public sphere. The term 'boys' club' has come into rather wide use to describe the culture of Australian parliaments and some other circles of public life (such as sporting associations and corporate business). The words of Carmen Lawrence, quoted at the start of this chapter,[58] echo the description of the culture of boys' peer groups offered by group socialisation theorists,[59] and suggest that under certain conditions this culture continues to thrive and develop—and to categorise females as other—through adult life.

A fourth contribution concerns the changes in patterns of marriage and divorce.[60] A number of writers have argued that the extension of women's roles to include long-term labour-force participation has upset the previous (rough) balance between the breadwinner and homemaker roles.[61] Women no longer need a male breadwinner to get by, and even a very low-income single mother may feel she is better off than she would be in an unhappy relationship. At the same time, changing lifestyles mean that a man can get by without a wife, and is likely to prefer singlehood to a low-quality marriage. In consequence, only relationships of reasonable quality are likely to persist, and since high-quality heterosexual relationships are quite hard to achieve, a high rate of breakdown is to be expected. As we have seen, the best-quality relationships are those where both partners are relatively high on femininity (or communion). It follows that (at least in modern societies) anything that promotes the status of these qualities within the male gender role is likely to promote family stability and have benefits for individuals, families and the wider community.

Student exercises

1   Discuss the incident described in this chapter of a boy wearing his sister's dress to kindergarten. What reaction do you think he received from his teacher, from the other children, and from other parents? Do differing reactions constitute different contexts? How do children learn the behaviour that is acceptable for their gender, especially when they receive conflicting messages?

2   In adulthood, how does the nature of same-sex and cross-sex friendships operate to maintain gender differences?

3   What role do parents take in the socialisation of gender in their children? Which other agents in society are seen as more powerful in this regard than parents? Discuss the research evidence used to justify the relative importance of parents and other societal agents in this regard.

Notes

1   Carmen Lawrence, MHR and former premier of Western Australia, commenting on her difficulties as a parliamentarian. Cited in *Sydney Morning Herald*, 25 October 1997, p. 45.

2   Parliament of the Commonwealth of Australia, *Boys: Getting it Right: Report on the Inquiry into the Education of Boys*, Australian Government Publishing Service, Canberra, 2002, Foreword, unnumbered.

3   E. Maccoby & C. Jacklin, *The Psychology of Sex Differences*, Stanford University Press, Stanford, CA, 1974.

4   See H. Eisenstein's *Contemporary Feminist Thought*, Allen & Unwin, Sydney, 1984, for a concise summary.

5   E. Erikson, *Childhood and Society*, Norton, New York, 1963, p. 411.

6   Parliament of the Commonwealth of Australia, 2002.

7   Parliament of the Commonwealth of Australia, 2002.

8   Parliament of the Commonwealth of Australia, 2002.

9   S. Golombok & R. Fivush, *Gender Development*, Cambridge University Press, Cambridge, 1994.

10 Scales such as the Bem Sex Role Inventory and the Australian Sex Role Inventory ask subjects to rate themselves on sets of adjectives that have been judged to be more 'typical' of males or females: for example 'assertive' and 'compassionate'. For an example of this approach, see J. Antill, S. Cotton & S. Tindale, 'Egalitarian or Traditional: Correlates of the Perception of an Ideal Marriage', *Australian Journal of Psychology*, 35, 1983, pp. 245–57. For the relation to maths achievement, see J. Hyde, E. Fennema, M. Ryan & L. Frost, 'Gender Comparisons of Mathematics Attitudes and Achievement: A Meta-analysis', in *Psychology of Women Quarterly*, 14, 1990, pp. 299–324.

11 Australian Bureau of Statistics, *Labour Force 1996, Australia*, catalogue no. 6203.0, Australian Government Publishing Service, Canberra, 2002.

12 M. Bittman, S. Hoffmann & D. Thompson, *Men's Uptake of Family-friendly Employment Provisions*, Social Policy Research Centre, University of New South Wales, 2002.

13 M. Bittman & J. Pixley, *The Double Life of the Family*, Allen & Unwin, Sydney, 1997.

14 Australian Bureau of Statistics, *Australian Social Trends 2001*, Australian Government Publishing Service, Canberra, 2001.

15 Australian Bureau of Statistics, *Social Trends 2002*, Australian Government Publishing Service, Canberra, 2002.

16 Golombok & Fivush, 1994.

17 M. Siegal, 'Are Sons and Daughters Treated More Differently by Fathers than by Mothers?', *Developmental Review*, 7, 1987, pp. 183–209.

18 J. Dunn, I. Bretherton & P. Munn, 'Conversations about Feeling States Between Mothers and their Young Children', *Developmental Psychology*, 23, 1986, pp. 132–9; R. Fivush, 'Exploring Sex Differences in the Emotional Content of Mother–child Conversations about the Past', *Sex Roles*, 20, 1989, pp. 675–91.

19   See Golombok & Fivush, 1994, pp. 23–8 for a good discussion of the Baby X studies.
20   Maccoby & Jacklin, 1974.
21   L. Serbin, K. Powlishta & J. Gulko, 'The Development of Sex Typing in Middle Childhood', *Monographs of the Society of Research in Child Development*, 58, 2, 1993, serial no. 232; C. Patterson, 'Children of Lesbian and Gay Parents', *Child Development*, 63, 1992, pp. 1025–42.
22   Golombok & Fivush, 1994; E. Maccoby, 'The Two Sexes and their Social Systems', in *Examining Lives in Context*, eds, P. Moen, G. Elder Jr & K. Lüscher, American Psychological Association, Washington, DC, 1995, pp. 347–64.
23   D. Plomin & D. Daniels, 'Why are Children in the Same Family So Different From One Another?', *Behavior and Brain Science*, 10, 1987, pp. 1–16; F. Reiss, 'Genetic Influence on Family Systems: Implications for Development', *Journal of Marriage and the Family*, 57, 1995, pp. 543–60.
24   See for example J. Dunn, *Young Children's Close Relationships: Beyond Attachment*, Sage, London, 1993.
25   See for example J. Harris, 'Where is the Child's Environment? A Group Socialisation Theory of Development', *Psychological Review*, 102, 1995, pp. 458–89.
26   L. Kohlberg, 'A Cognitive-developmental Analysis of Children's Sex-role Concepts and Attitudes', in *The Development of Sex Differences*, ed, E. Maccoby, Stanford University Press, Stanford, CA, 1966, pp. 82–173.
27   K. Bussey, 'The First Socialization', in *Australian Women: New Feminist Perspectives*, eds, N. Grieve & A. Burns, Oxford University Press, Melbourne, 1986, pp. 90–104.
28   Maccoby, 1995.
29   Maccoby, 1995.
30   B. Thorne, *Gender Play: Girls and Boys in School*, Open University Press, Buckingham, 1993.
31   Harris, 1995, p. 486.
32   D. Perry & K. Bussey, 'The Social Learning Theory of Sex Difference: Imitation is Alive and Well', *Journal of Personality and Social Psychology*, 37, 1979, pp. 1699–712; K. Bussey & A. Bandura, 'Influence of Gender Constancy and Social Power on Sex-linked Modeling', *Journal of Personality and Social Psychology*, 47, 1984, pp. 1292–302.
33   Golombok & Fivush, 1994, provide a good review.
34   M. Signorella, R. Bigler & L. Liben, 'Development Differences in Children's Gender Schemata about Others: A Meta-analytic Review', *Developmental Review*, 13, 1993, pp. 1106–26.
35   Bussey, 1986; Bussey & Bandura, 1984.
36   K. Bussey & A. Bandura, 'Self-regulatory Mechanisms Governing Gender Development', *Child Development*, 63, 5, 1992, pp. 1236–50.
37   Harris, 1995, pp. 465–7.
38   Harris, 1995.
39   Harris, 1995, p. 472.
40   Thorne, 1993.
41   When asked if the girls took part in these conflicts he showed surprise at the question and replied, 'Oh no! They're up on the hill doing their ring-a-ring-a-rosy'.
42   E. Maccoby, 'Gender and Relationships: A Developmental Account', *American Psychologist*, 45, 1990, pp. 513–20.

43 D. Tannen, 'Gender Difference in Topical Coherence: Creating Involvement in Best Friend's Talk', *Discourse Processes*, 13, 1990, pp. 73–90; also D. Tannen, *You Just Don't Understand: Men and Women in Conversation*, Morrow, New York, 1990.

44 Thorne, 1993, p. 94.

45 S. Milligan & K. Thomson, *Listening to Girls*, Australian Education Council, Canberra, 1991. See also B. Davies, 'The Discursive Production of the Male/Female Dualism in School Settings', *Oxford Review of Education*, 15, 3, 1989, pp. 229–42; M. Clark, *The Great Divide: The Construction of Gender in the Primary School*, Curriculum Development Centre, Canberra, 1989.

46 Clark, 1989, p. 34.

47 Thorne, 1993, p. 123.

48 N. Chodorow, 'Family Structure and Feminine Personality', in *Women, Culture and Society*, eds, M. Rosaldo & L. Lamphere, Stanford University Press, Paolo Alto, 1974, p. 50. See also a critique of this view by J. Norton, 'Deconstructing the Fear of Femininity', *Feminism and Psychology*, 7, 1997, pp. 441–7.

49 N. Galambos, D. Almeida & A. Petersen, 'Masculinity, Femininity and Sex Role Attitudes in Early Adolescence: Exploring Gender Intensification', *Child Development*, 51, 1990, pp. 1905–14.

50 D. Bush & R. Simmons, 'Gender and Coping with the Entry into Early Adolescence', in *Gender and Stress*, eds, R. Barnett, L. Beiner & G. Baruch, Macmillan, New York, 1987, pp. 185–217.

51 G. Levy & D. Carter, 'Gender Schema, Gender Constancy and Gender Role Knowledge', *Developmental Review*, 25, 1989, pp. 444–9.

52 Australian movies such as *Puberty Blues* and *Blackrock* describe variations on this theme. See also B. Brown, 'Peer Groups and Peer Cultures', in *At the Threshold: The Developing Adolescent*, eds, S. Feldman & G. Elliot, Harvard University Press, Cambridge, MA, 1990, pp. 171–96.

53 Maccoby, 1995, p. 353.

54 Antill, Cotton & Tindale, 1983; J. Antill, 'Sex-role Complementarity versus Similarity in Married Couples', *Journal of Personal and Social Psychology*, 45, 1983, pp. 145–55; J. Antill & J. Cunningham, 'The Relationships of Masculinity, Femininity and Androgyny to Self-esteem', *Australian Journal of Psychology*, 32, 1980, pp. 195–207.

55 Maccoby, 1995, p. 361.

56 Bittman & Pixley, 1997.

57 J. Hubbard & J. Coie, 'Emotional Correlates of Social Competence in Children's Peer Relationships', *Merril-Palmer Quarterly*, 40, 1994, pp. 1–20.

58 Carmen Lawrence, cited in *Sydney Morning Herald*, 25 October 1997, p. 45.

59 Harris, 1995; Maccoby, 1990.

60 See A. Burns & C. Scott, *Mother-headed Families and Why They have Increased*, Lawrence Erlbaum, Hillsdale, NJ, 1994.

61 Some research has taken up these issues. See for instance J. Coates, *Woman Talk: Conversation Between Women Friends*, Blackwell, Oxford, 1996; M. Monsour, B. Harris & N. Kurzweil, 'Challenges Confronting Cross Sex Friendships: "Much Ado about Nothing"', *Sex Roles*, 31, 1994, pp. 55–77.

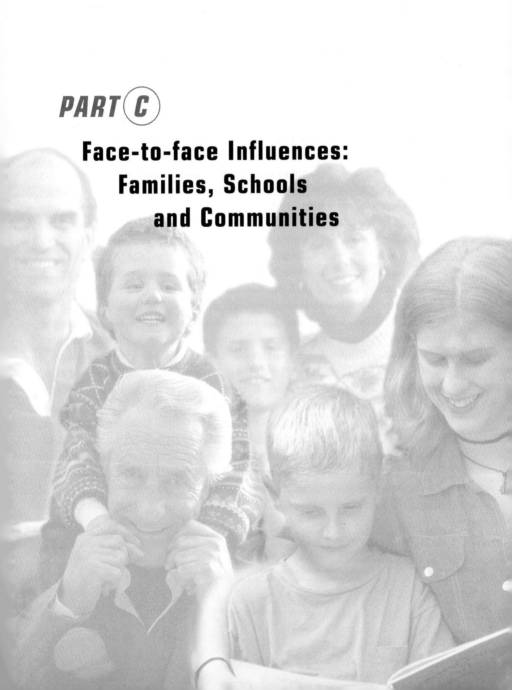

PART Ⓒ
Face-to-face Influences:
Families, Schools
and Communities

In Part C we turn from the characteristics of individuals to examine in more detail the contexts of children's development. The three chapters in this section explore the ways in which contexts can influence the behaviour and choices of the people within them and the ways in which children, families and communities actively shape the contexts in which they participate. We have chosen three contexts that play a major part in the lives of children: families, educational settings and neighbourhoods.

Families, child care and schools impinge directly on children, and on a daily basis. Children who live in families where domestic violence is a reality and a constant threat, or children who attend a high-quality pre-school, for example, will be affected by those contexts, actively adapting to the characteristics of those settings in a way that affects their future lives. The degree and kind of effect will be influenced by the nature of their participation, the kind of interactions they have with other people in those contexts, and by their personal perceptions of the contexts.

Chapter 5 examines families as a changing context, presenting some ways of thinking about families and considering features of family life that influence the development of children. Families are also considered in their community context. The impact on families of television, videos and the Internet and the spillover from parents' work are considered along with parenting approaches to reduce risk for children and prepare them for life beyond the family.

Chapter 6 steps outside the home to consider other face-to-face contexts encountered by children and families, particularly in child care and schools. These settings offer both risks and opportunities for children, and have multiple consequences for children, families and communities. The importance of the relationship between these contexts and others in which children and families are involved—Bronfenbrenner's mesosystem—emerges strongly in this chapter.

The wider context of neighbourhood or community can also have considerable impact on children's lives. Chapter 7 deals with community links for children and families and the importance of community social capital for children's development. It explores the impact of social isolation for children and families as well as the features of successful intervention programs.

In all of these contexts, children and their families make an active contribution to shaping and changing the contexts in which they participate. How this happens, and how programs of prevention and intervention can help, are among the key issues in Part C.

Families as a Context for Children

Jennifer Bowes and Johanna Watson

Families in all societies are commonly expected to care for and nurture children, to provide financially for their members, and to transmit cultural and moral traditions and values.[1]

The teacher asked us to draw pictures of our family. I did one of you and Mummy and Mikey and me, but isn't it funny, the others were putting in their Nannas and aunties and uncles and all sorts of people like that.[2]

Families are a primary context for child development. Most children grow up in families and, in their early years especially, families have a major impact on children's lives, influencing their developing patterns of thinking, feeling and behaviour. Although children may spend a lot of their time in other contexts from their early years, the emotional intensity of families means that learning in this context is likely to be extensive and long lasting.

Families influence children's development in a number of direct and indirect ways. Parents, siblings and members of the extended family can exert an individual influence on children, but that influence is more than an individual one because it occurs in the context of family. Any learning within a family is magnified by reinforcement from other family members.

Families also tend to operate as self-contained systems in that they develop their own ways of dealing with problems, of allocating resources of time and affection, and of maintaining patterns of harmony or discord. Such patterns are learnt by children living within families, whether these patterns are subsequently accepted or rejected.

Family units cannot be seen as fully self-contained, however. In the same way that individuals need to be seen in terms of their connections with other family members, families themselves cannot be understood in isolation from their community and cultural contexts. Even the question of what a family *is* remains subject to cultural interpretation. When Anglo-Australians refer to family, for example, they are likely to be referring to their immediate nuclear family whereas Indigenous Australians use the term 'family' to refer to an extended kin network.[3] Children are likely to include family pets as well as people in their depictions of family.

Although families are widely recognised as being the primary and most influential force in shaping the developmental outcomes of their children, the community in which they live affects how, and the ease with which, they parent their children. The influence of families in their community contexts on the development of children is the focus of the chapter.

In exploring the nature of families as a context for children's development, the first part of the chapter asks three questions. What are families like? How do families operate and what are the consequences for children? How are families connected to communities and what are the consequences for children? The chapter begins by considering the diverse range of families, and the changing nature of families, within Australian society. Having established that it is impossible to talk about the family as a prototype, we look at two models of family functioning: the family life cycle approach and family systems theory.

The chapter then moves beyond the predominantly self-contained approach to families offered by family systems theory to consider in more detail how links with others outside the family unit play a part in the well-being and socialisation of children. It is argued that families cope or fail to cope with the stresses of daily living and with the inevitable crises of family life through a combination of resources from within and outside the family unit. We discuss just what it is that makes some families more resilient and others more vulnerable, and factors within and outside families are again seen to play a part.

When considering families it is easy to lose sight of the individuals within them. Our concern here is with children and the effects of growing up in a family on their development. Broadly speaking, families can provide opportunities for children's development and they can pose risks for children. Families also stand between children and the wider society. They can operate to protect children from risks outside the family or can expose them to those risks. Equally, families can assist their children to gain access to aspects of the wider society that are beneficial for their development, or they can shield their children from useful contact with the world outside.

Contexts

What are families like?

Despite fears expressed by politicians and the media that the family as an institution is in decline, 82 per cent of Australians lived in families in 2001.[4] What is slowly changing is the public perception of what defines 'family'. The stereotype of most households in Australia consisting of a nuclear family with a father-breadwinner married to a mother who is at home caring for dependent children is misleading. In fact, this group makes up only a small and decreasing proportion of families.[5]

The assumption that children have to be present for a household to be seen as a family is also under question. Couple families with children are forming a decreasing proportion of all families (47 per cent in 2001).[6] There are increasing numbers of couples without dependent children who still consider themselves to be a family (increased 33 per cent between 1986 and 2001).[7] Many of these are older couples whose children no longer live at home or are no longer dependent on them. It is not difficult to agree that such couples fall within the definition of family. If couples whose children have left home are still families, the term may then apply equally to other couples who do not have children (either because they have not had them yet or because they have chosen not to, or cannot have, children).

The line is very thin between what constitutes a family and what does not. Although they may not be married, a young man living with his girlfriend and her child from a previous relationship would still fall within the currently accepted definition of family. If they were renting a house together, however, but had stronger emotional ties to other people, this would probably be seen as shared accommodation. The definition of family, while certainly applying to people with a 'blood tie', also increasingly applies to those with an emotional commitment to each other.

In this case, we might ask, does a couple have to consist of a male and a female to count as a family? In the 1996 census, for the first time, homosexual couples with or without dependent children were counted as families. Again there is assumed to be a strong emotional tie or some kind of joint commitment. Definitions of family, then, refer consistently to personal relationships formed through kinship and residence, although definitions are fluid, changing over time and in different cultural groups. In its report on the 2001 census, the Australian Bureau of Statistics defined family as comprising 'two or more persons, one of whom is at least 15 years of age, who are related by blood, marriage (registered or de facto), adoption, step or fostering, and who are usually resident in the same household'.[8]

Changes in Australian families

Despite the changes in definition of family and the decline of the traditional family type, most Australian children grow up in families. Improved contraception, the legalisation of abortion and the widely publicised detrimental effects of institutionalisation have resulted in nearly all children growing up in a family even if it is not their biological family. There are now only 200 children growing up in institutions in Australia and 500 in correctional centres.[9]

Several factors contribute to the decline of the 'traditional' family type. The most obvious area of change has been in the work patterns of men and women and, in particular, the increased participation of women with dependent children in the paid workforce. In 2001, 56 per cent of children aged fifteen years or under had both parents in paid employment, compared with 41 per cent in 1981.[10] The labour force has also been restructured, with an increase in the number of jobs that are part-time (28 per cent of all jobs)[11] and casual (27 per cent of all jobs).[12]

Despite the increased dependence of families on the wages of both parents, however, the patterns of women's involvement in the labour force are consistent with family responsibilities being assumed mainly by mothers rather than fathers. As their children grow older, more mothers join the paid labour force and mothers are more likely to shift from part-time to full-time work.[13] By contrast, patterns of fathers' participation in the workforce are unaffected by the ages of their children.[14]

The other major change in family type has been one-parent families (an increase of 53 per cent between 1986 and 2001). One-parent families now make up 23 per cent of all families with dependent children. More than one in five children under fifteen years of age are now living with one parent, who is generally their mother (20.3 per cent of families with dependent children are headed by a single parent mother and 2.7 per cent are headed by a single parent father).[15]

In addition, about three-quarters of couples in Australia now live together before they marry, in contrast to patterns of the mid-1980s.[16] De facto relationships are now recognised by law, and many couples are choosing not to marry. This trend not to marry may partly explain why close to a third of children in Australia are now born outside a formal marriage.[17]

Although most Australian children grow up in families, children's experiences of childhood differ as a function of the structure of their family, their parents' socio-economic circumstances and the cultural background into which they are born.

Structural diversity in Australian families

The definition of 'family' may be changing generally but, even within an individual family group, family membership alters as children are born, parents divorce and remarry and grandparents die. It is predicted that 26 per cent of newborns in 1999 will never marry and 32 per cent could be expected to divorce.[18] Remarriages are even more prone to breakdown than first marriages.[19] As a result of marriage breakdown, the increase in births outside marriage and, to a lesser extent, death of a spouse, about one in five children in Australia is living in a one-parent family, and more have experienced or will experience this at some stage in their lives. Most couple families with children include the natural or adopted children of both parents. In the other 11 per cent of couple families with children, 6 per cent are step-families, 4 per cent are blended families that contain both natural and step-children and 1 per cent are families that include foster children, nieces, nephews or other unrelated children.[20]

Diversity in socio-economic circumstances

The increasing gap between the rich and poor in Australia contributes to a corresponding difference in the experience of childhood depending on the material and social resources of the family.

The expectation of health and good health care, combined with a low birth-rate[21] and a greater use of prenatal testing, has led to an assumption by more affluent women that they will have one or two perfect children. The emphasis for these children is no longer just on surviving. They are encouraged to 'fulfil their potential', with many families who can afford to do so investing resources in private education and extra tuition fees for their children. Academic and sporting achievements are not only hoped for but expected in these families, and anything merely average may be regarded as a disappointment. These expectations for children have led to less emphasis on children's useful contributions to the family in terms of work in the home or of money. At the other end of the spectrum, for children from more disadvantaged families, opportunities are fewer and further between, and there seems to be an increasing sense of social alienation as they struggle to find the money even to be able to join in school excursions. University education is increasingly out of reach for children of poor families in Australia. As tuition fees rise, the proportion of students from lower socio-economic-group families completing the more expensive university courses is decreasing.[22]

Cultural diversity in Australian families

Australia is a country characterised by the migration of a diverse range of people. The first Australians, or Indigenous Australians, currently comprise 2 per cent of Australia's population of 18.8 million people.[23] The British colonised Australia during the eighteenth century and this is reflected in the population today. The three most common ancestries reported in the 2001 census were Australian (people born in Australia of various ancestries including Indigenous people), English and Irish. Immediately following the Second World War, migrants were from Europe (largest groups from the ancestry census question were from Italy, Germany, Poland and the Netherlands). More recently, people of Lebanese, Vietnamese, Indian, Chinese and many other ancestries (160 in all) have joined the Australian population. In the 2001 census, over half of children aged less than fifteen were reported as having Australian ancestry, with most having been born in Australia and having at least one Australian-born parent.[24] Within some ancestry groups, notably Vietnamese, Lebanese and Chinese, many families speak a language other than English in the home. The diversity of languages and cultures in Australia adds to our social wealth as well as challenging the English language and Anglo-Saxon cultural dominance of many services for children and families in Australia.

Indigenous families

In the 2001 census, 410,000 people answered that they were of Aboriginal or Torres Strait origin.[25] While most live in major cities or in regional centres, proportionally more Indigenous than non-Indigenous people live in remote areas of Australia. As a group, Aboriginal and Torres Strait Islander people suffer multiple disadvantages: poor health, a higher rate of infant mortality, a reduced life expectancy compared to non-Indigenous Australians, lower rates of employment, lower rates of educational achievement, higher rates of incarceration, a high incidence of domestic violence and child abuse and neglect, and limited infrastructure and services in remote areas.[26] Many of the social problems affecting Indigenous families have been linked to the history of their experiences after the arrival of the British (see Chapter 9). While forecasts for the general Australian population over the next few decades are for more older people than children in the population, in the Indigenous population, there are more children than older people. In New South Wales, for example, Indigenous children represent 4.2 per cent of the under-12 population.[27] This has implications for services for Indigenous and Torres Strait Islanders, particularly health and education, as there are a large number of dependants and relatively few adults to provide for them. In addition, Indigenous parents are often poor, young and relatively uneducated—characteristics that point to a need for parenting support.[28] High levels of domestic violence and abuse also create an unpredictable and sometimes dangerous backdrop for Indigenous children.[29]

   This need for support is counteracted to some extent by the strong sense of family and community in Indigenous culture, which leads to a lesser sense of isolation than might be experienced by non-Indigenous families in the same circumstances. Life expectancy, however, is twenty years less than for non-Indigenous Australians[30] so that grandparents are not as available to support families and children. Given the age distribution of the Indigenous population, the geographic remoteness of many communities, poor access to fresh food and high rates of injury and illness, it is not surprising that there is a high need for health and social services for families.

How do families operate?

Life cycle approach

An approach to the description of families that has focused on common changes in families over time has been the family life cycle approach. Early models[31] put forward a simple life-course for families: marriage, the birth of children, the moving away from the family home by the children (empty nest) and finally the death of partners. Each point of transition was seen to be a major and predictable point of stress for families. Later writers have criticised the simplicity and inflexibility of this approach to family life cycle, arguing that the birth of children can occur before marriage or indeed without marriage, that partnerships can be dissolved not only by death of one partner but by divorce or separation.[32] In addition, it is no longer certain that children will leave home when they reach adulthood. For financial reasons and because many young people are dependent on their parents owing to unemployment or further study, children may still be living at home into middle adulthood. This model also implies that any digression from the 'normal' timetable is abnormal, stigmatising the families and children concerned and pays no attention to extended family. Recent developments of the family life cycle approach have incorporated a focus on transitions and their associated stress for families and a view of families as multigenerational.[33] It is important, however, in considering times of major stress for families, to keep in mind that families may perceive seemingly identical events as more or less stressful, and that the way that family members cope with such stresses also varies according to the characteristics of individuals in the family and their relationships with one another. An example can be seen in research on the effects of divorce on children. For children who have been witnesses of marital conflict or the victims of domestic violence over a long period, parental separation and divorce can lead to positive as well as negative outcomes.[34]

Dunlop[35] found in a longitudinal study of the effects of divorce on Australian children that a key feature of children who were well adjusted three years after their parents' divorce was a good and continuing relationship with at least one of their parents. This is not to deny that divorce is a source of stress in the lives of children at the time, and a source of enduring unhappiness for some. The example is raised to show that the same event can affect families and individuals within families quite differently.

We have seen that families can be viewed in many different ways and that they differ over time, both historically and during a family's life cycle. Families are similar, however, in that for most children they are the most influential and immediate context for development. As a way of understanding how families operate, family systems theory, described in the next section, offers an approach that goes beyond the mother–child focus, which characterised most research on family influences until recent years.

Family systems approach

Tolstoy in the first sentence of *Anna Karenina* wrote, 'All happy families resemble one another, but each unhappy family is unhappy in its own way.'[36] Family systems theory attempts to isolate the dimensions of life within families that make them happy or unhappy, although most research and clinical attention has focused on unhappy families.

A number of theories about the family as a system have been proposed. Generally, whichever systems theory one examines, the basic premises are the same.[37] First, the context for the child is seen as part of an interactional system whereby behaviours of individual members are caused and maintained by the interactions between all family members.

These interactions are seen as circular in nature rather than in one direction only (as from parent to child, or from child to parent). For instance, cheerful gurgling babies will attract positive attention and elicit smiles from their parents. This in turn reinforces the happy response of the child, further encouraging positive responses from the parents. Second, each family has its own unique style of interacting, bound by the implicit family rules and accepted roles of each member. When two households combine in a step- or blended family, the differences in these implicit rules can lead to some misunderstandings.

In most accounts of family systems theory, healthy families are seen to be ones where communication is open and the 'rules' of family are flexible and can adapt to changing demands. If there are too many sub-messages, such as tight-lipped agreement that really means 'No', the communication is not so open and successful negotiation becomes more difficult. Families also need to be able to adapt to developmental changes in their children: the parental demands and expectations placed on a five-year-old will be quite different from those placed on a fifteen-year-old.

According to the family systems approach, a final premise of systems theory is that families are expected to be in some kind of balance. As long as the implicit rules are followed, the feedback from other family members is fairly positive. If, however, rules are flouted, the feedback becomes negative and the family tips out of balance. This happens in all families, and can usually be dealt with within the family without undue distress (such as when children do not come home until after the curfew or leave a mess around for others to clean up). In some families, however, the flouting of the rules is more serious and contravenes not only implicit family rules but also societal ones. For instance, when the person flouting the rules is a parent who is unable to function effectively due to alcoholism, or when they abuse their children, the levels of distress are proportionally greater. Often the relative powerlessness of children within a family means they are the members most likely to become distressed.

Systems concepts are most commonly applied in therapeutic settings, and they may assist therapists and counsellors in working out strategies to help families to function more effectively. However, the family systems model falls into the same trap as the life cycle model as it is strongly based on the cultural norms of the day. It is deficit based and seeks cause in 'dysfunction'. For instance, in the same way that the family life cycle model sees 'marriage' as normal, the family systems model emphasises the importance of a strong marital relationship. By implication, a lack of a marital subsystem is necessarily deficient despite the research evidence suggesting it is not crucial to the adjustment of children. If a strong marital relationship is positively associated with positive outcomes, but not an essential component, the research question then becomes what is it about the marital relationship that contributes to positive child outcomes? If the essential element is support provided by a close and caring relationship, could a strong supportive extended family or friends be as effective in providing this support?

Family systems theory also implies fine tuning to keep the family in balance. It seems underpinned by the notion of a comfortable middle class, reasonably well-adjusted family where children are merely testing family limits. It is insufficient as a model to deal with such community-based issues as binge drinking in the wider Australian society or petrol sniffing in some Indigenous communities.[38]

Consequences

Influence of parenting on children

We turn now to the influence of parents on children. Parenting behaviour needs to be seen in historical and cultural context.[39] In many ways, approaches to parenting are influenced by current societal values and expectations as well as cultural traditions. There are 'fads' in parenting, ranging from the scientific approach of strictly timed and regulated care of babies during the 1940s in Australia to the preoccupation with the self-esteem of children during the 1980s.[40]

Although there is a wide range of parenting behaviours worldwide and within the different cultural groups in Australian society, a great deal of research on parenting has been conducted in Western developed countries and this needs to be kept in mind when reading about parenting in the following section of the chapter.

Parent–child relationships

Parent–child relationships are usually defined on two dimensions, closeness (also called warmth, affection, affiliation or acceptance) and flexibility (also called adaptability, power or control).[41] Of these two dimensions, closeness is probably the most important. Shonkoff and Phillips (2001) argue that 'from birth to death, intimate and caring relationships are fundamental to successful human adaptation' (p. 27) and the relationships in the early years are the building blocks upon which 'fragile' or 'sturdy' foundations for future relationships are built.[42] Children need at least one warm and caring relationship where their caregiver can read the child's emotional cues and respond to them in a timely manner. Maternal negativity seems particularly damaging.[43]

This finding underlines the fact that when it comes down to it, the most important thing that parents can give children is the unconditional and irrational positive regard that Bronfenbrenner listed in his summary of what every child needs.[44]

Parenting style

Warmth and control were identified by Baumrind as the two dimensions that underlie parenting styles. Baumrind began her research into parenting style with two studies in the USA on the effects of different child-rearing techniques on pre-school children's sociability, self-reliance, moodiness and self-control.[45] She made observations and conducted interviews in the children's homes and at their university-associated pre-school. From these early studies she isolated three parenting styles: authoritative, permissive and authoritarian. She found that the authoritative style, a mixture of warmth and control, was linked with children who were cheerful, socially responsive, self-reliant, achievement oriented, and cooperative with adults and peers. Children of parents who were permissive (high in warmth with little control) or authoritarian (low in warmth and high in control) showed less positive outcomes, particularly in terms of achievement motivation.

Baumrind's parenting styles have been questioned in terms of their cultural specificity. The high academic performance of Chinese-American children whose parents tended to have an authoritarian rather than authoritative approach to parenting provided a challenge to the model as did the identification of another style of parenting among Chinese parents, *guan* or training, characterised by more emotionally distant and controlling parenting.[46]

Despite the wealth of research on parenting style, the impetus for particular approaches cannot be seen as stemming only from the parents. The characteristics of children themselves can elicit differing styles of parenting. An authoritative style, for example, may be the parental response to an already competent child with an 'easy' temperament. A more authoritarian style might be adopted with a child who has a more 'difficult' temperament or with an 'easy' child who is behaving badly in public or when the parent is tired.[47]

Fathers and parenting

The inclusion of fathers in accounts of parenting is a relatively new phenomenon. Research on fathering has shown that fathers differ from mothers in the amount of time they spend with their children and in the ways they interact with their children. Fathers spend more time in play with their children, particularly outdoor and rough-and-tumble play, whereas mothers are more involved in caretaking activities and play indoors with their children, using toys and books.[48] There is evidence of fathers taking a more active role in child care over the last two decades but this change has been slow. It should be noted that a great deal of research on fathering has been conducted in two-parent families. Many fathers, living apart from their children, have no contact or less regular contact with their children and need to negotiate a new kind of father–child relationship and set of behaviours. Less is known about fathering under these circumstances.[49]

Parental practices

The family is a setting where children learn many of the values, skills and behaviours that they take with them through life. Much of their learning is through shared participation in family activities and through observation of parents, siblings and extended family members.[50] Different families develop their own common culture of rituals, habits, norms and expectations that form the context of children's learning.[51]

Involvement of children in household tasks, for example, can play a large part in teaching them to take responsibility for themselves and others. The relative emphasis on individual and communal responsibility in relation to children's contribution to household work has been shown to vary in different cultures.[52] Observation within the family of different behaviours such as acts of kindness to others or violence and abuse is a powerful means of learning patterns of values and ways of relating to other people in later life.

Parents also teach their children values, skills and behaviours through direct instruction or coaching, letting them know explicitly what is expected of them or conveying messages through stories.[53] Discipline is another way that parents teach their children acceptable behaviour, using a range of techniques including physical punishment, withdrawal of love and inductive reasoning or explaining to children why they should behave a certain way.[54]

A longitudinal study of Canadian children has shown that parents change their parenting practices as their children get older,[55] reducing their responsiveness steadily from high levels in the early years and increasing their use of reasoning and firmness, with a marked increase in both when children are around the age of seven. The study has found that the benefits of positive parenting practices were equally strong for rich and poor families. Poor parenting practices were associated with child behavioural problems.[56]

Managing work and family

With the increasing involvement in paid work of women in Australia over the past two decades,[57] part of parenting involves management of work and family responsibilities. This has been made more difficult for dual earner and single-earner families by a shift in Australia away from standard working hours to longer hours of work and to 'flexible' but 'unsocial' working hours involving early mornings, evenings and weekends. There is considerable concern over the impact this could be having on parents and their relationships with their children and each other.[58] In addition, there has been a trend towards more casual work, with one in three positions now offered on a casual basis. This has led to greater financial insecurity, which has a detrimental effect on family well-being.

In general, mothers have coped with competing demands of work and family by adjusting their involvement in paid work, by either not working or working part-time when their children are young.[59] Some fathers have taken on the role of primary caregiver for their children or have reduced their working hours in order to be more involved with their children although workplaces tend to be less understanding of such work adjustments by fathers than by mothers.[60] Some employers have responded to the family responsibilities of their workers by instituting family-friendly policies such as opportunities for leave, working reduced hours or job sharing.[61] Informal cultural pressure at work, however, often means there is a reluctance by workers to take advantage of these provisions. In addition, child care is difficult for parents to organise as places and trained staff are insufficient in formal child care such as long day care centres and family day care schemes, especially for children under two years, and child care hours are generally structured around a standard working day. As a result, parents are making a patchwork of formal and informal care arrangements, which has led to a third to a half of Australian children in their first three years attending two or more care settings a week.[62]

Influence of siblings

A great deal of children's social understanding, including how to share and how to fight and resolve disputes comes from their interactions with siblings. Older brothers and sisters, for example, often act as tutors to younger children, teaching them games, what to expect at school, and skills such as how to skip or climb trees. They can also act as gatekeepers for their younger siblings, managing their access to, or protecting them from, children outside the family. In turn, older children can learn how to be prosocial from their interactions with younger children.

An indirect way in which children are influenced by siblings is through observing their parents with brothers and sisters. Watching their siblings get into trouble with parents, for example, can teach children about acceptable behaviour and legitimate excuses. Listening to the explanations given by parents to miscreant siblings can teach children reasons for avoiding such misdeeds themselves.[63] With current trends towards smaller families in Australia, these benefits of growing up with siblings may be available to fewer children in the future, with children learning how to interact with peers in more formal contexts such as child care and school (see Chapter 6). Parents can and do treat siblings differently, which is one of the reasons given for why siblings are often so different from one another in personality and adjustment. A recent study has shown that such differential treatment relates to the age of the children and is more likely to occur in poorer families, in larger families and in families with low marital satisfaction.[64]

Influence of the extended family

Support from within the extended family is a crucial resource for families. Without support in the form of information, and financial and practical help such as grandparents' assistance in the care of young children, families become isolated and their children suffer.

It is unusual in Australia for members of the extended family to live in the household of 'nuclear' families, although this is more likely in Aboriginal and Torres Strait Islander households, reflecting a wider kinship system.[65] Nevertheless, families in Australia tend to keep in touch with extended family by telephone and through visits. Although members of the extended family can be a source of great support for families, they are not always willing to act in that role and, where help is provided, there may be emotional costs.[66] In some family circumstances, such as domestic violence or chronic illness, or where family members undermine more than they help, external support from agencies other than extended family is more appropriate.

The role of grandparents in the lives of children has been of increasing interest to researchers and policy makers. Grandparents are living longer and having a longer period of shared lives with their grandchildren.[67] When grandchildren are of pre-school age and their parents are in the workforce, many grandparents act as regular part-time caregivers and increasingly are awarded custodial care of their grandchildren when parents are unable to care for them. In this way, they often take on shared parenting roles in the care of their grandchildren.[68]

Issues of family obligations within the extended family can vary according to cultural group. This is particularly so in the care of elderly parents. A higher sense of filial responsibility is felt for parents born in southern or eastern Europe and Asia than for Australian-born 'Anglo' parents.[69]

Resources and support beyond the family

Although the family is the most powerful influence on children's lives, it does not operate in a vacuum. Families are influenced by the neighbourhood in which they live and the material resources and social support available to them from their local community. Families can be assisted by practical, emotional and informational support from informal sources in the community such as friends and neighbours and from formal sources such as health and educational services provided by local councils or state and Commonwealth governments. In recent years there has been a shift in research towards understanding the influence of community on family functioning and towards providing services at community level to improve child and family well-being. These issues are discussed in more detail in Chapters 7 and 11.

How are families and communities connected and what are the consequences for children?

Families do not affect children solely in terms of their internal dynamics. They also influence children's interactions with the world outside the family. Factors inside and outside the family affect its performance of three functions essential for children's well-being and development: the provision of resources and opportunities; protection from risks; and preparation for life beyond the family (socialisation).

Families as providers of resources and opportunities for children

Children can benefit in their development from a number of different kinds of resources that a family can provide for them. In his assessment of the importance of fathers in children's lives, Amato used Coleman's analysis to create a theoretical framework for his discussion.[70] That framework of the human, financial and social capital that parents provide to children in addition to their genetic inheritance is used below. As discussed in Chapter 1, such resources from families act together with the child's personal characteristics and forces outside the family to build resilience in children.

Human capital

In using the term 'human capital', Amato was referring to parents' skills and knowledge, indicated particularly by their education level and employment status. Well-educated parents confer educational advantages on their children not only in what they can teach them but in their familiarity with educational institutions, their procedures and expectations. When parents, particularly mothers, have little education, this is seen as a risk factor for children, affecting the resources available to children and their aspirations.[71]

A similar situation holds for parental employment. Employed parents bring home information to their children about the world of work. At the same time, children learn from employed parents about the work ethic and are influenced in their aspirations for employment and for further education.[72] Children with unemployed parents are relatively disadvantaged. Unemployment has a disorganising effect on family functioning, leading to lower family integration. In unemployed families fathers lose status, mothers gain in influence, and daughters, especially, are involved more in family decisions and forced to be independent at a younger age than girls in less deprived families.[73]

Unemployment also adds to family stress, and financial hardship compromises parents' ability to respond to their children's needs. This combination is a potent risk factor for child abuse and neglect, with researchers on the economic antecedents of child abuse warning that 'the loss of jobs in a community may endanger the well-being of children'.[74]

Financial capital

Amato includes income and the goods and experiences purchased with income in his definition of financial capital.[75] An adequate income for families can mean greater choice and opportunity, and family functioning that is not subject to the unrelenting financial stress that poverty brings. A family's income determines the resources available to children. Resources include material goods such as clothing, food and housing. In addition, parents can open up or restrict opportunities for their children by their choice (or their lack of choice in the matter) of where they live, and the resources of that community such as public transport and educational, cultural and recreational facilities; by their choice of child care and the schools the children attend; and by the friends they allow or encourage their children to make. Such choice is governed very much by income.

Poverty and low income are risk factors for children. Apart from restricting material resources and educational opportunities, poverty affects children through the stress it places on parents and the parental 'irritability and anger [that] may fester in chronic conditions'.[76] In a United States study, Brooks-Gunn found family functioning to be quite different for poor, near-poor, middle-income and affluent families, with poorer families having less predictable and stable family patterns of operation.[77] According to Radke-Yarrow, Richters and Wilson, 'the context of family chaos...alters the quality of relationships in the family, the ways in which networks of relationships are organised in the family, and the factors that are critical influences on the child'.[78]

The effects of low income and poverty on children can be far-reaching, and are mediated by a range of factors. Brooks-Gunn summarised the research in this way: 'The well-being of children is drastically reduced by being reared in poverty. Many factors seem to be associated with decreases in social, cognitive, emotional and physical well-being: economic disadvantage, poor schooling, residence in areas of highly concentrated poverty, young maternal age, single parenthood, low maternal education, and unemployment.'[79]

The effects of poverty appear to be cumulative, in that persistent poverty has a much greater effect on children's intelligence levels, for example, than transient poverty.[80]

In Australian society, poverty or near poverty is a feature of life for just over one out of every four children.[81] According to Birrell and Rapson, 'the fundamental distinguishing feature of poor families (relative to the middle-class group) is that 43 per cent were headed by a single parent, almost always the mother'. The authors concluded that 'poor families are shouldering a major part of the burden of raising Australia's children'.[82]

Social capital

Social capital relates to the relationships between people. This includes the relationships within the family and extended family as well as relationships with community members. An important resource in the development and maintenance of relationships is time spent with other people. Parents who build up relationships with neighbours, chat to other parents at school activities, and welcome friends to their home provide children with an outward-looking and trusting model of social relationships and a sense of being embedded in their community. When communities are high in social capital, there are better outcomes for children and for their parents as parents feel more supported and less stressed.

There has been much concern about the effects of parental employment involving non-standard and long working hours on parents' time to talk to their children, to help and comfort them, to teach them about life, or even just to be present and available for them.[83]

Time together provides opportunities for parents and children to develop family stories and rituals. Monitoring of children's activities has been shown to be particularly important for school performance and behaviour in children.[84] Time-use surveys suggest that mothers tend to reduce their recreational and social time to ensure that their children do not suffer from lack of time spent with them.[85] How parents use the time they spend with children is another matter. Canadian parents changed their patterns of behaviour according to the child's age, with declines between two and eleven years in all measured activities: laughing with the child, praising the child, talking or playing with the child, engaging in special activities with the child such as hobbies, games or sports and, a less frequent activity at all ages, reading to the child.[86] An Australian study of dual-earner parents with children in the middle-childhood years indicated that time with children was rarely one-to-one 'quality time' but rather was spent in different activities or passive activities together such as watching television.[87] It may have always been the case, however, that parents and children were engaged in different activities during a great deal of their time together. Nevertheless, opportunities to spend time together without distractions so that family talk is possible appear to be declining as television and computers dominate the home and families rarely sit down to meals together.[88]

When children have two parents living with them, the coparenting relationship is an additional source of social capital for children. Children can learn such skills as conflict resolution, open communication and how to provide emotional support to others by observing a strong coparenting relationship. Conversely, children who observe parents engaged in conflict, hostility or violence do not have access to the social capital from parents to enable them to learn more positive patterns of behaviour and their emotional security is likely to be compromised.[89]

Social capital available to children is also influenced by the psychological and physical health of parents, their parenting style and behaviours, and the support provided within the family, including the extended family. As we have seen, parenting style is important for child outcomes. In addition, particular parenting practices have been linked to children's cognitive development. These include parents' sensitive structuring of learning experiences based on their monitoring of children's current level of development. Children's progress in learning to read, for example, has been improved by intervention programs that teach parents to read more responsively to their children, to read more often, and to use the method of paired reading as their child progresses through school.[90]

Responsive parenting is less likely to be present when parents are not attentive to their children's signals—at times when, for example, they are depressed, abusive, or suffering from multiple stresses so overwhelming that they are unable to attend to the needs of others. It is also less likely when the children's signals are difficult to interpret—in cases where children, for instance, have disabilities that make it difficult for them to communicate, or have received very little stimulation from birth. Parents also find it difficult to respond sensitively to children who are defiant, aggressive or hard to manage.[91]

Families as protectors of children

As well as trying to ensure safety around the home, parents act as 'gatekeepers' for children's exposure to the risks of the world outside the family. Parental fears of injury or abduction of their children have meant that many parents do not allow their children to walk or ride bicycles to the shops, to school or to friends' houses, or to use public transport without adult supervision.[92] Paradoxically, these protective measures also prevent children from learning skills they will need when they leave home, and so may not be protective in the long term.

In high-risk neighbourhoods possible dangers are visible, as explained by the mother of a three-year-old boy from a Melbourne inner-city housing block: 'I don't really approve of the neighbourhood for children. There's a lot of things happening...He mostly plays in the back and people have found used syringes. I'm very worried about that so I try and avoid taking him outside. You can always find drunk people in the lifts and stairways. It's not a very good place to bring up children.'[93]

Keeping children inside the home for their protection, however, is isolating and means that children will be less active and more likely to watch television and play computer games. The world outside the family is not only 'out there'. It enters family homes as an uninvited guest through television, videos, computer and video games and the Internet. Garbarino argues that parents and society have an obligation to protect children from a toxic environment of adult issues and the general 'nastiness' of a violent and uncivil society, as it appears on the electronic media.[94] Others have argued that television and other electronic media portray the world as a more violent place than it really is, inculcating mistrust and fear in children and in parents, who may respond by being overprotective. Parents are urged to monitor their children's use of the electronic media, but children appear to be successful in evading their parents' attempts at regulation. Bronfenbrenner suggests that the behaviour children learn from television is not the main issue for child development so much as the behaviour it prevents: 'the talks, the games, the family festivities, the arguments through which much of the child's learning takes place and his [sic] character is formed'.[95]

Preparing children for life beyond the family

In addition to providing resources for children and protecting them from risks, families socialise children, teaching them cultural values and acceptable ways of behaving. Families transmit cultural values, often through everyday practices. In urban middle-class Anglo-Australian families, for example, it is acceptable for children to argue that they should not have to clean up all the mess if another child helped to create it. By contrast, such negotiation is not acceptable in urban comparable Chinese families.[96] Through this kind of everyday parental request to clean up at home, and from the negotiation that sometimes follows, children learn about cultural values and their relative importance.

Another important aspect of families as a context for children is the degree of fit between families and other contexts in which the child participates. Families can be seen as training grounds for children's participation in the wider society. In families, for instance, children learn about relationships with others, the importance of literacy and education, and ways to work or avoid work.[97] There are, however, important differences between the 'social contract' in the home and that in other settings such as the workplace. Whereas contexts outside the home often operate on an exchange model—a model of reciprocal obligations and rewards—relationships at home are generally assumed to operate under a more communal model, where the contribution of each family member is seen to benefit the family as a whole, and reciprocity, at least in the short term, is not a central expectation.[98]

Families as contexts for children

In summary, families may differ greatly in their structure and functioning but they are central contexts in the lives of children, offering them support and protection and preparing them for life beyond the family. The ability of families to perform these roles is determined by their resources, human, financial and social. Even in the most advantaged families, however, support and assistance are needed from outside the family for coping with the stresses of family life and child-rearing. Families cannot be seen as standing alone in children's lives. They are tied to other social systems and institutions such as schools, and to their local communities. These issues are explored in the following chapters.

Student exercises

1   If current demographic trends continue, especially in terms of smaller numbers of children born in Australia, what do you see as the consequences for children of the future, their families and communities?

2   Discuss the impact of the birth of a first baby on families. What are the features of the family itself that may impact on their adaptation to this life event? What are the contextual influences beyond the immediate family that might affect the impact of this event on family members?

3   Do you think that the intrusion of society into the home by way of electronic media such as television, video and computers is potentially harmful to children's development? In what ways do you think it could affect children and their parents? Is it the responsibility of parents to restrict and monitor children's use of these media, especially within the family, or should this be a responsibility of society?

4 Much of children's learning about aspects of the world, relationships and behaviour occurs in the context of the family. Discuss the nature of what children learn from family life and how that learning can transfer, appropriately or inappropriately, to other contexts such as child care, school and work.

Notes

1   R. Hartley, 'Families, Values and Change: Setting the Scene', in *Families and Cultural Diversity in Australia*, ed, R. Hartley, Allen & Unwin, Sydney, 1995.

2   M. Young and P. Wilmott, 1962, cited in M. O'Brien, P. Alldred & D. Jones, 'Children's Constructions of Family and Kinship', in *Children in Families: Research and Policy*, eds, J. Brannen & M. O'Brien, Falmer Press, London, 1996, p. 95.

3   B. Hunter & M. Gray, 'Family and Social Factors Underlying the Labour Force Status of Indigenous Australians', *Family Matters*, 62, 2002, pp. 18–25.

4   Australian Bureau of Statistics, *Australian Social Trends*, Canberra, 2003a.

5   There are now only 11.5 per cent of families who fit this stereotype—Australian Bureau of Statistics, 2003a.

6   Australian Bureau of Statistics, 2003a.

7   Australian Bureau of Statistics, 2003a.

8   Australian Bureau of Statistics, *Census of Population and Housing: Selected Social and Housing Characteristics*, 2003b, p. 35.

9   Australian Bureau of Statistics, 2003a.

10   Australian Bureau of Statistics, *Labour Force Australia (2002)*, Australian Government Publishing Service, Canberra, 2003c.

11   Australian Bureau of Statistics, *Labour Special Article: Full and Part-time Employment*, Australian Government Publishing Service, Canberra, 2001b.

12   Australian Bureau of Statistics, *Special Article: Casual Employment*, Australian Government Publishing Service, Canberra, 2002d.

13   Australian Bureau of Statistics, 2003a.

14   The patterns of women's involvement in the labour force are consistent with family responsibilities being assumed mainly by mothers rather than fathers—Australian Bureau of Statistics, 2003c.

15   One-parent families now make up 15 per cent of all families and 23 per cent of all families with dependent children. Australian Bureau of Statistics 2003a.

16   Australian Bureau of Statistics, *Special Article: Marriage and Divorce in Australia*, Australian Government Publishing Service, Canberra, 2002b; See also D. de Vaus, L. Qu & R. Weston, 'Changing Patterns of Partnering', *Family Matters*, 64, 2003, pp. 10–15.

17   Australian Bureau of Statistics, 2003a.

18   Australian Bureau of Statistics, *Marriages and Divorces Australia*, Australian Government Publishing Service, Canberra, 2002c.

19   Australian Bureau of Statistics, 2002b. In 1996 there was a 60 per cent divorce rate for remarried couples.

20   Australian Bureau of Statistics, 2003a.

21   An average of 1.75 children born to each woman of child-bearing age in 2001. Australian Bureau of Statistics, 2003a.

22   Commonwealth Department of Education, Science and Training, *Higher Education: Report for 2003 to 2005 Triennium*, Australian Government Publishing Service, Canberra, 2003, p. 19. Table 2.5 shows that the proportion of disadvantaged students in higher education (low socio-economic status, non-English speaking, rural or isolated or Indigenous background) has decreased by 2.4 per cent between 1991 and 2003.

23   Australian Bureau of Statistics 2003a.

24   Australian Bureau of Statistics, 2003a.

25   Australian Bureau of Statistics, 2003a.

26   Australian Institute of Health and Welfare, *The Health and Welfare of Australia's Aboriginal and Torres Strait Islander Peoples 2001*, 2001.

27   Australian Institute of Health and Welfare, 2001.

28   J. Watson, 'Determined to be Self-Determined', paper presented at the Frozen Futures Conference, Sydney, November 2002.

29   Australian Institute of Health and Welfare, *Child Protection in Australia, 2001–2002*, 2003.

30   Australian Institute of Health and Welfare, 2001.

31   For an account of early models and a suggested alternative, see D.T. Rowland, 'Family Diversity and the Life Cycle', *Journal of Comparative Family Studies*, 12, 1991, pp. 1–14.

32   T.A. Laszloffy, 'Rethinking Family Development Theory: Teaching with the Systemic Family Development (SFD) Model', *Family Relations*, 51, 2002, pp. 206–14.

33   Lazloffy, 2002.

34   E.M. Cummings & P. Davies, *Children and Marital Conflict: The Impact of Family Dispute and Resolution*, The Guilford Press, New York, 1994.

35   R. Dunlop, 'Family Processes: Towards a Theoretical Framework' in *Images of Australian Families*, ed, K. Funder, Longman Cheshire, Melbourne, 1991, pp. 122–35.

36   L. Tolstoy, *Anna Karenina*, trans. A. & L. Maude, Penguin Books, Harmondsworth, 1954, p. 3.

37   D.H. Olson, 'Circumplex Model of Marital and Family Systems: Assessing Family Functioning', in *Normal Family Processes*, ed, F. Walsh, The Guilford Press, New York, 1993.

38   A. Franks, *Indigenous Services in the Northern Rivers Region of NSW*, NSW Health, Sydney, 2001.

39   Rogoff, B., *The Cultural Nature of Human Development*, Oxford University Press, New York, 2003; S. Harkness & C. Super, eds, *Parents' Cultural Belief Systems*, The Guilford Press, New York, 1996.

40   C. Hardiment, *Dream Babies*, Oxford University Press, Oxford, 1984. It is interesting to note that preoccupation with children's self-esteem has also been shown to be culturally specific. A cross-cultural study of stories that mothers told about their children showed that mothers from Taipei often told stories of their child's transgressions and how they provided discipline and guidance for their child. In contrast, American mothers rarely told stories about their child's transgressions. When they did, they minimised the wrongdoing using humour. In contrast to the Taiwanese mothers, the American mothers were concerned not to damage their child's self-esteem. P.J. Miller, J.A. Hengst & S. Wang, 'Ethnographic Methods: Applications from Developmental Cultural Psychology', in *Qualitative Research in Psychology: Expanding Perspectives in Methodology and Design*, eds, P.M. Camic, J.E. Rhodes & L. Yardley, American Psychological Association, Washington, DC, 2003, pp. 219–41.

41   H. Bee, *The Developing Child*, Harper Collins, New York, 1992.

42   J. Shonkoff & D. Phillips, *From Neurons to Neighbourhoods: The Science of Early Childhood Development*, National Academy Press, Washington, 2001.

43   K. Deater-Deckard & J. Dunn, 'Multiple Risks and Adjustments of Young Children
     Growing Up in Different Family Settings', in *Coping with Divorce, Single Parenthood and
     Remarriage: A Risk and Resiliency Perspective*, ed, E.M. Hetherington, Lawrence Erlbaum,
     Mahwah, NJ,1999, pp. 47–64.

44   U. Bronfenbrenner, 'Principles for the Healthy Growth and Development of Children', in
     Marriage and Family in a Changing Society, ed, J.M. Henslin, The Free Press, New York,
     1989, pp. 235–41.

45   D. Baumrind, 'Child Care Practices Anteceding Three Patterns of Preschool Behavior',
     Genetic Psychology Monographs, 75, 1967, pp. 43–88; D. Baumrind, 'Current Patterns of
     Parental Authority', *Developmental Psychology Monographs*, 4, 1, pt 2, 1971.

46   L. Steinberg, S.M. Dornbusch & B.B. Brown, 'Ethnic Differences in Adolescent
     Achievement: An Ecological Perspective', *American Psychologist*, 47, 1992, pp. 723–9.

47   L.K. Mekertichian & J.M. Bowes, 'Does Parenting Matter? The Challenge of the
     Behaviour Geneticists', *Journal of Family Studies*, 2, 1996, pp. 131–45.

48   M.E. Lamb, 'Fathers and Child Development: An Introductory Overview and Guide', in
     The Role of the Father in Child Development, ed, M.E. Lamb, John Wiley & Sons, New York,
     1997, pp. 1–18; L. Craig, 'Caring Differently: A Time Use Analysis of the Type and Social
     Context of Child Care Performed by Fathers and Mothers', Discussion Paper No. 116,
     Social Policy Research Centre, University of New South Wales, Sydney, 2002; R.D. Parke
     & R. Buriel, 'Socialization in the Family: Ethnic and Ecological Perspectives', in *Handbook
     of Child Psychology*, ed, N. Eisenberg, Wiley, New York, 1997.

49   Lamb, 1997; R.D. Parke, 'Fathers and Families', in *Handbook of Parenting*, vol. 3, ed, M.H.
     Bornstein, Lawrence Erlbaum, Mahwah, NJ, 1995; also Parke & Buriel, 1996, pp. 27–63.

50   Rogoff, 2003.

51   F.F. Furstenberg, 'Social Capital and the Role of Fathers in the Family', in *Men in Families*,
     eds, A. Booth & A.C. Crouter, Lawrence Erlbaum, Mahwah, NJ, 1998, pp. 295–301.

52   J.M. Bowes, C.A. Flanagan & A.J. Taylor, 'Adolescents' Ideas About Individual and Social
     Responsibility in Relation to Children's Household Work: Some International
     Comparisons', *International Journal of Behavioral Development*, 25, 2001, pp. 60–8; J.M.
     Bowes, M-J. Chen, Q.S. Li & Y. Li, 'Reasoning and Negotiation About Child
     Responsibility in Urban Chinese Families: Reports from Mothers, Fathers and Children',
     International Journal of Behavioral Development, 28, pp. 48–58; J. Goodnow, 'From Household
     Practices to Parents' Ideas About Work and Interpersonal Relationships', in *Parents'
     Cultural Belief Systems*, ed, S. Harkness & C. Super, The Guilford Press, New York, 1996,
     pp. 313–44.

53   V. Kolar & G. Soriano, *Parenting in Australian Families*, Australian Institute of Family Studies,
     Melbourne, 2001.

54   M.L. Hoffman, 'Conscience, Personality, and Socialization Techniques', *Human
     Development*, 13, 1970, pp. 90–126.

55   R.K. Chao & J.D. Willms, 'The Effects of Parenting Practices on Children's Outcomes',
     in *Vulnerable Children*, ed, J.D. Willms, University of Alberta Press, Alberta, 2002, pp.
     149–65.

56   Chao & Willms, 2002.

57   Australian Bureau of Statistics, 2003a, p. 123.

58   Australian Bureau of Statistics, 2003a; J. Buchanan & L. Thornwaite, 'Paid Work and
     Parenting. Charting a New Course for Australian Families', Report prepared for the
     Chifley Foundation, University of Sydney, Sydney, 2001; L. Strazdins & R.J. Korda,

'Around-the-Clock: Parent Work Schedules and Children's Well-being in a 24-hour Economy', in Proceedings of the Work, Health and Families Forum, Canberra, August 2003, <http://www-nceph.anu.edu.au/Health_For_Life/publications>, accessed 5 May 2004; R. Weston, L. Qu & G. Soriano, 'Implications of Men's Extended Work Hours', *Family Matters*, 61, 2002, pp. 18–25.

59   Buchanan & Thornwaite, 2001.

60   K. Hand & V. Lewis, 'Fathers' Views on Family Life and Paid Work', *Family Matters*, 61, 2002, pp. 26–9.

61   G. Russell & L. Bowman, *Work and Family: Current Thinking, Research and Practice*, report prepared for the Department of Family and Community Services, Canberra, 2000.

62   J. Goodfellow, 'Multicare Arrangement Patchworks: The Multiple Use of Formal and Informal Childcare in NSW', report prepared for the Office of Childcare, NSW Department of Community Services, Sydney, 1999; J. Bowes, S. Wise, L. Harrison, A. Sanson, J. Ungerer, J. Watson & T. Simpson, 'Continuity of Care in the Early Years? Multiple and Changeable Childcare in Australia, *Family Matters*, 64, 2003, pp. 30–5.

63   J. Dunn, *The Beginnings of Social Understanding*, Harvard University Press, Cambridge, MA, 1988; C. Herrara & J. Dunn, 'Early Experiences with Family Conflict: Implications for Arguments with a Close Friend', *Developmental Psychology*, 33, 5, 1997, pp. 869–81.

64   R. Plomin & D. Daniels, 'Why are Children in the Same Family so Different from Each Other?', *Behavioral and Brain Sciences*, 10, 1994, pp. 1–16; J.M. Jenkins, J. Rasbash & T.G. O'Connor, 'The Role of Shared Family Context in Differential Parenting', *Developmental Psychology*, 39, 2003, pp. 99–113.

65   Indigenous families are more likely to live in extended families reflecting a wider kinship system. Only 4 per cent of Australian households in 1992 contained extended family members. Aboriginal and Torres Strait Islander households are mostly one-parent households (86 per cent). See D. de Vaus & I. Wolcott, eds, *Australian Family Profiles: Social and Demographic Patterns*, Australian Institute of Family Studies, Melbourne, 1997.

66   C. Millward, 'Intergenerational Family Support', *Family Matters*, 39, 1994, pp. 10–13.

67   P.K. Smith & L.M. Drew, 'Grandparenthood', in *Handbook on Parenting: Becoming a Parent*, vol. 3, ed, M.H. Bornstein, Lawrence Erlbaum, Mahwah, NJ, 2002, pp. 141–73.

68   C. Millward, 'Work Rich, Family Poor? Non-standard Working Hours and Family Life', *Family Matters*, 61, 2002, pp. 40–7; V.L. Bengston, 'Beyond the Nuclear Family: The Increasing Importance of Multigenerational Bonds', *Journal of Marriage and the Family*, 63, 2001, pp. 1–16; J. Goodfellow, 'Grandparents as Regular Child Care Providers: Unrecognised, Under-valued and Under-resourced', *Australian Journal of Early Childhood*, 28, 2003, pp. 7–17; J. Laverty, The Experience of Grandparents Providing Regular Child Care for their Grandchildren, unpublished MEd (Hons) thesis, University of Western Sydney, 2003.

69   de Vaus & Wolcott, 1997.

70   P.A. Amato, 'More than Money? Men's Contributions to their Children's Lives', in *Men in Families*, eds, A. Booth & A.C. Crouter, Lawrence Erlbaum, Mahwah, NJ, 1998, pp. 241–78.

71   C. Flanagan, 'Families and Schools in Hard Times', in *New Directions for Child Development*, no. 46, eds, V.C. McLoyd & C.A. Flanagan, Jossey-Bass, San Francisco, 1990, pp. 7–26.

72   J.M. Bowes & J.J. Goodnow, 'Work for Home, School or Labor Force: The Nature and Sources of Children's Understanding', *Psychological Bulletin*, 119, 1996, pp. 300–21; Flanagan, 1990.

73   Flanagan, 1990; R.K. Silbereisen, S. Walper & H.T. Albrecht, 'Family Income Loss and

Economic Hardship: Antecedents of Adolescents' Problem Behavior', in Economic Stress: Effects on Family Life and Child Development, New Directions for Child Development, no. 46, eds, V.C. McLoyd & C.A. Flanagan, Jossey-Bass, San Francisco, 1990, pp. 27–46.

74   V.C. McLoyd & C.A. Flanagan, 1990; L.D. Steinberg, R. Cataleno & D. Dodley, 'Economic Antecedents of Child Abuse and Neglect', Child Development, 52, 1981, p. 975.

75   Amato, 1998, p. 243.

76   M. Radke-Yarrow, J. Richters & W.E. Wilson, 'Child Development in a Network of Relationships', in Relationships within Families: Mutual Influences, eds, R.A. Hinde & J. Stevenson-Hinde, Clarendon, Oxford, 1988, p. 56.

77   J. Brooks-Gunn, 'Children in Families in Communities: Risk and Intervention in the Bronfenbrenner Tradition', in Examining Lives in Context, eds, P. Moen, G.H. Elder Jr & K. Lüscher, American Psychological Association, Washington, DC, 1995, pp. 467–519.

78   Radke-Yarrow, Richters & Wilson, 1988, p. 63.

79   Brooks-Gunn, 1997, p. 87;

80   G.J. Duncan, J. Brooks-Gunn & P.K. Klebanov, 'Economic Deprivation and Early Childhood Development', Child Development, 65, 1994, pp. 296–318.

81   A. Harding & A. Szukalska, 'A Portrait of Child Poverty in Australia in 1995–1996', paper presented at the Australian Institute of Family Studies Conference, Melbourne, November 1998.

82   B. Birrell & V. Rapson, 'Poor Families, Poor Children: Who Cares for the Next Generation?', People and Place, 5, 3, 1997, pp. 45–53.

83   L. Strazdins, R.J. Korda, D. Broom, L. Lim & R. D'Souza, 2003; R. Weston, L. Qu & G. Soriano, 2002.

84   A.C. Crouter, S.M. MacDermid, S.M. McHale & M. Perry-Jenkins, 'Parental Monitoring and Perceptions of Children's School Performance and Conduct in Dual- and Single-earner Families', Developmental Psychology, 26, 4, 1990, pp. 649–57.

85   M. Bittman & J. Pixley, The Double Life of the Family: Myth, Hope and Experience, Allen & Unwin, Sydney, 1997.

86   C. Cook & J.D. Willms, 'Balancing Work and Family Life', in Vulnerable Children, ed., J.D. Willms, University of Alberta Press, Alberta, 2002, pp 183–98.

87   C. Liossis-Vernados, 'Dual Working Parents and Their Families', unpublished PhD thesis, University of Queensland, 1997.

88   J. Garbarino & K. Kostelny, 'Parenting and Public Policy', in Handbook of Parenting, vol. 3, ed, M.H. Bornstein, Lawrence Erlbaum, Mahwah, NJ, 1995, pp. 419–36.

89   P.T. Davies, G.T. Harold, M.C. Goeke-Morey & E.M. Cummings, 'Child Emotional Security and Interparental Conflict', Monographs of the Society for Research in Child Development, 67, 3, 2002, serial no. 270.

90   S. Meadows, Parenting Behaviour and Children's Cognitive Development, Psychology Press, Hove, 1996.

91   K.E. Barnard & L.K. Martell, 'Mothering', in Handbook of Parenting, vol. 3, ed, M.H. Bornstein, Lawrence Erlbaum, Mahwah, NJ, 1995, pp. 3–26.

92   M. Owen, 'Children's Pedestrian Risk and Opportunity in a Disadvantaged Community', unpublished PhD Thesis, Macquarie University, Sydney, 2001.

93   T. Gilley & J. Taylor, Unequal Lives? Low Income and the Life Chances of Three Year Olds, Brotherhood of St Laurence, Melbourne, 1995, p. 100.

94   J. Garbarino, 'Growing up in a Socially Toxic Environment. Life for Children and Families

in the 1990s', in *The Individual, the Family, and Social Good*, ed, G.B. Melton, University of Nebraska Press, Lincoln, NA, 1995, pp. 1–19; J. Garbarino, *Raising Children in a Socially Toxic Environment*, Jossey-Bass, San Francisco, 1995.

95   U. Bronfenbrenner, 'Developmental Ecology Through Space and Time' in *Examining Lives in Context*, eds, P. Moen, G.H. Elder Jr & K. Lüscher, American Psychological Association, Washington, DC, 1995, p. 170.

96   J.M. Bowes, M-J. Chen, Q.S. Li & Y. Li, 2004.

97   Goodnow, 1996; S. McNaughton, *Patterns of Emergent Literacy*, Oxford University Press, Auckland, 1995; Bowes & Goodnow, 1996.

98   J.J. Goodnow, 'Differentiating Among Social Contexts: By Spatial Features, Forms of Participation, and Social Contracts', in *Examining Lives in Context*, eds, P. Moen, G.H. Elder Jr & K. Lüscher, American Psychological Association, Washington, DC, 1995, pp. 269–301.

From Home to the World Beyond:

The Interconnections among Family, Care and Educational Contexts

Catherine Neilsen-Hewett, Pamela Coutts
and Alan Hayes

The historical changes in families, as described in Chapter 5, have clear consequences for children, families and communities. This chapter explores the links between families and the contexts beyond them, focusing particularly on child care and, to a lesser extent, school. This brings into relief some of the processes that socialise children for life in the wider community. It illustrates the ways in which contexts are interconnected, and demonstrates how specific developmental consequences for children depend on the combination of their individual characteristics and the experiences they have at home and in the wider context of child care and school. The quality of experiences in each context is seen as the key determinant of developmental outcomes.

The chapter examines the following:
* the contemporary context of child care
* the influence of culture, beliefs and values on care and educational settings
* some of the sources of variation, such as child and family characteristics, social class, ethnicity and system differences
* the evidence of differential effects on children's development of group size, quality and duration of time in care and, particularly related to school, the effect of culture on academic achievement.

Contexts

Family life, care and education

In the past three decades, Australian families have undergone significant shifts in structure and composition, and these shifts have had dramatic impacts on the lives of children. While the nuclear family remains the most prevalent type of family in Australia (77 per cent), increasing numbers of children are now living in mother-only (20.3 per cent) or father-only households (2.7 per cent).[1] An increase in the number of marriages ending in divorce and trends towards women having children outside marriage underlie this familial landscape.[2] Within families there has been a dramatic reduction in the number of children. In Australia, the trend for fewer children has led to the average household now having only 1.5 children under the age of fourteen years. The impact on the children's experiences of family life has been equally dramatic. Hernandez talks of 'children's new lives' in these families.[3] They are now more likely to have fewer siblings, a better educated mother and a family with reduced options for dividing child care and household work.

The context of contemporary Australian child care

In contemporary Australia, men and women are frequently faced with the challenge of having to balance both family and paid work. Today, more than half (57.1 per cent) of all couple families with children under fifteen years, have both parents in paid employment.[4] Further, the proportion of women who are employed has increased dramatically in recent years, with 70 per cent of those aged twenty-five to thirty-four now being employed outside the home. This has meant an increased demand for child care. Many families have unmet needs for child care,[5] and workplaces vary in the extent to which they accommodate the family responsibilities of their employees.[6] Taken together, these changes have direct implications for children, their families and the communities in which they live.

Over 1.5 million Australian children under twelve years of age, or almost half of their age group, experience some type of formal or informal child care. Twenty-five per cent of children under the age of three years use formal care arrangements and this increases to seventy-three per cent when children are aged four years.[7] Approximately one-third of children use informal care arrangements[8] and a significant proportion of families make child care arrangements that involve a mixture of formal and informal child care.[9] For many families with both parents in the workforce, non-parental care is their only option; child care is not a luxury but a necessity. As such, child care has multiple roles and functions. It serves care and educational needs, as well as the economy of families and the wider society, and enables opportunities for equal employment of women.[10] The prevalence of child care, in some form, has led Silverstein[11] to suggest that the key focus of concern should not be on the possible adverse effects of child care, but rather on the consequences of not providing children with quality care.

The most striking characteristic of existing child care provisions is its diversity. 'In Australia, the provision of early childhood education cuts across a number of jurisdictional boundaries. As a result there are variations in the way early childhood education is defined and in the types of settings that are considered to offer early childhood education'.[12] Child care takes a variety of forms, from informal care provided by family members, friends and neighbours to formal long day care, after-school care and occasional care. Irrespective of the type, child care experiences need to be seen in the context of those available in the home. Experiences across the two types of context, home and care, may complement each other,[13] or one may compensate for the lack of particular experiences in the other.[14] The degree of responsiveness to the needs of individual children is an essential aspect of the different care contexts.[15]

The outcomes of child care are related to the quality of care received, and how care settings link with the other contexts in which children develop.[16] The diversity of services to choose from means that children's care experiences vary markedly in terms of content and quality. High-quality care can enhance socio-emotional functioning, cognitive abilities and school performance.[17] Concerns have been raised, however, that early and extensive child care poses risks for infants on the basis of the theory that healthy development requires stable and continuous caregiving from one adult caregiver.[18]

The importance of context

Three phases of child care research have been identified.[19] The first wave was characterised by simple contrasts between children reared at home and children enrolled in centre-based care. It had a strong focus on social-emotional development using attachment theory to frame the questions asked and the measures employed. In the second wave, the research focus shifted to identification of specific features of care environments that were related to the different developmental outcomes for children. More recently, a third wave has taken into account the impact of wider social influences on children's experiences in child care, and the influences of child and family characteristics on developmental effects. The research in this wave seeks to evaluate children's experiences within their social, economic and political context.

Progressively, child care research has moved beyond a narrow definition of the influences of particular types of care on children. The focus has turned increasingly to the interplay of program processes, staff experiences, family experiences and child characteristics. Of particular importance are the quality of the child care environment, the characteristics of children and families, and the social context in which child care programs operate.

Ochiltree and Edgar summarise the situation as follows:

> A vast array of influences interact to affect child outcomes: the interrelationships between the child's parents, or parent and partner(s); the home environment and neighbourhood; the level of family income and parent education; and the wider social, political and economic context which dictates norms of 'appropriate' behaviour for girls and boys and influences the way in which parents and partners combine their private caring tasks with the task of earning a living.[20]

McGurk, Caplan, Hennessy and Moss have argued that a critical aspect of the ecology of the child care experience is the 'social, political and moral zeitgeist within which child care is embedded'.[21] Again this highlights the importance of considering social context in understanding children's development.

Child characteristics, family factors and child care

Children's experiences at home and in the child care setting are related. Cumulatively and independently, they influence children's development. As such, development is multiply determined: by characteristics of the child, such as temperament, neurological integrity and impairment; by environmental factors, such as quality of relationships and interactions with parents and siblings and peers, and quality of non-parental care; and by factors in the child's larger social environment, including the immediate neighbourhood and the broader culture. These factors operate in a complex and integrated fashion to influence children's development.

The individual characteristics of children such as temperament and gender need to be considered in understanding the effects of non-parental care. Recent research by Watamura et al.[22] suggests that not all children are similarly affected by the amount of time spent in non-parental care. The authors examined the cortisol levels of infants and toddlers enrolled in full-day centre-based child care as an indicator of child stress. They found that teacher ratings of children's social fearfulness were associated with larger cortisol increases over the day for those children. Watamura et al. suggest that infants and toddlers who are more temperamentally fearful show greater stress responses to full-time centre-based care and as such may find the child care environment particularly challenging. Differences in vulnerability to the child care environment have also emerged among boys and girls. The NICHD Study[23] reported that among children who experienced more than thirty hours per week in non-parental care, boys were more likely than girls to be insecurely attached at age fifteen months. Together these findings highlight the need to take into account child characteristics when explaining the effects of non-parental care.

Findings from the study conducted by Watamura et al. draw our attention towards the role of peers in shaping children's day care experience. Centre-based care, in particular, brings children in contact with many same-age peers and provides opportunity for interaction and play that may otherwise be absent for children from the smaller families that are characteristic of Australia today. The importance of other children for children's social, emotional and cognitive development has been clearly underscored in research on children's peer relationships[24] yet researchers have failed to account sufficiently for the role of peers in understanding the effects of child care. 'The interactions with peers in the child care environment have the potential to be both risky and beneficial'.[25] Interestingly, in the study by Watamura et al. the children who were found to be shy and fearful, were seen by their teachers to play less frequently and less comfortably with other children. Clearly, further research is needed to untangle the complex relationships among child characteristics, peer experiences, the child care environment and adjustment outcomes.

Developmental outcomes of care also reflect the interrelationships among children's home environments, their individual differences, and non-parental care. Richters and Zahn-Waxler[26] suggested that family background factors directly affect outcomes. In examining the relationship between children's attachment security, child care and home experiences, Howes et al.[27] found that the social behaviour of toddlers reflects their experiences both at home and in the child care setting. Toddlers with insecure attachments to their mothers and caregiver demonstrated the least ability to engage in interactions with caregivers while in care. Children with insecure attachments to their mothers but secure attachments to caregivers exhibited more socially competent behaviours than those children who were deprived of secure relationships in both settings.

Further, Ahnert and Lamb[28] found mothers of German children enrolled in child care compensated for the time away from their children by increasing the intensity and regularity in which they interacted with their children at home. The amount of attention children received was comparable to what they would have received had they not been in centre-based care. Similar results have been found in Australian research on mothers working full-time.[29] Recent research findings from the Competent Children Project[30] found that early child care services and home resources play complementary roles with regard to children's competency levels.

Experience in early childhood education appears to nourish children's social, communicative, and problem-solving competencies in particular, while family resources may be important for children's cognitive competencies, as well as their social skills. Home activities were also associated with higher levels of cognitive competencies.[31]

In the National Institute of Child Health and Development (NICHD) Study of Early Child Care,[32] similar associations were found between family, economic and psychological factors and child care experiences. Economic factors were most consistently associated with the amount and nature of non-parental care, which was linked with reduced family size, lower maternal education, higher maternal income, longer hours of maternal employment, and the mother's beliefs about the benefits of maternal employment.

In the USA and Canada, socio-economic status has been linked with the type of care parents choose for their children.[33] Much less socio-economic variability exists in Sweden than in the USA or Australia. Sweden's long-standing political commitment to gender equality has led to the creation of a publicly subsidised daycare system of exceptionally high quality.[34] As a result of the quality control measures, there is less correlation between the standard of care received and the socio-economic background of children exposed to centre-based care in Sweden than in the USA, Canada or Great Britain.[35] Cross-national comparisons highlight the importance of accounting for cultural and social influences on the child care experience.

Child care occurs in the context of family circumstances and events as well as beyond them.[36] Each context affects the other and can only be understood in relation to the other. Previous approaches to understanding child care outcomes have underestimated the complexity of developmental processes. Children are not only influenced by their social and physical environments, but they also shape them.[37] Issues related to quality of care, amount of care, attachment security and socio-emotional, linguistic and cognitive development can be more clearly understood within an ecological model of childcare.

The importance of quality of care

The quality of care has been viewed as an important variable in influencing children's development.[38] In linking quality care to child outcomes it is necessary to consider what constitutes quality of care and how this can be measured. The quality of non-parental care is a multidimensional construct[39] encompassing the physical environment, social policy, the educational curriculum, staff training, child/staff ratios, group sizes and interpersonal relations.[40] Measurement typically involves global measures of program features (for example, ratings of program environmental features) and measures of dynamic processes (for example, caregivers' interaction behaviour). Ruopp et al.[41] argued that proper assessment of care quality involves both specifying the goals of care and understanding the specific indicators of quality. In examining the quality of the child care experience, researchers have focused on structural and philosophical characteristics of early child care as well as the quality of programs. The National Day Care Study (NDCS)[42] proposed that the debate on child care quality focus on three variables: group size, caregiver-to-child ratio and caregiver qualifications. Findings from the study suggested that, of the three, group size had the most consistent and pervasive effects on teacher and child behaviour and on later cognitive performance. In this study, caregiver-to-child ratio had less effect on pre-schoolers' functioning than on toddlers' and infants'. Higher caregiver-to-child ratios were associated with less distress in infants and toddlers. Better caregiver qualifications were associated with more social interaction between caregiver and children, with more cooperation and task persistence among children, and with increased involvement of children in activities. While much of the subsequent research has focused primarily on these three features, a number of additional structural characteristics have been considered, including staff turnover, caregiver stability, programming, health and safety provisions, available space and equipment.

High-quality care has been associated with short and long-term cognitive, social and emotional benefits for children's development. A recent study conducted by Helburn and colleagues[43] found that children in higher quality settings exhibited more advanced language development and pre-maths skills, displayed advanced social skills, were more positive towards their child care experiences, and had warmer relationships with their teachers. In examining the relationship between child care quality and social development, Phillips, McCartney and Scarr[44] found that children from better quality programs were more sociable, more considerate, less anxious and more task oriented than children who were exposed to lower quality care. Similar links have emerged from the NICHD longitudinal study where high-quality care, increases in the quality of care, and experience in centre-type arrangements were associated with better pre-academic skills and language abilities at four years.[45]

An important issue related to the quality of care is whether the negative effects associated with child care quality are short lived or have longer term implications for children's development. In examining the possible long-term consequences of child care quality, Vandell, Henderson and Wilson[46] found that poor-quality care was predictive of children's adjustment at eight years of age. Children exposed to lower quality care were less sociable, showed more problematic behaviours, and had more negative self-perceptions than children who had experienced high-quality care. Significant continuity was found between their behaviour in the child care centres and their functioning four years later.[47] While these results underline the importance of quality of care in influencing long-term development, there is a need for caution in interpreting these results as they did not control for family factors other than socio-economic status, and the sample size was small.

Amount of time in care

Along with the quality of care, the amount of time children spend in non-parental care has emerged as an important determinant in predicting adjustment outcomes among children. Findings from a body of research suggest that a history of extensive and continuous non-parental care is associated with poorer socio-emotional outcomes.[48] Amount of time in care has also been linked with poorer mother–infant interactions. Evidence from the NICHD study[49] showed that more time in care was associated with less sensitive mothering and less harmonious mother–infant interactions at six, fifteen, twenty-four and thirty-six months. The ongoing NICHD child care study has shown that time in child care through the first four and half years of life was important in predicting children's social competence. More hours in child care were associated with more behaviour problems in pre-school and kindergarten, lower levels of social competence and more conflict with teachers. This relationship held after controlling for variations in family background factors, maternal sensitivity and child care quality. Findings highlight the impact of cumulative quantity of non-parental care; while some evidence pointed to more hours during infancy predicting later maladjustment, other findings suggested that it was the amount of care experienced in the third and fourth years that best predicts poor outcomes for children.

Several studies, however, have found that quality and type of care are factors that are as important, or more so, in predicting outcomes for children than time spent in care. Crockenberg[50] concluded that: 'given that much of the variance in child behaviour was associated with amount of care was shared with quality and type of care, it appears that negative effects occur primarily when children spend long hours in poor-quality, centre-based care'.[51] Findings from the Sydney Family Development Project support this contention, finding no significant correlation between quantity of care and behaviour problems, attachment, school social adjustment, and teacher–child conflict,[52] with quality of care emerging as the most important predictor of child outcomes. Ungerer et al.[53] have argued that child care research needs to be interpreted in its cultural context. In countries such as Australia where quality of centre-based care is monitored through an accreditation system, time in care is less likely to have the detrimental effects found in research in the USA where quality of child care is more variable.

Congruence between home and care setting

Child care and family characteristics are linked. A problem in examining quality care in isolation from the influences of other contexts is the possibility that group differences do not result solely from the quality of the child care experiences, but reflect the complex interplay of child care, familial and individual differences in the child. More recently researchers have focused on variations in both the quality of non-parental care and the child's home environment and family circumstances.[54]

Findings from a longitudinal study examining the impact of family quality on children's behaviour illustrate that marital dissatisfaction, conflict and marital status lead to increased behaviour problems in children.[55] Research by Goelman and Pence[56] in the United Kingdom found that low-resource families (for instance single mothers with little education and low incomes) were more likely than families with more advantages to enrol children in low-quality centres. In the British Child Health and Education Study[57] social and family factors were found to influence the type of experiences of children in pre-school. Children from lower socio-economic classes, ethnic minorities, one-parent families and large families were poorly represented in organised pre-school educational facilities, with most of these children attending Local Education Authorities nursery schools. The characteristics of the families or the children themselves may influence both their placement in care of varying quality and their developmental outcomes.[58]

Researchers adopting a more ecological approach to understanding the effects of child care have begun to examine the quality of care that children receive at home (in, for example, the NICHD Study and the Thomas Coram Child Care Project). In examining the protective role of child care for children from disadvantaged backgrounds, Caughy, DiPietro and Strobino[59] found heightened reading and mathematical ability in children from low-income homes who entered care earlier and/or had more years in care. In contrast, children whose home environments promoted cognitive development and socialisation actually had lower scores if they had been cared for outside their homes. These findings highlight the complex relationship between the individual child, the environment and the processes of development. The differences in effects for low- and high-risk children 'will necessitate longitudinal research designs that measure the broad continua of individual, familial and extra-familial (including child care quality) attributes, while addressing the moderating impact of environmental and biological factors'.[60] That quality of care affects positive socio-emotional and cognitive development is strongly supported by longitudinal research.[61]

Culture, social policy, child care programs and child development outcomes

Many of the inconsistencies in research findings regarding the effects of child care on development are attributable to the different social contexts in which the research was conducted.[62] Moss and Melhuish suggest that in order to interpret findings from studies dealing with characteristics of child care, 'it is important to situate these findings in their social context, since this will have a major influence on child care arrangements and on children's experience in individual settings'.[63] They suggest that the social context influencing child care is both extensive and complex. Lamb and Sternberg[64] noted that economic, demographic, ideological and historical forces in a society influence the manner in which services are provided.

Great importance is now placed on research that acknowledges the interplay between development and socio-cultural influences. Contemporary societies vary with respect to policy and practice in the area of children's services.[65] The underlying issues that shape service provision include beliefs about children as a societal or family responsibility, about opportunities available to women for equal employment status with men, and about child care as education or welfare. While there may be strong differences across and within national contexts in child care provision, in the Australian context child care policy seeks to ensure that care is of high quality, accessible, and affordable to families from different social, economic and cultural backgrounds.[66]

The values and beliefs specific to the society determine the manner in which services to families and children are provided, affecting their organisation and delivery. In countries where there is significant gender inequality in employment, there is less public support for child care and less value is placed on the need for quality care. This is apparent in service provisions in the USA and the United Kingdom. In these market-driven economies it is considered that if the 'market place' needs women in the workforce then the market will provide women with child care services.[67] This has been a less than optimal framework within which to develop quality children's services. In northern European countries, child care is provided largely through public programs. In these countries there is greater gender equality for employment, and child care programs are viewed as early education. There are stronger beliefs in these countries that children are a responsibility of the whole society,[68] as extensive national support combines with a sense of public responsibility for children's services. As a result, the quality of care is high.

In Australia, opinion appears to be divided as to whether child care provisions are a public or private responsibility.[69] Through the 1980s and into the 1990s, the Commonwealth government agenda for child care, under the Children's Services Programs, had a strong economic rationale to encourage women with dependent children to return to the workforce. Economic considerations influenced political decisions to fund increases in child care places, with particular support going to community-based services (see Chapter 10). A stronger 'market approach' to the provisions and funding for child care services has since developed with the growth of more private child care providers and child care companies represented in the stock exchange.[70]

Given the inconsistencies in research findings on the effects of child care on development attributable to the different social contexts in which the research was conducted, caution should be used in drawing parallels between different countries because of culturally specific factors that influence the context of child care.

As the discussion to date shows, research that acknowledges the interface between development and socio-cultural influences is important. The extent to which research findings from one context may be generalised to contexts in which different social conditions operate is limited. It is important to examine child care effects within specific social contexts as the interconnections of children, families and communities vary across contexts.

Consequences

Key outcomes of exposure to child care

Attachment security

As discussed earlier, initial research examining the outcomes of child care focused on the potential negative effects on mother–child relationships and children's socialisation, reflecting concerns that young children might not fare as well emotionally in large groups as they do in the more intimate surroundings of their homes.[71] Initial evaluations of early child care programs were greatly influenced by the debate about attachment, with researchers claiming that extensive non-maternal care in infancy was associated with an insecure attachment to the significant adults in their lives.[72] A key assumption of attachment theory is that early social experiences, particularly the mother–infant relationship, play a key role in later development.[73] In a review examining early research on the effects of non-maternal care on children's attachment and development, Belsky and Steinberg[74] concluded that children were not harmed by the child care experience, and that children's relationship with their mothers was not in jeopardy. While this review represented a 'change in perspective', it was criticised on methodological grounds, in that many of the studies examined only high-quality centres and did not consider other important variables such as family background.[75]

In one of the first multistudy analyses linking early child care and attachment classifications, Belsky and Rovine[76] reported that infants who experienced twenty or more hours per week in non-maternal care in the first year of life were significantly more likely to be insecurely attached to their mothers, as measured at twelve and eighteen months. Similar results were reported by Lamb, Sternberg and Prodromidis.[77] Together these reports suggest a negative relationship between extensive care and secure attachment.

The picture, however, may not be as clear as suggested by the reports of Belsky and Rovine, and Lamb, Sternberg and Prodromidis. More recent research conducted by Roggmann et al.[78] found no significant relationship between non-maternal care and attachment. Findings from the NICHD Study of Early Child Care[79] indicate that the effects of child care on attachment depend on the complex interplay of the characteristics of the child care setting, the duration of exposure, the gender of the child, and children's prior relationships outside the context of child care. In a later report, associations between child care and attachment were reported to occur under conditions of insensitive mothering.[80] The results showed that less sensitive mothering in combination with long hours per week in care increased the risk of children being classified as insecurely attached to their mothers. The authors argue that more hours in care serve as an additional risk factor for children already experiencing poor mother–child interactions. Findings from these studies provide strong support for the argument that attachment security is not directly related to child care arrangements.

Socio-emotional development

There have been mixed results from research into the short- and long-term effects of early child care experiences on children's social and emotional development. Measures of children's socio-emotional development have involved conflict resolution;[81] interactions with peers;[82] social self-perceptions and self-concept;[83] teacher–child relationships;[84] sociometric status;[85] and externalising behaviours such as child hostility.[86]

In assessing children's development it is important that researchers study developmentally appropriate behaviour. For example, behaviour related to security of attachment is important for an infant sample, and peer relations are important for pre-schoolers. As expectations of what children can do differ from society to society,[87] it is particularly important that measures of socio-emotional competency are multidimensional and reflect their environment.

The Swedish Childrearing Project[88] aimed to compare and contrast the relative effects of centre care and home care on children's short- and long-term social development. Data were collected from children, classmates, teachers and mothers, providing multiple perspectives on children's socio-emotional adjustment. Outcome variables included children's interactions with peers and adults, as well as their values and attitudes towards moral problems, sex roles and friendships. A strength of this study is that it followed children over time (that is, it was a prospective design), as this allowed researchers to observe children directly at home and in the centre settings, rather than having to rely on retrospective ratings and the recollections of mothers and child care staff.

The Swedish researchers found significant differences on follow-up measures at one and five years of age between centre-based children and those cared for at home. At one year of age, centre-based children interacted with adults less often than their home-based peers. At five years of age a similar pattern of interactions was evident, with children from home-based care continuing to interact more with adults. By contrast, centre-based children tended to interact with peers. Some caution should be taken before directly comparing the social interaction patterns of the two groups, as children were observed in different environments (that is, centre-based children at the centre, and home-based children in their homes). Perhaps if the centre-based children had also been observed at home, where there are fewer or no children to interact with, they might also have displayed higher levels of interaction with adults. Again, it is essential that researchers carefully consider the contextual influences on children's behaviour.

To address this issue, Hagekull and Bohlin[89] assessed the effects of child care quality on children's socio-emotional development with reference to child and family characteristics. Quality of child care was systematically related to children's socio-emotional behaviours both concurrently and over time, with those exposed to high-quality care showing more positive emotions at home, independent of family and child characteristics. In a study of the social competencies of New Zealand children, Wylie et al.[90] showed that family income and mother's educational qualifications were the strongest predictors of children's social adjustment. Children from lower socio-economic groups had lower scores on measures of social skills and social interaction with peers. Again it is clear that, in evaluating children's socio-emotional adjustment, it is important for researchers to include variables related to both the family and non-parental care settings.

Cognitive and language development

A number of studies have assessed the short- and long-term effects of exposure to child care on cognitive and language development and have found small but detectable gains in children's academic performance,[91] from infancy through to the high school years.[92]

Social class is an important variable in understanding the findings for cognitive and language development of children in care. Studies of at-risk and economically disadvantaged samples in high-quality care interventions show heightened cognitive performance in children exposed to early childhood education compared with children who did not have this experience.[93] Findings from a study conducted by Howes[94] suggest that early child care history continues to influence children's behaviours even after three years of exposure to high-quality elementary schooling. Concurrent and short-term outcomes were associated with child care quality and stability, with stable and high-quality care predicting positive school adjustment for both boys and girls.

In examining the protective role of daycare participation for the cognitive development of low-income children, Caughy, DiPietro and Strobino[95] found daycare participation during the first three years of life to be positively related to subsequent development of mathematical and reading skills. For mathematics, centre-based care in particular exerted a stronger protective influence over the developmental effects of an impoverished environment.[96] These findings demonstrate the compensatory role that child care can play in children's cognitive development.

Osborn, Butler and Morris,[97] in reporting the results of a five-year longitudinal study, demonstrated the association between attendance at a nursery school, playgroup or day nursery and children's behaviour and cognitive ability. Children exposed to pre-school education performed better on tests assessing conceptual maturity and fine motor skills at the age of five. A significant predictor of antisocial behaviour in children at five years was frequency of attendance. Those who attended any type of pre-school institution for more than five sessions a week, however, were more likely to have higher antisocial behaviour scores than were non-attendees or children who attended fewer than five sessions per week.

The relationship between duration of care and measures of academic achievement was examined in a thirteen-year longitudinal study conducted by Fergusson, Horwood and Lynskey.[98] The researchers found that high levels of exposure (two to three years) to early education were associated with small improvements in school achievement at thirteen years. This occurred even when confounding factors were controlled for factors such as parental education, socio-economic status, position in family, child ethnicity, infant feeding methods, early mother–child interactions, and child's birthweight.

The ongoing Gotenburg Child Care Study[99] has shown that while the type of early child care experienced was important in predicting children's cognitive performance at the age of eight, measures of cognitive abilities taken at forty months were the best predictors of later development. This study highlights the importance of adopting an ecological model in understanding children's development. Characteristics of children and their child care settings were related to later cognitive performance. Children who spent more months in centre-based care before they were forty months showed higher cognitive ability than children who started later and/or spent less time in care. The quality of non-parental care was predictive of verbal abilities in later years.

The quality of care emerges as a key variable in promoting children's cognitive and language development. In research by McCartney,[100] for example, language development was positively predicted by the amount of speech caregivers directed towards children (a dimension of child care quality). Other dimensions of child care quality such as small group size, teacher training, and educational activities involved in the programs have been linked with cognitive development. Lamb[101] argues that children's adjustment—cognitive, linguistic or socio-emotional—is a product of their current and past circumstances and experiences, and that non-parental care should not be regarded as exerting a disproportionate influence.

It is taken for granted that, as with families, child care settings and schools are agents of socialisation in which children—regardless of their ethnic or socio-economic backgrounds—are expected to have certain common experiences and develop skills, values and attitudes that will help them develop into tolerant, responsible, socially competent and educated members of society. It is also assumed that settings must be organised according to the age and educational level of the child in order to encourage this development, and that they must become increasingly differentiated so that the student has expanding opportunities to establish independence at both the personal and curriculum level. It is interesting to note that this latter assumption is rarely challenged. The result has been relative uniformity, encouraged in some respects by aspects of legislation, in the child care and schooling experiences of children across Australia. Consequently it is a straight-forward task to describe the 'typical' child care, primary classroom and secondary school in Australia at the beginning of the twenty-first century.

From home and care to school

Children usually begin their formal schooling by joining a same-age coeducational classroom of twenty to twenty-five children, with a female teacher. The feminisation of the Australian teaching profession is increasing, according to Australian Bureau of Statistics figures, with the proportion of male teachers declining nationwide from 25.8 per cent to 20.9 per cent in primary schools and from 49.4 per cent to 44.9 per cent in secondary schools over the past decade.[102] Many students complete primary school with little, if any, direct experience of male teachers, and in the company of a set of classmates with whom they have been placed for the previous six years of schooling. In contrast to the continuity of the peer group noted above, in some areas of disadvantage in New South Wales the annual student mobility rate is in excess of 25 per cent.[103] At a school level, the constant change in the student population makes it difficult for staff to perform the welfare function society increasingly expects of them. At a student level, this dislocation of schooling and lack of continuity is yet another contributing factor to potential disadvantage, and in terms of the focus of this chapter, the likelihood of increased peer difficulties.

Secondary school presents many children with major challenges. Most children change schools between the primary and secondary years, since there are relatively few middle (grades 5–8) or kindergarten to grade 12 schools across Australia. In addition, many children change from the public to the non-government sector at this point. Regardless of school type, students are likely to join a larger school community, experience a variety of teachers each year, mix with a different group of peers according to each subject, and have a choice (albeit a limited one) of subject options. Moreover, the emphasis in the secondary system across Australia remains on an academic, competitive curriculum, and much of the focus, especially in the latter years of schooling, is directed towards performance in the final credentialling examination. Most schools at the beginning of the twenty-first century also continue to emphasise the importance of attendance, punctuality, conformity of uniform and routines—which, as Preston and Symes[104] argue, encourage socialisation to the work ethic. In these respects school organisations, structures and bureaucracy have altered little since the 1970s.

It is tempting, as noted earlier, to underestimate the diversity of experiences available across the educational sector. For instance, not all children enter same-age classrooms. Across Australia there are many one- and two-teacher schools, especially in remote rural areas: in 2001 within New South Wales alone 108 government primary schools (kindergarten to grade 6) had a total enrolment of twenty-one or less. In such circumstances the structural parallels between the school setting and an extended family are far closer than in a primary school of 800 students, and the transition from home to school presumably a less daunting one.

Schools also vary according to whether they are in a government secular system or set up by a private group or organisation to follow a particular charter, whether it be on religious, ethnic or pedagogical grounds. Cutting across all these variations is the extent to which schools are linked to their immediate community or neighbourhood. An interesting example is provided by the Northern Territory, where Aboriginal community schools provide a curriculum designed by the local community and taught in the local language. The differences in experience between children in such settings and those taught in a large urban school, following a centrally prescribed curriculum, are marked.

There is also great diversity in the ethnic mix of classrooms, with some schools, particularly in certain areas of the large cities, having a majority of students from recent-migrant, non-English-speaking backgrounds, whereas others in more established or country areas have a higher proportion of children from Anglo-Australian backgrounds.

The greatest diversity in the educational system, however, is exhibited in the more subjective features of school and schooling and in the values held about schooling. The following section examines some of the variations in the school culture across the Australian educational system, and the sources of some of these variations.

Culture, beliefs and values

From the point of view of critical theorists, no school curriculum is value neutral as all knowledge is socially constructed. It is not surprising, therefore, that there are systematic differences across settings in terms of beliefs and values held. Some of these are a result of school types, others a consequence of family characteristics. The most obvious difference is between government and private school systems. By definition, government schools are secular and do not see any part of their role being to transmit or encourage values and beliefs that are specifically linked to particular religious or philosophical viewpoints. This restriction does not hold for schools in the private sector. As a consequence, for instance, children in some fundamentalist Christian private schools in the 1990s are being taught a version of science—creationist science—that is consistent with the religious views of those schools but is disputed by the majority of science researchers. This example may be an extreme instance of the influence of the educational system on the views expressed, but it demonstrates the point clearly. In this case the values are to do with the primacy of certain forms of information (in this case a literal interpretation of the Scriptures) rather than on so-called scientific evidence.

As is the case for child care, the factors most commonly considered to influence values about schooling are family characteristics such as socio-economic status (SES), gender and ethnicity. The evidence has been largely indirect and comes from a research base that has considered the link between family backgrounds and school success in terms of educational outcomes. Traditionally, a deficit model has been used whereby certain 'inadequacies' in family backgrounds (for example low SES) have been linked to lower educational benchmarks such as school completion rates, university entry, and performance on achievement measures. Governments have attempted to compensate for these factors by providing greater resources for certain schools and certain groups, for example through initiatives such as the Disadvantaged Schools Program. Such models target 'at-risk' groups rather than individuals, assuming that the general societal factors are the principal determinants of success or failure.

In contrast, reproduction theorists argue that school success relates to the extent to which the beliefs, values and overall culture of the school correspond with those of the students.[105] In this viewpoint the notion of cultural capital, or the extent to which the contexts of child development ultimately enrich the whole culture of a society, plays a key role.

Interconnections between families and schools

The most direct and obvious link between a school and its community is through its parent body. During the 1970s, when it was commonly argued that the role of schools should be as agents for social change, the emphasis was on a school-based curriculum. The argument was that children would be best served by curricula that reflected the needs of the community in which the school was set. It was subsequently argued that such an approach advantaged those middle-class children from families of high social capital whose values most closely matched those of their teachers. Nevertheless the movement foundered for far more pragmatic reasons, namely the recognition by teachers that to create school-based programs within staffing constraints verged on the impossible.

The shift more recently has been to centrally based curriculum structures, but the emphasis on links with parents has changed to an emphasis on their participation. In New South Wales, schools are expected to have school councils with parent representation. It is widely accepted that parent participation is a good indicator not only of parental interest but of how directly parents assist the learning and development of their children. A recent publication by the Australian Parents Council espouses this viewpoint in that it argues that 'parent participation has the potential to break a cycle of failure and set in motion a cycle of success'.[106]

This viewpoint seems consistent with the 'reproduction' view of education but appears to overlook several features of Australia's multicultural society. Within Australia, parental participation varies according to class and ethnicity, whereas teachers are predominantly from Anglo-Australian middle-class backgrounds. More importantly, as a recent doctoral thesis demonstrated,[107] for certain ethnic groups patterns of parent participation may not reflect the values held about education. Duchesne argues strongly that a belief system sits within a particular social and cultural context. In her case study of Vietnamese- and Anglo-Australian families whose children attended the same schools, the Vietnamese parents were considered by the teachers to have less than satisfactory parent participation in their children's schooling and were deemed to be less interested. Despite this, the children succeeded—largely, Duchesne argues, as a result of a congruence between the values held about the importance of education and the practices the families encouraged in their children. These Vietnamese parents considered teachers to be experts, with education seen as the opportunity to improve their lives, and so they encouraged their children at every step. The Anglo-Australian parents, by contrast, participated as teachers expected them to, but had a view of education that was less positive: their participation was as much an effort to monitor the school and to express discontent as to assist actively in their children's education. The implication is that there may be more than one successful developmental path in a multicultural society, and we should be cautious in interpreting actions without some understanding of the underlying beliefs and values.

Policy influences

One recent change in society's perceptions of the role of schools has had great impact. The rhetoric of the market economy is now used by policy-makers and parents alike. Education is seen by many as a commodity, not a right. The emphasis is on schools performing a 'value-added' function, and of being accountable to their 'customers'. This philosophic shift has implications for the ways that schools are seen as settings for the development of young children.

To take a simple example: since 1989 there has been deregulation of the 'zoning' system for New South Wales government schools. In effect this means that parents are not required to send their children to the local government school but can approach any school that has room and staff available. Parents now 'shop around' for the school they feel best suits the needs of their child. In principle this freedom of choice and the resultant accountability are admirable, but they may have unintended implications for the education of young children. It has been estimated that 15 per cent of infant/primary state enrolments are now 'out of area', compared with 30 per cent for secondary.[108] This has consequences not only for the schools, which are forced to join in the effort to market and publicise themselves—presumably taking time and energy from an already crowded schedule—but for the children. If, for instance, families take the opportunity for their children to attend a school near the parents' workplace rather than near their home, and especially if after-school care is located at the school, children have limited opportunities to establish friendship networks based on their neighbourhoods. There is a discontinuity and isolation between school and home communities. For young children in particular, friendships are established from the neighbourhood and from the circle of children with whom they are in close contact. Out-of-area schooling, particularly for children who are too young to use public transport without supervision and so are reliant on parents for their travel, means that the parents increasingly act as gatekeepers for the children's access to age mates. Given that Garbarino[109] considers that both schools and neighbourhoods have the potential to provide a supportive community to foster resilience, we may be unwittingly reducing the possible support networks for our children.

A second issue to do with parental choice is linked to socio-economic measures. It may be those parents who already hold substantial 'social capital' and have the resources of time and energy to investigate schooling options that make these decisions for their children. Others may accept the de facto option of the neighbourhood school.

Change and its consequences

The most obvious change facing education is to do with technology. Technology will cause us to rethink some of the traditional ways of teaching, learning and communicating with the school community. Certainly the way technology is used to support the teacher has changed rapidly over the past ten years, even though many of the school structures, organisations and routines have remained essentially the same. Most schools are now linked to the Internet, and beginner teachers are expected to demonstrate competency in the use and application of technology. Increasingly, technology will be used to change the ways in which children are taught and in the amount and kind of personal interaction they engage in. But the implications go beyond this. Technology causes us to reconsider our definition of literacy, for instance. Will we consider the fifty-year-old who can read and discuss a complex novel but cannot and does not want to learn about information technology to be more or less literate than the fifteen-year-old who can access all the information that is needed to answer any assignment question from the Internet, can follow complex plots and subplots on interactive video games and stories, communicates hourly with friends by texting (using SMS technology) but is poor at traditional text-based comprehension and writing?

The intriguing question that is relevant to the present chapter is what impact these changes will have on the traditional parent–child and parent–teacher relationships, and on the ways in which the school and its community communicate and interact. For the next generation, technology has the possibility of changing in some critical aspects the relative status of parents and children in certain domains—for instance, as the children exhibit expertise in technology that their parents may not have. It has the possibility of redefining class differences, not so much in terms of traditional socio-economic measures but in terms of access to and knowledge of technology. In rural and remote areas of Australia, for instance, technology, especially the Internet, has come some way to redress traditional difficulties about access of resources. Those presently knowledge disadvantaged are those who have limited or unreliable access, and this may be caused by either economic or technological factors.

Technology also has the capacity to help us redefine the school community, and parent involvement may have to be reconceptualised. Schooling has always played an important role in supporting and encouraging the social aspects of children's development, acting *in loco parentis*. The challenge of the increasing role played by technology is to ensure that the interpersonal support so necessary for resilience in children is not diminished, and that school settings remain a positive context for development, whether as a physical or a virtual presence.

Student exercises

1   Reflect on your own transition to child care or school. What were the factors that determined your experience of this change of context?

2   The second major transition is from primary to secondary school. In what respects are the same issues important? What additional factors impact on a student's experience of this change of context?
3   Briefly describe some of the programs in your local area that are designed to assist children to make the transition to school.
4   Which factors are particularly important in determining the degree of match between the home and care contexts?
5   In what ways might the cultural backgrounds of children influence their experience of child care or school?

Notes

1   Australian Bureau of Statistics, *Australian Social Trends*, catalogue no. 4102.0, Australian Bureau of Statistics, Canberra, 2003a.
2   E.M. Hetherington & M. Stanley-Hagan, Parenting in Divorced and Remarried Families, in *Handbook of Parenting, Vol. 3, Being and Becoming a Parent*, ed, M.H. Bornstein, Lawrence Erlbaum, Mahwah, NJ, 2002, pp. 287–315; M. Weinrub, D.L. Horrath & M.B. Gringlas, 'Single Parenthood', in *Handbook of Parenting, Vol. 3, Being and Becoming a Parent*, ed, M.H. Bornstein, Lawrence Erlbaum, Mahwah, NJ, 2002, pp. 109–40.
3   D.J. Hernandez, 'Child Development and the Social Demography of Childhood', *Child Development*, 68, 1, 1997, pp. 149–69.
4   Australian Bureau of Statistics, 2003a.
5   F. Maas, 'Child Care Needs of Working Families in the 1990s', *Family Matters*, 26, 1990, pp. 59–63.
6   C. Kilmartin, 'Working Mothers Throughout the Decade', *Family Matters*, 26, 1990, p. 49; G. Russell, 'Sharing the Pleasures and Pain of Family Life', *Family Matters*, 37, 1994, pp. 13–19.
7   Australian Bureau of Statistics, 2003a.
8   Australian Bureau of Statistics, 2003a.
9   J. Bowes, S. Wise, L. Harrison, A. Sanson, J. Ungerer, J. Watson & T. Simpson, 'Continuity of Care in the Early Years? Multiple and Changeable Childcare in Australia, *Family Matters*, 64, 2003, pp. 30–5.
10   M. Sims & T. Hutchins, 'The Many Faces of Child Care: Roles and Functions', *Australian Journal of Early Childhood*, 21, 1996, pp. 21–46.
11   I. Silverstein, 'Transforming the Debate About Child Care and Maternal Employment', *American Psychologist*, 46, 1991, pp. 1025–32.
12   A. Rice & F. Press, *Early Childhood Education in New South Wales: A Comparative Report*, report for the NSW Department of Education and Training commissioned by the Strategic Research Directorate, 2003.
13   K. Deater-Deckard, R. Pinkerton & S. Scarr, 'Child Care Quality and Children's Behavioral Adjustment: A Four-year Longitudinal Study', *Journal of Child Psychology and Psychiatry*, 37, 1996, pp. 937–48.
14   H. McGurk, M. Caplan, E. Hennessy & P. Moss, 'Controversy, Theory and Social Context in Contemporary Child Care Research', *Journal of Child Psychology and Psychiatry*, 34, 1993, pp. 3–23; I. J. Schweinhart & D.P. Weikart, 'A Summary of Significant Benefits: The High/Scope Perry Pre-School Study Through Age 27', in *Start Right: The Importance of*

Early Learning, ed, C. Ball, Royal Society for the Encouragement of Arts, Manufacture & Commerce, London, 1994, pp. 97–102.

15   S. Scarr, *Mother Care/Other Care*, Basic Books, New York, 1984; S. Scarr & M. Eisenberg, 'Child Care Research: Issues, Perspectives, and Results', *Annual Review of Psychology*, 44, 1993, pp. 613–44.

16   National Institute of Child Health and Human Development Early Child Care Research Network, 'Characteristics of Infant Childcare: Factors Contributing to Positive Caregiving', *Early Childhood Research Quarterly*, 11, 1996, pp. 267–306.

17   B. Andersson, 'Effects of Public Day-care: A Longitudinal Study', *Child Development*, 60, 1989, pp. 857–66; B. Andersson, 'Effects of Day-care on Cognitive and Socioemotional Competence of Thirteen-year-old Swedish School Children', *Child Development*, 63, 1992, pp. 20–36; C. Howes, 'Can the Age of Entry into Child Care and the Quality of Child Care Predict Adjustment in Kindergarten?' *Developmental Psychology*, 26, 1990, pp. 292–303; M. Lerner, L. Gunnarsson, M. Cochran & S. Haggund, 'The Peer Relations of Children Reared in Child Care Centers or Home Settings: A Longitudinal Analysis', paper presented at the Biennial Meeting of the Society for Research in Child Development, Kansas City, April 1989; National Institute of Child Health and Human Development Early Child Care Research Network, 'Child-care Structure Process Outcome: Direct and Indirect Effects of Child Care Quality on Young Children's Development', *Psychological Science*, 13, 2002, pp. 199–206.

18   J. Belsky & M.J. Rovine, 'Nonmaternal Care in the First Year of Life and the Security of Infant–parent Attachment', *Child Development*, 59, 1988, pp. 157–67; M. Hojet, 'Can Affectional Ties be Purchased?: Comments on Working Mothers and their Families', *Journal of Social Behavior and Personality*, 5, 1990, pp. 493–502.

19   J. Belsky, 'Two Waves of Day-care Research: Developmental Effects and Conditions of Quality', in *The Child and Day-care Setting*, ed, R. Ainslie, Praeger, New York, 1984, pp. 1–34; J. Belsky, 'Parental and Nonparental Child Care and Children's Socioemotional Development: A Decade in Review', *Journal of Marriage and the Family*, 52, 1990, pp. 885–903; C.D. Hayes, J.L. Palmer & M.J. Zaslow, 1990, *Who Cares for America's Children? Child Care Policy for the 1990s*, National Academy Press, Washington, DC, 1990, p. 291; Scarr & Eisenberg, 1993.

20   G. Ochiltree & D. Edgar, 'Today's Child Care, Tomorrow's Children!', AIFS Early Childhood Study Paper no. 7, Australian Institute of Family Studies, Melbourne, 1995, p. 20.

21   McGurk et al., 1993, p. 19.

22   S.E. Watamura, B. Donzella, J. Alwin & M.R. Gunnar, 'Morning-to-Afternoon Increases in Cortisol Concentrations for Infants and Toddlers at Child Care: Age Differences and Behavioural Correlates,' *Child Development*, 74, 2003, pp. 1006–20.

23   National Institute of Child Health and Human Development Early Child Care Research Network, 'The Effects of Infant Child Care on Infant-Mother Attachment Security', *Child Development*, 68, 1997, pp. 860–79.

24   C. Howes, The Earliest Friendships, in *The Company They Keep*, eds, W.M. Bukowski, A.F. Newcomb & W.W. Hartup, Cambridge University Press, New York, 1996, pp. 66–86: G. Ladd, 'Peer Relationships and Social Competence During Early and Middle Childhood', *Annual Review of Psychology*, 50, 1999, pp. 333–59; C.M. Neilsen-Hewett, 'Children's Peer Relations and School Adjustment: Looking Beyond the Classroom Walls', unpublished PhD thesis, Institute of Early Childhood, Macquarie University, 2001.

25   R.A. Fabes, L.D. Hanish & C.L. Martin, 'Children at Play: The Role of Peers in Understanding the Effects of Child Care', *Child Development*, 74, 2003, pp. 1039–43.

26   J.E. Richters & C. Zahn-Waxler, 'The Infant Day Care Controversy: Current Status and Future Directions', *Early Childhood Research Quarterly*, 3, 1988, pp. 319–36.

27   C. Howes, C. Rodning, D.C. Galluzzo & L. Myers, 'Attachment and Child Care: Relationships with Mother and Caregiver', *Early Childhood Research Quarterly*, 3, 1988, pp. 403–16.

28   L. Ahnert & M.E. Lamb, 'Shared Care: Establishing a Balance Between Home and Child Care Settings', *Child Development*, 74, 2003, pp. 1044–9.

29   M. Bittman, S. Hoffman & D. Thompson, 'Men's Uptake of Family-Friendly Employment Provisions', Social Policy Research Centre, University of New South Wales, 2002.

30   C. Wylie, J. Thompson & A.K. Hendricks, *Competent Children at 5: Families and Early Education*, NZCER, Wellington, 1997.

31   Wylie et al., 1997, p. xiii.

32   National Institute of Child Health and Human Development Early Child Care Research Network, 'Child Care and Child Development: The NICHD Study of Early Child Care', in *Developmental Follow-up: Concepts, Domains and Methods*, eds, S.L. Friedman & H.C. Haywood, Academic Press, San Diego, CA, 1994, pp. 377–96.

33   M.K. McKim, B. Stuart & D.L. O'Connor, 'Infant Care: Evaluation of Pre-care Differences Hypotheses', *Early Education and Development*, 7, 1996, pp. 107–19.

34   H. Wessels, M.E. Lamb & C.P. Hwang, 'Cause and Causality in Daycare Research: An Investigation of Group Differences in Swedish Child Care', *European Journal of Psychology of Education*, XI, 1996, pp. 231–45.

35   Howes, 1990; E.C. Melhuish & P. Moss, 'Child Care in the United Kingdom in Historical Perspective', in *Child Care in Context: Cross-Cultural Perspectives*, eds, M.E. Lamb, K.J. Sternberg, C.P. Hwang & A.G. Broberg, Lawrence Erlbaum, Hillsdale, NJ, 1992, pp. 157–83.

36   National Institute of Child Health and Human Development Early Child Care Research Network, 1994.

37   Hayes, Palmer & Zaslow, 1990.

38   M.E. Lamb, 'Nonparental Child Care: Context, Quality and Correlates', in *Handbook of Child Psychology, Vol. 4: Child Psychology in Practice* (5th edn), eds, W. Damon, I.E. Sigel & K.A. Renninger, Wiley, New York, 1998, pp. 73–134.

39   B. Hagekull & G. Bohlin, 'Child Care Quality, Family and Child Characteristics and Socioemotional Development', *Early Childhood Research Quarterly*, 10, 1995, pp. 505–26.

40   McGurk et al., 1993; G. Ochiltree, 'Effects of Child Care on Young Children: Forty Years of Research', AIFS Early Childhood Study Paper no. 5, Australian Institute of Family Studies, Melbourne, 1994; Scarr & Eisenberg, 1993; NICHD, 2002.

41   R. Ruopp, J. Travers, F. Glantz & C. Coelen, *Children at the Centre: Final Report of the National Day Care Study*, Abt Associates, Cambridge, MA, 1979.

42   Ruopp et al., 1979.

43   S. Helburn, ed, *Cost, Quality and Child Outcomes in Child Care Centers*, University of Colorado, Denver, CO, 1995.

44   D.A. Phillips, K. McCartney & S. Scarr, 'Child Care Quality and Children's Social Development', *Developmental Psychology*, 23, 1987, pp. 537–43.

45   National Institute of Child Health and Human Development Early Child Care Research Network, 'Early Child Care and Children's Development Prior to School Entry: Results from the NICHD Study of Early Child Care', *American Educational Research Journal*, 39, 2002, pp. 367–87.

46   D.L. Vandell, V.K. Henderson & K. Wilson, 'A Longitudinal Study of Children with Child Care Experiences of Varying Quality', *Child Development*, 59, 1988, pp. 1286–92.

47   D.L. Vandell, V.K. Henderson & K. Wilson, 'A Follow-up Study of Children in Excellent, Moderate, and Poor Quality Child Care', paper presented at the Biennial Meeting of the Society for Research in Child Development, Baltimore, MD, April 1987.

48   J. Belsky, 'Developmental Risks (still) Associated with Early Child Care', *Journal of Child Psychology and Psychiatry*, 42, 2001, pp. 845–59; National Institute of Child Health and Human Development, 2003.

49   National Institute of Child Health and Human Development Early Child Care Research Network, 'Childcare and Mother–child Interaction in the First 3 Years of Life', *Developmental Psychology*, 35, 1999, 1399–413.

50   S.C. Crockenberg, 'Rescuing the Baby from the Bathwater: How Gender and Temperament (may) Influence how Child Care Affects Child Development', *Child Development*, 74, 2003, pp. 1034–8.

51   Crockenberg, 2003.

52   L.J. Harrison & J.A. Ungerer, 'The Sydney Family Development Project: Family and Child Care Predictors at Age Six', paper presented in the symposium, Longitudinal Studies of Early Childhood in Australia, J. Bowes (Chair), at the Australian Association for Research in Education Conference, Brisbane, December 2002; J.M. Love, L. Harrison, A. Sagi-Schwartz, M.H. van Ijzendoorn, C. Ross, J.A. Ungerer, H. Raikes, C. Brady-Smith, K. Boller, J. Brooks-Gunn, J. Constantine, E.E. Kisker, D. Paulsell & R. Chazan-Cohen, 'Child Care Quality Matters: How Conclusions May Vary with Context, *Child Development*, 74, 2003, pp. 1021–33.

53   Love et al., 2003.

54   W.S. Barnett, 'Long-term Effects of Early Childhood Programs on Cognitive and School Outcomes', *The Future of Children*, 5, 1995, pp. 25–50.

55   J.M. Najman, B.C. Behrens, M. Andersen, W. Bor, M. O'Callaghan & G.M. Williams, 'Impact of Family Type and Family Quality on Child Behavior Problems: A Longitudinal Study', *Journal of American Academic Child Adolescent Psychiatry*, 36, 1997, pp. 1357–65.

56   H. Goelman & A.R. Pence, 'Effects of Child Care, Family and Individual Characteristics on Children's Language Development: The Victoria Day Care Research Project', in *Quality in Child Care: What Does Research Tell Us?*, ed, D.A. Phillips, National Association for the Education of Young Children, Washington, DC, 1987, pp. 89–104.

57   A.F. Osborn, N.R. Butler & A.C. Morris, *The Social Life of Britain's Five-year-olds*, Routledge & Kegan Paul, London, 1984.

58   Hayes, Palmer & Zaslow, 1990.

59   M.O. Caughy, J. DiPietro & M. Strobino, 'Day-care Participation as a Protective Factor in the Cognitive Development of Low-income Children', *Child Development*, 65, 1994, pp. 457–71.

60   Deater-Deckard, Pinkerton & Scarr, 1996, p. 947.

61   For example the Competent Children Project, 1993; B. Hagekull & G. Bohlin, 'Quality of Care and Problem Behaviors in Early Childhood', paper presented at the Biennial Meeting of the Society for Research in Child Development, New Orleans, LA, March 1993; National Institute of Child Health and Human Development, 1994.

62   Love et al., 2003.

63   P. Moss & E. Melhuish, *Maternal Employment and Child Care in the First Three Years After Birth*, Report prepared for the Department of Health and Social Security, London, 1988, pp. 4–5.

64   M.E. Lamb & K.L. Sternberg, 'Sociocultural Perspectives on Nonmaternal Child Care', in *Child Care in Context: Cross-cultural Perspectives*, eds, M.E. Lamb, K.L. Sternberg, C.P. Hwang & A.G. Broberg, Lawrence Erlbaum, Hillsdale, NJ, 1992, pp. 1–23.

65   Lamb & Sternberg, 1992.

66   D. Brennan, *The Politics of Australian Child Care: From Philanthropy to Feminism*, Cambridge University Press, Cambridge, 1994; J. Wangmann, 'Towards Integration and Quality Assurance in Children's Services', AIFS Early Childhood Study Paper no. 6, Australian Institute of Family Studies, Melbourne, 1995.

67   Hayes, Palmer & Zaslow, 1990; J.E. Wilkinson, B. Kelly & C. Stephen, 'A Participatory Methodology for the Evaluation of Innovation in the Context of the Integrated Pre-school Services', *Early Child Development and Care*, 108, 1995, pp. 35–49.

68   S.B. Kamerman, 'Child Care Policies and Programs: An International Overview', *Journal of Social Issues*, 47, 1991, pp. 179–90.

69   Brennan, 1994; Wangmann, 1995; F. Press & A. Hayes, *OECD Thematic Review of Early Childhood Education and Care Policy*, Australian Background Report prepared for the Commonwealth Government of Australia, 2000.

70   Economic Planning and Advisory Commission, Child Care Task Force, *Future Child Care Provision in Australia: Child Care Task Force Interim Report*, Australian Government Publishing Service, Canberra, 1996; Economic Planning and Advisory Commission, Child Care Task Force, *Future Child Care Provision in Australia: Final Report*, Australian Government Publishing Service, Canberra, 1996.

71   Barnett, 1995; D.S. Gomby, M.B. Larner, C.S. Stevenson, E.M. Lewitt & R.E. Behrman, 'Long-term Outcomes of Early Childhood Programs: Analysis and Recommendations', *The Future of Children*, 5, 1995, pp. 6–24.

72   J. Bowlby, *Maternal Care and Mental Health*, World Health Organization, London, 1951; M. Rutter, *Maternal Deprivation Re-assessed*, Penguin, New York, 1981.

73   Ochiltree, 1994.

74   J. Belsky & L. Steinberg, 'The Effects of Day Care: A Critical Review', *Child Development*, 49, 1978, pp. 929–49.

75   D. Phillips & C. Howes, 'Indicators of Quality in Child Care: Review of Research', in *Quality in Child Care: What Does Research Tell Us?*, ed, D. Phillips, National Association for the Education of Young Children, Washington, DC, 1987, pp. 1–19.

76   Belsky & Rovine, 1988.

77   M. Lamb, K. Sternberg & M. Prodromidis, 'Nonmaternal Care and the Security of Infant–mother Attachment: A Reanalysis of the Data', *Infant Behavior and Development*, 15, 1992, pp. 71–83.

78   L.A. Roggmann, J.H. Lanlois, L. Hubbs-Tait & L.A. Reiser-Danner, 'Infant Day-Care Attachment and the "File Drawer Problem"', *Child Development*, 65, 1994, pp. 1429–43.

79   National Institute of Child Health and Human Development, 1996; National Institute of Child Health and Human Development Early Child Care Research Network, 'The Effects of Infant Child Care on Infant–mother Attachment Security: Results of the NICHD Study of Early Child Care', *Child Development*, 68, 1997, pp. 860–79.

80   National Institute of Child Health and Human Development Early Child Care Research Network, 'Child Care and Child Development, Childcare and Family Predictors of Preschool Attachment and Stability from Infancy, *Developmental Psychology*, 37, 2001, pp. 847–62.

81 Vandell, Henderson & Wilson, 1988.

82 Helburn, 1995; C. Howes, 'Relations Between Early Child Care and Schooling', *Developmental Psychology*, 24, 1988, pp. 53–7; National Institute of Child Health and Human Development, 1994; Wylie et al., 1997; National Institute of Child Health and Human Development, 2003.

83 Helburn, 1995; NICHD Study, 1994 (see note 32); M. Whitebrook, C. Howes & D. Phillips, *Who Cares? Child Care Teachers and the Quality of Care in America*, final report of the National Child Care Staffing Study, Child Care Employee Project, Oaklands, CA, 1990.

84 Helburn, 1995; National Institute of Child Health and Human Development, 2003.

85 Lerner et al., 1989.

86 Howes, 1990.

87 Wylie et al., 1997.

88 M. Cochran, 'A Comparison of Group Day Care and Family Childrearing Patterns in Sweden', *Child Development*, 48, 1977, pp. 702–7; M. Cochran & L. Gunnarsson, 'A Follow-up Study of Group Child Care and Family-based Childrearing Patterns', *Journal of Marriage and the Family*, 47, 1985, pp. 297–309; Lerner et al., 1989.

89 Hagekull & Bohlin, 1993; Hagekull & Bohlin, 1995.

90 Wylie et al., 1997.

91 For example D.M. Fergusson, L.J. Horwood & M.T. Lynskey, 'A Longitudinal Study of Early Childhood Education and Subsequent Academic Achievement', *Australian Psychologist*, July 1994, pp. 110–15.

92 For example Andersson, 1992; National Institute of Child Health and Human Development, 2003.

93 J.R. Berrueta-Clement, L.J. Schweinhart, W.S. Barnett, A.S. Epstein & D.P. Weikart, 'Changed Lives: The Effects of the Perry Preschool Program on Youths through Age 19', in *Monographs of the High/Scope Educational Research Foundation*, 8, 1984.

94 Howes, 1988.

95 Caughy, DiPietro & Strobino, 1994.

96 Caughy, Dipietro & Strobino, 1994, p. 466.

97 Osborn, Butler & Morris, 1984.

98 Fergusson, Horwood & Lynskey, 1994.

99 A.G. Broberg, H. Wessels, M.E. Lamb & C.P. Hwang, 'Effects of Child Care on the Development of Cognitive Abilities in 8-year-olds: A Longitudinal Study', *Developmental Psychology*, 33, 1997, pp. 62–9.

100 K. McCartney, 'Effect of Quality Care Environment on Children's Language Development', *Developmental Psychology*, 20, 1984, pp. 244–60.

101 M. Lamb, 'Infant Care and Practices and the Application of Knowledge', in *Applied Developmental Psychology*, eds, C.B. Fisher & R.M. Lerner, McGraw-Hill, New York, 1994, pp. 23–45

102 Australian Bureau of Statistics, 2003

103 T. Vinson, *Reports of the Inquiry into the Provision of Public Education in New South Wales*, NSW Teachers Federation and Federation of P & C Associations of NSW, Sydney, 2002, p. 22.

104 N. Preston & C. Symes, *Schools and Classrooms: A Cultural Studies Analysis of Education*, Longman, Melbourne, 1997.

105 See for example P. McLaren, *Life in Schools*, Longman, White Plains, NY, 1989.

106   Australian Parents Council, *Children's Learning: The Parent Factor*, Australian Government Publishing Service, Canberra, 1996, p. 31.

107   S. Duchesne, *Parental Beliefs and Behaviours in Relation to Schooling*, unpublished PhD thesis, School of Education, Macquarie University, 1996.

108   *Sydney Morning Herald*, 13 October 1997.

109   J. Garbarino, *Raising Children in a Socially Toxic Environment*, Jossey–Bass, San Francisco, 1995.

Isolation in Rural, Remote and Urban Communities

Maureen Fegan and Jennifer Bowes

We've been moving all the time, four times in the last five years, looking for cheaper places to live, feeling isolated living here, restricted in where we can go on a discount fare ticket.[1]

The community of Wemba Wemba is located on the New South Wales border on the Murray River across from Swan Hill. In many ways this community lives in an isolated, 'overlooked pocket'. They have nothing where they are. For services they have to cross the river to Victoria. Otherwise the closest services in New South Wales, where they live, is Albury, some 200 kms away. Occasionally one of the services from Swan Hill might come across the river for a visit.[2]

In this chapter we consider the role of communities in the support of families and children. To illustrate the importance of community influences, we discuss the benefits of well-functioning and adequate community links, then highlight difficulties encountered by families who are cut off from their communities, or who live in communities that are themselves isolated. We examine links between families and communities, discuss the impact of social change on the extent and form of isolation, and consider what it can mean for children and families to be excluded from community support. We conclude by identifying strategies and examples of innovative, ongoing and effective service models that have been used successfully in the Australian context to combat the negative effects of isolation. The first task, however, is to clarify how we are using the term 'community'.

Contexts

What is a community?

'How should we define a community?' is one of the oldest questions in social science. A single definition that everyone agrees with still remains elusive.[3]

What size is a community? Is it a few streets or a whole town?' Does size matter at all? Or are the social characteristics that some people share more relevant to our definition, such as religion, ethnicity, culture or traditional place. The term 'community' is increasingly being used very broadly to describe 'a social group that shares some common social characteristics and whose members are conscious of belonging to that group, with no necessary assumptions that the group in question is limited to a particular locality or that its members are personally known to one another'.[4]

While 'community' means different things to some people and to some groups[5] and while such differences can frequently be divisive,[6] in this chapter we suggest that the social networks among people and the core services available to them are what matters to everyone in a community.

People's perceptions of their community also matter. We return to a recurring theme in the book that a crucial component of context is 'in the eye of the beholder'. If families perceive their local area as a community of which they are a part, despite distance from neighbours or lack of facilities, then they will behave as if it is a community. This perception will lead to behaviour that has benefits for the families and children within it. Parents and children will also be more likely to believe that they have something to contribute to the community themselves.

If, on the other hand, individuals or families believe that they are isolated from their community, even if they do have a network of family and friends, they will behave in ways that reflect their perceptions of isolation. They will be disadvantaged in relation to other families by not making use of the resources that communities can provide.

How can communities support families and children?

Communities provide families and children with infrastructure and the social links that have been referred to as social capital. Community investment in children enables neighbourhoods to bring direct benefits to their lives through provision of a variety of contexts such as children's services, schools, play-grounds, libraries, cinemas and theatres, community groups, and venues where peer groups can play or gather safely. Access to wider societal contexts through transport links or technology, such as the Internet, may also be offered.[7]

Affluent neighbourhoods can offer more of these resources to families and children. These resources, along with more positive parental behaviours and greater community regulation, have been found to influence the higher ver-bal skills and fewer behavioural problems found in more affluent neighbour-hoods in Canada and the USA.[8]

In terms of the less tangible social links through which communities con-fer benefits on families and children, the idea of social capital is a useful one. There is an increasing recognition that accounts of Australia's wealth and well-being need to include assessment of our 'social capital' as well as our 'economic capital'. 'Social capital refers to the processes between people which establish networks, norms and social trust and facilitate coordination and cooperation for mutual benefit.'[9]

As part of his social capital theory, Coleman[10] outlined several dimensions of community resources. Communities high in social capital, according to Coleman, had the following characteristics: relationships that were dense and complex, information networks that were seen as accessible and helpful, rela-tively clear-cut norms and sanctions about parental and child behaviour, per-ceived opportunities for advancement (for example good schools, job opportunities, the chance to be a valued community member), and percep-tions of stability of residence in the area.

When social capital in a community is high, there are many potential ben-efits for children. Parents and children are supported by relationships with people outside the immediate family. When problems arise, those people are a resource for families to turn to for help and advice. Access to information about health and safety issues, children's development and community serv-ices also provides considerable support for families, especially when the peo-ple who hold the information are seen as helpful, and families know where to go for information relevant to their needs.[11]

Children benefit from the community support of social networks both directly and indirectly. They benefit directly from the friendships, information and emotional support that can come from their own friends and from the friends of their parents. Indirect effects flow to children from the influence of parents' networks on their parenting beliefs, attitudes and behaviour.[12] Another indirect effect is the protective influence of a community's shared code of conduct. A shared code of conduct that also respects the social and cultural uniqueness of families and communities has benefits for children in two ways. First, norms and sanctions regarding children's behaviour and shared neighbourhood goals and expectations for children can lead to a kind of collective socialisation, with a network of like-minded adults concerned with the well-being and development of children in the local area.

Second, such norms and sanctions within a community can help prevent maltreatment of children by family members or others. The emotional support provided by community networks can provide a buffer against stressful circumstances and assist parents to handle their own emotions and control violent impulses towards family members.[13]

When families are isolated from the community, these benefits are not available to them. The next section of the chapter will examine the forms that isolation can take and some of the effects of isolation on families and children.

Rethinking isolation

The first point to make is that isolation is not the same as solitude. Being alone, braving the elements, functioning independently, enjoying solitary endeavours and demonstrating resilience can all be positive experiences for individuals and for families. Certainly such attributes characterise many of the positive aspects of life in urban, rural and remote Australia. Kingwill noted the positive as well as negative aspects of solitude when she wrote, 'It is difficult to capture the richness of some forms of "isolation" or the despair of others'.[14] Our concern in this chapter, however, is with those families, and the children within those families, who suffer as a result of their isolation.

Forms of isolation

While geographic or physical isolation is perhaps the most easily recognised form in Australia, isolation has many causes, and children and families experience it in different ways. They may be isolated because they live in very remote areas, in valleys or mountains with difficult access or where there are particularly harsh climatic conditions, such as dust, floods or snow. They may be cut off from their local neighbourhood by a six-lane highway, or they may be isolated because of poor health, disability or special needs. They can be culturally isolated because they speak a different language, or have different-coloured skin or different traditions from the families around them. They may be 'the newcomer' in an established neighbourhood, or the last of a town's 'original' inhabitants. They may be isolated through lack of money to buy food or clothing, to reciprocate hospitality, to pay for a school excursion or to provide a child's birthday party.[15]

Alternatively, their isolation may be due to lack of education, telephone or transport. For Indigenous Australians, isolation from traditional lands can mean isolation from cultural and individual identity.[16]

During times of war or other international conflict, some families may become socially isolated because of their ethnicity or because their religious customs are seen as suspicious.[17]

Sometimes communities make informed choices to deliberately embrace selected types of isolation from mainstream values and customs. Examples include alcohol-free or 'dry' communities and communities grounded in common ethnic, religious or sexual identity. Yet this does not necessarily protect them from suffering the negative effects of isolation from other mainstream benefits such as access to health services, schooling or social standing and respect.

Even in the most densely populated cities, people who live in close physical proximity to one another can still suffer from a lack of connection with their neighbours, or with other community networks. Many families experience more than one form of isolation, often simultaneously, and this compounds their risk of suffering negative outcomes. One-parent families, for example, can be isolated within their families (no partner to assist with child rearing) as well as from connections to the community. As numbers of one-parent families increase in Australia, particularly in regional areas, this source of isolation for families is of particular concern.[18]

Social change and isolation

Several writers have voiced concern that society is changing in ways that make it increasingly difficult for people to establish or to maintain social links, even in the same local community.[19] As Garbarino wrote of families in the USA: 'Families are on their own. Family privacy, economic prosperity, and mobility patterns all separate parents and children from traditional sources of support and feedback, e.g., the church, elders, kin and neighbors. Isolation is contagious; we become estranged from each other and all families lose the social support of close and caring loved ones.'[20]

In Australia, one factor is the high mobility of families within and between states.[21] Frequent moves have been shown to have a negative impact on children's problem behaviours and school achievement but the degree of effect depends on the number of moves, existing problems in the family and the support available to families through income, parents' education, or assistance from other families in the new area.[22] Children whose families move between Australian states can also be disadvantaged by the disparity of state-mandated ages for school entry and by the lack of agreed national curriculum and related assessment criteria. High rates of mobility, however, can be seen as less of a threat to individuals than to the integration of social networks in communities.[23]

Another factor affecting community links is that the high cost and insufficient availability of housing has led to an increase in the number of families living in apparent segregation from the wider community, in concentrations of public housing or in mobile homes within caravan parks. Some families live permanently in designated caravan parks while others have more transient lifestyles, moving regularly between caravan parks or campsites. Life can be stressful for families living in caravan parks for a number of reasons, not the least being the intensity of close living. Children in this situation are also at increased risk of truancy and non-enrolment at school.[24]

In addition, the numbers of people who are homeless continue to rise.[25] Their options are limited and bleak: to move between the houses of relatives or friends, to live in cars, to sleep rough or, as is happening increasingly in Australia, to use the refuges for homeless people that until recently have mainly housed homeless men.[26] These individuals and families, often cut off from the support of their extended families, live on the fringes of society, unable to make the social ties that are available to established families in a neighbourhood.[27]

Within the wider society of Australia at present, there is disturbing evidence of a growing economic and social divide between rich and poor. Some researchers have referred to areas within our largest cities as 'urban ghettos'—areas with high concentrations of poverty, unemployment, violence and social distress that is manifested in crime, delinquency, domestic violence, child abuse and suicide.[28] At the same time more affluent areas, Cox argues,[29] are developing a fortress mentality, putting up physical and psychological walls to ward off perceived dangers from 'outsiders' within their own wider community.

Prosperity in the USA, Garbarino argues,[30] has led to greater isolation in terms of increased distance between members of the extended family, and greater family privacy. Home-based entertainment for children through computer and video games, backyard swimming pools and the highly organised after-school activities of many mean that the need for children to mix with other children from the neighbourhood is diminished, and children are effectively discouraged from developing community ties.

Isolation has many guises

The pressures of school life too can be isolating for both children and families. Children from some neighbourhoods have to travel long distances daily to reach their nearest school. Others do so as part of an increasing drift of students away from local state schools to selective or private schools, frequently located outside the student's home neighbourhood. Increased travel time reduces the time for 'play' in the local context. It also decreases opportunities for frequent, incidental contact centred around school and neighbourhood activities between family members and neighbours. Unless schools accept the responsibility to facilitate contact between students, their families and communities, children and families may be at risk of isolation from these aspects of traditional support once found in the local neighbourhood.

Changes in work patterns also militate against the formation and maintenance of social relationships beyond families. Unemployment leads to increased social isolation by reducing opportunities to meet others in the workplace, and by restricting the financial capacity of the unemployed to participate in wider society. Unemployment in rural areas often means relocation to the larger regional centres or to the cities to find work, making it more difficult to maintain family and community ties. Many people who are in employment are now working longer hours,[31] a pattern that leaves little time for family relationships and less for friends outside the workplace.

Social changes that affect community living and involvement are also taking place in rural Australia. National and international trends and policies are contributing to a downturn in the rural economy that has seen rural incomes drop and many small towns suffer.[32] Centralisation of services in larger towns or cities has led to many small towns experiencing the closing of schools, hospitals and other essential services, a reduction in railway services, and fewer jobs—including those in areas of public utility such as electricity and water delivery.[33] Such reduced social infrastructure can increase the isolation of whole communities and change the age profile of small towns and regional centres as young people leave to seek employment.[34]

As regional towns become larger and more like cities, and the infrastructure of smaller rural towns diminishes, informal social interaction at the local bank, supermarket or government agency is less likely. Travel to regional centres often involves high costs in travelling and working time, fuel and convenience. Such factors can make the development of community social ties difficult for rural or remote families, make it harder for them to attract and retain workers such as teachers and doctors to their neighbourhoods, and can result in considerable stress for children.

Periods of prolonged drought can also have a devastating effect on families, especially in many parts of rural and remote Australia. Families can lose crops, breeding stock and livelihoods. Some are forced to sell up and move away, leaving local or itinerant workers such as shearers, station hands or fruit-pickers with reduced job opportunities. Yet as McNicholl wrote, even when the rains come 'many in both the farming and small business sectors will exit the bush taking with them our most valuable resource, their children. Without access to a young, enthusiastic and skilled workforce the future for rural and remote Australia is indeed bleak.'[35]

The general social trends we have described do tend to increase the pressures on families and the risk of social isolation. The frequency of families changing place of residence, the intensity of modern living and the effects of economic trends, especially in rural areas, all militate against the establishment and maintenance of close and enduring local social networks for families and for their children.

Geographic isolation

While families who experience isolation, irrespective of cause, have much in common, physical or geographic isolation presents particular challenges and can magnify the collective impact of other negative aspects of isolation. This is particularly true in the Australian context.

Australia is a large country with a relatively small population. It is one of the most highly urbanised countries in the world, with the majority of the population of each state or territory living in or around large cities mostly located near the coast. Those living in areas classified as rural tend to cluster around large regional towns. Consequently, Australia has considerable areas of remote, sparsely populated outback land frequently characterised by harsh, hot and dry climatic conditions. This has usually meant that planning models used by governments often bypass the particular needs of very small communities, particularly those in remote areas.

In a country such as Australia, with its vast distances, families can live hundreds of kilometres from the next family or the nearest town, and this has implications for children and their parents. Young children who live in rural and remote isolated circumstances often have limited choices and opportunities to be with children of their own age for social interaction or for educational activities. This is equally true for their parents. Lack of opportunity to see their child interacting with other children, or to talk with other parents and professionals, can erode parents' confidence in their ability to monitor progress in their child's development and learning. For some families virtually the only source of comparison is via television. Socially isolated families living in urban communities may be at similar risk. Images of the idealised child, family and childhood contained in many television programs project quite unrealistic models for Australian parents. This too can undermine parents' confidence in their own abilities and lead to inappropriate expectations for children. Parental uncertainty and anxiety often have negative implications for the quality of parent–child interaction.[36]

All families, including those living in urban areas, need access to information that helps them gain a realistic understanding of their child's development and of the possible impact of developmental changes on family life. Families living in isolated circumstances, but particularly in geographic isolation, are often deprived of incidental encounters with other children and other parents within the local neighbourhood, encounters that can provide such information, reduce the intensity of uncertainty and alleviate parental anxiety.

Parents in rural and remote areas often live long distances from most, if not all, of their extended families. Outside the larger cities, transport costs are high and public transport frequently non-existent, particularly in remote areas. While some families can and do use telephones to stay in touch over long distances, economic considerations often necessitate shorter or less frequent calls. Physical separation from family members, especially grandparents, limits access to this source of regular interpersonal support.[37] The Internet has the potential to make access to others easier and less expensive for isolated families.[38] This will only work if families have access to computers and the knowledge of how to use them, a situation that is less likely in rural than urban centres, particularly among Indigenous families.[39]

The challenges of geographic isolation can perhaps be seen most starkly in times of emergency or ill health. The nearest hospital may be more than a day's journey away by car, and childhood illness can be a time of extreme stress for families. When a child is hospitalised there may be no close neighbour or family member to help care for other children in the family. The range of health professionals such as doctors, physiotherapists, dentists and psychologists that is available in cities and often in regional centres does not exist in geographically isolated towns.

Although living in rural and remote communities poses many challenges for families, it also offers many advantages. In the words of one professional familiar with the problems of families in remote areas:

> People in remote areas do not want to replicate urban lifestyles and solutions; they are understandably proud of their self-reliance. Community development objectives must reinforce this [self-reliance], and not undermine the strength and independence of these people. Rural Australia is made of company towns, Aboriginal communities, small rural towns, regional centres and remote areas with dispersed families. All of these communities are made up of people who need the broadest possible holistic approach to their services.[40]

Social isolation

Communities do not need to be geographically isolated to experience threats to social cohesion. Many newer suburbs on the outer rims of Australian cities, for example, are depleted in social capital. Such areas often have high levels of unemployment and little community infrastructure. When few residents have access to cars and there is little or no public transport, and not even footpaths to allow safe walking with infants in strollers, residents are effectively isolated in their homes. Financial concerns also mean that parents are so drained by their efforts to look after themselves and their own families that they have no emotional resources left to provide help or support for their neighbours.[41]

Families in such neighbourhoods frequently do not know where to turn when they need help. They often cannot even contact the relevant societal agencies because they are unaware of the procedures for obtaining assistance from them. Gaining access to information is made even more difficult for parents with low levels of literacy or education or from culturally and linguistically diverse backgrounds, and these factors can further increase family isolation.

Consequences

How does isolation affect children and families?

Irrespective of how isolation has come about, lack of access to the resources that community links provide can result in non-involvement in the community, alienation, loneliness, low self-esteem, boredom, intolerance, lack of motivation and vulnerability for adult family members. Isolation can also have a negative impact on family functioning and disadvantage or impair children's development.

For some, the negative effects of isolation may be temporary, while for others they may seem almost insurmountable. The adolescent who has no choice but to leave the support of family and friends and the familiarity of the local community to attend boarding school or university, for example, may experience considerable disruption at least in the short term. So too may the few remaining adolescents in a small town when most other young people have moved to the city for employment. Yet their long-term prospects for social support are quite different from those of an elderly widow in the country forced to move hundreds of kilometres away from her community to the only available nursing home. Government policies, economic priorities and town planning all interact with an individual's own realities, perceptions and life chances to determine the experience of isolation at different points in the life cycle.

Social isolation and child abuse

One of the most extreme negative outcomes of isolation has been found in the well-documented links between socially isolated families and child maltreatment. Social isolation increases the risk of all forms of domestic violence, including child abuse. As Cox writes, 'the more private and disconnected families are, the more difficult it is to identify signs of abuse or even inadequate levels of care'.[42] Child abuse is one of the most serious possible outcomes of social isolation, and it has clear costs to children, families and communities.

When areas are low in physical and social capital and families are socially isolated, collective socialisation may be low.[43] In this type of situation, families and children are at risk of violence and abuse resulting from the stresses of few resources and the lack of contact with others who might act to curb this behaviour. This is a conclusion drawn by researchers into child abuse in the USA[44] and Australia,[45] who have found geographic pockets of high levels of child abuse within neighbourhoods. The feature distinguishing these areas from others close by that did not have such high levels of abuse was the social isolation of the families. Their isolation from the human resources of their community placed them and their children at risk.

Many researchers, however, see family violence as linked to the overall balance of stress and supports in the community where families live.[46] Families already experiencing high levels of stress due to low income, the demands of single parenthood, or the presence of a child with a chronic illness or disability, for example, may maltreat their children if they are socially isolated or if another major isolating stress such as unemployment is added.[47]

There are, however, structural differences between communities, and sometimes between urban and rural communities, that can affect not only the likelihood of domestic violence, but also the possibilities of escape from abusive relationships. Hornosty,[48] for example, found that several structural factors made it particularly difficult for rural women in Canada to report abuse or to leave abusive relationships. These included physical isolation, lack of transportation and support services, limited employment opportunities, and conservative cultural norms and beliefs about women, marriage and the family. Hornosty concluded that understanding the local community factors that make it more difficult to escape an abusive situation is an essential first step in identifying appropriate intervention strategies. Attention to community infrastructure and attitudes is important too for approaches to the prevention of child abuse.

Successful interventions for isolated families

In these times of social and economic change, families living in all forms of isolated circumstances are increasingly at risk of disadvantage and sometimes despair. Their social and economic circumstances make the delivery of services to address their needs more difficult, but at the same time more necessary than ever. The challenges of providing support for families and alleviating the negative effects of isolation need to be met in a variety of creative and innovative ways.

Some service and community development strategies used to combat isolation and to support the emergence of community resilience have been particularly effective in the Australian context. The examples that follow illustrate interventions involving 'outsiders'; those begun by parents to address a particular need; and interventions that attempt to coordinate the services of several government departments.

Intervention by 'Outside' agencies: CONTACT Incorporated

Particularly in rural and remote areas, communities have to be very resourceful to help families establish social ties and gain access to the health and educational services of the wider society. In many cases, individuals or organisations from outside these communities are needed as a catalyst if such resourcefulness is to emerge and be sustained.

One example of the use of such a strategy is the CONTACT Program, which was launched as an ongoing project for the International Year of the Child in 1979. CONTACT Incorporated is a community-managed program for isolated children, families and communities. The program's charter is to provide information, resources and support for people caring for young children in isolated circumstances. The CONTACT definition of isolation encompasses social, emotional, cultural, educational, economic, intellectual, physical, geographic and locational disadvantage. It acts to break down isolation by bringing information to isolated children, their families and communities, and to the professionals working with them. While working extensively across urban, rural and remote communities in New South Wales, CONTACT Incorporated is also proactive in initiating and influencing policies, service models and practices that address isolation across Australia.

The CONTACT experience suggests that strengthening the capacity of the communication, information and support networks that surround families is the most effective long-term strategy for addressing the challenges of isolation. The program works to achieve this in a number of ways. CONTACT staff provide regular support and resources to the parents, children's services, early childhood nurses and teachers and others who are involved in the care of young children. Staff also work closely with local communities to identify local needs and priorities, and to facilitate policy changes to address those needs.

Individuals and services throughout New South Wales can access CONTACT support and resources directly through its city office, while the fieldwork component of the project enables staff to visit remote communities regularly. Through personal contact, telephone discussions and correspondence, staff stay in touch, answer enquiries and initiate and support local community networks. Following each field visit, CONTACT staff prepare reports that are then returned to local communities to provide a written 'picture' of existing and potential social networks. This process empowers local people to become more fully involved in identifying and strengthening community links within their local areas.

In addition, CONTACT produces and disseminates information about children's development, parenting, community arts and crafts and community services. Resources are designed to assist in building caregiver competence and confidence to combat isolation and to interact effectively with young children. To assist individuals and local communities to locate other relevant services, CONTACT also prepares and distributes a list of community services and organisations of particular relevance for carers of children with disabilities.

Material from CONTACT resources is often disseminated more widely by local newspapers, or by other support agencies or community groups.

As well as providing information, CONTACT encourages the formation of interest groups. 'Contact Activity Days', involving story-telling, arts and craft activities and early childhood programs, are an ongoing feature of the project and are designed to encourage people out of their isolation. Activity days are particularly welcomed in rural and remote communities. Invitations are extended to all in the community and, though families are involved in the various activities provided, parents may also choose to have private discussions with visiting professionals such as teachers, psychologists and health workers. This model of inclusion provides opportunities for all families, including those at risk of child abuse, to have access to potentially supportive community networks and to individual counselling. It differs from other programs that are targeted at families or children categorised as 'at risk'.

CONTACT is also actively involved in the support of mobile children's services designed to offer more regular and ongoing support for child–adult interactions in remote and disadvantaged areas. A mobile service reaches isolated or disadvantaged communities by car, bus, plane or train, and provides staff with an appropriate range of equipment to support the educational programs offered. Mobiles service socially, culturally and geographically isolated areas and disadvantaged locations on a regular basis.

Working in a mobile service requires resourcefulness and a range of equipment to deal with the problems of physical isolation. Two pre-school teachers providing a mobile service for isolated families in Queensland explained their life 'on the road':

> We've held playgroups alongside bars, next to racecourses and…on a property lawn with a territorial goanna and in a dirt backyard in the middle of a dust storm…With the roads we travel, you need to be prepared for anything [their four-wheel-drive contains not only preschool equipment but camping gear, an axe, tyre tubes, jumper leads, air compressor, fluorescent lights, tools, shovels, a high-frequency radio and a satellite phone]. We take emergency food supplies. As we are sometimes the only people visiting, many families ask us to bring out a variety of items—a pane of glass, a set of electric dehorners, nappies, spare tyres.[49]

CONTACT has found that one of the advantages of the mobile service model is that it can respond to the specific educational needs of children while at the same time offering children and families support in the wider social, health and safety areas.[50] Yet those on the 'front line' of service delivery are themselves at risk of professional and personal isolation. To combat this, CONTACT supports ongoing networking and professional development for mobile staff including organising National Mobile Musters (week-long residential training conferences) for those working in rural and remote parts of Australia.

Mobile services are just one of a range of flexible strategies required if the diverse needs of children and families who live in isolated circumstances are to be met effectively. CONTACT also works closely with government representatives, community organisations and local communities to identify unmet needs including gaps in service provision and to find innovative and cost-effective ways of addressing them. For example, within New South Wales, in the western region CONTACT identified ways of including children with additional needs in children's services,[51] and statewide it helped implement child health initiatives for Indigenous children, and assisted in the establishment of 'in home' care arrangements for isolated farming families.

Having access to a service that actually meets their child's specific needs can make a big difference for families. Highlighting the benefits of in-home care, for example, Pitman wrote, '[it] is proving to be a great relief for families living in isolated areas. It has helped some families to employ a governess to supervise their children's schooling and has supported other busy mothers who need help with station work, beyond the homestead. All in all it is a very worthwhile service that has taken the pressure off families who were near breaking point'.[53]

CONTACT also considers the needs of non-English-speaking, itinerant workers and their children who travel to various country regions for seasonal harvests and the transition to school needs of geographically isolated children living in rural and remote areas who have little or no access to children's services and who will start their formal schooling via Distance Education.

Education and professional qualifications can provide young people with a career pathway that encourages them to leave rural Australia in search of education and employment.[54] CONTACT and growing numbers of community organisations are strong advocates for supporting lifelong learning within communities.[55] Macquarie University, for example, offers a program for Indigenous workers in children's services that enables them to become qualified early childhood teachers. The program enables them to remain in their communities working in local services after graduation.[56]

Intervention by parents: the Isolated Children's Parents' Association

The formation of community groups around 'tasks in common', and the new social networks that often emerge as outcomes from parents' joint endeavours, each play a part in establishing community 'protection' against the effects of isolation. Shared recognition of their children's needs, and their own actions to have these needs met, unite parent groups at the local level. Many established early childhood services, playgroups, schools, hospitals and early intervention programs for children with special needs, for example, have benefited from the advocacy and voluntary support of families.

An example of such a parent-initiated group is the Isolated Children's Parents' Association of Australia (ICPA Australia). Gaining access to education for their children is an ongoing challenge for families living in isolated rural and remote areas. ICPA was formed in 1971 by a group of parents who shared a common need 'following the closure of the Bourke School Hostel in New South Wales and a parallel denial of schooling to isolated schoolchildren throughout outback Australia'.[57]

At this time Australia was experiencing a rural recession, continuing drought, rising production costs, reduced commodity returns and limited job opportunities throughout rural and remote areas. Many families were moving into larger towns seeking employment and needed affordable boarding institutions to enable their children to go to school. Variations of this scenario have escalated rather than diminished over the ensuing years.[58]

ICPA brings together parents from around Australia who together are influential advocates for the educational needs of geographically isolated children. 'Membership includes a cross section of Australia's rural and remote population and includes fishermen, miners, itinerant employees, farmers, pastoralists and small business owners'.[59] Over the years their repeated representations to government have helped bring about changes in government awareness of and responses to the needs of children living in rural and remote areas. These include the introduction in 1973 by the Commonwealth government of the 'Assistance for Isolated Children Scheme' (AIC). The AIC provides a Distance Education Allowance for children who learn at home, a Boarding Allowance for those children who attend a school hostel or boarding school facility, and a Second Home Allowance to assist in the establishment of a second home, to enable children to attend school on a daily basis.[60] In recent years, ICPA Australia has advocated strongly for the implementation of mobile children's services, including in-home child care for families that do not have access to any other child care services. Increasingly mobile services have become a lifeline for those families who are able to access them.[61]

At state level, ICPA NSW has successfully lobbied for an effective school travel scheme as well as for improved access to correspondence lessons via distance education. Distance education has been revolutionised by the establishment of distance education centres, decentralised schools of the air, and by the use of new communication technology.[62] Rapid advances in information technology now offer exciting opportunities for geographically isolated children who learn at home to interact more with peers.

'Whole-of-government' Approach: Schools as Community Centres

Government responsibility is organised in terms of multiple tiers (local, regional, state and national levels) and of separately managed departments in such areas as health, education, community services and housing. Families' needs and communities' needs, however, do not work in this fragmented way just as it is in urban areas. It is difficult, for example, to separate the needs of a family living in a geographically isolated region into children's issues, education issues, or broader family or health issues.

Joint departmental projects can overcome artificial legislative or administrative barriers that hinder service delivery, and can increase the responsiveness of departmental programs and procedures to community needs. An example of such an interdepartmental project is the Schools as Community Centres program in New South Wales. This program commenced in 1995 as a pilot project in four disadvantaged communities in New South Wales. The project was a joint venture between the state government departments of Health, Community Services, and Education and Training. The Department of Housing joined the venture in 1998.

The program's aim is to influence the planning and integration of service delivery to meet the needs of disadvantaged families. It is targeted at families with children aged from birth to eight years, with a priority on children in the first five years to promote the health, well-being and school readiness of those children. The objectives of the program and the strategies designed to meet them recognise both the commonality and the uniqueness of local social contexts as well as family and community needs.

An evaluation of the New South Wales Inter-agency School Community Centres Pilot Project confirmed that the project successfully met its objectives. This was demonstrated by:

- enrolments in transition-to-school programs increased significantly
- Aboriginal families and workers developed strategies to meet family needs
- the level of age-appropriate immunisation increased in all four sites
- emergent literacy behaviours increased at all centres
- children involved with the project demonstrated a smooth transition to school
- families participated in joint action to address community needs
- departmental staff commented on increased inter-agency cooperation
- referrals to local services increased
- departments engaged in joint planning.[63]

The use of a local facilitator to connect families, service agencies and communities is a feature of the Schools as Community Centres program that has contributed to its success at least in its pilot phase. Another key feature of the program is the use of a local school as a base for work with the community. Making the school a site for activities with pre-school-aged children and their families has had many benefits in terms of children's school readiness, and for the schools themselves in terms of greater parental involvement once children have started school. Parental involvement assists not only children's education but also their health outcomes such as increased immunisation rates. Communities can also benefit. For example, on one site of the inter-agency pilot program, parents mobilised parental and local council assistance to build a path through a neighbouring swamp to assist children walking to the school.

The ability of government departments to work together in such a way, and the effectiveness of strengthening communities to benefit families and children, is the subject of the ongoing evaluation of the program.

The Schools as Community Centres program has been incorporated into the New South Wales Cabinet Office's Families First initiative and by 2003 was expanded to twenty-three schools. Further expansion is likely as Families First planning is completed across New South Wales.

The Families First initiative, as its website explains, is the New South Wales Government's 'prevention and early intervention strategy that helps parents give their children a good start in life. The strategy aims to connect parents to each other for support and to build communities and services that support families with children 0–8 years. The Families First strategy is jointly delivered by five government agencies, including the Department of Education and Training, in partnership with parents, communities and local government'.[64]

Implementation of strategies such as Families First demonstrates evolving recognition by policy makers of the many benefits the whole-of-government approach offers for the planning and delivery of community services.

Intervention programs can be aimed at children or families 'at risk', or they can be general prevention programs such as CONTACT that are directed towards all families in a particular geographic area or local community. An issue in policy discussions is the target of these programs. Programs differ in their focus on parents, children, both, or parents and children in interaction.[65] There is some concern in the USA that intervention and policy aimed at adults only do not necessarily flow on to the benefit of children, and that there is a need to intervene with children directly.[66] Two-generation programs that provide services for children and parents have been shown in research from the USA to lead to the best outcomes for children, families and communities.[67]

The best way to design and implement such interventions is still uncertain although it is clear that building positive relationships is a key element. Whether facilitators should be paid workers or unpaid volunteers, and profes-sionally trained or trained specifically for the program, are two of the ongoing debates in this area. The importance of having local residents in these roles, however, is widely acknowledged,[68] as is the importance of building up com-munity infrastructure to help overcome family isolation.[69]

Leaving aside these wider issues of intervention and returning to implica-tions for practitioners, several principles have emerged from our review of isolation problems to guide those who work with isolated children, families and communities. In general terms, policy-makers, teachers, health professionals and community workers need to be aware:

- of the special challenges posed by all forms of isolation and, in particular, by geographic and social isolation
- that while some of the problems caused by isolation are common across communities, others can only be understood and addressed at the local level
- that strategies that involve communities in the identification of, and solutions to, their own local problems are more likely to be effective for both individuals and communities
- that we need to recognise the contradiction that sometimes strong group identity within communities can prevent inclusion of those deemed to be 'outsiders'
- that the processes used to prevent or address isolation can themselves increase community resilience, social infrastructure and social capital
- that if we are to avoid 'blaming the victim', we cannot assume that all people and all communities can be equally resilient, innovative or resourceful in addressing the negative effects of isolation
- that while external intervention including professional staff can support communities they must be careful not to undermine existing support agencies, including the voluntary sector
- that any form of community development or intervention must at the very least 'do no harm'.

In conclusion, there is no single intervention model that can alleviate all forms of isolation, support all children and strengthen all families and all communities. There are, however, some tried and true characteristics of flexible model-building that have emerged from community development programs around the world. Ruth Cohen from the Bernard van Leer Foundation writes that many specifically targeted early childhood education programs, for example, can and do become catalysts for wider community development. Such programs reflect a 'model' for sustaining processes of individual and community growth. Cohen describes this model as:

> a marvellously fluid, continually adapting combination of individuals of all ages, races, classes who listen to others, adapt what they learn to their own environments, then alter what they do as circumstances and people change. These are individuals who know what they want for their communities and their children and who have a vision for the future. They live in rural and urban areas all over the world and, even though they speak different languages, they understand each other.[70]

With a shared language of individual endeavour, advocacy, social policy and just practice we can 'rethink' isolation, combat its negative outcomes and, in so doing, strengthen those 'buffers' of community capital and infrastructure that best protect children and strengthen their families and communities.

Student exercises

1   Think about the community in which you live. First, look up the statistical descriptors of your neighbourhood. This information can be found in publications of the Australian Bureau of Statistics or from their website at <http://www.abs.gov.au>. Consider such factors as:
   • local employment patterns (including unemployment rates, shift work, casual or seasonal employment)
   • socio-economic status
   • demographic composition (for example, proportions of young and old; married/partnered/living alone)
   • family composition; household size
   • where people live (houses, flats, farms, nursing homes, caravan parks)
   • where children go to school and how they get there
   • languages spoken in the community (and availability of interpreters)
   • rates of car ownership (also ask who has a driving licence and who has access to a car)
   • costs of living (rents, petrol, food, schooling and so on).
   Then walk around your local neighbourhood, observe closely, and think about the possible work, play and friendship patterns of the people who live there. What types of factors might influence these? You might consider public transport (is it available and how much does it cost?), roads and their impact on people, the availability of community resources such as shops, banks, schools, medical support, housing stock and population density.
   Identify community meeting places or other resources that provide opportunities for contact between people such as children's services, schools, parks, halls, churches and clubs.
   Consider how town planning contributes to or inhibits interactions between people. Some questions you might ask include the following. Where are the roads? Are they easy to cross safely? Are there footpaths? Where can children play or ride a bicycle safely? Are there opportunities for incidental contact between neighbours? Where can teenagers and young adults gather? What leisure alternatives are available to them?
   Find out if there are any family support programs available in the local area. Are there playgroups or meetings for members of other self-help associations such as the Nursing Mothers Association or the Country Women's Association? Are family support programs available locally such as Good Beginnings, Parents as Teachers and Schools as

Community Centres? Who can provide local families with accurate advice on how to choose properly fitting child restraints for their children? Who is authorised and available locally to make certain they are correctly fitted in cars and other vehicles?

How easy was it for you to access this information? How would families who are experiencing isolation find out about these networks?

2   Consider the various types of social networks and community supports that may or may not be available to the people who live in your community. Who might be experiencing isolation? What sorts of isolation? What could be done to alleviate the negative effects of isolation? Would you rate your local community as high or low in social capital? Why?

3   Think about yourself and the people and places that are important to you.

• Have you ever experienced feelings of isolation? If so, write down how it felt. Then describe any influences you think may have contributed to the experience of isolation and identify any factors that may have alleviated its negative aspects.

• What strategies have you (or might you) put in place to prevent yourself becoming personally or professionally isolated?

• What contributions do you make (or might you make in the future) to the social capital of your community?

Find examples of innovative programs to strengthen families and communities and compare their characteristics to the programs described in this chapter. Use the following websites as starting points for your search:

Australian Institute of Criminology: <http://www.aic.org.au>
Australian Institute of Family Studies:<http://www.aifs.org.au>
Community Builders: <http://www.communitybuilders.nsw.gov.au>
Community Building: <http://www.communitybuilding.vic.gov.au>
Family Action Group: <http://www.newcastle.edu.au/centre/fac>
Families First: <http://www.familiesfirst.nsw.gov.au>

Notes

1   Mother of three-year-old, living in inner-city Melbourne. T. Gilley & J.Taylor, *Unequal lives? Low Income and the Life Chances of Three Year Olds*, Brotherhood of St Laurence, 1995, p. 95.

2   Comments of Aboriginal Field Worker, in Z. Kutena, *Identified Needs of Remote and Isolated Aboriginal Children, Families and Communities in New South Wales: An Overview*, CONTACT Incorporated, Sydney, 1995, p. 93.

3   S. Shaver & J. Tudball, *Literature Review on Factors Contributing to Community Capabilities: Final Report*, Report for the Department of Family and Community, Social Policy Research Centre, University of NSW, 2001.

4   A.S. Rossi, 'Contemporary Dialogue on Civil Society and Social Responsibility', in *Caring and Doing for Others: Social Responsibility in the Domains of Family, Work and Community*, ed, A.S. Rossi, University of Chicago Press, Chicago, 2001, p. 31.

5   M. Dodson, *My People and Place: Why Does Place Matter?* Keynote Address, People, Places, Partnerships Conference, University of New South Wales, Sydney, April 2003; J. Ife, *The Place of Human Rights in Community*, Keynote Address, People, Places, Partnerships Conference, University of New South Wales, Sydney, April 2003.

6   D. Brennan & B. Cass, 'The Communitarian Imaginery: Deconstructing the Concept of "Community" in Australia's Welfare Reform Debate', paper presented at the National Social Policy Conference, 'Competing Visions', University of New South Wales, Sydney, June 2003, <www.sprc.unsw.edu.au/nspc2001/index.htm>, accessed 5 June 2003.

7   J. Brooks-Gunn, 'Children in Families in Communities: Risk and Intervention in the Bronfenbrenner Tradition', in *Examining Lives in Context*, eds, P. Moen, G.H. Elder Jr & K. Lüscher, American Psychological Association, Washington, DC, 1995, pp. 467–519; G. Hugo, 'Australia's Future Population: Where Will They Live?', in *Australia's Population Challenge*, eds, S. Vizard, H.J. Martin & T. Watts, Penguin Books, Melbourne, 2003.

8   The study comparing children from affluent and poor neighbourhoods in Canada confirms previous findings in the USA. See D.E. Kohen, J.E. Brooks-Gunn, T. Leventhall & C. Hertzman, 'Neighbourhood Income and Physical and Social Disorder in Canada: Associations with Young Children's Competencies', *Child Development*, 73, 2002, pp. 184–6.

9   E. Cox, *A Truly Civil Society: 1995 Boyer Lectures*, ABC Books, Sydney, 1995, p. 15.

10   J.S. Coleman, 'Social Capital in the Creation of Human Capital', *American Journal of Sociology*, 94, 1988, pp. 94–120.

11   Brooks-Gunn, 1997.

12   M. Cochran & S. Niego, 'Parenting and Social Networks', in *Handbook of Parenting*, ed, M.H. Bornstein, Lawrence Erlbaum, Mahwah, NJ, 1995, pp. 393–418.

13   J. Garbarino & A. Crouter, 'Defining the Community Context for Parent–child Relations: The Correlates of Child Maltreatment', *Child Development*, 49, 1978, pp. 604–16.

14   S. Kingwill, *Isolation: A Key Factor which Affects Australian Families and Their Children: Implications of CONTACT Inc. Initiatives for Commonwealth Policies and Priorities in Education and Child Support*, Submission to Employment, Education and Training Reference Committee, 1995, p. 2.

15   J. Taylor & A. Fraser, *Eleven Plus: Life Chances and Family Income*, Brotherhood of St Laurence <http://www.bsl.org.au/pdfs/11plus.pdf>, accessed 29 August 2003.

16   Dodson, 2003.

17   R. Kattan, 'What Counts in the Quality of Life Education', paper presented at the People, Places, Partnerships Conference, University of New South Wales, Sydney, April 2003.

18   Australian Bureau of Statistics, *Australian Social Trends, 2003*, Australian Government Publishing Service, Canberra, 2003a; B. Birrell, V. Rapson & C. Hourigan, 'The Origin of Home-Parent Connections in Metropolitan and Regional Australia', *Family Matters*, 62, 2002, pp. 11–17.

19   Coleman, 1988; Cox, 1995; J. Garbarino, 'Growing up in a Socially Toxic Environment: Life for Children and Families in the 1990s', in *The Individual, the Family, and Social Good*, ed, G.B. Melton, University of Nebraska Press, Lincoln, NA, 1995, pp. 1–19.

20   J. Garbarino & R.H. Abromowitz, 'The Family as a Social System', in *Children and Families in the Social Environment*, ed, J. Garbarino, Aldine de Gruyter, New York, 1992, p. 94.

21   In the five-year period 1981 to 1986, 46 per cent of five- to nine-year-olds and 39 per cent of ten- to fourteen-year-olds moved house either once or twice. B.A. Fields, 'Children on the Move: The Social and Educational Effects of Family Mobility', in *Children Australia*, 22, 3, 1997, pp. 4–9.

22   D.J. De Witt, D.R. Offord & K. Brown, *The Relationship Between Geographic Relocation and Childhood Problem Behaviour*, Applied Research Branch Strategic Policy Human Resources Development, Quebec, 1998, <http://www.hrdc.rhc.go.ca/arb/publications/research/abw-98-17e.html>, accessed 13 November 2001; Fields, 1997.

23   M. Larner, 'Local Residential Mobility and its Effects on Social Networks: A Cross-cultural Comparison', in *Extending Families: The Social Networks of Parents and their Children*, eds, M. Larner & D. Hendersen Jr, Cambridge University Press, Cambridge, 1990, pp. 205–29.

24   G. Eddy, ed., *Insite*, 13, The National Dissemination Program of the Family Action Centre, August 1997, p. 4.

25   I. O'Connor, *Our Homeless Children: Their Experiences*, Report to the National Inquiry into Homeless Children by the Equal Rights and Equal Opportunity Commission, Sydney, 1989.

26   M. Horn, 'Families and Homelessness: Prospects and Policies for the 21st Century', paper presented at the Fifth Australian Family Research Conference, Brisbane, November 1996.

27   Mission Australia website: <http://www.mission.com.au> accessed 19 October 2003.

28   R.G. Gregory & B. Hunter, *The Macro Economy and the Growth of Ghettos and Urban Poverty in Australia*, Centre for Economic Policy Research, ANU Discussion Paper No. 325, Canberra, 1995.

29   Cox, 1995.

30   J. Garbarino, *Children and Families in the Social Environment*, Aldine de Gruyter, New York, 1992.

31   J. Buchanan, G. Considine, T. Bretherton & B. van Wanrooy, 'Hours of Work in Australia: Recent Trends and Challenges for Policy', in *Work, Health and Families: Forum Proceedings*, Australian National University, Canberra, 2003.

32   Council of Social Services of New South Wales (NCOSS), 'The Issues Paper', in *Rural Communities Looking Ahead: Papers, Abstracts and Notes from the New South Wales Rural Social Policy Conference*, Dubbo, June 1995, pp. 1–8; P.J. Smailes, 'Socio-economic Change and Rural Morale in South Australia, 1982–1993', *Journal of Rural Studies*, 13, 1, 1997, pp. 19–42.

33   Smailes, 1997; J. Wearne, 'Local Government in Rural and Remote Communities', in *Rural Communities Looking Ahead: Papers, Abstracts and Notes from the New South Wales Rural Social Policy Conference*, Dubbo, June 1995, pp. 28–31.

34   Three times as many young people aged 15–24 years left country areas in the five years to 2001 than arrived during that time. Australian Social Trends, 2003.

35   Isolated Children's Parent's Association, 'Isolated Children's Parents' Association Submission to the National Inquiry into Rural and Remote Education', 1999, <http://www.icpa.com.au>, accessed 19 September 2003.

36   M. Fegan, 'CONTACT: Facilitating Adult–child Interactions in the Australian Context', paper presented at the China–Asia–Pacific Conference, Beijing, China, 1995, p. 1.

37   Fegan, 1995, p. 2.

38   U. Stephens, *Strengthening Communities Resource Kit*, New South Wales Premier's Department, Sydney, 2001.

39   E.A. Daly, *Implications of Development in Telecommunications for Indigenous People in Remote and Rural Australia*, Discussion Paper No. 219, Centre for Aboriginal Economic Policy Research, Australian National University, Canberra, 2001.

40   S. Vardon, *Report from the Australian Remote and Isolated Children's and Family Services Mobile Muster*, CONTACT, Birdsville, 1991.

41   Garbarino & Crouter, 1978.

42   Cox, 1995, p. 32.

43   Brooks-Gunn, 1997.

44   J. Belsky, 'Child Maltreatment: An Ecological Integration', *American Psychologist*, 35, 4, 1980, pp. 320–35; C.J. Coulton, J.E. Korbin, M. Su & J. Chow, 'Community Level Factors and Child Maltreatment Rates', *Child Development*, 66, 1995, pp. 1262–76; Garbarino & Crouter, 1978.

45   T. Vinson, E. Baldry & J. Hargreaves, 'Neighbourhoods, Networks, and Child Abuse', *British Journal of Social Work*, 26, 1996, pp. 523–43.

46   Garbarino & Crouter, 1978; Coulton et al., 1995.

47   Belsky, 1980.

48   J. Hornosty, 'Wife Abuse in Rural Regions: Structural Problems in Leaving Abusive Relationships—A Case Study in Canada', in *With a Rural Focus: An Edited and Refereed Collection of Papers with a Rural Focus presented to the Annual Conference of the Australian Sociological Association Inc.*, ed, F. Vanclay, Deakin University, 1994, pp. 21–34.

49   *Land*, 24 July 1997.

50   J. Jeremy, 'Australia: Generating a Sense of Community', *Bernard van Leer Foundation Newsletter*, 78, 4, 1995, pp. 5–6.

51   Isolated Children's Parent's Association, 1999.

52   Isolated Children's Parent's Association, 1999.

53   Isolated Children's Parent's Association, 1999, p. 37.

54   Stephens, 2001, p. 13.

55   Isolated Children's Parent's Association, 1999.

56   R. Hughes, A. Fleet & J. Nicholls, 'Both-Ways Learning: The Development of an Indigenous Bachelor of Teaching', *Change: Transformations in Education*, 6, 2003, pp. 67–74.

57   J. McLellan, 'Access to Education', in NCOSS, 1995, p. 71.

58   Isolated Children's Parent's Association, 1999, p. 1.

59   Isolated Children's Parent's Association, 1999, p. 1.

60   Isolated Children's Parent's Association, 1999, p. 2.

61   J. Pittman, 'Early Childhood Report', paper presented at the Isolated Children's Parents' Association 30th Annual Conference, Adelaide, <www.abc.net.au/rural/ICPA2001/ECE.htm>, accessed 11 June 2003.

62   McLellan, 1995.

63   R. Cant, *Interagency Schools Community Centres Pilot Project Evaluation Report*, Department of Education and Training: Social Systems and Evaluations, 1997.

64   For further information see <http://www.familiesfirst.nsw.gov.au>.

65   Brooks-Gunn, 1997.

66   A.J. Cherlin, 'Policy Issues in Child Care', in *Escape from Poverty: What Makes a Difference for Children?*, eds, P.L. Chase-Lansdale & J. Brooks-Gunn, Cambridge University Press, Cambridge, 1995, pp. 121–37; P.L. Chase-Lansdale & M.A. Vinovskis, 'Whose Responsibility? An Historical Analysis of the Changing Roles of Mothers, Fathers, and Society', Chase-Lansdale & Brooks-Gunn, 1995, pp. 11–37.

67   J. Brooks-Gunn, 'Do You Believe in Magic? What We Can Expect from Early Childhood Intervention Programs', *Social Policy Report of the Society for Research in Child Development*, 17, 2003, pp. 3–14.

68   G. Vimpani, 'How Can We Improve Access to Services for Families with Young Children? The Need for New Models of Interagency Collaboration', paper presented at the Fifth Australian Family Research Conference, Brisbane, November 1996.

69   R.D. Parke & R. Buriel, 'Socialization in the Family: Ethnic and Ecological Perspectives', in *Handbook of Child Psychology*, ed, N. Eisenberg, Wiley, New York, 1997, pp. 463–552.

70   R. Cohen, 'Eighty-seven and Still Going Strong', *Bernard van Leer Foundation Newsletter*, 87, October 1997, p. 36.

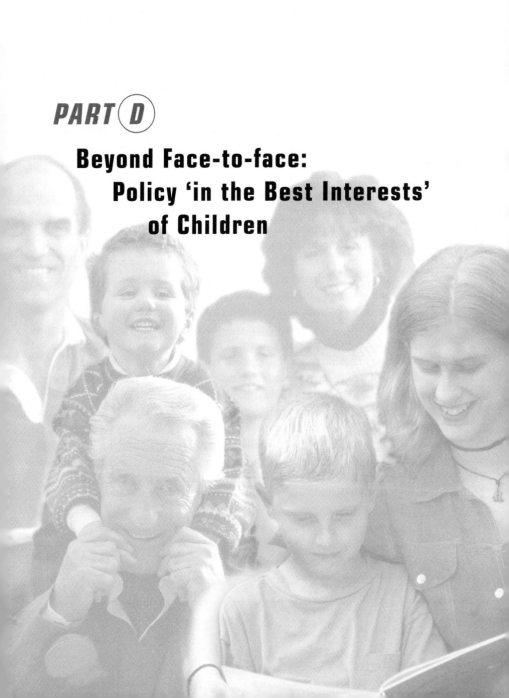

PART D

Beyond Face-to-face:
Policy 'in the Best Interests'
of Children

In this part we consider some examples of the wider social context as it plays a direct role in the lives of children. The examples are the removal of children from their families as part of the child protection system, the special case of removal of Indigenous children from their families—the stolen generations—and the policies on children's services in Australia. All three examples have used the best interests of the children as part of their justification.

Important aspects here are the beliefs that have been held about what is best for children, the decisions about what are appropriate means for implementing those beliefs, and the resources available to those who actually undertake the implementation. Some discrepancies that can emerge between these aspects are described in each of the three chapters. For example, Chapter 8 presents a clear picture of the dilemmas in the child protection system. Australian states, through their laws, accept responsibility for protecting children from abuse and neglect, yet the systems developed to help such children in themselves expose children to risk. The debate over whether children in need of protection are better cared for by the state or by their families is ongoing, and has implications for the direction of government initiatives in prevention and intervention.

In the case of Indigenous children, discussed in Chapter 9, the policy espoused by legislators and Protectors was that of merging and, later, assimilation, into the white population. However, this overlooked both the desire of Indigenous people to live within their own culture and the unwillingness of much of the white population to assimilate them. It also overlooked the fact that the institutions that received the children were nearly always grossly under-resourced. The consequence was that official Australian policy maintained into the 1970s practices that had long been known to be detrimental to child development and to Indigenous families and communities.

The final example of the effect of social policy on children, families and communities comes from the field of children's services. Chapter 10 presents an historical account of changing policy in this area, discussing particularly the impact of current changes in child care policy, and policy in other areas such as employment, on the daily lives of families and children. The chapter shows that 'in the best interests' of children was only a minor theme among many put forward to justify changes in resources for this sector.

Child Protection and Substitute Care:

The Responsibility of Families, Community and State

Judy Cashmore

Becoming a parent in the biological sense hardly ensures that an adult will consistently maintain the standards of upbringing that are widely regarded in society as necessary or desirable. It seems legitimate for society—through the force of law if necessary—to act when such standards are not achieved. There is a strong popular sense of society's duty to protect children, and social workers already involved with families where a child is killed may be bitterly accused of negligence and incompetence for not having used more fully and willingly the powers of the state.[1]

One of the main areas of contention involving children, families and the state is the extent to which the state is seen as having a legitimate interest in exercising control over the upbringing and education of children and in intervening in the private domain of the family. While child-rearing is regarded as primarily the responsibility of families, ensuring the safety, welfare and well-being of children is now generally accepted as a responsibility of the state. This is because the state has a vested interest in children's development and in their capacity to participate in and contribute to society, and because the state is increasingly seen as having a role in protecting and upholding children's rights. The role of the state in most Western societies now includes providing education for all school-age children (unless they and their parents choose non-government schooling), offering cash income support and other forms of assistance to families with children, and directly intervening when the family is not able to or fails to provide adequate care and protection for children.[2] Where families do not properly meet their responsibilities, a range of responses from the state may follow. These include deducting funds from parents' wages to provide maintenance for their children; initiating investigations and court action to establish the need for, and to secure, orders to protect the child; and, as a last resort, removing children from the care of their parents. The main focus of this chapter is on these latter responses, the context in which the state intervenes to protect children, and the consequences for children when this happens.

Contexts

Parental/state responsibility for children

The general acceptance that the state has some responsibility for children marks a significant change over the last hundred years or so from a laissez-faire minimalist view of the role of the state and the common law conceptualisation of children as the 'property' of their fathers.[3] In particular, over the last decade or so, changes in family law and child welfare law in common law countries have signalled a clear shift from a narrow definition of parental rights over children to a broader definition emphasising duties and responsibilities to their children.[4] As Coady[5] explains, a 'parental right' is the right to look after the rights of the child, and in that way is more like a duty than a right. It does, however, give the parent the power to make certain decisions for those children who are not able to make decisions for themselves. But this is not an unqualified power. For if parents consistently act in a way that clearly harms the child, the right is forfeited.

The limits to that parental right have also been more clearly delineated by landmark cases (*Gillick v West Norfolk* and *re Marion*) that articulate the notion of parental responsibility and the separability of children's interests from those of their parents. Both cases concerned adolescent female sexuality—in the case of *Gillick*, the right of a doctor to prescribe contraceptives without parental knowledge, and in *re Marion*, the rights of the guardians of an adolescent girl with an intellectual disability to consent to her sterilisation. In *Gillick*, the House of Lords determined that parental authority is 'a dwindling right', which 'starts with a right of control and ends with little more than advice' as the child matures.[6] In *re Marion*, one of the High Court judges (McHugh J) outlined the duties of parents and clearly stated that children's interests are separable and may be in conflict with those of their parents, in which case a parent has 'no authority to act on behalf of his or her child'.[7]

Evidence of the increasing recognition of the state's responsibility for children and of its duty of care towards them comes in the form of the United

Nations Convention on the Rights of the Child and in recently revised child welfare legislation.[8] The UN Convention formalises what children might expect from the state, while still recognising the primacy of children's relationship with their parents and their family (although Australia and other countries that have ratified the Convention are still clearly stronger on rhetoric than on action).[9]

The notion of the state's duty of care towards children also underlies recent and proposed changes to child welfare legislation in Australia and the United Kingdom in relation to children's right to contact with their parents after parental separation and in relation to the reporting of abuse and neglect and the screening, recruitment, and probity checks of people who care for children.[10] The need to find an appropriate balance between the rights and needs of children and other vulnerable people, the duty of care of service providers, and the civil liberties of employees, remains a contentious and difficult issue.

Defining abuse and neglect

Although there may be general acceptance of the state's responsibility in relation to the safety, welfare and well-being of children, views vary markedly on the particular circumstances in which state intervention is seen to be warranted. While there is likely to be agreement about the need to intervene when children are sexually abused, deliberately burnt, severely beaten or neglected to the point where their health and development are jeopardised, there is little agreement about less extreme forms of parental behaviour, and when these cross the line to become abusive or 'not good enough'. When does constant belittling become emotionally abusive, minimal supervision become neglectful, and bodily punishment physically abusive rather than 'reasonable chastisement'? What form of intervention is warranted? Under what circumstances?

These are necessarily subjective judgments that are 'defined within the context of the normative and deviant child rearing behaviour of the time'.[11] Awareness and concern about child abuse have increased markedly since the late 1960s, and definitions and interpretations of what is abusive have broadened from the 'battered babies' described by Kempe 'to the physical abuse of children of all ages, to failure to thrive, neglect, psychological and emotional abuse, and sexual abuse'.[12] More recently, definitions of abuse have been extended to include exposure to domestic violence[13] as concern and understanding about its effects on children's psycho-social and emotional development have increased.[14]

While beliefs about what constitutes acceptable and abusive behaviour towards children have varied over time, they are also culturally determined, and they may vary across subgroups within a culture (for example, social class). This can create some difficulties for a multicultural society such as Australia, a dilemma clearly articulated by Korbin: 'Failure to allow for a cultural perspective in defining child abuse and neglect promotes an ethnocentric position in which one's own set of cultural beliefs and practices are [*sic*] presumed to be preferable to others. On the other hand, a stance of extreme cultural relativism, in which all judgements of humane treatment of children are suspended, may be used to justify a lesser standard of care for some children.'[15]

Korbin identified three levels at which definitions of abuse may be formulated to provide some direction in resolving the definitional difficulties that are exacerbated when these levels are confounded. The first level includes 'practices which are viewed as acceptable in the culture in which they occur, but as abusive or neglectful by outsiders'.[16] This is where cultural conflict is most likely. It is useful for those of us who are members of Western cultures and apt to regard our own values as superior to be reminded that many Western child-rearing behaviours (such as leaving babies and infants to sleep alone in separate rooms and the use of 'controlled crying') are regarded by the members of some other cultures as abusive.

The second level involves 'idiosyncratic abuse or neglect', which includes those behaviours that 'fall outside the range of acceptability' for that society. Although cultures vary in what they deem acceptable, cross-cultural conflict is less likely at this level. For example, while some societies accept fondling of infants' genitals for soothing the child, fondling older children or fondling for adult sexual gratification falls outside the boundaries for acceptable behaviour across cultures.

The third level concerns societal conditions such as poverty, homelessness and lack of health care that are beyond the control of individual parents. While societies vary in the extent to which they tolerate these conditions, and in their capacity to change them, it is clear that the same tolerance level does not apply uniformly within societies. For example, while such conditions would not be condoned for mainstream culture, they are endemic among particular minority groups, such as the Australian Aboriginal population. At the same time, there is increasing concern that 'cultural relativism' and fear of 'over-intervention' are doing just what Korbin warned against—justifying a lesser standard of care for some groups of children, such as Aboriginal children.

It is clear then, as Korbin[17] and others have pointed out, that 'there is no universal standard for optimal child care nor for child abuse and neglect' across or within cultures. In practice, however, child abuse and neglect are operationally defined by the decisions people make in referring suspected abuse and neglect to child protection services, and by the responses of those agencies to the referrals.[18] Different definitions may apply at different stages of the process, depending on the purpose, the expected consequences, and the perceived responsibility and degree of harm involved. The result is that cases may take different routes through the system, with more or less intervention, depending on skills and the type of professional making the decision, their understanding of the legislative, policy and practice guidelines they are expected to follow, the information available to them, and their perceptions of the harm caused to the child and the assessed responsibility of the perpetrator for that harm.[19]

Incidence of reported child abuse and neglect

What do the available figures tell us about the prevalence of child abuse and neglect in Australia? How many children are abused and neglected? How reliable are the figures? Are child abuse and neglect increasing?

The figures on reported abuse and neglect—or more accurately, the number of notifications of children to the statutory authorities—in Australia, the United Kingdom and the USA have shown a massive increase over the last thirty years or so. The best and most recent Australian figures[20] (based on an agreed general definition of abuse and neglect used by the Australian Institute of Health and Welfare) indicate that over 198,000 notifications of child abuse and neglect were recorded nationally by state and territory departments for the year 2002–03 in relation to just over 131,000 children. This is more than four times the number of children reported a decade ago (45,974 in 1991–92) and many times more than the numbers in the 1960s and 1970s.

The interpretation of these figures,[21] and particularly the recent escalation in the figures, is subject to intense debate. As Scott and Swain point out: 'Some see it as a social problem of epidemic proportions with ever-rising child abuse notifications perceived as evidence of the disintegration of the family in modern society. Others see a "child protection industry" with a vested interest in making exaggerated claims and perpetuating the public perception of an epidemic.'[22]

Like most complex issues, there is no simple answer, but the 'best fit' is most likely to lie somewhere between the extreme positions and to include a number of factors and qualifications.[23] While expanded definitions of abuse and neglect, together with mandatory reporting, have clearly contributed to an increase in awareness and reporting, there is also evidence that the increase reflects an increasing incidence of and awareness of parental substance abuse, domestic violence, and parental mental illness or disability.[24]

Cultural background and family type, with underlying poverty in both cases, are also significant factors that affect the rate of reported child abuse and neglect, with Aboriginal and Torres Strait Islander children, and children from one-parent families, both over-represented. Depending on the state or territory, Aboriginal children were from two to nearly eight times more likely than other children to be the subject of a substantiated notification, particularly for neglect.

Children from one-parent families are also significantly over-represented in reported and substantiated child abuse and neglect statistics. Approximately 20 per cent of children under the age of fifteen in Australia live in female-headed one-parent families,[25] but they make up approximately 40 per cent of substantiated notifications of child abuse and 50 per cent of substantiated neglect cases. Financial stress, social isolation and lack of support are more common among one-parent than two-parent families, and these are significant risk factors for abuse and neglect.

'Causes' of child abuse and neglect

Physical and emotional abuse and neglect

The over-representation of Aboriginal children and children from female-headed one-parent families points to some of the recognised risk factors for physical and emotional abuse and neglect—poverty, unemployment, lack of resources, social stress and isolation. For example, a number of studies have shown increased rates of child abuse and neglect for communities containing higher proportions of single parents, low-income families, unemployment, substance abuse, and other forms of economic and social stress.[26] These factors do not directly cause child abuse and neglect but, together with other factors associated with the carer, the child and the family, they clearly increase the risk of abuse and neglect, especially when they are not counteracted by protective factors such as social and community support.[27]

At the individual carer level, some of the main risk factors for physical and emotional abuse and neglect are a history of being abused or neglected as a child, depression, substance abuse, poor impulse control and low self-esteem. There is also evidence that abusive carers are more likely to have unrealistic expectations of the child's behaviour (for example, to expect that toddlers can be toilet-trained without 'accidents'), and to attribute negative explanations to the child ('he's just crying to get at me').[28] While most parents who were abused or neglected as children do not go on to abuse their own children, there is some evidence to suggest that those who do so are more likely to be hypersensitive and negatively reactive to babies' crying and to stressful and non-stressful mother–child interactions[29] and that a history of abuse may indeed result in exaggerated stress responses or hyperreactivity.[30]

At the child's level, a number of factors have also been found to increase the risk of abuse and neglect. These include the child's developmental stage, vulnerability, health status, disability and behaviour. Young children are both more vulnerable to abuse and neglect and more likely to be abused and neglected than older children, but adolescents are also at greater risk than pre-adolescent children. As Belsky[31] points out, young children may be at greater risk of maltreatment for several reasons. They spend more time with their carers and are more physically and emotionally dependent on them. Physical force is more likely to be used to control them, and they have more difficulty regulating their emotions than older children. Both toddlers and adolescents also display oppositional behaviour in asserting their independence, and it seems likely that this behaviour increases their risk of maltreatment.[32] Children who put a strain on family resources in other ways by having poor health, a disability, being unwanted or too closely spaced are also more likely to be at increased risk of maltreatment, not only within Western industrialised societies, but cross-culturally.[33]

Children's behaviour as a risk factor is less clear-cut. While a mismatch between the parent's and the child's temperament may increase the risk of maltreatment, the evidence seems to point to children's behavioural problems being more likely to be a consequence of maltreatment than a cause of it.[34] In fact, it seems likely that it is the parent's responses and attributions about the child's behaviour that explain or predict abusive response rather than the child's behaviour itself. Abusive parents tend to report more problem behaviours by their children than are reported by outside 'observers', and they are also more likely to rely on physical punishment and less likely to support and reward children's positive behaviours.[35] Although maltreated infants and toddlers may display behaviour problems that make them difficult to manage, interventions to increase mothers' sensitivity and knowledge about children's development have shown some success.[36] It is clear that child maltreatment can have many causes, with a number of risk factors at the level of the individual carer and child, the family environment, the community context, and even at the societal level in determining the value of children and the tolerance of violence. According to this developmental–ecological approach, maltreatment occurs when 'stressors outweigh supports and risks are greater than protective factors'.[37] There are therefore multiple pathways to physical and emotional abuse and neglect.[38]

Sexual abuse

The preceding discussion of 'causes' focused on physical and emotional abuse and neglect and excluded sexual abuse. This is because the causes of child sexual abuse are recognised as being significantly different from the causes of other forms of child maltreatment, although they are still insufficiently understood.[39] While personal and/or socio-economic disadvantages are recognised as risk factors for physical and emotional abuse and neglect, their association with child sexual abuse is much weaker. 'Unlike neglect (which is often seen as a function of poverty) and physical abuse which is often related to a range of stresses, sexual abuse cuts across the whole socioeconomic spectrum. It exists in all types of communities and at all socioeconomic levels.'[40] The best predictor of sexual abuse is still gender: the vast majority of sexual abuse perpetrators are male and the majority of the children in *reported* cases are female.

Consequences

There is a substantial literature on the consequences or the effects of abuse and neglect on children's behaviour and socio-emotional development.[41] The adverse outcomes that have been associated with abuse and neglect include problems in attachment and trust, poor self-esteem and self-regulation, aggressive behaviour and depression. More recently, there has been significant attention to the effects on young children's brain development and the underlying neurobiological processes that are thought to mediate the longer term outcomes.[42] This has galvanised the focus of a range of professionals who are presenting this as evidence for the need for early intervention to prevent difficult-to-reverse adverse outcomes.

It is also important to note that many of the social and familial factors known to increase the risk of child maltreatment are also significant predictors of other social problems concerning children. Poverty, social isolation, harsh and inconsistent parenting, parental rejection, family conflict and violence have also been identified as risk factors for juvenile offending, youth suicide and homelessness. Furthermore, there is evidence that young children who are abused and neglected are at increased risk of being aggressive and involved in criminal behaviour as adolescents.[43] Working to decrease the risk factors and increase the protective factors early in children's lives is therefore likely to have additional pay-offs, not only in preventing child abuse and neglect, but also in tackling juvenile crime, homelessness and youth suicide.

Responding to child abuse and neglect

The origins of child maltreatment lie at several different levels, and correspondingly the response needs to occur at different levels, and to take both a short- and a long-term perspective.[44] Unfortunately the main response has been *after* maltreatment has occurred and been identified, and it is directed at an individual level—to the particular child and family involved. It is reactive rather than proactive, preventive and community-based, although increasingly there are programs such as home visiting and other early intervention programs that aim to prevent child abuse and neglect by developing family and community supports.[45] Their functions are outlined later.

Over the last decade, however, there has been increasing concern in the USA, the United Kingdom and Australia about the failure of the system to respond to and provide appropriate services for the ever-increasing numbers of child protection reports that concern families and children *in need* rather than reports of children *being harmed*. Concerns about the focus, and the effectiveness and efficacy of the statutory investigative response were clearly articulated during the 1990s in both the United Kingdom and the USA[46] and more recently in Australia. The common concern was that the child protection system had become overly forensic and legalistic in its response—that it was investigating problems or 'incidents' but not helping or supporting children and families in need, and not protecting children from further abuse or neglect. Indeed, the Dartington research in the United Kingdom indicated that families were often less receptive and less likely to receive services after being reported to the child protection authority than before it. As Scott[47] and Melton[48] and others have argued, in these systems, the focus is on 'What happened?', not 'How is the child?' and 'What can we do to help?'

The intent of recent legislative and policy changes has therefore been to try to shift the focus from forensic investigation of 'abusive incidents' to an assessment of the needs of the child and the family and to widen the responsibility of other agencies to provide the necessary services. The bigger challenge is to build a system that encourages early intervention and prevention so that fewer children in future need to be subjected to the more intrusive end of statutory intervention.

Children in out-of-home care

Removing children from their family in a transfer of guardianship to the state is the most serious form of intervention the state can take, and is increasingly a measure of 'last resort'. Only a small proportion of children who are the subject of a substantiated allegation of child abuse or neglect are found to be 'in need of care and protection', necessitating a court order, and even fewer are removed from their homes or have guardianship transferred from their parents. While overall approximately 88 per cent of children in out-of-home care are on a care and protection order, some children (some of whom have a disability) are placed in care on a 'voluntary' basis by their parents when they are unable to provide adequate care. In 2002–03, over 12,800 children entered care, and 9077 were discharged from care, bringing the total number of children in out-of-home care in Australia on 30 June 2003 to 20,297 (4.2 children per 1000 aged 0–17 years in the population). Once again, Indigenous children were heavily over-represented, with 22.8 children per 1000 in care, making Indigenous children over six times more likely to be in care than non-Indigenous children.

Placement of children in out-of-home care
The most common placement for children in Australia who enter care is foster care (51 per cent in 2002–03), followed by relative care (40 per cent) with

the exception of New South Wales where relative care placements are now more prevalent than non-relative foster carers (57 per cent compared to 34 per cent). The reasons for the increase in the numbers of children placed with relatives are both ideological and pragmatic. Relative care fits with notions of family preservation but is also cost effective and practical because of the shortage of foster carers and the difficulty of finding suitable placements for children in need of care. It also has particular advantages for Indigenous children and is consistent with traditional practices of caring for children within their kinship groups. While some research points to positive benefits for children in relative care, especially in terms of stability and continuity of family contact, much of the research is descriptive and limited in relation to outcome measures for children.[49] There are also concerns about the lack of proper assessment and support for relative carers. Many relative carers are grandmothers, who are older, single and living in relative poverty, and called on to care for young children with minimal financial and practical support.

The second trend in out-of-home care is the radical shift away from residential care to family-based placements. In 2002–03, only 5 per cent of children and young people in care in Australia were in residential care. In 1961, the figure was closer to 46 per cent.[50] This shift has occurred across the Western world, 'fuelled by cost considerations, abuse enquiries, research about children's development and attachment needs, notions of "normalization" and "least restrictive environments" and a belief in the importance of families for children'.[51] It has, however, been more exaggerated in Australia so that a much lower proportion of children and young people in out-of-home care are now in residential care than in other countries such as the United Kingdom (15 per cent in 1999) and the USA (approximately 20 per cent). There is now increasing concern about the lack of options for children and young people, especially for 'hard to place' adolescents. The difficult and challenging behaviours of some young people are putting serious strain on the out-of-home care system, which does not have the specialist services to meet their needs. It means that individual packages are 'strung together' for some of these young people at great expense and for containment purposes, with no assurance of meeting the mental health, educational and safety needs of the young people involved. There is, however, renewed and increasing interest in Australia in the development of a range of therapeutic models of care for these young people, following overseas examples of specialist services.

Permanency planning

For many children who enter care, their stay in care is short-lived and intended to be so. In line with the now generally accepted principle that children should so far as possible remain within their families, the preferred option for permanency in most jurisdictions is for children to return to their families as soon as circumstances have changed to allow them to return safely and to be cared for adequately.

The national figures for Australia indicate that nearly 24 per cent of children in care in 2002–03 had been in care for less than six months, and 36 per cent for less than twelve months.[52] The most obvious interpretation of these cross-sectional figures is positive—that children are able to return home within relatively short periods. The problem revealed by the only Australian longitudinal study of children entering care is that most (69 per cent) of the 129 children who were entering care had already been in care before the entry into care that brought them into this study.[53] Similarly, other studies overseas have found that a significant proportion of children returned home re-enter care within twelve to twenty-four months.[54] This means that a significant number of children are 'oscillators', cycling in and out of care.[55] The concern is that current policies, intended to overcome the earlier problem of children drifting *in* care without proper planning and moving through multiple changes of placements, are now moving children in and out of care or leaving them at home in unsafe and inadequate care for too long. Their 'recycling' or delayed entry to care means that when they do come into care they do so with significant levels of disturbance and attachment difficulties, increasing the likelihood of further placement breakdowns and 'corroding the very core of the capacity of a child to develop trust'.[56]

Perhaps the most contentious issue in child welfare policy and practice is how and when to draw the line and ensure some certainty and permanence in the lives of children in (or in and out of) out-of-home care. The problem of children in out-of-home care 'drifting in care' without proper planning, with multiple changes of placements and consequent instability and insecurity has been recognised since the 1970s and most jurisdictions have attempted to implement policies and practices, backed by changes in legislation, to promote timely, long-term decision-making for children in care. The reality is that such certainty and permanence continue to be difficult to achieve.

Where reunification with the parents or within the extended family is not a realistic option, other permanent plans are meant to be put in place but the order of choice tends to vary across countries. In the USA, the *Adoption and Safe Families Act* of 1997 actively promotes adoption as the preferred option for children who cannot return home and prescribes strict time limits within which a decision must be made and parental rights terminated. Official funding policy also penalises states that do not meet their targets for adoption from foster care.[56] The intention is to try to force decision-makers to make the hard decision to terminate parental responsibility, but such policies have not dealt with the perceived unfairness of a system that has provided few resources to assist parents to make the required changes (particularly drug rehabilitation). Further, the concern is that such policies cause workers and judges to make decisions to return children home too quickly in order to avoid having to terminate parental rights, a move that may jeopardise the child's safety and well-being.[57]

Adoption is also encouraged in the United Kingdom but the stance is not so 'tough', and long-term foster care is still accepted as a reasonable option.[58] In Australia, adoption by carers is much less common with only twenty-nine children being adopted by their carers in the year 2002–03.[59] There appear to be a number of reasons for the very low rate (and under-utilisation) of adoption of children from care in Australia. Again these are both ideological and pragmatic. The ideological objections relate to the severing of legal ties with the biological family and the cultural inappropriateness of the concept of adoption within Indigenous communities, especially given the history of the 'stolen generations'. Practically, many carers cannot afford to lose the carer allowance for the children, and many workers do not have the time and the skills to process the adoption, especially if the parents are not contactable and willing and able to give consent. In many cases, children are also in the care of relatives and so adoption by a relative is neither necessary or appropriate.

Children's experience in care
The difficulties facing children in care and, in particular, children who drift *in* care and in and out of care, are well documented. While some children experience a series of 'broken' placements, numerous workers, changes of school, and little contact with their parents, siblings and other relatives, a number of children in care do well in stable long-term foster care. When compared with children in the community who are not in care, however, children in care are generally significantly behind in their school performance and educational achievements, and their emotional well-being and physical and mental health are often significantly poorer. They often have difficulty forming and maintaining intimate relationships, and may display asocial or antisocial behaviours.[60] The reasons why children in care do more poorly than other children are complex and relate to their early adverse environment and pre-care experiences, and to some extent to their in-care experience and lack of security in care.[61] There is increasing evidence that children who come into care later have higher levels of disturbance (and lower chances of remediation) than those who enter care early. This is in line with the earlier discussion about the 'damage' to children who 'oscillate' or cycle in and out of care.

It is important, however, to recognise that the findings of various comparative studies depend on the study design. While point-in-time comparisons of children in care with children not in care in the general population generally indicate poorer outcomes for children in care, longitudinal studies of children in care have shown that children's cognitive performance and their social and emotional adjustment generally improve over time in care,[62] especially in the context of stable care.[63] Furthermore, children who remained in care were 'better off' in terms of their behavioural and emotional adjustment and 'quality of life' than children who returned home from care or whose entry into care was delayed.[64]

The critical role of stability in care and, more importantly, children's perceived emotional security, is evident in several overseas studies[65] and recently in a longitudinal study of young people leaving care in Australia. Cashmore and Paxman[66] found that young people who had spent at least 75 per cent of their time in care in one long-term placement were better off than those who had not, even if they were not living in that placement when they were discharged from wardship. They attended fewer schools, were happier, were more likely to have completed at least Year 10 at school, to report being able to 'make ends meet', to be satisfied with what the Department had done for them, and to be less likely to say they missed out on affection and 'things other kids had', and less likely to have thought about or attempted suicide.[67] Perceived emotional security was, however, a more powerful predictor of positive outcomes, and young people who indicated that they had felt secure and that they were loved while they were in care were also doing better five years after leaving care than those who had never felt there was someone who loved and cared about them.

Leaving care

The risks for children and young people in out-of-home care continue beyond childhood and their time in care. Increasing expectations by government that parents are responsible for the children's post-secondary education fees and living expenses into their twenties means that many young people living with their parents now often remain at home until they are in their early to mid-twenties, and they may leave and return several times before they finally live independently. By contrast, young people in care who may have little continuity or stability are often discharged from care at the age of sixteen or eighteen, with little financial and social support, and with poor prospects for employment and good stable accommodation. Cashmore and Paxman[68] found, for example, that half the young people discharged from wardship were unemployed twelve months later and on average had changed accommodation three times during that period. In addition, a third of the young women had a child or were pregnant, and two-thirds had thought about or attempted suicide.

Although the state clearly has a duty to continue providing support and to assist the young people for whom it has assumed guardianship to make the transition to independent adulthood, this responsibility has been recognised only recently. After-care and leaving-care services were established in 1997 by the New South Wales government, and other states are beginning to move in the same direction. These services are not intended to take over responsibility from the agencies that provide substitute care for these children and young people, but to assist them in their task. Unfortunately a number of the contracts for substitute care services do not make adequate allowance for the work and costs involved in preparing young people for leaving care, and for providing after-care service.

As the ALRC/HREOC report recommended, what children and young people in care clearly need is a Charter for Children in Care that guarantees, among other things, 'appropriate assistance in the transition from care' and, while they are in care, 'regular reviews of their case plan and circumstances in care', 'therapeutic support or additional educational assistance', and 'a safe living environment'.[69]

Improving the response to child abuse and neglect

Although there have been some significant advances over the past thirty years or so in the recognition of child abuse and neglect and in the acceptance of some communal responsibility for child protection and care for children who can no longer live with their families, the situation is still far from adequate and there are at least three areas in which some improvements can be made. These include proper resourcing, early intervention and prevention, and participation by children and families in the decisions that affect their lives.

Proper resourcing

The lack of resources in the field of child protection and out-of-home care, especially in terms of professionally qualified, well-supervised and supported workers is not new and in many areas is getting worse.[70] But it is unlikely that there will ever be enough resources, so more effective measures, including prevention and early intervention, are needed to manage and hopefully reduce the supply side of the equation over the longer term. Evidence-based practice is also essential to work out what measures and approaches are effective with what children and families in what circumstances and to implement those approaches.

Early intervention and prevention

The aim of early intervention and prevention is, of course, to forestall abuse and neglect. This means taking action before problems develop to the point where full-scale protective intervention is necessary—action that must often be early in the life of the child, or when there are early indications of problems such as emotional disturbance or behaviour problems in the child. The need for more services and coordinated early intervention in relation to children with behavioural problems is pressing because these are the children who tend to 'fall between the gaps' of the available services and often end up being suspended or expelled from the school or even pre-school system, and are later involved in the care system or juvenile justice system.

Early intervention programs can be universal (available, say, to all parents or all first-time parents), or more specifically focused or targeted to particular social or demographic groups (for example young single mothers, teenage mothers, or parents experiencing stress and isolation as a result of poverty or other problems). The aim of a number of existing community-based programs and services such as family (or child and family) support programs, early intervention programs, and home visiting programs is specifically to intervene early to prevent child abuse and neglect. They do so by providing a range of information, advice and support services to families at the neighbourhood/community level. Unfortunately many are being forced to give priority to families already in crisis—a demand that usually denies them the 'luxury' of focusing on prevention. On the positive side, there is an increasing recognition of the need to support and coordinate these services and to integrate and use other universal services, such as child care, in a more effective way to assist children at risk and their families.

Participation of children and families

Perhaps the greatest potential for change in the child protection and substitute care systems lies in greater participation in the system by children and their families, including members of the extended family. There is already some evidence to that effect in the role that associations such as CREATE,[71] formerly the Australian Association of Young People in Care, are playing as advocates for children in care.

In many ways, children involved in the child protection system and their families face similar difficulties in having their voices heard, and for similar reasons. Probably the biggest barriers are attitudinal. Children and young people tend to be treated as the 'objects of concern', who either lack the capacity or competence to participate or who should not be burdened with the responsibility. Similarly, their parents tend to be seen as the cause of the concern relating to the child, and to lack the capacity to be involved—or perhaps even to have forfeited the right to be involved. Underlying these attitudes is also the issue of control, and the unwillingness in some cases of workers to give up control to families.

Other more structural reasons for this lack of involvement are the absence of guidance or requirements for workers to involve children and families in this way, a dearth of training for workers, and families' and children's ignorance of the processes. Even when some participatory processes do occur, they are likely to be mere tokens if there is no adequate preparation for the family and workers have no real commitment to it. For example, despite the requirements for working together and partnership with parents in the *Children Act 1989* (UK), British research indicates that fewer than half of the parents asked about their involvement in child protection cases said that they had contributed to the plans, and only about a third said they took part in the decision-making.[72] A number of studies asking children and young people for their views on and experience in taking part in decision-making about their lives, have indicated significant difficulties for them being heard but positive benefits when they are.[73]

The positive signs are that there is now clear acknowledgment of the participation rights of children and families in decision-making processes that affect them in the child protection system.[74] There are new models that encourage participation (for instance family group conferences) and there is evidence of the benefits of participation. These include improved practice, better outcomes for children and their families, and greater commitment and compliance with decisions by families.[75] As *Messages from Research* points out, 'A great deal of social work research shows that clients will co-operate even if it is against their obvious personal interests as long as they see the process as "just"'.[76]

Turning the rhetoric into reality and establishing a whole-of-government commitment to participation and inter-agency collaboration are of course continuing challenges. It requires continuing commitment from government and the community to really make it happen: to ensure that children are protected from abuse and neglect and that those who are in the care of the state are properly provided for. Children are a community responsibility, and the price of not providing adequate care for them will be paid by the community in the long term.

Student exercises

1   To what extent do you think that child protection is a community responsibility? What do you think are the barriers to community responsibility in this area?
2   Why is it difficult to provide clear definitions of child abuse and neglect?
3   What are some of the risk factors for child abuse and neglect? How do you think they operate to increase the likelihood of children being abused or neglected?

Notes

1   L. Fox Harding, *Perspectives in Child Care Policy*, Longman, London, 1991, pp. 1–2.
2   Australian Law Reform Commission/Human Rights and Equal Opportunity Commission, *Seen and Heard: Priority for Children in the Legal Process*, Report no. 84, 1997
3   Fox Harding, 1991.

4   R. Dingwall, J. Eekelaar & T. Murray, *The Protection of Children: State Intervention and Family Life* (2nd edn), Avebury, Aldershot, 1995.

5   M.M. Coady, 'Reflections on Children's Rights', in *Citizen Child: Australian Laws and Children's Rights*, ed, K. Funder, Australian Institute of Family Studies, Melbourne, 1996, p. 22.

6   Although it is no longer assumed that parents always act in the best interests of their children, there is still some way to go before children's rights are recognised in the same way as are adults' rights. For example, children are still the only group in our society who may legally be hit. Physical punishment that can be justified as 'reasonable chastisement' would constitute assault if 'applied' to an adult. J. Cashmore & N. de Haas, *Legal and Social Aspects of the Physical Punishment of Children*, Commonwealth Department of Human Services and Health, Canberra, 1995; *Gillick v West Norfolk v Wisbeck Area Health Authority and Department of Health and Social Security* (1986) (*Gillick* case).

7   *Secretary, Department of Health and Community Services v JWB* (1992) 175 CLR 340 (*Marion's* case).

8   Fox Harding, 1991; For example, the *Children's Act* UK 1989 and the *NSW Children and Young Person's (Care and Protection) Act* 1998.

9   J. Cashmore, 'Children: Non-contractual persons?', in *The New Contractualism?*, eds, G. Davis, B. Sullivan & A. Yeatman, Macmillan, Melbourne, 1997, p. 58.

10   Royal Commission into the New South Wales Police Service, *Final Report vol. V: The Paedophile Inquiry*, 1997; *NSW Children's Commission Green Paper*, NSW Government, Sydney, 1997.

11   D. Scott & S. Swain, *Confronting Cruelty: Historical Perspectives on Child Protection in Australia*, Melbourne University Press, Melbourne, 2002, p. xii.

12   Kempe, 1978, cited in D. Gough, 'Defining the Problem', *Child Abuse & Neglect*, 20, 1996, p. 994.

13   NSW Child Protection Council, *Interagency Guidelines for Child Protection Intervention*, 1997.

14   P. Jaffe, D. Wolfe & S. Wilson, *Children of Battered Women*, Sage, Newbury Park, CA, 1990.

15   J.E. Korbin, 'Cross-cultural Perspectives and Research Directions for the 21st Century', *Child Abuse & Neglect*, 15, Supplement 1, 1991, p. 68.

16   Korbin, 1991, p. 68.

17   Korbin, 1991.

18   Gough, D., 'Defining the Problem', *Child Abuse & Neglect*, 20, 1996, pp. 993–1002.

19   H. Dubowitz, M. Black, R.H. Starr & S. Zuravin, 'A Conceptual Definition of Child Neglect', *Criminal Justice and Behavior*, 20, 1993, pp. 8–26; Gough, 1996; S.J. Rose & W. Meezan, 'Defining Child Neglect: Evolution, Influences and Issues', *Social Service Review*, 67, 1997, pp. 279–93.

20   The national figures from the Australian Institute of Health and Welfare are the most reliable figures available but there are some significant differences between the states in relation to their legislation, policy and practice, and significant problems with the reliability of the state-based data collection processes.

21   The proportion of notifications that were investigated in 2002–03 ranged from 36 per cent in Victoria, 41 per cent in New South Wales, to 96 per cent in Western Australia, reflecting significant differences in the way in which the state jurisdictions define and respond to notifications. For example, in Victoria and New South Wales, 'the definition of a notification is very broad and may include family issues that are responded to without a formal investigation process. In contrast, in Western Australia and Tasmania, reports to the departments are screened before being classified as a notification' and 'only those where maltreatment is

indicated are classified as a notification'; most of these are investigated. Australian Institute of Health and Welfare (AIHW), *Child protection Australia 2002–03*, AIHW catalogue no. CWS 22, AIHW (Child Welfare Series no. 34), Canberra, 2004, p. 12.

22 Scott & Swain, 2002, p. 186.

23 Furthermore, the statistics 'raise more questions than they answer' (Scott & Swain, 2002, p. 186). Changes in the definition of what constitutes reportable 'abuse and neglect' and changes in the reporting, recording and response to child abuse and neglect mean that any comparisons over time and across jurisdictions using recorded child maltreatment figures are problematic. The statistics also refer to recorded reports or notifications to the statutory authority; they do not indicate the actual prevalence of abuse and neglect. It is clear that not all child abuse and neglect comes to the notice of the relevant authorities, and that some of the reports that should have been recorded and looked at more closely should not have been screened out, as inquiries following the deaths of young children and babies previously notified to the authorities have pointed out (NSW Child Death Review Team, *Second Annual Report 1996–1997*, Sydney, 1998). There is therefore an unknown 'dark figure'—the number of children who have been abused and/or neglected but not recorded or not substantiated as being so.

24 See A. Tomison, 'Child Maltreatment and Substance Abuse', National Child Protection Clearing House Discussion Paper No. 2, Australian Institute of Family Studies, Melbourne, 1996a; A. Tomison, 'Child Maltreatment and Mental Disorder', National Child Protection Clearing House Discussion Paper No. 3, Australian Institute of Family Studies, Melbourne, 1996b; A. Tomison, 'Exploring Family Violence: Links Between Child Maltreatment and Domestic Violence', *Issues in Child Abuse Prevention*, no. 13, Australian Institute of Family Studies, Melbourne, 2000; NSW Child Death Review Team, *Second Annual Report 1996–1997*, Sydney, 1998.

25 Australian Bureau of Statistics, *Social Trends 2003*, catalogue no. 4102.0, Australian Government Publishing Service, Canberra, 2003a.

26 J. Garbarino & D. Sherman, 'High Risk Neighbourhoods and High Risk Families: The Human Ecology of Child Maltreatment', *Child Development*, 51, 1980, pp. 188–98; J. Garbarino & K. Kostelny, 'Neighborhood-based Programs', in *Protecting Children from Abuse and Neglect: Foundations for a New National Strategy*, eds, G.B. Melton & F.D. Barry, The Guilford Press, New York, 1994, pp. 304–52; B. Gillham, G. Tanner, B. Cheyne, I. Freeman, M. Rooney & A. Lambie, 'Unemployment Rates, Single Parent Density, and Indices of Child Poverty: Their Relationship to Different Categories of Child Abuse and Neglect', *Child Abuse & Neglect*, 22, 1998, pp. 79–90; D. Weatherburn & B. Lind, *Social and Economic Stress, Child Neglect and Juvenile Delinquency*, NSW Bureau of Crime Statistics and Research, Sydney, 1997.

27 J. Belsky, 'Etiology of Child Maltreatment: A Developmental–ecological Analysis', *Psychological Bulletin*, 114, 1993, pp. 413–34. A number of studies have shown increased rates of child abuse and neglect—for example in communities where there is a higher proportion of single parents, low-income families, substance abuse, and other forms of economic and social stress—indicating the importance of the 'social fabric' that surrounds families: Garbarino & Sherman, 1980; Garbarino & Kostelny, 1994; Weatherburn & Lind, 1997.

28 Belsky, 1993.

29 A.M. Frodi & M.E. Lamb, 'Child Abusers' Responses to Infant Smiles and Cries', *Child Development*, 51, 1980, pp. 238–41; D.A. Wolfe, 'Child-abusive Parents: An Empirical Review and Analysis', *Psychological Bulletin*, 97, 1985, pp. 462–82.

30   D. Cicchetti, 'Child Maltreatment: Implications for Developmental Theory and Research', *Human Development*, 39, 1996, pp. 18–39.

31   Belsky, 1993.

32   M.A. Straus, R.J. Gelles & S.K. Steinmetz, *Behind Closed Doors: Violence in the American Family*, Anchor Books, Garden City, NJ, 1980.

33   Korbin, 1991.

34   Belsky, 1993.

35   Belsky, 1993; E.E. Whipple & C. Webster-Stratton, 'The Role of Parental Stress in Physically Abusive Families', *Child Abuse & Neglect*, 15, 1991, pp. 279–91.

36   J. Brooks-Gunn, L.J. Berlin & A.S. Fuligini, 'Early Childhood Intervention Programs: What About the Family?', in *Handbook of Early Childhood Intervention* (2nd edn), eds, J.P. Shonkoff & S.J. Meisels, Cambridge University Press, Cambridge, 2000, pp. 549–88; C. Goddard, *Child Abuse and Child Protection*, Churchill Livingstone, Melbourne, 1996.

37   J.D. Osofsky & M.D. Thompson, 'Adaptive and Maladaptive Parenting: Perspectives on Risk and Protective Factors', in *Handbook of Early Childhood Intervention* (2nd edn), eds, J.P. Shonkoff & S.J. Meisels, Cambridge University Press, Cambridge, 2000 pp. 54–75.

38   Belsky, 1993, p. 427.

39   D. Daro, *Confronting Child Abuse: Research for Effective Program Design*, The Free Press, New York, 1988; J. Kaufman & K. Zigler, 'The Prevention of Child Maltreatment: Programming, Research, and Policy', in *Prevention of Child Maltreatment: Developmental and Ecological Perspectives*, eds, D.J. Willis, E.W. Holden & M. Rosenberg, Wiley & Sons, New York, 1992, pp. 269–95.

40   Daro, 1988, p. 110.

41   See for reviews: M. Augustinos, 'Developmental Effects of Child Abuse: Recent Findings', *Child Abuse & Neglect*, 11, 1987, pp. 15–27; D. Cicchetti & V. Carlson, eds, *Child Maltreatment: Theory and Research on the Causes and Consequences of Child Abuse and Neglect*, Cambridge University Press, New York, 1989; D. Cicchetti, S.L. Toth & A. Maughan, 'An Ecological-transactional Model of Child Maltreatment', in *Handbook of Developmental Psychopathology* (2nd edn), eds, A.J. Sameroff & M. Lewis, Kluwer Academic Publishers, Dordrecht, Netherlands, 2000. pp. 689–722; B. Egeland, T. Yates, K. Appleyard & M. van Dulmen, 'The Long-Term Consequences of Maltreatment in the Early Years: A Developmental Pathway Model to Antisocial Behavior', *Children's Services: Social Policy, Research, & Practice*, 5, 4, 2002, pp. 249–60; F.W. Putnam, 'Ten-year Research Update Review: Child Sexual Abuse', *Journal of the American Academy of Child & Adolescent Psychiatry*, 42, 2003, pp. 269–78.

42   D. Glaser, 'Child Abuse and Neglect and the Brain—A Review', *Journal of Child Psychology and Psychiatry*, 41, 2000, pp. 97–116.

43   P. Salmelainen, 'Child Neglect: Its Causes and Its Role in Delinquency', *Crime and Justice Bulletin*, 33, 1996; C. Smith & T.P. Thornberry, 'The Relationship Between Childhood Maltreatment and Adolescent Involvement in Delinquency', *Criminology*, 33, 1995, pp. 451–81.

44   J.A. Durlak, 'Common Risk and Protective Factors in Successful Prevention Programs', *American Journal of Orthopsychiatry*, 68, 1998, pp. 512–20.

45   See Chapters 7 and 11.

46   See the *Child Protection: Messages from Research* publications in the United Kingdom and the report by the US Advisory Board on Child Abuse and Neglect (1990), which proclaimed a national emergency in relation to the child protection crisis in the USA.

47   D. Scott, 'A Vision for Family Services: Support and Prevention that Works for Families at Risk', Keynote Presentation at Forum, A Vision for Family Services and Prevention that Works for Families at Risk, Sydney, 30 April 2003a.

48   G.B. Melton, 'Chronic Neglect of Family Violence: More than a Decade of Reports to Guide US Policy', *Child Abuse & Neglect*, 26, 2002, pp. 569–86.

49   F. Ainsworth & A.N. Maluccio, 'Kinship Care: False Dawn or New Hope?', *Australian Social Work*, 51, 4, 1998, pp. 3–8.

50   D. Scott, 'Opening Comments', Presented at CAFWAA Symposium 'When Care is Not Enough', Canberra, 17 September 2003b.

51   C.M. Sultmann & P. Testro, *Directions in Out of Home Care: Challenges and Opportunities*, PeakCare Qld Inc., Paddington, Qld, 2001, p. 10.

52   Australian Institute of Health and Welfare (AIHW), 2004b.

53   P.H. Delfabbro, J.G. Barber & L. Cooper, 'Placement Disruption and Dislocation in South Australian Substitute Care', *Children Australia*, 25, 2, 2000, pp. 16–20; P.H. Delfabbro, J.G. Barber & L.L. Cooper, 'Predictors of Short-term Reunification in South Australian Substitute Care', *Child Welfare*, 82, 2002, pp. 27–51. In this South Australian study of all children aged four to seventeen entering a new placement over a twelve-month period, 25 per cent of children had returned home within four months and 39 per cent within twelve months; most (90 per cent) who returned home within two years had already returned by eight months.

54   R. Bullock, M. Little & S. Millham, *Going Home: The Return of Children Separated from their Families*, Dartmouth, Aldershot, 1993; B. Minty, 'A Review of the Effects of Living Long-term in Substitute Care in the Context of a Discussion of Outcome Criteria', *Social Work & Social Sciences Review*, 8, 2000, pp. 169–93; Minty, 2000.

55   Bullock, Little & Millham, 1993.

56   Scott, 2003.

57   J. Cashmore, 'What Can We Learn from the US Experience on Permanency Planning?', *Australian Journal of Family Law*, 15, 2001, pp. 215–29.

58   H.N. Taussig, R.B. Clyman & J. Landsverk, 'Children Who Return Home from Foster Care: A 6-Year Prospective Study of Behavioural Health Outcomes in Adolescence', *Pediatrics*, 108, 2001, pp. 1–7.

59   Australian Institute of Health and Welfare, *Adoptions Australia 2002–03*, AIHW catalogue no. CWS-21 (Child Welfare Series 33), Canberra, 2004a.

60   The 'official hierarchy of desirable placement options' in the United Kingdom, according to Minty (2000) is reunification, fostering by relatives, adoption, foster care with approved non-relatives and residential care.

61   P.D. Steinhauer, *The Least Detrimental Alternative: A Systematic Guide to Case Planning and Decision Making for Children in Care*, University of Toronto Press, Toronto, 1991.

62   Minty, 2000.

63   D. Fanshel & F.B. Shinn, *Children in Foster Care: A Longitudinal Study*, Columbia University Press, New York, 1978.

64   J.G. Barber, P.H. Delfabbro & L.L. Cooper, 'Placement Stability and the Psychosocial Wellbeing of Children in Foster Care', *Research on Social Work Practice*, 13, 2003, pp. 409–25.

65   B. Davidson-Arad, D. Englechin-Segal & Y. Wozner, 'Short-term Follow-up of Children at Risk: Comparison of the Quality of Life of Children Removed from Home and Children Remaining at Home', *Child Abuse & Neglect*, 27, 2003, pp. 733–50; L. St Clair

& A.F. Osborne, 'The Ability and Behaviour of Children Who Have Been in Care or Separated from their Parents', *Early Childhood Development and Care*, Special Issue, 28, 1987, p. 3; Taussig, Clyman & Landsverk, 2001; L. Garnett, *Leaving Care and After*, National Children's Bureau, London, 1992; J. Lahti, 'A Follow-up Study of Foster Children in Permanent Placements', *Social Service Review*, 56, 1982, pp. 556–71.

66   J. Cashmore & M. Paxman, *Wards Leaving Care: A Longitudinal Study*, NSW Department of Community Services, Sydney, 1996, p. xiii; J. Cashmore & M. Paxman, 'Meeting the Needs of Children in Care: How Can We Do Better? The "Attachment" Needs of Young People Leaving Care', Presentation at Australian Institute of Family Studies Conference, Melbourne, February 2002.

67   Cashmore & Paxman, 1996

68   Cashmore & Paxman, 1996.

69   Australian Law Reform Commission/Human Rights and Equal Opportunity Commission, 1997.

70   Community Services Commission, *Annual Report 1996–97*, Sydney, 1997; Royal Commission into the New South Wales Police Service, 1997.

71   CREATE website at <http://www.create.org.au>, accessed 3 September 2003.

72   J. Thoburn, A. Lewis & D. Shemmings, *Paternalism or Partnership: Family Involvement in the Child Protection Process*, HMSO, London, 1995.

73   J. Cashmore, 'Facilitating the Participation of Children and Young People in Care', *Child Abuse & Neglect*, 26, 8, 2002, pp. 837–47.

74   Department of Health, *Child Protection: Messages from Research*, HMSO, London, 1995.

75   Department of Health, 1995.

76   Department of Health, 1995, p. 47.

Strong State Intervention:

The Stolen Generations

Ailsa Burns, Kate Burns and Karen Menzies

Sixteen children, all related one way or another, were removed from the mission on a day Julia has never forgotten…The assembled children were loaded onto the truck very suddenly and their things thrown in hastily after them. The suddenness and the suppressed air of tension shocked the mothers and the children and they realised something was seriously wrong…children began to cry and the mothers to wail and cut themselves…The tailgate was slammed shut and bolted and the truck screeched off with things still hanging over the back and mothers and other children running after it crying and wailing.[1]

The National Inquiry into the Separation of Aboriginal and Torres Strait Islander Children from their Families concluded that over the period 1910–70 between one in three and one in ten children were forcibly removed from their families and communities and, in some places and at some times, a much higher proportion. The Inquiry further concluded that 'not one Indigenous family escaped the effects of forcible removal',[2] with many affected over a number of generations. Why and how did the Australian authorities take this extreme action, and what were the outcomes? In this chapter we consider these questions, drawing extensively on the findings of the National Inquiry.

Contexts

Child removal: early events and beliefs

In line with their belief that education of the children in European ways was best for Indigenous populations, the Australian colonial authorities made early efforts to school Aboriginal children. Aboriginal families were initially willing to let their children attend, but by 1833 the only Aboriginal school operating in New South Wales had just four pupils.[3] A 'problem' noted by government authorities was the strength and attraction of the Indigenous lifestyle: 'We had an institution here, in Governor Macquarie's time, where the native children were educated, and turned out of it at the age of puberty good readers and writers; but being all associated together, and their native instincts and ideas still remaining paramount, they took to their old ideas again as soon as freed from thraldom.'[4]

To overcome this problem of 'reversion' to Aboriginal ways, the separation of Indigenous children from their families and communities became an entrenched aspect of colonial protection policy. On the reserves and missions children were housed in dormitories, and contact with their families was strictly limited. In some states the Chief Protector of Aborigines was made the legal guardian of all Indigenous children, overruling the rights of parents.

By the late nineteenth century it had become apparent that while the full-descent Aboriginal population was diminishing, the mixed-descent population was increasing. The colonial authorities had been prepared to supply basic food and shelter to the dwindling full-descent population, but the growth in the mixed-descent numbers raised other issues.

First, there were genetic considerations. In accordance with the Darwinist ideas of the day, 'half-castes' were regarded as potentially undesirable characters who needed to be carefully controlled, since they were likely to inherit 'the worst traits of both races'. In the Northern Territory, where white settlers were few, they were considered to be positively dangerous.[5] But they were also regarded as having greater developmental potential. James Isdell, for example, an early Protector in Western Australia, argued, 'The half-caste is intellectually above the aborigine, and it is the duty of the State they be given a chance to lead a better life than their mothers'.[6]

Second, the existence of the mixed-descent children raised humanitarian and religious issues. Many of the mothers were without any form of support from the white fathers of the children and unable to provide for them, and some children were rejected by their communities because of their parentage. Without help, their futures were bleak. In addition, the missionaries wished to convert them to Christianity. An alternative to removal would have been to provide the mothers with some support, but this option was ruled out by the belief that children of mixed descent should be merged into white society.

Third, the increasing mixed-descent population raised financial and labour-force issues. Governments were not prepared to support this expanding population as 'dependants'. Moreover, the Australian economy needed labour if it was to develop. The approach taken by state governments in collaboration with missionaries was to step up efforts to separate Aboriginal children from their families at an early age, remove them to institutions for basic education plus religious and vocational training, and send them to work as domestics, farmhands or labourers as soon as they reached their early teens.

Comparisons with the state's approach to non-Indigenous children

In some ways the removal policy was consistent with the state's approach to white children whose parents were regarded as exerting a bad influence. For these children, too, institutionalisation was seen as removing children from 'the irregular and immoral habits of the Parents' and educating them in 'religious as well as industrious habits'.[7]

However, there were critical differences between the approach of the state to Indigenous and to white children. Aboriginal culture was regarded by the state as both degenerate and seductive, so that it was especially important to remove children at an early age, before strong ties could be formed. There were different opinions as to what age was best. One official argued that children should be taken away as soon as they were born, because 'If they are in the wurley for a week it is bad for them'.[8] Other authorities favoured removal when children were two or four years old, thereby avoiding the costs involved in caring for babies, but before their Aboriginal identity was too strongly forged. The male administrators emphasised that though separation might be painful at the time, it was for their own good: 'In some cases, when the child is very young, it must of necessity be accompanied by its mother, but in other cases, even though it may seem cruel to separate the mother and child, it is better to do so, when the mother is living, as is usually the case, in a native camp.'[9]

To combat the influence of Aboriginal culture, the authorities made special efforts to sever family ties. A woman missionary explained how it was done:

> The Mission desired to give the half-caste children such a training as would help them to merge into the white population. They were unable to do so as long as the Home was in close proximity to an aboriginal camp. Some of the little ones had relatives in the Oodnadatta camp, and it was not possible to segregate them from their own people. The only way to do this was by taking them away where they could no longer see the natives or hear the sounds of

corroboree...After much prayer for guidance, it was decided to remove the children to a place further south, where there were no aborigines.[10]

Other strategies used to detach the children from Aboriginal culture included not allowing the parents to see their children, giving them new names, not telling them who their family were (this included separating children from siblings who were also in state custody: 'splitting the litter'), telling them that their parents were dead or had rejected them, intercepting and destroying correspondence, forbidding the use of Aboriginal languages, not telling (lighter-skinned) children that they were Aboriginal, and telling them that Aborigines were inferior, and should be avoided.[11]

A second difference between the state's approach to Aboriginal children and to white children lay in their different legislative treatment. In a number of states, the Chief Protector was the guardian of all Aboriginal children from the moment they were born. This allowed him or his delegate to remove children without the need to prove that removal was in the interests of the child, as was the case with white children. In Queensland and Western Australia the Chief Protectors were able to use their powers to force all Indigenous people onto large, highly regulated settlements and missions, to remove children from their mothers around the age of four and place them in dormitories and training schools, and then to send them off the missions and settlements to work.

Many personal accounts describe the experience of those who were removed. For example, one woman who herself had been taken away at birth, who had been brought up in four different institutions, and subsequently had her own three children taken, described four generations of removal, starting with a tribal grandmother, and extending over three states:

> My grandmother was taken from up Tennant Creek...they brought her down to The Bungalow [an institution at Alice Springs]. Then she had Uncle Billy [at age 14] and my Mum [at age 15] to an Aboriginal Protection Officer. She had not much say in that from what I can gather...When she was 15 and a half they took her to Hermannsburg and married her up to an Aranda man...When Mum was 3, they [took her] from Hermannsburg, putting her in The Bungalow until she was 11. And then they sent her to Mulgoa mission in NSW. From there they sent her to Carlingford Girls' Home [New South Wales] to be a maid. She couldn't get back to the Territory, and she'd had a little baby...In the end [they told her] 'We'll pay your fare back on the condition that you leave the baby here'. So she left her baby behind and came back to the Territory, and then she had me and my brother and another two brothers and a sister and we were all taken away as soon as we were born.[12]

Though government policy targeted mixed-descent children, and the legislation expressed this policy in terms of amount of 'Aboriginal blood', in practice skin colour was the deciding factor. Officials who visited the camps and settlements to remove the mixed-descent children selected those of light colour, while the parents tried to hide or camouflage them by blackening their skins. One submission to the National Inquiry described how:

> Every morning our people would crush charcoal and mix that with animal fat and smother that all over us, so that when the police came they could only see black children in the distance. We were told always to be on the alert, and, if white people came, to run into the bush or run and stand behind the trees as stiff as a poker, or else hide behind logs or run into culverts and hide. Often the white people...would come into our camps. And if the Aboriginal group was taken unawares, they would stuff us into flour bags and pretend we weren't there. We were told not to sneeze. We knew if we sneezed and they knew that we were in there bundled up, we'd be taken off and away from the area...During the raids on the camps it was not unusual for people to be shot...You can understand the terror that we lived in...[13]

The development of government policy during the twentieth century

Up until 1937 the various state governments acted independently on Aboriginal issues, although their philosophies were quite similar. In that year the first national conference was held, and it concluded with an agreement that all states (except Tasmania, which did not attend) would adopt consistent policies aimed at 'assimilation'. 'Assimilation' differed from the previous policy of 'merging' or 'biological absorption' in that it presumed a much more intensive intervention by the state. It also often involved the idea that Aboriginality would in time be 'bred out' through intermarriage with the white population.[14] In line with the assimilationist view that Aboriginal communities were 'just like groups of poor whites',[15] over the next thirty years responsibility shifted from the Aboriginal protection authorities to state child welfare departments. The legislation permitting the removal of Aboriginal children on the ground of their 'blood' was repealed, and they now came under the same child welfare laws as white children, and could be removed if they were found by a court to be 'neglected', 'destitute' or 'uncontrollable'.

Despite this change, the procedures were much the same: the same police and other officials who previously removed children on the basis of race now utilised the neglect and destitution provisions of the child welfare legislation to remove even larger numbers. Destitution was easy to prove as most Aboriginal families were very poor; neglect was used to characterise Aboriginal mores such as frequent travelling and sharing child-rearing across the extended family; and children who resisted schooling or indeed were excluded from school could be classed as uncontrollable.

Many witnesses to the 1997 National Inquiry described their bitterness regarding the 'neglected' and 'uncontrollable' tags that resulted in their removal from happy homes to strange, regimented and poorly resourced institutions, where food could be short and discipline harsh.[16]

The increasing numbers of Indigenous children being removed put considerable pressure on state welfare budgets and charitable agencies. From the late 1940s, fostering with white families rather than institutionalisation became more common: it was cheaper and it found support in child development theory, which increasingly stressed the importance of children's relationship with a primary caregiver. Adoption of Aboriginal children by white families was also promoted: for the state it had the advantage of transferring the cost and responsibility onto the adopting parents. What was overlooked was that for Aboriginal children the experience of being separated not only from family and community, but from other Aboriginal children, was intensely isolating and distressing.

Assimilation through education was another form of removal. In the more remote communities and the Northern Territory, Aboriginal parents were persuaded or coerced into allowing their children to be taken to cities to live in hostels or with white families while attending school. In line with this policy, governments gradually removed the rights of schools authorities to refuse to enrol Aboriginal children, but European parents (and their children) made their dislike of Aboriginal children known.

By the later 1960s it had become clear that despite the high level of state intervention, Aboriginal people were not being assimilated. They were resisting attempts to break up their families and communities and seeking each other out after being forcibly separated. At the same time, the white population was continuing to discriminate against them in employment, housing and social security rights. Instead of becoming respectable working members of white society, these Aboriginal children were moving into the criminal justice system or having their own children taken from them. By this time, also, Bowlby's writings[17] on the destructive effects of maternal deprivation were well accepted in respect of non-Aboriginal children, and the discrepancy between policies for black and for white children was becoming more obvious.

In 1967 the Commonwealth acquired joint responsibility for Aboriginal affairs. The policies of the Whitlam Government, elected in 1972, included support for Aboriginal self-determination, and the new government provided funding for Indigenous groups to challenge the removal policy. There was an immediate decline in the numbers being removed, and a sympathetic response from welfare agencies. The traumatic nature of removal, and the lifelong problems that stemmed from it, began to be appreciated among some welfare staff. After extensive lobbying, the National Inquiry was set up to investigate the effects of child removal, and its report was made public in 1997.

Child removal: the practice

The program was carried out with minimal resources. Australia was not a wealthy country, the state governments had limited budgets and staff, and they had many other commitments to which they gave higher priority. In addition, the economic depressions of the 1890s and 1930s were very severe in many parts of the country. Thus while the aims of the removal policy were ambitious, the practice was sparsely funded and heavily reliant on the services of local police, missionaries, and the kind of staff prepared to work for low pay in often overcrowded children's institutions.

The institutions differed in size, in whether they were close to or separate from adult settlements and camps, and in operating style, religious affiliation, and relationship to the wider community. What they had in common was limited funds and staff, which meant limited food (and in some cases water), limited space, limited protection from the weather, and limited adult attention. Illness and child mortality rates were often high. On Groote Eylandt almost 50 per cent of one generation of mixed descent suffered from leprosy, owing, according to the Chief Protector, to 'low resistance following years of improper feeding'.[18] In addition, inadequate staffing meant that harsh methods of management and control were often resorted to, including severe physical punishment, denial of food, forced standing and kneeling for long periods, heavy work assignments, head-shaving, and every kind of shaming. A Queensland woman recalled that: 'We were called the dormitory girls. But the kids who slept out on the verandah...they were the pee-the-beds...Maybe you'd pee the bed [just] one night, but you were transferred from your bed out onto the verandah. You slept on a mattress on the floor and all you were called was pee-the-beds..."Tell the pee-the-beds it's time to get up." No identity at all. Absolutely nothing.'[19]

Conditions in some Northern Territory institutions were particularly harsh, and further exacerbated in the 1920s by the severe drought that devastated central Australia at that time. At the Half-caste Home outside Darwin, by 1928 there were seventy-six inmates living in a 'house large enough for only one family'.[20] At The Bungalow, which comprised three corrugated-iron sheds on land opposite the police station, there were about fifty children and ten adults, and rations were scarce. One submission by a man removed from his mother at the age of three described his experience at The Bungalow:

> There's where food was scarce again. Hardly anything...night time we used to cry with hunger, y'know, lice, no food. And we used to go out there to the town dump...we had to come and scrounge at the dump, y'know, eating old bread and smashing tomato sauce bottles and licking them. Half of the time our food we got from the rubbish dump. Always hungry there...

That's another thing—culture was really lost there, too. Because religion was drummed into us, y'know, when we'd be out there and we'd have knuckle-up and that, we were that religious we'd kneel down in prayer...We had to pray every time you swear or anything, you'd go down on your hands and knees...they pumped that religion into us.[21]

Despite the emphasis on religious and moral training, sexual abuse was a problem, both within the institutions and when girls were sent out to domestic service, often returning pregnant. Archbishop Donaldson, visiting Barambah settlement in 1915, noted that of the girls sent out to service 'over 90 per cent come back pregnant to a white man'.[22] The baby would then be removed in its turn, creating a cycle that could continue for generations. A particularly hated feature of places like Barambah was the dormitory system, whereby mothers and siblings were housed in the same institution, but in different dormitories, with contact prevented.

Of all the children's homes, Colebrook in South Australia has been most commonly cited as a success story. A number of its alumni became leading figures in Aboriginal affairs, and others made successful careers in teaching, nursing and administration. Colebrook had the advantage of being staffed over the period 1927–52 by two exceptional women, who are described with respect and affection in alumni memoirs. As well as themselves acting as consistent parent figures, Matron Hyde and Sister Rutter supported their children's emotional needs by encouraging attachments between the older girls and younger children: 'When you were in Colebrook the older kids...sort of took the young ones under their care. So you got your love in a different way. Matron couldn't give everybody hugs and loves and kisses, but that minder was more like my mother...she took that place as that warm caring person and each one had their older one looking after them.'[23]

Even so, Colebrook children shared with those in other institutions the problems of scarce resources, staff turnover, and loss of cultural identity, as many memoirs make clear: 'Colebrook started with Sister Hyde and Sister Rutter. They *were* Colebrook...What we had was constant love and attention from the two ladies, although often we were short on food...Those kids went through hell on earth after they had gone.'[24]

As a source of income, the institutions sent their children out on work assignments, as servants and labourers, sometimes from an early age. A common complaint of those sent out was that they 'never saw' any of the money they earned, which was paid to the institutions and, in theory, kept in trust for them.[25] In 1941 Commonwealth child endowment was extended to Aboriginal children, and this money came to the institutions rather than to the parents, providing another source of funding. Nevertheless income usually remained inadequate, and there were constant reports of poor conditions and overcrowding in the children's homes. One solution, especially after 1940, was to move children into welfare homes for non-Aboriginal children and, if they had been declared 'uncontrollable', into juvenile justice institutions. A 1980 report noted that in New South Wales '17.2 per cent of children in corrective institutions are Aboriginal…[of whom] 81 per cent…are not in their home regions [and] 34 per cent had no contact with either parents or relatives…10.2 per cent of [all] children in non-government children's homes are Aboriginal [and] 15.5 per cent of children in foster care are Aboriginal'.[26] The Aboriginal population of New South Wales at the time was about 1 per cent of the total.

Fostering and adoption

Besides institutionalisation, fostering and adoption were the options for removed children. From early on, some children were taken into non-Aboriginal homes in this way. It was also common for children to experience a mix of placements, moving from institution to foster home and then back again to the institution—perhaps a number of times. Among removed people making submissions to the National Inquiry, one-quarter had spent their entire time in a single institution, 14 per cent had lived for the whole period with a non-Aboriginal family, and 54 per cent had spent time in both. The proportion of children who were fostered or adopted increased in the 1950s and 1960s, when the institutions could no longer cope with the large numbers involved, and child welfare thinking had come to the view that institutions were less desirable than family rearing. Placement in white families was preferred, as this was seen as helping children to assimilate more quickly. The arrangements made were often very casual. The Victorian government noted that:

> An informal placement takes place when some person…considers that there are Aboriginal children in the area who are at risk. Contact is then made with some resource person who may have contact with a group of people who will accept care and responsibility for these children at a minute's notice…the children are placed informally with various other people and as has happened on many occasions, when parents request the return of their children, some cannot be traced…It is often difficult to identify these children as it is not uncommon for the 'foster parents' to change the name of the child.[27]

One consequence of this uncontrolled approach was that a very mixed group of people were able to foster or adopt children. Some adoptive parents were 'fantastic', and strong attachments were formed. Other removed children described foster parents who were mentally ill, cruel, sexually predatory, exploitative of the child's labour, or just insufficiently caring. Waters, who interviewed a number of those removed and subsequently adopted or fostered, noted that:

things seem to have gone quite well until they got into the teenage years. Then they started to become more aware…that they were different…It was the impact of what peers were doing and saying which seemed to be most distressing to them. And sometimes their families didn't deal with that very well. They were dismissive. 'Look, the best thing to do is just forget you were ever Aboriginal' or 'Tell them that you came from Southern Europe'…But in none of those families was there a sense that one way to manage this situation was to recapture your sense of Aboriginality. There seemed to be no honour and dignity in being an Aboriginal, even if you'd been brought up by a family.[28]

Even the most sensitive of adoptive parents often knew little of the child's background, which meant that it could be very hard to trace the biological parents. In some cases there were no records. In other cases the birth records, when found, showed the name of the adoptive mother or some other person rather than that of the birth mother. Adopting parents themselves described being deceived: being told, for example, that their adopted child was an orphan, and later finding it had been removed from a mother who continued to seek it.[29]

As the adoption stories illustrate, a terrible weakness in the removal philosophy was its failure to prepare the white community for 'merging' or 'assimilation'. The removed children ran into discrimination, prejudice and racism at school, in their peer groups, in the workforce and on the streets. Some were racist themselves, having been told from an early age that Aboriginal people were undesirables, and to be avoided ('Our instructions were quite explicit: run across the park, don't talk to the natives.').[30] The individualist philosophy underlying assimilation—that 'given a chance', each individual should be able to make his or her own way in mainstream society—also overlooked (or, more accurately, denied) the developmental importance of a sense of cultural identity, except where the culture was that of the assimilationists.

Consequences

Child removal: the outcomes

As we have seen, implementation of the removal policy varied with time and place, and there was no attempt to conduct an ongoing evaluation of the effects. However, the 1994 national survey of Indigenous people[31] conducted by the Australian Bureau of Statistics provides one means of assaying the effects of the policy. It compared those who had or had not been taken away on a number of measures of life success. These can be compared with the stated aims of the policy, which, as we have seen, included 'rescuing' children from their family situation, and providing them with a higher level of education than they would otherwise receive, a greater commitment to the workforce, better earning potential, improved health, a more law–abiding lifestyle, and more personal stability and morality.

The findings were of failure on all these counts: there was either no difference between the groups, or those taken away fared worse. (It should be remembered that the survey was conducted in the 1990s, so that most removals would have occurred after 1940, rather than in earlier times.) In educational achievement and employment status there were no significant differences between the two groups, although those not taken away were a little more likely to be employed (see Table 1).

Table 1 Post-school qualifications and employment status of Indigenous adults twenty years and above[32]

Qualification	Taken away	Not taken away
Higher education	1.9%	2.0%
TAFE	1.9%	1.8%
Other	0.6%	1.0%
None	95.6%	94.8%
Not stated	—	0.3%
Employment status		
Employed non-Community Development Employment Program	22.8%	25.0%
Employed CDEP	8.2%	8.5%
Unemployed	22.2%	20.0%
Not in labour force	39.2%	38.3%
Not applicable	7.6%	8.2%

Income in both groups was very low, with under 6 per cent from either group earning more than $30,000 per annum. More of those taken away had incomes in the $8000–$16,000 range (39.9 per cent compared with 16.7 per cent), while those not removed were more likely to be in the $0–$3000 range (21.5 per cent compared with 13.3 per cent). Social security payments available at the time fell in the $8000–$16,000 range, suggesting that the group taken away were likely to be living in more settled areas and receiving social security, while those not taken were more likely to be living in remote communities and not doing so. The policy's aim of cutting government costs had thus also failed.

The figures also show that the policy had negative effects on health and crime. Those taken away in childhood were twice as likely to have been arrested more than once in the past five years (22 per cent as against 11 per cent).[33] Self-reported health status (which has been shown to be a good measure of subsequent morbidity and mortality) was worse in the removed group, 29 per cent of whom described their health as only fair or poor, compared with 15 per cent of the non-removed.

A smaller-scale longitudinal study comparing those removed or not in childhood found psychological distress to be very high in both groups.[34] Overall, two-thirds of all participants were described as distressed throughout the three years of the study, with depression the most common diagnosis. However, distress was far higher in the removed (90 per cent) than the non-removed group (45 per cent). Factors that offered protection against the development of depression and other psychiatric problems included a strong Aboriginal identity, frequent contact with one's extended family, and a knowledge of Aboriginal culture—all of which were much weaker in the removed group. The removed group also had a lower level of education, less stable living arrangements, and weaker social relationships. And these people were twice as likely to have been arrested by police and convicted of an offence, three times more likely to have been in jail, and twice as likely to use illicit substances, including intravenously. Similar finding were reported in a 1970s study of clients seeking assistance from the Victorian Aboriginal Legal Service for criminal charges, 90 per cent of whom were found to have been in placement—either in institutions or in foster or adoptive homes. In New South Wales the comparable figure was 90–95 per cent, with most placements having been in white families.[35] Another comparative study, this time concerned with educational outcomes, looked at removed and non-removed Aboriginal students who were taking a bridging course at Monash University. It found that those not removed had better self-esteem and more positive relationships, and did better in their studies, whereas the removed appeared 'held back because they were still dealing with all the emotional stuff'.[36]

Intergenerational effects

An important aim of the removal policy was that of 'breaking the cycle' of behaviour seen as undesirable. This is a difficult aspect to evaluate, but the outcome appeared to be the opposite: the institution of a new cycle of ineffective parenting. Topp[37] compared parenting among Aboriginal people in Victoria with that in remote communities in central Australia where there had been few removals:

> In central Australia I never saw any infants with feeding or sleep difficulties and whenever I saw infants who were unsettled it was because they were unwell. Young mothers were clearly well supported and advised by their relatives and they had a strong belief in what they were doing. In contrast in Victoria…I saw many young mothers with very little idea of how to interact with their young infants, how to feed them, how to rear and discipline their older children or how to set limits. Removal of children from their families and

from their culture has at the very least resulted in loss of role models for them to learn their parenting skills.

Brady[38] makes a similar distinction regarding petrol-sniffing. She found that this addiction was rare in pastoral communities where the pastoralists had not interested themselves in their Aboriginal workers' family life, but more common in settlements where government or mission staff had been more intrusive, and traditional tribal authority undermined.

Kamien's[39] 1972 study in Bourke, New South Wales, adds to this picture. Many of the Aboriginal adults in Bourke had themselves been separated in childhood. Among their children, Kamien found that one-quarter of the boys aged five to fourteen and one-third of the girls had substantial behavioural problems. Kamien commented that nearly all the Bourke children experienced 'inconsistency, unpredictability, and a conflict of values with the dominant white society'.[40] Waters noted in his clinical work with Aboriginal families that:

> Not only has the legacy of impaired interpersonal relationships and poor self-worth rendered them more liable to unplanned parenthood, but they make poor parents and their children in turn have often been taken into care for having been abused or neglected. Such parents are often disorganised, impatient, capricious and ultimately demoralised, feeling unable to provide for their children what they missed out on and often being painfully aware that the experience of childhood they are providing for their children [is] not dissimilar to that which they experienced.[41]

Another expert witness to the National Inquiry noted that the separated children could, as adults, be 'afraid of the dependency of their children', and unable to meet their needs, despite a 'yearning to look after their kids consistently'.[42]

Were there any positive outcomes? There is no ready answer. There was considerable variation across institutions, and at different times, but there is no research relating these variations to outcomes. Some removed children went on to notable achievements; but, as Table 1 shows, their overall education and occupation levels were a little lower than those of the non-removed, who also had access to schooling. It has to be remembered, too, that child mortality in the Aboriginal camps was often high, and some mothers were unable to keep their children because of destitution and/or community rejection, and surrendered them voluntarily to the missions. Thus removal may have saved some (or many) lives. However, we lack research in these areas.[43]

What developmental processes are important?

How can developmental psychology help us to better understand these outcomes? An obvious issue is that of attachment. In his 1951 report on the effects of institutionalisation, Bowlby[44] described a range of damaging outcomes, including impaired cognitive and language development, inability to form close relationships, hostility, depression, substance abuse, and what he termed 'affectionless character': a readiness to delinquent or criminal behaviour associated with absence of feeling for the victims. Bowlby attributed these deficits to 'maternal deprivation', that is, the absence of a stable mothering figure to whom the infant and child would become attached. This primary attachment to the mother formed the template for all later attachments, and without it later attachments would be deficient. The primary attachment also provided the child with a sense of security and well-being, and the presence of the attachment figure gave the child a 'secure base', from which it was able to venture out to explore and enjoy the world. Absence or loss of the mothering person damaged the child's sense of security, hindering all aspects of development and rendering the child prone to passivity, anxiety, rage and despair.

There has been debate over some of Bowlby's ideas: for example whether infants need a *single* primary caregiver (what about fathers?). But his findings were from the beginning extremely influential, and throughout the Western world at least there was a rapid move away from institutionalisation of children and towards fostering, family support and small family-type group homes. At the same time, and in order to describe the nature of maternal deprivation more exactly, a number of researchers studied children living in group homes in different countries. They concluded that young children can generally cope with more than one major caregiver, but that what they need to develop normally are sustained interactions with caring and responsive people. If these conditions are not present, the child risks failing to develop an understanding of their own feelings and aims, or those of others, or a cohesive sense of self.[45]

The many destructive outcomes attributed to maternal deprivation appear to apply only too well to the removed children. Given the general acceptance of Bowlby's views, and the retreat from institutionalisation of non-Aboriginal children, how was it then that Indigenous children continued to be removed into the 1970s? One answer appears to be that those in authority saw these children's situation as different from that of children in general, and believed that they would be worse off if they continued to live in their own communities. The records present many expressions of this view, for example the following: '[The] half-caste, who possesses few of the virtues and nearly all of the vices of whites, grows up to be a mischievous and very immoral subject; it may appear to be a cruel thing to tear an aborigine child from its mother, but it is necessary in some cases to be cruel to be kind.'[46]

Other examples have already been cited. It is of interest that from early on some Aboriginal women appreciated that this perception was the root of the problem, and attributed it in part to the fact that the white authorities were men, who lacked understanding of the feelings of women and children:

> In many things the white people mean well, but they have so little understand-
> ing. My experience has convinced me that, sociologically, the Native Depart-
> ment is working on wrong lines...The same law that applies to the white race
> should apply to the native races in that particular...Our native mothers have all
> the natural feeling of mothers the world over, and to many of them the admin-
> istration of the Native Department by men only, is stark tragedy.[47]

A second question concerns the operating style of the children's homes. Given the increased understanding of developmental needs after Bowlby's classic work, why were they permitted to operate in such unsatisfactory ways? The answer here is lack of resources, and the difficulty of recruiting and keep-ing suitable staff. Inexperienced staff often held responsibilities beyond their capacities, and 'the burdens placed on [them] and the stresses and frustrations they experienced, were no doubt responsible for the brutal punishments that often occurred'.[48] The National Inquiry also documents many instances of sexual abuse, and given the known tendency of institutions to draw pae-dophiles, this comes as no surprise.

Emotional abuse is another form of abuse, harder to define, but generally considered to include bullying, terrorising, shaming, humiliation, denigration and discrimination. Stories told to the National Inquiry and elsewhere[49] demonstrated a distressing variety of such abuse, including many particular incidents that had remained vivid in the victims' memories over decades.

To 'maternal deprivation', then, we must add the effect of physical, sexual and emotional abuse in some cases. The detrimental effects of physical abuse are by now well documented, and include low self-esteem, anxiety, anger, depression, lack of empathy with the sufferings of others, substance abuse, and increased likelihood of oneself becoming a child-abuser.[50] In the case of sex-ual abuse, confusion over sexual identity and sexual norms, dissociation, emo-tional numbing and guilt are also reported, and parenting problems are again a feature.[51] As with other forms of abuse, emotional abuse is linked with low self-esteem and poor mental health in adulthood.

Running through all of these aspects is a third theme that is central to per-sonality development: that of identity, in this case ethnic/cultural identity. It is well documented that the achievement of a coherent sense of identity is an important developmental task, with adolescence usually a critical time.[52] Occupational and sexual identity has generally been seen as the core of per-sonal identity, with ethnic/cultural identity a more peripheral aspect. This seems a fair description of the experience of members of the mainstream cul-ture. For example, at the time of writing, one of the authors was involved in a survey that asked respondents to nominate their 'cultural group'. Most of the Anglo-Australians bypassed this question, or gave joke answers such as WASP and SNAG. For them, cultural identity was a non-issue. However, as Chapter

3 notes, minority-group individuals often find themselves categorised by others in terms of their group rather than as individuals. For them, in consequence, coming to terms with this attributed group membership is a central aspect of personal identity. This was the case for the removed children, who were consistently reminded of their ethnicity, usually in a denigratory way. One woman, removed in the 1940s as a baby, told how:

> There was a big poster at the end of the dining room and it used to be pointed out to us all the time [in] religious instruction…They had these Aborigine people sitting at the end of this big wide road and they were playing cards, gambling and drinking. And it had this slogan…'Wide is the road that leads us into destruction' which led up into hell. The other side they had these white people, all nicely dressed, leading on this narrow road and 'Narrow is the road that leads us into the kingdom of life or the Kingdom of God'.[53]

Other stories were sometimes of worse, sometimes of milder identity devaluations, as in the advice from foster parents to 'tell them you came from southern Europe'. In each case, however, it sooner or later became clear that 'merging' or 'assimilation' was not the ready option envisaged by the policy-makers because, even if they wished to merge, the European population was not prepared to accept and absorb them simply as individuals. The developmental task of achieving coherent and positive identity development thus involved achieving a cultural identity. Personal stories describe many ways in which it was sought, and many failures. An insightful account was given by a man removed from his family in the 1950s and placed in an Anglican boys' home.

> When they took us away, we could only talk Aboriginal, we only knew one language, and when we went down there, well we had to communicate somehow. Anyway, when I come back I couldn't even speak my own language. And that really buggered my identity up. It took me 40 odd years before I became a man in my own people's eyes, through Aboriginal law. Whereas I should've went through that when I was about 12 years of age.[54]

Conclusion

In 1980 the Aboriginal family tracing and reunion agency Link-Up was established in New South Wales, since when it has extended across the country. Subsequently the Aboriginal Child Placement Principle—that when Aboriginal or Torres Strait Islander children are to be placed in substitute care, they should wherever possible be placed within their own culture and community—was introduced. Today it is recognised in all Australian jurisdictions, either in legislation or in policy, although its implementation remains problematic.

Responses at the state and territory level to other recommendations made in the report have varied, reflecting the priorities of the governments that have been in office. These recommendations included the setting up of a national compensation fund for people affected by forcible removal, and that all Australian parliaments acknowledge and formally apologise for their role in the policy. As at 2003 no compensation fund had been created, the Howard Government taking the view that 'there is no practical or appropriate way to address [the issue].'[55] All states and territories had officially apologised to the stolen generations. However, the Federal Government had refused to do so, instead expressing 'regret that indigenous Australians suffered injustices under the practices of past generations.'[56]

At the same time, the Federal Government spent over $10 million in court costs defending against individual claims for compensation. Two claimants (Lorna Cubillo and Peter Gunner) lost their court case when the High Court supported earlier rulings that the events in question were so long ago that key witnesses had either died or were unable to give evidence.[57] Another claimant (Joy Williams, who sued the State of New South Wales) lost her case on similar and other legal grounds. Community attitudes to these issues continue to be divided. On National Sorry Day (28 May 2000), some quarter of a million people walked across the Sydney Harbour Bridge in support of reconciliation between Aboriginal and non-Aboriginal Australians.

Student exercises

1　The 'stolen generations' themselves suffered greatly from being removed from their families. What do you see as the 'ripple effect' of these policies and practices? Discuss the impact on succeeding generations and on Aboriginal communities of these events.

2　At different historical times, and even during the same era, the interpretation of the words 'in the best interests of the children' has differed markedly. Why was removal of Aboriginal children from their families seen as being in their best interests? Discuss how this differs from policies and practices concerning Aboriginal children and their families today. Compare this interpretation of the 'best interests' policy with policies and practices concerning non-Indigenous children at the same time (for example, the sending from England to Australia of children from disadvantaged backgrounds; adoption laws and practices).

3　The report of the National Inquiry into the Separation of Aboriginal and Torres Strait Islander Children from their Families, *Bringing them Home*, suggested that the policies and practices documented in the report amounted to genocide, or the deliberate destruction of a race of people. Do you agree that this was a case of genocide?

4   How can Bowlby's theories about the detrimental effect of maternal deprivation be reconciled with the 'best interests of children' presented as a defence for the policies that led to removal of Aboriginal children from their families?

5   What do you see as appropriate community and government responses to the continuing effects of the removal policy?

Notes

1   Human Rights and Equal Opportunity Commission (HREOC), *Bringing Them Home*, HREOC, Sydney, 1997, p. 142.

2   HREOC, 1997, p. 37.

3   C. Rowley, *The Destruction of Aboriginal Society*, Penguin, Ringwood, 1970, p. 91.

4   Rowley, 1970, p. 92.

5   See B. Cummings, *Take This Child*, Aboriginal Studies Centre, Canberra, 1990.

6   HREOC, 1997, p. 104.

7   *Historical Records of Australia, Additional Instructions to Governor Bligh, 20.11.1805*, HRA Series I, Vol VI, Government Printer, Sydney, 1915, pp. 18–19.

8   Secretary of the SA State Children's Council, quoted in C. Mattingley & K. Hampton, *Survival in Our Own Land*, Hodder & Stoughton, Sydney, 1992, p. 160.

9   Chief Protector Spencer of the Northern Territory, quoted in Cummings, 1990, p. 17.

10   Violet Turner, quoted in Mattlingley & Hampton, 1992, p. 213.

11   HREOC, 1997, Chapter 10; R. van Krieken, *Children and the State*, Allen & Unwin, Sydney, 1991, p. 108.

12   HREOC, 1997, pp. 147–9.

13   HREOC, 1997, p. 27.

14   HREOC, 1997, pp. 30–2; Public Submission by James Miller to the National Inquiry. See also R. Manne, 'The Stolen Generation', *Quadrant*, January/February 1998, pp. 53–63.

15   J. Bell, 'Assimilation in NSW', in *Aborigines Now: New Perspectives in the Study of Aboriginal Communities*, ed., M. Reay, Angus & Robertson, London, 1964, p. 68.

16   See for example HREOC, 1997, Chapter 10.

17   J. Bowlby, *Maternal Care and Mental Health*, World Health Organization, London, 1951.

18   A. Markus, *Governing Savages*, Allen & Unwin, Sydney, 1990, pp. 46–59.

19   HREOC, 1997, p. 84.

20   Cummings, 1990, p. 20.

21   HREOC, 1997, p. 134.

22   Quoted in R. Kidd, 'You Can Trust Me, I'm With the Government', paper presented at One Family, Many Histories Conference, 13–15 September 1994, Brisbane.

23   Faith Thomas, quoted in Mattingley & Hampton, 1992, pp. 215–18.

24   Faith Thomas, quoted in Mattingley & Hampton, 1992, pp. 215–18.

25   See for instance HREOC, 1997, pp. 171–2.

26   NSW Parliament, *Report of the NSW Aboriginal Children's Research Project to the Select Committee of the Legislative Assembly upon Aborigines*, NSW Government Printer, Sydney, 1981, p. 292.

27   HREOC, 1997, p. 67.

28   B. Waters, in HREOC, 1997, p. 158.

29   HREOC, 1997, p. 66.

30   HREOC, 1997, p. 174.

31   Australian Bureau of Statistics, *National Aboriginal and Torres Strait Islander Survey*, Australian Government Publishing Service, Canberra, 1994.

32   Australian Bureau of Statistics, *National Survey of Indigenous People*, 1994, cited in HREOC, p. 14.

33   Australian Bureau of Statistics, 1994, p. 58.

34   J. McKendrick, HREOC, 1997, p. 22.

35   E. Sommerlad, HREOC, 1997, p. 190.

36   H. Siggers, HREOC, 1997, p. 192.

37   J. Topp, HREOC, 1997, pp. 225–6.

38   M. Brady, *Heavy Metal*, Aboriginal Studies Press, Canberra, 1992, pp. 183–90.

39   M. Kamien, *The Dark People of Bourke*, 1972, cited in HREOC, 1997, p. 225.

40   Kamien, 1972, quoted in HREOC, 1997, p. 225.

41   B. Waters, HREOC, 1997, p. 222.

42   N. Kowalenko, Public Submission to the National Inquiry.

43   G. Seagrim & R. London, *Furnishing the Mind: A Comparative Study of Cognitive Development in Central Australian Aborigines*, Academic Press, Sydney, 1980, provides an interesting comparison of removed and non-removed children on cognitive tasks.

44   Bowlby, 1951. See also Bowlby's *Attachment and Loss*, 3 vols, Basic Books, New York, 1969–80.

45   See for example S. Provence & R. Lipton, *Infants in Institutions*, International Universities Press, New York, 1962; M. Rutter, *Maternal Deprivation Re-assessed*, Penguin, New York, 1981; B. Tizard, *Adoption: A Second Chance*, Open Books, London, 1977; L. Robins & M. Rutter, eds, *Straight and Devious Pathways from Childhood to Adulthood*, Cambridge University Press, Cambridge, 1990; E. Clarke & J. Hanisee, 'Intellectual and Adaptive Performance of Asian Children in Adoptive American Settings', *Developmental Psychology*, 18, 1982, pp. 595–9.

46   J.M. Drew, WA Parliamentary Debates, quoted in P. Biskup, *Not Slaves, Not Citizens*, University of Queensland Press, 1973, p. 142.

47   Gladys Prosser, a Noongar mother, quoted in the WA Legislative Council by the Hon. H. Seddon, *Hansard*, 22 November 1938, WA Government Printing Office, Perth, p. 2246.

48   Cited in Cummings, 1990, p. 119.

49   See for instance Mattingly & Hampton, 1992.

50   R. Malinovsky-Rummell & D. Hansen, 'Long-term Consequences of Childhood Physical Abuse', *Psychological Bulletin*, 114, 1994, pp. 68–79.

51   K. Kendall-Tackett, L. Williams & D. Finkelhor, 'Impact of Sexual Abuse on Children', *Psychological Bulletin*, 113, 1993, pp. 164–80.

52   A. Waterman, 'Identity Development from Adolescence to Adulthood', *Developmental Psychology*, 18, pp. 341–58.

53   HREOC, 1997, p. 157.

54   HREOC, 1997, p. 203.

55   Senator John Herron, Minister for Aboriginal and Torres Strait Islander Affairs, 'Bringing Them Home—Commonwealth Initiatives', media release, Canberra, 26 August 1999.

56   Hon. John Howard, *Hansard*, Commonwealth of Australia: House of Representatives, Statement on the Motion of Reconciliation, 26 August 1999.

57   P. O'Brien, 'Are We Helping Them Home?', paper on the Surveys of Progress in the Implementation of the *Bringing Them Home* Recommendations, Parliament House, Canberra, 13 November 2002; A. Buti, 'Unfinished Business: The Australian Stolen Generations', *Murdoch University Electronic Journal of Law*, 7, 4, 2000, <http://www.murdoch.edu.au/elaw/>, accessed 19 November 2003.

(10)

Child Care and Australian
Social Policy

Deborah Brennan

Children's services are firmly entrenched on the Australian political agenda
and are an accepted part of social provision in this country. Since the 1990s,
however, there has been a fundamental transformation in the philosophy
underlying the provision of such services and the nature of the services provided. The ideals of the community-based, non-profit child care movement
that previously underpinned Commonwealth policy no longer hold sway; they
have been superseded by a far more hard-edged, market-driven approach. The
number of child care places has grown, but most of the recent growth has been
in out-of-school-hours care, family day care and private for-profit services.
Caring for children is now big business with major child care corporations
listed on the stock exchange and their owners featured in *Business Review
Weekly*'s list of Australia's richest individuals.

The rights and needs of children do not play a major part in current policy debates: the children's services program is firmly focused on the needs of
adults—parents and employers. As a result of Commonwealth Government
policy initiatives, begun by Labor and extended by the Coalition, the for-
profit sector is now the major provider of centre-based long day care in Australia. Although total outlays on child care have increased under the Howard
Government, the amount spent on most individual children has been cut;
thus costs have risen, especially for families who choose to use non-profit

services. It is increasingly difficult for families to use services in a flexible way to support their particular needs.

This chapter explores the transitions that have taken place in the philosophy underlying children's services in Australia since their inception in the 1890s. The central argument is that, as the program has become more tightly focused on work-related care, and as community-owned services have been sidelined in favour of privately owned businesses, the needs and interests of children have become increasingly marginalised. The chapter emphasises the significance of a range of policy debates such as paid maternity leave and work/life balance as well as those directly related to child care service provision.

Contexts

Early kindergartens and day nurseries

The earliest group care services for children in Australia were set up by philanthropic organisations such as the various Kindergarten Unions (which were established in all states between 1895 and 1911), the Sydney Day Nursery Association (1905) and the Victorian Day Nurseries Association (1910). The establishment of kindergartens and day nurseries was closely linked with the founding of staff training colleges. In New South Wales, for instance, the first free kindergarten was opened in 1896 and students were enrolled in the Kindergarten Training College the following year. Students worked in the kindergartens during the mornings, and undertook the more theoretical aspects of their studies in the afternoons. The close ties between the preparation of staff and the administration of services have long been regarded as a strength of the early childhood field.

The founders of children's services in Australia were not narrowly focused on the provision of kindergartens and day nurseries; they had much broader social goals. Their work included home visits to the families of the children enrolled in their services, and the establishment of supervised playgrounds in the inner suburbs.[1] Considerable effort was put into the preparation of staff to work with children in the early years of school, promoting the idea that 'early childhood' extended beyond the pre-school years into the first part of formal school.

A story from these early years that illustrates the broad social commitment of the early activists concerns Lillian de Lissa, a key figure in children's services in South Australia and after whom the de Lissa Institute was named. In the account de Lissa left of her efforts to establish kindergartens in Adelaide, she acknowledged that, at first, the inner-urban families she attempted to work with were quite suspicious of her efforts. None of them had heard of a kindergarten and they were understandably wary of someone who, for no apparent reason, wanted to take care of their children for the whole morning.

Once the first kindergarten was opened, however, it proved extremely popular, and the mothers who used it decided that they would like to see the idea extended to a neighbouring area. Accordingly, a group of them went to a nearby suburb, where they spent a week keeping house and caring for the children of women they did not know. They did this to enable the second group of women to spend time observing how kindergartens were run, so that they, in turn, could have such a service set up in their own neighbourhood. Lillian de Lissa commented: 'I was more stirred by this than by anything that had happened in my life up to that time, because I saw a vision of a new world; a world in which women, as women, would begin to think about children who were not their own and who would work for them and their well being though they themselves were getting nothing out of it.'[2]

This statement encapsulates an essential element of what the movement for children's services has historically been about in Australia: improving and expanding the provision of services not simply *for one's own children*, but for the children of the whole community.

Child Care Act 1972 (Cth)

By the 1960s most state governments had begun to provide assistance for pre-school education, but the provision of day care remained in the philanthropic sphere. As the demand for women's labour became more pressing and the women's liberation movement emerged, the Commonwealth Government became the focus of sustained claims for assistance with child care services that would support parental employment.

The *Child Care Act 1972* (Cth) marked the beginning of the Commonwealth Government's large-scale involvement in funding child care. Introduced by the then Minister for Labour and National Service, the Act was designed to facilitate the labour-force participation of mothers of young children. The scope of the legislation was strictly limited: it authorised the Commonwealth to provide financial assistance only to non-profit, centre-based long day care. In the early 1970s, virtually the only recognised voices in the children's services field were those of the established philanthropic-cum-educational bodies. Feminists were beginning to become active around child care issues, but were still very new players in the field and did not have access to government ministers. The philosophy of the Act inevitably reflected the dominance of the traditional organisations and their ethos of professionalism. Thus there was no debate about parent participation in the running of services, for example, as this had never been part of the early childhood tradition. Nevertheless the legislation had a clear focus on children through its insistence that funded services meet defined quality standards. The original funding formula, established by the Child Care Act, tied funding to the employment of trained staff. The ratios and staff qualifications built into the Act were those laid down by the Australian Pre-school Association (precursor of Early Childhood Australia). Although it had significant limitations, the Child Care Act was extremely important. Its very existence was an acknowledgment that affordable, quality child care was beyond the reach of ordinary families. As one of the government speakers in the parliamentary debate commented, 'child care which is beneficial to the child's overall development is prohibitively costly for the large body of parents and...the child minding arrangements that most parents could afford fall far short of the quality required in the interests of child welfare...'[3] Further, the Act embodied the idea that it was appropriate for the Commonwealth to assume responsibility in an area traditionally seen as an extension either of child welfare or of education (and therefore the province of the states).

Another development of the 1970s was the emergence of the community child care movement. Participants in this movement called for the provision of free child care centres, available to all parents, regardless of their reasons for use. They cautioned against a narrow, work-related focus, arguing that child care services should not simply be designed to free women to work outside the home during the day at dreary, exhausting labour that left them with the housework to do at night: 'To only want day care on the grounds that it will give us a chance to prove we are as good as men in a man's world is to entirely miss the point of the new feminism'.[4]

Rather, they saw child care as part of a broad social revolution that would lead to less rigid sex role and generational stereotypes, and provide opportunities for individuals to maximise their choices concerning work, leisure and child-rearing, depending upon individual temperament and ability. Ideas about children's liberation, as well as women's liberation, were embedded in this philosophy. Children should be liberated from the oppression of adults, just as women should be liberated from male oppression. One way of achieving this was to permit and encourage children to develop strong ties to people other than family members.

> In our society, the nuclear family (read 'mother') has been held to be fully responsible for the development and socialisation of the child under school age. Women's Liberation holds this to be an unreasonable and unsatisfactory method of childrearing. The recently formed Women's Liberation 'Community Controlled Child Care' action groups...denies the assumption that the ideal environment for the small child is home with mother, all day every day.[5]

Although the legislation enabling the Commonwealth Government to fund child care was passed in the last days of the McMahon Coalition Government, it was under the Whitlam Labor Government (1972–75) that Australian child care policy development and funding really got under way. During the short life of this government early childhood educators, philanthropic organisations and feminists vied with one another to influence government policy and determine expenditure priorities.

The Whitlam era was a turning point in the politics of child care. It was a period when crucial lessons about policy-making, policy implementation and bureaucratic politics were learned by feminists.[6] These years were also a period of struggle and uncertainty for the women who had previously dominated the traditional early childhood organisations, and whose role as expert advisers to government on matters pertaining to the care and education of young children had hitherto gone unchallenged.

Within the government itself ministers and bureaucrats clashed over the most desirable direction for child care policy and the most appropriate department (education or social security) for this policy function. From mid-1973 onwards, official Labor policy called for 'a comprehensive child care service [which would] provide support for women to participate more fully in society'.[7] This policy had been devised by feminists within the party, particularly the New South Wales Labor Women's Committee, and was strongly supported by the Prime Minister's Adviser on Women's Affairs, Elizabeth Reid. In mid-1974 the Labor Government announced that it intended to establish a Children's Commission so that by 1980 'all children in Australia [would] have access to services designed to take care of their physical, social and recreational needs'.[8]

Despite this visionary ideal, the Whitlam Government in fact allocated most of its child care funding to sessional pre-schools run by traditional organisations such as the Kindergarten Unions. This happened largely because the government used a model of funding that relied on submissions from the community, and which thus gave the edge to organised groups that were familiar with bureaucratic procedures. It was also the result of sustained opposition to the children's services program by state governments and a range of vested interests both inside and outside the bureaucracy.[9]

Following the dismissal of the Whitlam Government in late 1975, uncertainty surrounded the future of Commonwealth-funded child care. The Coalition Government led by Malcolm Fraser was committed to reducing Commonwealth expenditure and to encouraging a greater role for families and the market in responding to social needs such as child care. Despite this, most of the central components of the children's services program survived the Fraser Government (1975–83), although funding was substantially curtailed.

This outcome was the result of the determined efforts of a small number of committed people. A key role was performed by Beryl Beaurepaire, a close friend of the Prime Minister and Vice-President of the Victorian Liberal Party. Beaurepaire was appointed Convenor of the first National Women's

Advisory Council in 1976 and used this position to lobby strenuously for a range of women's issues including child care. Senator Margaret Guilfoyle, Minister for Social Security (1975–80) and Minister Assisting the Prime Minister on Child Care Matters (1975–76) was also sympathetic to the need for children's services, especially long day care. Women in the bureaucracy (especially the Women's Affairs Branch) developed economic arguments to support the case for switching priorities to long day care.[10]

In addition to all these 'insider' efforts, the activities of various state-based lobby groups became far more effectively coordinated. These included Community Child Care (which by this time existed in both Victoria and New South Wales), the Women's Trade Union Commission, the Family Day Care Association and the Ethnic Child Care Development Unit. In 1983 the National Association of Community Based Children's Services (NACBCS) was formed. NACBCS aimed to represent the interests of all types of community-based children's services and, in particular, to overcome traditional divisions between home-based and centre-based care.

The Hawke and Keating Labor Governments

The politics of child care under the Hawke and Keating Labor Governments (1983–96) presented a distinct contrast with that of previous administrations and raised new issues and dilemmas. During these years, care policy was shaped by persistent tension between the government's economic and social justice objectives. Labor's economic goals in this period included reducing both public expenditure and the budget deficit. In the context of this climate of fiscal austerity, advocates of expanded child care provision found it necessary to use economic arguments to support their case. The close relationship between the government and the Australian Council of Trade Unions (ACTU), as expressed through the Accord, was also significant here. Under the Accord, the unions agreed to exercise wage restraint in return for increases in the social wage (the latter being broadly understood to include health, social welfare and community services such as child care) and a government commitment to reducing unemployment.

The ACTU took up the child care issue in a number of ways: it pressed for increases in the provision of community-based and work-related services; it urged the government to ensure that fees in subsidised services were kept at reasonable levels; and it helped to coordinate campaigns for improvements to the pay, working conditions and career structures of child care workers. During these years, the ACTU became a far more significant player than feminist groups and community child care advocates. As a result of this, and also because of the government's broader economic agenda, child care provision was increasingly tied to the needs of the labour market.

In the late 1980s a bitter struggle erupted within the government over the very existence of publicly funded child care, and especially over subsidies to middle- and high-income families.[11] For a time it appeared that child care might be entirely handed over to the private sector. This did not eventuate but, in 1991, following a period of sustained lobbying by private operators and pressure from the ACTU, the government extended subsidies to users of private, for-profit child care centres.

This represented a profound shift in government policy. The move was vigorously opposed by the community child care movement and most feminist organisations on the grounds that the care of children should be a public responsibility rather than a profit-making activity. Concerns were also voiced about the failure of most private centres to provide care for babies and toddlers. The standard of care offered in some private centres was also an issue. Research conducted by the Australian Bureau of Statistics had shown that commercial centres had fewer qualified staff than community-based services, employed four times as many staff under eighteen years, and had fewer ancillary staff.[12] The industrial conditions in commercial centres were also of concern, particularly the propensity of some operators to hire very young staff and dismiss them when they became eligible for adult wages. In response to these concerns, the Labor Government introduced an accreditation system, the Quality Improvement and Assurance System, which covered both private and community-based long day care centres.

Accreditation focuses particularly on the quality of interactions within each centre; it is thus quite separate from the licensing of the premises, which remains a state responsibility. In the words of June Wangmann (a Sydney-based academic and a key player in the accreditation debate): 'Regulations only deal with issues which affect children before they come in the door—the number of toilets, ratio of staff, the qualifications they hold. Accreditation looks at how staff interact with children'.[13] The idea behind accreditation was that public subsidies should only be available to centres that participated in this process, thus ensuring that public monies would not go to services that were in any way substandard. Accreditation has since been extended to family day care and out-of-school-hours care.

During the Labor years the role of the Commonwealth was increasingly defined as that of supporting other players, notably employers, commercial providers and state governments. Budgetary constraints resulted in pressure from Treasury to limit capital expenditure. Further efforts were made to focus child care provision on work-related needs and to limit access by other users such as parents at home. Attempts to shift policy in this direction were met by strong community resistance and were only partly successful.

Not long after the extension of subsidies to the private sector, Labor proposed the introduction of a 'two-tier' system of child care assistance (then called fee relief), in which work-related and non-work-related care would attract different rates of subsidy. This proposal was intended to discourage non-employed parents from using long day care, family day care and out-of-school-hours care by forcing them to pay higher fees.[14] Almost all users in this category would have been, by definition, one-income households, and the suggestion that they could afford to pay more for their child care than two-income households provoked a strong reaction. Particular concern was expressed about the possibility that children at risk of abuse might lose their access to child care.

Another problem concerned families with unemployed adults. With the national rate of unemployment at the time hovering around 9 per cent, Labor's two-tiered fee relief was regarded by many as an attack on unemployed families. The two-tier fee relief proposal was withdrawn after intensive campaigning by a range of organisations. Nevertheless, the incident had been instructive in demonstrating the kinds of thinking, and the pressures, that were at work within the government and the bureaucracy. The proposal has since re-emerged in a number of guises.

With child care increasingly seen by governments as an adjunct to labour-force participation, the feminist-inspired, community child care ideal of a national system of non-profit services based around the needs of children and their families has receded into the background. Community-owned long day care services now represent only 14 per cent of all Commonwealth-funded child care services.[15]

The shift to private, for-profit long day care

The broad thrust of policy change under the Hawke and Keating Labor Governments, extended and reinforced by the Howard Government, was to encourage competition between commercial and non-profit providers by subsidising consumer demand. More specifically the changes included the extension of child care assistance to users of for-profit centres; the active encouragement of expansion in this sector at the expense of the community sector; and the withdrawal of operational subsidies from long day care centres from July 1997 and out-of-school-hours care services from January 1998.

The winding back, almost to a standstill, of new non-profit services, together with the explosive, unplanned growth of for-profit care, resulted in the marginalisation of the community-based child care system. Less tangibly, it has contributed to a government approach to child care that targets the individual family as the recipient of services and ignores the community and social purposes of such care. Thus, despite significant levels of government funding, child care is increasingly constructed as a 'private' problem, which individual families can 'solve' by choosing to use a commercial service, a publicly owned service or its own internal resources.

Apparently reluctant to 'intrude' on private sector investment decisions, Labor placed no limits or constraints on the growth of commercial care. It subsidised expansion in any location chosen by private businesses. To qualify for child care assistance, a service simply had to open for a certain number of hours per day and weeks per year, be licensed by the relevant state or territory authority and be registered with the Quality Improvement and Accreditation System. The government did insist, however, that planning principles be applied to the non-profit sector. This led to the absurd situation whereby the minuscule growth of community-based child care (from 42,000 places in 1991 to 46,300 places in 1997) was subject to planning criteria, while the massive expansion of for-profit care (from 32,000 to 121,600 in the same period) was not subject to any planning guidelines at all. There is still no over-all planning of the location of new private child care centres—even though the profits of these centres are underwritten by Commonwealth subsidies.

Ironically, a major justification for the extension of child care assistance to the commercial sector was that it would reduce the financial burden on the Commonwealth. This was to occur for two reasons: first, because the capital costs of new services would be borne by commercial providers; second, because such services would not receive operational subsidies. The government esti-mated that 28,000 places would become available in the first four years of the policy. In fact, this target was exceeded in the first year. The scale of growth was so great that the Commonwealth found itself footing a bill for child care assistance that exceeded Treasury's worst fears. The extension of child care assis-tance to the private for-profit sector produced a doubling of child care assistance outlays between 1991 and 1996. Moreover, the 'unpredictability and scale' of this growth meant that the program continually required additional funds to cover shortfalls in estimates.[16]

The new policy approach to children's services opened up extraordinary commercial opportunities. Centres were concentrated in areas to which retirees had moved with lump-sum superannuation payouts to invest—the sunny coastal areas of south-east Queensland and northern New South Wales. Since these were not areas with a high demand for care, proprietors had to offer inducements such as free bags of toys on enrolment, discounts at major chain stores and free consumer goods such as microwave ovens.[17] Clearly, it was worthwhile for the service owners to woo their customers in this way. As the *Business Review Weekly* reported: 'Generous federal govern-ment funding of child care, a variety of government financial assistance schemes for parents, tax loopholes and even exemption in some areas from fringe benefits tax are underwriting the success of this 1990s phenome-non…For many property owners and developers, including foreign resi-dents, the flood of government money is a lifesaver, and possibly a license [*sic*] to get rich.'[18]

The growth of corporate child care

Federal government largesse has led to child care becoming 'big business'. ABC Learning Centres, one of the largest corporate child care players, owns more than two hundred centres around the country. While this is a relatively small proportion of all services, some 20,000 children under school age are cared for in these centres each week. In 2003 ABC Learning Centres made an after-tax profit of nearly $12.1 million; owner Eddy Groves is one of Australia's richest men.[19] Corporate child care chains intend to grow rapidly. ABC Learning wrote to all community-based and non-profit services in New South Wales, offering to take them over. By the middle of 2005, it hopes to own an additional 127 centres as a result of an 'aggressive acquisition strategy', which is likely to involve taking over centres owned by private individuals as well. Several other companies have tried to enter the corporate child care field, but none has been as successful as ABC. A rival chain, Child Care Centres Australia, was listed on the stock exchange in late 2002, but it was taken over by Peppercorn Management Group within a year. Another business, FutureOne, has been absorbed by ABC Learning.

Intriguingly, many of the corporations that invested in child care have strong connections with the Liberal Party. ABC Learning Centres is chaired by Sally-Anne Atkinson, former Liberal mayor of Brisbane. Child Care Centres Australia was developed by Liberal powerbroker Michael Kroger in association with his father-in-law, former Liberal Party leader Andrew Peacock. And FutureOne was chaired by a former Victorian Liberal minister Vin Heffernan.

It is sometimes argued that substantial differences between 'private' and 'public' child care no longer exist, and that the more important distinction is between services that offer high- and poor-quality care. This is true in a limited sense: very good care is provided by some private operators, and not all community sector services are exemplary. However, the fundamental issue is far broader than this. As Eva Cox has argued:

> Good centres provide more than just units of service in terms of hours of care. They provide a structure of relationships between staff, management and parents that offer links and bonds. These develop social relationships and trust, extending past the individuals involved and create, in many communities, a network that allows informal supports to develop. They become communities. Losing these resources through centres being undercut in price by private or small group minders, will create other social and economic costs.[20]

Opposition to private sector dominance of children's services is thus not solely a question of current standards in the different sectors. It is a longer term issue. As community child care has declined as a percentage of all Commonwealth services, pressures to reduce licensing standards and to move away from the current system of accreditation towards industry self-regulation have intensified. It was this sector (not the private sector) that urged state governments to introduce licensing of child care services in the postwar decades: this sector that attempted to have licensing standards raised in line with contemporary research on group care; this sector that led the campaign for accreditation; and this sector that worked with trade unions to improve the wages and conditions of workers in children's services.

The for-profit sector as a whole will not promote these broader interests. To date, whenever state regulations have been under review, interventions by private child care lobby groups have, almost without exception, been directed towards driving standards down. From a business point of view, regulations governing staff qualifications, group sizes, adult/child ratios and basic health, nutrition and safety requirements are barriers to profit. In an industry with tight profit margins it is rational to try to reduce such 'costs'.[21] In 2003, Eddy Groves (owner of ABC Learning Centres) challenged the Queensland regulations concerning staffing in child care centres during lunchtime and during breaks.[22]

Another concern is that policies geared towards gender equality and intended to have beneficial effects for mothers and babies—paid maternity leave for example—could be seen as antithetical to the business interests of private child care providers. In the midst of an intense public debate about the possibility of introducing such a scheme in Australia, the 'Money' section of the *Weekend Australian* reported: 'The main area which could affect private child care companies is the proposal to introduce some form of paid maternity leave, which would affect demand for child care services as more women stayed at home longer after giving birth'.[23]

The potential for longer term consequences of the shift towards private, for-profit care is thus of concern. If standards are reduced, Australia could become more like the USA, a country where the regulatory framework for children's services is best described as 'chaotic'.[24] The federal government in the USA abandoned national regulations in 1980. Since then, enormous variations have arisen between the American states in the types of care that are regulated and the matters covered by regulation. In many states home-based carers are expected to register (although not if they care for fewer than three children), but there are no regulations or standards covering the service they provide. More than half the states have no regulations covering group sizes in centre-based care and, where regulations do exist, they vary widely. In the state with the tightest regulations, one staff member is required for every three infants; at the other extreme the figure is one to seven. For children aged three to five years, the ratios vary from one staff member per seven, to one per twenty.[25]

Besides the possibility of falling standards, the other major issue facing users of Australian children's services is cost. Between 1991 and 1998 child care became less affordable for families using long day care centres.[26] With the abolition of operational subsidies in July 1997, sponsors and management committees faced a difficult choice: reduce quality or increase fees. Research conducted by the National Association of Community Based Children's Services showed that fees in community-based child care rose by between $4 and $20 per week, with average increases of around $10 per week. Families reduced their hours of care and many turned to unsatisfactory informal ('backyard') and patchwork arrangements.[27] In 2000 the Commonwealth introduced the Child Care Benefit, amalgamating 'child care assistance' and the 'child care rebate'. At the same time, in response to sustained community pressure concerning the gap between Commonwealth assistance and the actual fees charged, the maximum amount of Child Care Benefit was increased by $7.50 per week. Research produced by the Department of Family and Community Services demonstrates that this rise has increased the affordability of child care (i.e. that it has not all been absorbed by services charging higher fees); however, it is clear that many families are still struggling to find decent child care that they can afford. A study comparing child care usage in Western Sydney and Barbara Pocock's research into work and family issues in Australia has shown that in a range of occupations and industries—including call centres, factories, hospitals and offices—parents work different shifts in order to avoid the costs and stresses associated with finding child care.[28]

Many families are caught in a very difficult bind. The reason for this is that the Howard Government has introduced, or amended, a range of social policies that make child care (and the opportunity for mothers to work) far more difficult. Journalist and commentator Anne Summers (a former head of the Office of the Status of Women and an adviser to Prime Minister Keating) calls this 'the breeding creed'.[29] How can this be true, if the number of child care places has increased and the affordability of care has been enhanced? The answer to this conundrum is that family choices about employment and child care are affected by many different factors. The availability and cost of child care are important, but so too are taxation levels, interest rates and housing costs. Research by the Canberra-based National Centre for Economic Modelling has shown that low-income families can sometimes be worse off if the mother increases her hours of work. This happens because as the family receives more income, family benefits are withdrawn, child care costs go up, more tax is taken and the rent charged for public housing rises. These effects are particularly sharp for low-income women with several children. A low-income woman with three children loses at least 60 per cent of her hourly wages once tax, reduced family assistance and increased child care costs are factored in.[30]

Consequences

Implications of policy for children and families

When considering the issues that will shape the future for children, their families and communities, it is essential to take a broad view of the relevant policy arenas. A vast range of policies—including those concerning employment, industrial relations, taxation, social security and immigration—can be considered as 'family policies'. Certainly, these are all areas that have a significant impact upon the resources, opportunities, constraints and choices available to family members. Thus it is inappropriate for children's advocates to restrict their involvement in public policy debates to those issues that are *obviously* about children and families. Rather, participation in a range of debates including taxation, social security, employment and the appropriate division of Commonwealth–state responsibilities is vital.

Industrial relations can be used as an example of why participation in a broader range of debates is so important. The transformation of patterns of employment and unemployment in Australia has been occurring since the early 1970s. Many of the changes are structural (long-term changes in production patterns, for example), while others are more directly political. Changes to the industrial relations environment have been a key element of the policy agenda of the Howard Government. During its first year in office the Howard Government introduced the *Workplace Relations Act 1996* (Cth), which aimed to shift primary responsibility for industrial relations to employers and employees at the workplace level and, indirectly, to contribute to making the labour market more flexible from the point of view of employers.

The restructuring of industrial relations (and especially the emphasis on establishing a flexible labour market) will profoundly affect the lives of children. Yet, while there is a good deal of political rhetoric about 'family friendly' workplaces, there is virtually no indication that the government has considered (or is concerned about) what the new environment might mean for children, nor has there been any significant agitation from children's advocates. It can readily be shown, however, that children and those who care for them are likely to be considerably affected by the Howard Government's industrial relations agenda.

Parents, children and the new world of work

The main features of the changing nature of work in Australia include a substantial increase in part-time and casual work (almost a quarter of the Australian workforce is now employed part-time, compared with only 10 per cent in the 1970s); far greater reliance on 'non-standard' forms of employment such as contract, seasonal and 'on call' work; substantial increases in overtime; more jobs requiring employees to do split shifts, twelve-hour shifts and weekend work; and a reduction in the proportion of jobs with fixed starting and finishing times. Less than half the workforce now works Monday to Friday, and one-quarter work at least part of the weekend. By the late 1990s 'only 7 per cent of workers work[ed] all their weekday hours between 9 am and 5 pm'.[31]

The new world of work requires that children, as well as their parents, 'adjust' to non-standard hours of employment. For example, given the growth in work patterns outlined above, many children have to contend with unpredictability in their parents' schedules; not knowing when they will be collected from the centre or family day care premises; and not having their parents at home in the evenings or on weekends. It is indeed ironic that a government professing to be strongly in favour of 'traditional family values' is encouraging employers to adopt patterns of work that effectively undermine stable family life for many Australian workers.

The much vaunted 'flexibility' of the new world of work can be very much a two-edged sword. Working hours and patterns of employment that enable employees to meet both the routine and the unexpected demands of family life are desired by working parents. However, if flexibility essentially means an increase in the amount of insecure part-time work, or if it means that more workers are required to work long hours or extra days at short notice, then major problems will arise.

Child care workers

The status, pay and conditions of workers in children's services have improved greatly over the last hundred years, especially in recent decades. In the early days, much of the work of caring for children was done, literally, 'for love, not money'. According to Ruth Harrison, a former principal of the Sydney Kindergarten Teachers' College, students were encouraged to believe that their work could not be valued in money and were taught that if they received a pay cheque they should respond 'with a sense of surprise and appreciation'.[32] Such an attitude is inconceivable these days. Unionisation among children's services workers has increased (although this varies markedly between service types) and a high proportion are employed under award conditions. Nevertheless, there are severe anomalies and injustices in regard to child care workers' pay. It took until June 2003 for child care workers in council-run centres in Victoria, to obtain a level of remuneration that puts them on a par with garbage collectors.[33] The Workplace Relations legislation introduced by the Howard Government in 1996 has profoundly changed the industrial relations environment for employees in children's services. The impact of the new legislation has been both direct (in terms of their own negotiations with employers) and indirect (through the pressures to provide services that meet the needs of an increasingly casualised, deregulated labour market).

The direct changes have impacted upon negotiations between employees and employers. Industrial relations arrangements within the children's services sector are extremely complex, varying with the type of service, whether it is private or community based, the sponsoring body, the state in which it is located, and other variables. Furthermore, the child care workforce is characterised by small, isolated workplaces, and both employees and employers often understand existing award conditions poorly. According to the Australian Centre for Industrial Relations Research and Teaching (ACIRRT), of the 71,000 or so child care workers employed in Commonwealth-funded services, over 90 per cent are women; some 14 per cent come from non-English-speaking backgrounds (these are mostly family day care providers); and 2 per cent are Aboriginal or Torres Strait Islanders. Furthermore, this is an industry with a high turnover of staff. Approximately 70 per cent have been working in the area for four years or less.[34]

Assessing the bargaining capacity of the child care sector in the context of enterprise bargaining, ACIRRT expressed concern about the capacity of both employers and employees in children's services to engage in constructive and effective enterprise bargaining (especially bargaining of a type that would have positive outcomes for employees). Following consultations with industry practitioners and professionals it noted:

- poor levels of understanding of industrial rights and existing award conditions among child care workers
- lack of knowledge of award conditions and industrial issues among employers
- 'paternalistic' management styles and structures in services resulting in weak bargaining positions
- the small size of most workplaces and the isolation of workers from others in the industry
- the tendency of some private and commercial services to focus on cost-cutting.

This vulnerable group of workers is now being asked to provide child care services to meet the needs of the new, 'flexible' labour market. There seems to be an assumption on the part of government that child care providers (owners, managers and workers) will somehow be able to absorb the changes in the labour market and broader society and reorganise their services to meet the new challenges. In the context of declining government support for children's services, this may prove to be an overwhelming task.

Conclusion

The community-based child care movement that once provided the spirit and philosophy behind Australian children's services policy has been marginalised and downgraded since the mid-1990s. Community-based, non-profit care and its antecedents—the nursery school and free kindergarten movements—were born out of a public vision of the well-being of children and families. The establishment of neighbourhood links, the building of support networks, and the task of working together in a common enterprise were features of the community-based child care movement that simply cannot be sustained in an environment where the great majority of services are built for the purpose of private profit.

The winding-down of community-managed services in which parents have a stake—not only because of their own needs, but also because of their concern for those of their fellow citizens—is a major loss. At the same time significant changes in society, such as the transformation of patterns of work and unemployment, are creating enormous pressures on children, families and communities. There is an urgent need, as we move further into the new millennium, to reinvigorate public debate about the links between children, parents and communities, and to reformulate the arguments for public support.

Student exercises

1   Discuss how the relationship between group care services and parents has changed since the establishment of the first day nurseries and kindergartens in Australia.

2   For what reasons did the Commonwealth government become involved in policy and funding of children's services? Do you think that these reasons would affect the services available to families and to children? What are the processes by which policy translates into effects on individual children and families?

3   How has the provision of children's services in Australia been influenced by the political actions of parents? Give some examples of parental involvement and discuss favourable and unfavourable contexts for change from the 'bottom up' (rather than from the 'top down').

4   How will changing patterns of work in Australian society affect families and, particularly, children? How can detrimental impacts on children and families be avoided?

5   What are the implications of the growth of 'corporate child care' in Australia?

Notes

1   P. Spearritt, 'The Kindergarten Movement: Tradition and Change', in *Social Change in Australia: Readings in Sociology*, ed, D. Edgar, Cheshire, Melbourne, 1974, pp. 583–96.

2   L. de Lissa, *Talks Given at the Golden Jubilee of the Kindergarten Union of South Australia*, Adelaide, 1955.

3   Commonwealth Parliamentary Debates, House of Representatives, vol. 81, 10 October 1972, p. 2289.

4   W. McCaughey, 'Day Care—Liberating Who for What?', *Dissent*, 28, Winter 1972, p. 7.

5   McCaughey, 1972, p. 3.

6   S. Dowse, 'The Women's Movement's Fandango with the State: The Movement's Role in Public Policy Since 1972', in *Women, Social Welfare and the State* (2nd edn), eds, C.V. Baldock & B. Cass, Allen & Unwin, Sydney, 1988, pp. 205–26.

7   Australian Labor Party, *Platform, Constitution and Rules*, Canberra, 1973, p. 17.

8   Quoted in D. Brennan, *The Politics of Australian Child Care: From Philanthropy to Feminism*, Cambridge University Press, Cambridge, 1994, p. 90.

9   Brennan, 1994, pp. 92–5; Dowse, 1988.

10   M. Sawyer & A. Groves, *Working from the Inside: Twenty Years of the Office of the Status of Women*, Australian Government Publishing Service, Canberra, 1994, p. 56.

11   Labor's Minister for Finance, Peter Walsh, described such subsidies as 'an affront to the canons of decency'.

12   Australian Bureau of Statistics, *Commercial Long Day Child Care Australia*, catalogue no. 4414.0, Australian Government Publishing Service, Canberra, 1989.

13   *Sydney Morning Herald*, 4 March 1993.

14   J. Gifford, *Child Care Funding Re-assessed: Operational Subsidies, Fee Relief and Taxation Measures*, Australian Early Childhood Association and National Association of Community Based Children's Services, Canberra, 1992, p. 36.

15   Family and Community Services, *1999 Census of Child Care Services: Summary Booklet*, 2000.

16   Department of Health and Family Services, *The Development of a National Planning Framework for Child Care*, Canberra, 1996, p. 5; Auditor-General, *Mind the Children: The Management of Children's Services*, Audit Report no. 42, 1993–1994, Australian Government Publishing Service, Canberra, 1994, pp. 37–41.

17   S. Loane, *Who Cares?*, Reed Books, Kew, Victoria, 1996, p. 249.

18   A. Ferguson, 'The Industries Set for Success', *Business Review Weekly*, 25 July 1995, p. 50.

19   A. Jackson, 'ABC Learning Acquisition Alert', *Sydney Morning Herald*, 15 September 2003; A. Horin, 'When Making Money is Child's Play', *Sydney Morning Herald*, 4 October 2003; *Age*, 4 September 2003.

20   Quoted in Economic Planning and Advisory Commission, Child Care Task Force, *Future Child Care Provision in Australia: Final Report*, Australian Government Publishing Service, Canberra, 1996, p. 37.

21   For a United States/Canadian perspective on these issues, see K. Teghtsoonian, 'Neo-conservative Ideology and Opposition to Federal Regulation of Child Care Services in the United States and Canada', *Canadian Journal of Political Science*, 26, 1993, pp. 97–121.

22   Horin, 2003.

23   A. Fraser, 'Is Making Money out of Childcare as Easy as ABC?', *Weekend Australian*, 12–13 October 2003, p. 32.

24   F. Pettitt & J. Wangmann, 'Children's Services in Other Countries', unpublished paper prepared for Economic Planning and Advisory Council Child Care Task Force, 1996, p. 39. (A shorter version of this paper is published in EPAC Task Force, *Interim Report: Commissioned Studies*, Australian Government Publishing Service, Canberra, 1996, pp. 153–74.

25   Pettitt & Wangmann, 1996. See also Teghtsoonian, 1993.

26   Australian Institute of Health and Welfare, *Australia's Welfare, 2001*, Canberra, 2001, p. 171.

27   National Association of Community Based Children's Services (NACBCS), *Care Versus Quality—The Results of a National Survey of Community Owned Children's Services*, NACBCS, Melbourne, 1997.

28   B. Pocock, *The Work/Life Collision*, Federation Press, Annandale, 2003.

29   A. Summers, *The End of Equality: Work, Babies and Women's Choices in 21st Century Australia*, Random House, Milson's Point, 2003.

30   M. Toohey & G. Beer, 'Is it Worth Working Now? Financial Incentives for Working Mothers Under Australia's New Tax System', paper presented at the 2003 Australian Social Policy Conference, Sydney, July 2003.

31   I. Watson, J. Buchanan, I. Campbell & C. Briggs, *Fragmented Futures: New Challenges in Working Life*, Federation Press, Annandale.

32   R. Harrison, *The Sydney Kindergarten Teachers' College, 1897–1981*, Sydney Kindergarten Teachers' College Graduates Association, Sydney, 1985, p. 354.

33   Australian Centre for Industrial Relations Research and Training, 'Child Care in a Changing Industrial Relations Environment', in EPAC Task Force, *Interim Report*, Australian Government Publishing Service, Canberra, 1996, pp. 8–9.

34   Australian Centre for Industrial Relations Research and Training, 1996, p 18.

Children, Families and Communities:

Looking Forward

Jennifer Bowes and Alan Hayes

This chapter takes the theoretical framework explored in the preceding chapters and examines its application to future challenges for children, families and communities in Australia. It explores the range of prevention and intervention programs developed to support children, families and communities and the need for interventions and wider policy support for children and families.

Contexts

A review of the issues

In Chapter 1 and throughout the book it has been argued that people create and modify contexts and that, at the same time, contexts create and modify people. People vary, however, in the extent to which they are able to modify their contexts. Some individuals are more capable of change than others; and some contexts allow greater scope for change, providing more opportunities for development of the personal characteristics that are necessary for achieving change. While individuals can learn strategies for change, contexts are more open to modification, not only to accommodate people's needs, but also to allow them scope to develop and become more resilient in the face of the challenges they encounter. As earlier chapters and this chapter show, contexts can be modified in a variety of ways to benefit children and families.

The prime focus of this book has been on the interconnections among people and their contexts. It has been argued that these contexts are important in understanding the differences in consequences for the individuals involved. It is clear from the examples provided in the preceding chapters that there is considerable variation in the contexts of development for Australia's children, families and communities. We have argued that to understand development it is necessary to know about both who is developing and where development is taking place. This is a considerable shift from earlier approaches to the study of development that focused on individual development without a central concern for context.

A second focus of the book has been on the pathways to developmental outcomes. The consequences of shifts in the wider social contexts that surround children, families and communities have been demonstrated in examples related to Australian policies and practices for families, child care, school, ethnic and Indigenous minorities, gender, and state care. These examples show the consequences that flow from contexts, including those close to children's everyday lives and those that are more distant.

A third, and related, focus has been on the importance of time, or the extent to which people and contexts change, both in the short term and over the longer sweep of historical time. Ours is an era of considerable change and, to some extent, all of the chapters have explored the impact of social change on children, families and communities. Again, the consequences that have been explored highlight the ways in which people and contexts mutually influence one another. Change of one element (person or context) tends to change the other, to a varying degree. As argued in the first chapter, contexts also vary according to whether their impact is direct (via processes of direct interaction) or indirect (through consequences that flow from changes at the level of government or society to communities or families, and then having an impact on children).

Direct and indirect influences function to increase or constrain opportunity for children and families, and in this way alter the developmental consequences for all family members. Contexts can be differentiated to the degree that they provide protective factors that reduce the impact of negative influences on children's development. Contexts can also be categorised in terms of the extent to which they operate to increase or reduce children's resilience. Abusive, neglectful or substance-abusing parents can, for example, dramatically elevate the risks to their children, as can some social policies and practices that, for example, remove children from their families or place them in detention centres. By contrast, policies that support families and strengthen their communities may act in a protective way even in settings of multiple risk by increasing the resilience of families and children. It may be difficult to determine in individual instances which children will be affected adversely by negative factors in their lives although we know that the greater the number of risk factors in a child's life, the greater the chances of negative developmental consequences.[1] Some children due to their own personal characteristics or protective aspects in the relationships that surround them will be remarkably resilient, while others will show vulnerability when confronted by similar disadvantage or challenges. For children and families, the balance between the challenges facing them and the resources they have to meet those challenges is the key concept when considering effective ways to provide support or timely intervention.

Impetus for change in Australia

As we have seen in previous chapters, there is a need in both policy and practice to consider how Australian society might best support its children. This need is additionally evident in the light of advances in child development research and recent changes in Australian society that have affected the well-being of children. The current renewed focus on the importance of the early years of human development stems from wider public awareness of research on brain development.[2] New ways of imaging the brain have allowed researchers to document changes in the connections between neurons that relate directly to the amount and type of stimulation experienced by infants. An infant who experiences responsive interaction with others develops a more complex set of connections in the brain than an infant who receives little stimulation or who is subject to abuse.[3] In addition, the first two years of life are a period of rapid brain development, with later childhood development more concerned with shedding and ordering the brain cells developed over the first two years of life.[4]

Research has shown that an infant who is chronically abused develops habits of fearful response that can be seen in physical form in the brain and fails to set up other neural connections in a period of the most rapid brain development in the life-span. When this happens, the brain is wired to respond to the environment in a way that may be maladaptive later in life,[5] although there is potential to recover cognitively from even severe early deprivation as has been found in a study of Romanian orphans adopted in the United Kingdom.[6] Although recovery is possible at any time in the life-span, the research on early positive and adverse effects of experience on the neural structure of the brain does highlight the importance of the early years of life in establishing a good foundation for children's later development.

The health and well-being of children in Australian society is another factor in the need for change. In their book, Keating and Hertzman highlighted 'modernity's paradox'.[7] In modern society we are confronted with a puzzling paradox. Market-based economies have generated enormous wealth but at the same time there is a growing perception of substantial threats to the health and well-being of children.

Australia, regrettably, reflects this paradox. For children in Australia, these threats include increases in the rates of health problems, including obesity, as well as unacceptable rates of child abuse and neglect, and youth suicide.[8] There is accumulating evidence of threats to the contexts in which children are growing up, with signs of growing disadvantage, social exclusion and vulnerability in some communities[9] and their accompanying implications for the cost of public services.[10] A major demographic change in Australia has been a rise in the proportion of children in one-parent families, most of which are headed by mothers. One-parent families are more likely to be in the bottom quartiles of income, again placing children in these families at increased risk of a range of developmental problems. The patterns are complex, however, with many individuals protected if their family is well functioning and community supports are available.

The extent of perturbation of relationships is clear in the data on divorce and remarriage. Marriage breakdown is another distressing reality of family life in Australia. The Australian Bureau of Statistics[11] estimates that, at current rates, 46 per cent of marriages will end in divorce. In 2001 divorce affected the lives of 1 per cent of children, or 53,000 young Australians. Second marriages are at higher risk of breakdown, with 54 per cent of women who remarry divorcing again. The figures for men are even higher, with 65 per cent subsequently divorcing. Of remarriages, 37 per cent will dissolve after ten years. The pattern these data reveal is of many children living in circumstances that make formation of stable relationships and the skills to sustain them problematic.

The complex and at times rapid succession of relationships experienced by many children clearly contributes to their risk of later behavioural adjustment and relationship disorders. In Australia, approximately one in four children under the age of eighteen has a parent who lives elsewhere.[12] Thirty per cent of Australian children are involved in one-parent, step- or blended families. Behavioural problems are more common in children living in such circumstances, particularly for boys.[13]

Irrespective of 'social address', however, separation and divorce increase the risk of behavioural and relationship problems. Although the data show that behaviour problems are often present prior to the separation, boys are particularly at risk for subsequent behaviour problems around the time that their father leaves the household on separation or divorce.[14] The effects of separation and divorce are clearly long term as reflected in the consistent findings of increased relationship and marriage problems and higher risk of separation and divorce for children who have themselves experienced the breakdown of their parents' relationship.[15]

The key variable influencing outcomes for children seems to be family functioning. Type of family seems less important than the extent to which the family functions well and provides models of social and behavioural adjustment. Using data from Canada's National Longitudinal Survey of Children and Youth, Racine and Boyle[16] found that behavioural and social adjustment problems were related to poor family functioning and became more pronounced over time. Children in dysfunctional families were on the average 40 per cent more likely to display such problems than those living in well-functioning families. They were also significantly more likely to show physical aggression and emotionally abusive behaviour. The effects were particularly marked during adolescence.

Living in a one-parent family increased the likelihood of behaviour problems, particularly if the mother showed depression. Racine and Boyle found that single parents were twice as likely to be depressed as those in married or de facto relationships. Children were twice as likely to show behaviour problems if their mother was depressed, and again, family functioning emerged as the major determining variable.[17]

Given the current rates of separation, divorce and remarriage, the extent of disturbance of family relationships in Australia is quite alarming. Children in one-parent, step- or blended families are also at risk of abuse and neglect.[18] Abuse is likely to be a significant predictor of mental illness risk and relationship difficulties.[19] Mental health problems also show a disturbing prevalence in the Australian community. Sawyer estimates that 14 per cent of all children aged from four to sixteen, or 522,000 children, have a mental health problem.[20] Again, mental health problems are likely to be strongly related to difficulties in forming secure attachments and stable relationships.

Consequences

Modifying contexts to strengthen children, families and communities

In response to the need to improve children's well-being in Australian society, a range of possible approaches is possible. The ecological approach described here highlights the importance of the modification of contexts as a means of increasing resilience and enhancing the development of children. The value of interventions to strengthen families and communities and enhance the contexts of children's development has been demonstrated particularly when they have focused on children and families who are socially excluded as a result of their personal or contextual characteristics, such as disability or low socio-economic status.[21] The provision of high-quality child care, for example, is gaining increasing attention as a way to avert developmental risks and build resilience through strong relationships and education.[22]

Intervention programs

Intervention programs are often referred to as 'early intervention' and there is evidence that programs targeted at the early years are important and effective.[23] It is important, however, to remember that intervention can be successful at other ages and all is not lost if children experience a disadvantaged start to life. 'Early intervention' needs to be used in a wider sense to refer to intervention early in pathways. Life trajectories are never straight lines set at birth. Circumstances and choices can change a pathway at any time during the life course. If young people have 'got in with the wrong crowd', for example, intervention is far more likely to be effective if it is attempted early rather than later in the pathway to crime. Recent research has suggested that trajectories of antisocial behaviour can be of several kinds, some of which may be more easily diverted than others.[24]

Approaches to intervention

There have been a number of different child and family support programs in Australia developed since the 1990s.[25] In the USA, family support programs have been operating over a considerable period of time, many since the 1970s. Over that time, the focus of programs has changed from programs that targeted disadvantaged individuals (children or teenage parents, for example) to programs that take a more ecological approach, seeking to change family and other contexts for children, particularly in their pre-school years.[26] More recent programs in Australia have sought to encourage community change to support children and families living in those communities.[27] A final broader level of intervention is through policy at the societal level, an issue explored later in the chapter. First, several examples of programs are presented from the USA and Canada to illustrate different approaches to intervention and their impact, based on research and evaluation of those projects.

Child or parent-focused programs

An example of a primarily child-centred approach to intervention is the High/Scope Perry Preschool Project.[28] The program itself took place over five years during the 1960s and participants have been followed into adulthood. Participants were pre-school-aged African-American children living in poverty and at risk of school failure. The central intervention was high-quality pre-school education for the children. Parents were supported to become partners in their children's education but were not the focus of the intervention.

This is a program often cited for the educational and social benefits for the children involved, and for the cost-effectiveness of high-quality early childhood education in helping to prevent the later educational and social costs associated with such high-risk groups. The program concluded that US$1 spent on high-quality early childhood education saves US$7 in later costs to the educational, welfare and criminal justice systems. As Brooks-Gunn[29] and Farran[30] point out, however, these programs are not magic and do not inoculate children for life. In this program and others, children failed to maintain their early gains, due in part, Farran argues, to a lack of follow-up in the school system.

The New Chance project targeted another disadvantaged group in the USA: teenage mothers who had dropped out of high school. In this program, the focus was on the young mothers rather than directly on their children, with services aimed at not only helping mothers to parent their infants and plan future pregnancies but also to give them the life and vocational skills to help them provide financially for the children. The extensive adult educational component of the project was conducted in a centre, and child care was provided. Outcomes for children and mothers in the program were disappointing.[31]

Much of the argument for the effectiveness of home visiting for improving outcomes for young children and parents comes from the careful, medically oriented research conducted by Olds and colleagues in the Elmira and the later Memphis home visiting projects.[32] In both sites, the aim of the project was to prevent a range of health and developmental problems in children from disadvantaged families by providing an intervention for new mothers based on regular home visits by trained nurses that began during pregnancy and continued over two years. The Elmira project targeted teenage parents who were poor or unmarried in Elmira, New York. Medical care and parenting were the focus of the visits and outcomes for the mothers were the focus of evaluations. The encouraging results of the project were largely replicated in the Memphis Home Visitation Program in a sample of African-American low-income, low-education, unmarried and unemployed women who were having their first child.

Two-generation programs

The federal government in the USA has implemented several nationwide intervention programs to assist disadvantaged families with young children. The most established and well-researched federal program is Head Start.[33] Head Start began in 1965 as a one-year child development program targeting disadvantaged children of pre-school age. Most Head Start programs involve a centre-based half-day program for children aged four. The program offers a comprehensive approach to child development, involving parents in training, education and oversight, and providing medical services and nutrition.

A more recent program initiative, Early Head Start,[34] was introduced in 1995 as a program offering services to low-income families with children aged zero to three in all states of the USA. Goals of the program include support of child development in a safe and developmentally enriched environment, as well as support for parents through a comprehensive and integrated array of services delivered by trained and paid staff. Community involvement in mobilising resources for families with young children is also emphasised in the program goals. Reflecting the age of the children in Early Head Start programs, services tend to be home-based rather than centre-based and include home visiting.

Head Start and Early Head Start, are good examples of two-generation programs that help parents attain economic self-sufficiency through education and job training and assist the parents and children through parenting education and services such as early childhood education, health services and high-quality child care that promotes the children's development.[35] In her review of research on the effectiveness of intervention programs for children and families, Brooks-Gunn[36] included the two-generation approach as one of three features needed for effective programs. The other two features were high quality and comprehensiveness (involving services from a range of agencies such as health, education and housing).

Interventions that focus on people and contexts

The Montreal Prevention Project,[37] is an example of a program that sought to modify the behaviour of boys identified by their teachers as disruptive by intervening directly with the children and indirectly by modifying their contexts at home and at school. The program emphasised the development of self-control strategies, and social skills training was provided for parents and teachers in techniques of facilitating the boys' social development, monitoring their behaviour and using effective discipline techniques. When the boys were twelve years of age, those who had been in the program showed higher achievement at school and less antisocial behaviour than a control group.

A program that is similar in its educational emphasis to the High/Scope Perry Preschool Project but which provided more extensive modification of the school context is the Chicago Child-Parent Centers.[38] This project has placed a much greater emphasis on parent involvement in the children's education (parents spend half a day per week assisting at the centres). The centres in this continuing program are part of the school system in Chicago and offer high-quality half-day pre-school programs and enriched education up to grades 3 and 4 for children from the most disadvantaged areas of the city. The program also offers nutritional and health services, including two meals a day for the children in addition to parent education. The success of this program compared with pre-school programs of a similar kind, can be attributed in part to the follow-up services that have continued to support children and families into the school years.[39]

Outcomes of intervention programs

Benefits for children of these programs have been found in a number of areas. Cognitive development has attracted the most interest from researchers, particularly in earlier studies such as the many investigations on the effects of Head Start that focused on IQ gains.[40] Most evaluations show gains in cognitive development for children who have participated in these programs when they are compared with children with the same background who did not participate. Often, however, the gains have not persisted beyond the first few years of school unless the children have had access to a continuing program such as the Chicago Child–Parent Centers program, which effectively changes the school context, making it more likely that gains made by program children in the preschool phase of the project will be maintained. In addition, a consistent finding is that programs do not appear to lift the children beyond fairly low levels of achievement, reflecting their disadvantaged backgrounds.

Many United States family support programs have been specifically concerned with preparing children better for school and have measured benefits for children in a range of outcomes beyond IQ. In a review of selected United States programs, Bowes found that levels of achievement in basic skills before and after school entry have shown mixed results. Some studies showed gains for program children while others have shown no differences between program children and a comparison group. A consistent picture has emerged, however, for other aspects of children's school experience. Many studies have shown that program children had less absenteeism from school, were less likely to repeat a grade or to be placed in a special education class, and were less likely to drop out before completing high school. At school, they were less likely to have problem behaviour.[41]

A major benefit of intervention programs, found in several studies, is a lowered incidence of abuse, neglect and use of physical punishment with children. Children whose families had participated in an intervention program were likely to have fewer accidents requiring hospitalisation and to have better health care including more health screenings and a greater likelihood of immunisation and other preventive health care. They were likely to benefit from more stimulation at home and more interest and involvement from their parents in education and schooling.[42]

While cognitive gains may not persist beyond the early years of school, longitudinal studies show long-term social outcomes for children including higher rates of employment and less criminal behaviour in adulthood.[43] The cost savings to society in major services such as welfare, education and the criminal justice system are clear.[44] These prevention programs in the early years of a child's life do appear to have immediate and long-term benefits for children, particularly the disadvantaged children who are generally the target of these programs.

Limitations of intervention programs

In the design of intervention programs and their evaluation, there has been a surprising lack of attention to the social support links of parents and ways to build social networks that will sustain families over the long term. Too often, it seems, families are seen as isolated units without ties to extended family or to friends. Child rearing without support from others as well as a lack of involvement of outsiders who are in a position to observe what is happening in a family, isolates many families and this isolation can raise the likelihood of abuse. Assisting the development or strengthening of social networks involving parents would seem to be an important activity for programs to achieve their aims. Social support can be built through holding group meetings or activities for parents and young children, or through setting up support groups such as 'mothers' groups', which have been shown to provide long-lasting supportive social networks for mothers and their families.[45] Attracting the participation of some isolated families is a particular challenge for many programs.

As Bronfenbrenner's ecological model suggests, aspects of parents' lives beyond the family can impinge on their ability to parent effectively. There is a large body of research that investigates how parents in the paid workforce reconcile the demands of work and home, and how this can have an impact on their parenting.[46] Little account has been taken of this research in the design or evaluation of support programs for parents who are also in the paid workforce.

Paid work is not the only external demand on parents. Other aspects of parents' lives such as substance abuse or care for elderly relatives need to be considered in order to have a total picture of how an external program can change parenting practices. These considerations of the total context of parents' lives are no doubt part of the day-to-day operations of a program. Sensitive program coordinators or home visitors make themselves aware of the total picture in order to tailor services appropriately for parents and children. What is missing is measurement of these additional contextual factors in the evaluative research on the programs beyond demographic details of employment or income levels.

There are limits to the effectiveness of family support programs. Some program evaluators have made the point in their reports that no matter how good programs are, they cannot counteract the effects of poverty on families.[47] The total life circumstances of families and the stresses flowing from those circumstances will often override the efforts of the best-intentioned parenting programs. Parenting programs are often designed to help parents work within existing constraints by focusing on parent–child interaction and parenting skills rather than dealing with the contexts that impose those constraints.

Changing life circumstances through education and employment training, however, has been a focus of several programs. Other projects such as the New Hope Project in Wisconsin, USA,[48] have attempted to affect the general circumstances of families through direct financial payments. The aim of the project was to raise the family income of full-time workers above the poverty level and also provide health insurance and child care subsidies. Targeting the environment of poor families rather than trying to 'improve parents' had a more positive impact for children, particularly boys, than more narrowly targeted programs. In Australia, Medicare and child care benefits are schemes that similarly alter the financial contexts in which families raise their children. Wider social policies such as these ultimately have the greatest effect on parenting.

A clear demonstration of the widespread benefits of national change in context is provided in the case of Sweden. In legislative changes such as their law to prevent physical punishment of children, social provisions such as universal free health and dental care for children, and generous leave provisions and other benefits for parents, Sweden has invested in the future through its commitment to children's right to a safe, non-violent and health-promoting environment. As a result, Sweden has a very low rate of child deaths through abuse and neglect and a low health budget. At a national level, Sweden demonstrates the value of preventive approaches.[49]

The evidence suggests that modifying social contexts is the most cost-effective means of increasing resilience and enhancing the development of our children, families and communities. Interventions that focus on children, families and communities, with an emphasis on enhancing parenting skills and strengthening family–community links can have significant and enduring benefits.

The interconnectedness of contexts and consequences

The consequences for those children, families and communities that are at risk do not occur in isolation. The model developed in this book highlights the interconnectedness of contexts and consequences. Within any society, changes in relative affluence, demography, social structures, community resources or government policies have implications for the society as a whole. Despite the rhetoric of improved quality of life for children, strengthening of their families and renewal of their communities, recent census and demographic data reveal a different reality in Australia.[50] For too many children, families and communities, these data paint a picture of poverty, diminished resources to cope in the face of increased risks, and limited social cohesion. This chapter has already highlighted changes in family structure, particularly the dramatic growth in one-parent families in Australia, and the effects on children of parental separation and divorce. Other trends also have implications for the nation as it enters the third millennium. The declining fertility rate is perhaps the most marked of the changes that have occurred.[51] For example, from the 1860s to 1996, the fertility rate dropped from six children per female to under two per female. The trend has been steady, apart from the rapid decline around the years of the Great Depression and the steep rise in the post-war 'baby boom'.[52] In the last two decades the decline has again accelerated. The recent decline in fertility has been explained in economic terms as a result of the increased cost of time for parenting and the reduced financial return from children over an increasingly longer period of dependence, given that children are living with their parents for longer than in previous generations. At the same time, and linked with the decline in fertility rate, family formation is increasingly delayed.[53]

Both female and male life expectancy have also increased considerably over the last hundred years. Of greater concern, however, is the marked bulge in the distribution of the population by age as the 'baby boomer' generation gets older.[54] The increasingly smaller proportion of young people in the Australian population will carry responsibility in their adult years for the health and aged care of the predominantly older citizens of the nation. Accordingly, the health and well-being of the current generation of children is all the more crucial in economic and social terms for the future of Australian society. At the same time, however, there is some sign of a lack of sympathy for families and children in Australian society. A letter to the *Sydney Morning Herald* in 2003,[55] for example, that opposed tax spending on child care and referred to having children as a 'lifestyle choice', voiced a disturbingly common attitude in Australia today. There seems to be a growing divide between families with and without children, and children are often regarded as a burden in public discourse rather than as an asset to society.

The trends in population and disadvantage converge when one considers the nation's children. Birth rates differ considerably by social class. In the least advantaged suburbs of the capital cities the birth rates are double those in the most affluent.[56] However, the average interval between generations for the most affluent is also almost double that for the least affluent (approximately twenty-nine years versus sixteen years). These figures highlight the link between disadvantage and birth rates, but disadvantage also influences the rates of infant mortality and morbidity (the occurrence of health and developmental problems). The numerous risk factors that lead to problems in childhood tend to be related, though not exclusively, to social class. The interplay of child, family and community factors is also seen in the areas of abuse and neglect, school failure and criminality, among others. These areas of social concern reflect similar sets of risk factors related to poverty, limited parental education, family problems, unemployment, and lack of connectedness to community. The impact on the health and well-being of children in disadvantaged communities is widespread.

A considerable body of evidence is accumulating on a phenomenon called the 'social gradient'.[57] The term refers to the linear increase, or decrease, in some aspect of development, health or well-being in direct relation to social status. The measures of social status may include education, income or occupation, among others. Keating and Hertzman provide compelling evidence of such gradients in many aspects of development, health and well-being. Among these they include data on the pre- and perinatal status of infants, child health, cognitive development, behavioural development, academic performance including literacy and numeracy outcomes, criminality and outcomes in adult life.[58]

As social status increases, outcomes across that range of areas of development, health and well-being are higher. These are of course population measures and there will be individual variation in outcomes with any social status group. The message is clear, however, that social status is a powerful indicator of outcomes, both within a development period and across life.

Of greater interest, however, are the cross-national comparisons that have been undertaken analysing gradients from a range of countries as well as exploring gradients from areas within a country. Here the overwhelming message is that the flatter the gradient, the less the difference between social groups, the higher the personal, social and economic capital of a society, and the lower the social problems.[59]

Starkly, socially differentiated nations, while having some high achievers, will adversely influence the life chances of those who are socially disadvantaged to an extent that has impacts on the overall development, health and well-being of the entire population.

The solution to the current problems will require commitment to prevention and a willingness to invest in preventive services such as child care, education and community development. Such services have been found to be the most cost-effective ways of reducing social and developmental risk and preventing their negative consequences, such as crime, educational underachievement and problems of health and well-being.[60]

It is vital to acknowledge the complexity of these issues and the need for community involvement in solutions. This entails rejection of simplistic solutions. Complex social issues cannot be dealt with merely by interventions with children or by strengthening families. As has been argued in this book, the evidence is that intervention and policy will need to be focused on all three elements: children, families and communities.

Student exercises

1   Thinking about the issues in your local community for children and families, what are the factors that would need to be considered in the design of an intervention program aimed at reducing the incidence of nominated problems? Some questions that you might consider are:

- How could a strength-based approach be used in planning the approach to intervention?
- What features would the program need to have to strengthen the children concerned, their families and the local community?
- Would the program be universal or targeted at particular groups?

2   What are the future implications for children, families and communities in Australia of a continuing decline in the fertility rate? In particular, how will parenting be affected by the resulting demographic shift to a society with a higher proportion of elderly people and a lower proportion of children? What are the implications for social policy?

Notes

1   Rutter, M., 'Resilience Reconsidered: Conceptual Considerations, Empirical Findings, and Policy Considerations', in *Handbook of Early Childhood Intervention* (2nd edn), eds, J.P. Shonkoff & S.J. Meisels, Cambridge University Press, Cambridge, 2000, pp. 651–82.

2   A report developed for the Ontario government and disseminated and discussed widely has been instrumental in this awareness: M. McCain & J.F. Mustard, *Reversing the Real Brain Drain: Early Years Study: Final Report*, 1999, <http://www.childsoc.gove.on.ca>, accessed 2 March 1999.

3   R. Shore, *Rethinking the Brain: New Insights into Early Development*, Families and Work Institute, New York, 1997; J.P. Shonkoff & D.A. Phillips, *From Neurons to Neighbourhoods: The Science of Early Childhood Development*, National Academy Press, Washington, 2000.

4   D.C. Farran, 'Another Decade of Intervention for Children who are Low Income or Disabled: What do we Know Now?', in *Handbook of Early Childhood Intervention* (2nd edn), eds, J.P. Shonkoff & S.J. Meisels, 2000, pp. 510–48.

5   Shore, 1997; Shonkoff & Phillips, 2000.

6   Rutter, 2000; T.G. O'Connor, M. Rutter, C. Beckett, L. Keaveney, J.M. Kreppner & the English and Romanian Adoptees Study Team, 'The Effects of Global Severe Privation on Cognitive Competence: Extension and Longitudinal Follow-up', *Child Development*, 71, 2000, pp. 376–90.

7   D.P. Keating & C. Hertzman, *Developmental Health and the Wealth of Nations*, The Guilford Press, New York, 1999, p. 1.

8   Australian Government Task Force on Child Development, Health and Wellbeing, *Towards the Development of a National Agenda for Early Childhood: Consultation Paper*, Commonwealth of Australia, Canberra, 2003.

9   Australian Bureau of Statistics, *Australian Social Trends 2003*, catalogue no. 4102.0, Australian Government Publishing Service, Canberra, 2003a.

10 S. Scott, M. Knapp, J. Henderson & B. Maughan, 'Financial Cost of Social Exclusion: Follow Up Study of Antisocial Children into Adulthood', *British Medical Journal*, 323, 2001, pp. 1–5.

11 Australian Bureau of Statistics, *Marriages and Divorces*, catalogue no. 3310.0, Australian Government Publishing Service, Canberra, 2002c.

12 J. Pryer & B. Rodgers, *Children in Changing Families: Life After Parental Separation*, Academy of the Social Sciences in Australia, 2002.

13   Y. Racine & M.H. Boyle, 'Family Functioning and Children's Behaviour Problems', in *Vulnerable Children*, ed, J.D. Willms, University of Alberta Press, Alberta, 2002, pp. 199–209.

14   Australian Bureau of Statistics, 2002c.

15   Australian Bureau of Statistics, 2002c.

16   Racine & Boyle, 2003.

17   Racine & Boyle, 2003.

18   D. Bennett & L. Rowe, *What to Do When Your Children Turn into Teenagers*, Doubleday, Sydney, 2003.

19   Bennett & Rowe, 2003.

20   M. Sawyer, 'Child and Adolescent Mental Health Issues: Future Directions', in *Investing in Our Children: Developing a Research Agenda*, ed, M. Prior, Academy of the Social Sciences in Australia, Canberra, 2002, pp. 83–94.

21   J. Brooks-Gunn, 'Do You Believe in Magic?' What We Can Expect from Early Childhood Intervention Programs', *Social Policy Report of the Society for Research in Child Development*, 17, 2003, pp. 3–14.

22   K. McCartney, 'The Family–Child Care Mesosystem', paper presented at the Johann Jacobs Foundation Workshop on Families and Development, Zurich, October 2003.

23   J. Bowes, 'Parents' Response to Parent Education and Support Programs', *Newsletter of the National Child Protection Clearinghouse*, 8, 2001, pp. 12–21; L. Sherrod, 'The Role of Psychological Research in Setting a Policy Agenda for Children and Families', in A. Higgins-D'Alesssandro & K.R.B. Jankowski, eds, *Science for Society: Informing Policy and Practice Through Research in Developmental Psychology, New Directions for Child and Adolescent Development*, no. 98, pp. 85–94, 2002; McCain & Mustard, 1999.

24   National Crime Prevention, *Pathways to Prevention: Developmental and Early Intervention Approaches to Crime in Australia*, Barton, ACT, National Crime Prevention, Attorney General's Department, 1999; J.J. Goodnow, 'Contexts, Diversity, Pathways: Linking and Extending', in *Hills of Gold: Rethinking Diversity and Contexts as Resources for Children's Developmental Pathways*, eds, C.R. Cooper, G. Coll, T. Bartko, H. Davis & C. Chatman, Lawrence Erlbaum, Mahwah, NJ, in press; D.S. Shaw, M. Gilliom, E.M. Ingoldsby & D.S. Nagus, 'Trajectories Heading to School-age Conduct Problems', *Developmental Psychology*, 39, 2003, pp. 189–200.

25   Examples of Australian programs can be found in K. Rigby, 'Psychosocial Functioning in Families of Australian Adolescent School Children Involved in Bully/Victim Problems', *Journal of Family Therapy*, 16, 1994, pp. 173–87; M.R. Sanders & C. Markie-Dadds, 'Triple P: A Multilevel Family Intervention Program for Children with Disruptive Behavior Disorders', in *Early Intervention and Prevention: Mental Health Applications of Clinical Psychology*, eds, P. Cotton & H. Jackson, Australian Psychological Society, Melbourne, 1996, pp. 59–85; G. Vimpani, M. Frederico & L. Barclay, *An Audit of Home Visitor Programs and the Development of an Evaluation Framework*, Report commissioned under the auspices of the National Child Protection Council by the Department of Health and Family Services, 1996; Australian National Crime Prevention National Anti-crime Strategy (Australia), 1999.

26   Farran, 2000.

27   An example is Clarenden Vale Connect in Tasmania where a facilitator worked in a disadvantaged community to build social capital in the community. This resulted in considerable benefits for children, families and the whole community. B. Wellesley, 'Connecting with Good Beginnings', *Every Child*, 8, 2002, pp. 10–11,

28   D.P. Weikart & L.J. Schweinhart, 'High/Scope Preschool Program Outcomes', in *Preventing Antisocial Behavior: Interventions from Birth through Adolescence*, eds, J. McCord &

R.E. Tremblay, The Guilford Press, New York, 1992, pp. 67–88; L.J. Schweinhart, H.V. Barnes & D.P. Weikart, *Significant Benefits: The High/Scope Perry Preschool Study through Age 27*, High/Scope Press, Ypsilant, MI, 1993.

29   Brooks-Gunn, 2003.

30   Farran, 2000.

31   See J. Bowes, *Parents' Response to Parent Education and Support Programs: A Review of Selected Programs in the USA*, Report to the Creswick Foundation, Macquarie University, unpublished report, 2000, for an account of this program and other family support programs in the USA.

32   H. Kitzman, D.L. Olds, C.R. Henderson, R. Tatelbaum, K.M. McConnochie, K. Sidora, D.W. Luckey, D. Shaver, K. Engelhardt, D. James & K. Barnard, 'Effect of Prenatal and Infancy Home Visitation by Nurses on Pregnancy Outcomes, Childhood Injuries, and Repeated Childbearing', *Journal of the American Medical Association*, 278, 1997, pp. 644–52; D.L. Olds, J. Eckenrode, C.R. Henderson, H. Kitzman, J. Powers, R. Cole, K. Sidora, P. Morris, L.M. Petitt & D. Luckey, 'Long-term Effects of Home Visitation on Maternal Life Course and Child Abuse and Neglect', *Journal of the American Medical Association*, 278, 1997, pp. 637–43.

33   E. Zigler & N. Hall, *Child Development and Social Policy*, McGraw-Hill, New York, 2000; E. Zigler & S.J. Styfco, 'Using Research and Theory to Justify and Inform Head Start Expansion', *Social Policy Report*, vol. vii, no. 2, Society for Research in Child Development, Washington, 1993.

34   Mathematica Policy Research Inc., 'Making a Difference in the Lives of Infants and Toddlers and Their Families: The Impacts of Early Head Start', 2002, <http://www.acf.dhhs.gov/programs/core/ongoing/research/ehs>, accessed 24 July 2003.

35   Institute for Research on Poverty, 'Two Generation Programs: A Roadmap to National Evaluations', *Focus*, 19, 1997, pp. 28–33; S. Smith, 'Two Generation Programs: A New Intervention Strategy and Directions for Future Research', in *Escape from Poverty: What Makes a Difference for Children?*, P.L. Chase-Lansdale & J. Brooks-Gunn, Cambridge University Press, Cambridge, 1995, pp. 299–314.

36   Brooks-Gunn, 2003.

37   R.E. Tremblay, L. Pagani-Kurtz, L.C. Masse, F. Vitaro & R.O. Pihl, 'A Bimodal Preventive Intervention for Disruptive Kindergarten Boys: Its Impact Through Mid-adolescence', *Journal of Consulting and Clinical Psychology*, 63, 4, 1995, pp. 560–8.

38   A. Reynolds & J. Temple, 'Extended Early Childhood Intervention and School Achievement: Age Thirteen Findings from the Chicago Longitudinal Study', *Child Development*, 69, 1998, pp. 231–46. See also Farran, 2000.

39   Farran, 2000; Sherrod, 2002.

40   J. Brooks-Gunn, 'Strategies for Altering the Outcomes of Poor Children and Their Families', in *Escape from Poverty: What Makes a Difference for Children?*, P.L. Chase-Lansdale & J. Brooks-Gunn, Cambridge University Press, Cambridge, 1995, pp. 153–202.

41   Bowes, 2000; Farran, 2000.

42   Bowes, 2000; Family Resource Coalition, *Family Support Programs and the Prevention of Child Abuse*, Family Resource Coalition, Chicago, IL, 1995.

43   Farran, 2000; M. Tomison, 'Preventing Child Abuse: Changes to Family Support in the 21st Century', *National Child Protection Clearinghouse Issues Paper*, no. 17, Australian Institute of Family Studies, Melbourne, 2002.

44   For an estimate of costs of antisocial behaviour in the United Kingdom, see S. Scott et al., 2001.

45   D. Scott, S. Brady, P. Glynn, 'New Mothers Groups as a Social Network Intervention: Consumer and Maternal Child Health Nurse Perspectives', *Australian Journal of Advanced Nursing*, 18, 4, 2001, pp. 23–9.

46   J. Bowes, 'Recommendations for Future Research: A Family Researcher's Perspective', in *International Research on Work and Family*, ed, S.A.Y. Poelman, Lawrence Erlbaum, Mahwah, NJ, 2003; A.C. Crouter, 'Mothers and Fathers at Work: Implications for Families and Children', paper presented at the Johann Jacobs Workshop on Families and Development, Zurich, October 2003.

47   Brooks-Gunn, 2003; J.C. Quint, J.M. Bos & D.F. Polit, *New Chance: Final Report on a Comprehensive Program for Young Mothers in Poverty and Their Children*, Manpower Demonstration Research Corporation, <http://www.mdrc.psiweb.com/Reports/>, accessed 21 March 2000.

48   C. Huston, 'From Research to Policy: Choosing Questions and Interpreting the Answers', in *Science for Society: Informing Policy and Practice Through Research in Developmental Psychology, New Directions for Child and Adolescent Development*, no. 98, eds, A. Higgins-D'Alesssandro & K.R.B. Jankowski, 2002, pp. 29–41, 2002; Sherrod, 2002.

49   J.E. Durrant, 'Trends in Youth Crime and Well-being Since the Abolition of Corporal Punishment in Sweden', *Youth and Society*, 31, 4, 2000, pp. 437–55; J.E. Durrant & G.M. Olsen, 'Parenting and Public Policy: Contextualising the Swedish Corporal Punishment Ban', *Journal of Social Welfare and Family Law*, 19, 4, 1997, pp. 443–61; UNICEF, *Official Summary: The State of the World's Children*, UNICEF, New York, 2003.

50   Australian Bureau of Statistics, 2003a.

51   P. McDonald, 'Low Fertility in Australia: Evidence, Causes and Policy Responses', *People and Place*, 8, 2000, pp. 6–21,

52   M. Bittman & J. Pixley, *The Double Life of the Family: Myth, Hope and Experience*, Allen & Unwin, Sydney, 1997.

53   D. de Vaus, 'Understanding Family Change', *Family Matters*, 62, 2002, pp. 52–5.

54   Bittman & Pixley, 1997.

55   *Sydney Morning Herald*, 13 November 2003, p. 12.

56   P. Boss, S. Edwards & S. Pitman, *Profile of Young Australians: Facts, Figures and Issues*, Churchill Livingstone, Melbourne, 1995.

57   G. Jack, 'Ecological Influences on Parenting and Child Development', *British Journal of Social Work*, 30, 2000, pp. 703–20; Keating & Hertzman, 1999; E. Sloat & J.D. Willms, 'A Gradient Approach to the Study of Childhood Vulnerability', in *Vulnerable Children*, ed, J.D. Willms, University of Alberta Press, Alberta, 2002, pp. 23–44.

58   Australian National Crime Prevention National Anti-crime Strategy (Australia), *Pathways to Prevention: Developmental and Early Intervention Approaches to Crime in Australia*, Barton, ACT, National Crime Prevention, Attorney General's Department, 1999.

59   Keating & Hertzman, 1999; Jack, 2000.

60   P.W. Greenwood, K.E. Model, C.P. Rydell & J. Chiesa, *Diverting Children From a Life of Crime: Measuring Costs and Benefits*, RAND Corporation, Santa Monica, CA, 1996.

Bibliography

Aboud, F.E., *Children and Prejudice*, Blackwell, Oxford, 1988.

Ahnert, L. & Lamb, M.E., 'Shared Care: Establishing a Balance Between Home and Child Care Settings', *Child Development*, 74, 2003, pp. 1044–9.

Ainsworth, F. & Maluccio, A.N., 'Kinship Care: False Dawn or New Hope?', *Australian Social Work*, 51, 4, 1998, pp. 3–8.

Amato, P.A., 'More than Money? Men's Contributions to their Children's Lives', in *Men in Families*, eds, A. Booth & A.C. Crouter, Lawrence Erlbaum, Mahwah, NJ, 1998, pp. 241–78.

American Psychological Society, 'Human Capital Initiative—Reducing Violence: A Research Agenda', *APS Observer Special Issue*, Report 5, 1997.

Andersson, B., 'Effects of Public Day-care: A Longitudinal Study', *Child Development*, 60, 1989, pp. 857–66.

Andersson, B., 'Effects of Day-care on Cognitive and Socioemotional Competence of Thirteen-year-old Swedish School Children', *Child Development*, 63, 1992, pp. 20–36.

Antill, J., 'Sex-role Complementarity versus Similarity in Married Couples', *Journal of Personal and Social Psychology*, 45, 1983, pp. 145–55.

Antill, J., Cotton, S. & Tindale, S., 'Egalitarian or Traditional: Correlates of the Perception of an Ideal Marriage', *Australian Journal of Psychology*, 35, 1983, pp. 245–57.

Antill, J. & Cunningham, J., 'The Relationships of Masculinity, Femininity and Androgyny to Self-esteem', *Australian Journal of Psychology*, 32, 1980, pp. 195–207.

Ashman, A. & Elkins, J., 'Learning Opportunities for All Children', in *Educating Children with Special Needs* (3rd edn), eds, A. Ashman & J. Elkins, Prentice Hall, New York, 1998, pp. 5–38.

Atkins, K. & Rollings, J., 'Informal Care in Asian and Afro/Caribbean Communities: A Literature Review', *British Journal of Social Work*, 22, 1992, pp. 405–18.

Auditor-General, *Mind the Children: The Management of Children's Services*, Audit Report no. 42, 1993–1994, Australian Government Publishing Service, Canberra, 1994.

Augustinos, M., 'Developmental Effects of Child Abuse: Recent Findings', *Child Abuse & Neglect*, 11, 1987, pp. 15–27.

Australian Bureau of Statistics, *Commercial Long Day Child Care Australia*, catalogue no. 4414.0, Australian Government Publishing Service, Canberra, 1989.

Australian Bureau of Statistics, *National Aboriginal and Torres Strait Islander Survey*, catalogue no. 4155.0, Australian Government Publishing Service, Canberra, 1994.

Australian Bureau of Statistics, *Labour Force, Australia April 1996*, catalogue no. 6203.0, Australian Government Publishing Service, Canberra, 1996.

Australian Bureau of Statistics, *Australian Women's Yearbook*, catalogue no. 4124.0, Australian Government Publishing Service, Canberra, 1997.

Australian Bureau of Statistics, *Births Australia*, catalogue no. 3301.0, Australian Government Publishing Service, Canberra, 1997.

Australian Bureau of Statistics, *Special Article: Casual Employment*, catalogue no. 6203.0, Australian Government Publishing Service, Canberra, 1999.

Australian Bureau of Statistics, *Disability, Ageing and Carers: Summary of Findings*, catalogue no. 4430.0, Australian Government Publishing Service, Canberra, 1999.

Australian Bureau of Statistics, *Australian Social Trends 2001*, catalogue no. 4102.0, Australian Government Publishing Service, Canberra, 2001a.

Australian Bureau of Statistics, *Labour Special Article: Full-time and Part-time Employment*, catalogue no. 6203.0, Australian Government Publishing Service, Canberra, 2001b.

Australian Bureau of Statistics, *Australian Social Trends 2002*, catalogue no. 4102.0, Australian Government Publishing Service, Canberra, 2002a.

Australian Bureau of Statistics, *Special Article: Marriage and Divorce in Australia*, catalogue no. 3310.0, Australian Government Publishing Service, Canberra, 2002b.

Australian Bureau of Statistics, *Marriages and Divorces, Australia*, catalogue no. 3310.0, Australian Government Publishing Service, Canberra, 2002c.

Australian Bureau of Statistics, *Australian Social Trends 2003*, catalogue no. 4102.0, Australian Government Publishing Service, Canberra, 2003a.

Australian Bureau of Statistics, *Census of Population and Housing: Selected Social and Housing Characteristics*, catalogue no. 2015.0, Australian Government Publishing Service, Canberra, 2003b.

Australian Bureau of Statistics, *Labour Force Australia (2002)*, catalogue no. 6203.0, Australian Government Publishing Service, Canberra, 2003c.

Australian Centre for Industrial Relations Research and Training, 'Child Care in a Changing Industrial Relations Environment', in *Interim Report: Commissioned Studies*, EPAC Task Force, Australian Government Publishing Service, Canberra, 1996.

Australian Government Task Force on Child Development, Health and Wellbeing, *Towards the Development of a National Agenda for Early Childhood: Consultation Paper*, Commonwealth of Australia, Canberra, 2003.

Australian Institute of Health and Welfare, *The Health and Welfare of Australia's Aboriginal and Torres Strait Islander Peoples, 2001*, AIHW, Canberra, 2001b.

Australian Institute of Health and Welfare, 'People with an Intellectual or Early Onset Disability in Australia', *Journal of Intellectual & Developmental Disability*, 28, 2003, pp. 79–83.

Australian Institute of Health and Welfare, *Adoptions Australia 2002–03*, AIHW catalogue no. CWS-21, AIHW (Child Welfare Series no. 33), Canberra 2004a.

Australian Institute of Health and Welfare, *Australia's Welfare, 2001*, AIHW, Canberra, 2001a.

Australian Institute of Health and Welfare, *Child Protection Australia, 2002–03*, AIHW catalogue no. CWS 22, AIHW (Child Welfare Series no. 34), Canberra, 2004b.

Australian Labor Party, *Platform, Constitution and Rules*, Canberra, 1973.

Australian Law Reform Commission/Human Rights and Equal Opportunity Commission, *Seen and Heard: Priority for Children in the Legal Process*, Report no. 84, 1997.

Australian National Crime Prevention National Anti-Crime Strategy (Australia), *Pathways to Prevention: Developmental and Early Intervention Approaches to Crime in Australia*, National Crime Prevention, Attorney General's Department, Barton, ACT, 1999.

Australian Parents Council, *Children's Learning: The Parent Factor*, Australian Government Publishing Service, Canberra, 1996.

Aylward, G.P., Gustafson, N., Verhulst, S.J. & Colliver, J.A., 'Consistency in the Diagnosis of Cognitive, Motor and Neurologic Function over the First Three Years', *Journal of Pediatric Psychology*, 12, 1987, pp. 77–98.

Bågenholm, A. & Gillberg, C., 'Psychosocial Effects on Siblings of Children with Autism and Mental Retardation: A Population-based Study', *Journal of Mental Deficiency Research*, 35, 1991, pp. 291–307.

Barbarin, O.A., Hughes, D. & Chesler, M.A., 'Stress, Coping and Marital Functioning among Parents of Children with Cancer', *Journal of Marriage and the Family*, 47, 1985, pp. 473–80.

Barber, J.G., Delfabbro, P.H. & Cooper, L.L., 'Placement Stability and the Psychosocial Wellbeing of Children in Foster Care', *Research on Social Work Practice*, 13, 2003, pp. 409–25.

Barnard, K.E. & Martell, L.K., 'Mothering', in *Handbook of Parenting*, ed, M.H. Bornstein, Lawrence Erlbaum, Mahwah, NJ, 1995, pp. 3–26.

Barnett, W.S., 'Long-term Effects of Early Childhood Programs on Cognitive and School Outcomes', *The Future of Children*, 5, 1995, pp. 25–50.

Baumrind, D., 'Child Care Practices Anteceding Three Patterns of Preschool Behavior', *Genetic Psychology Monographs*, 75, 1967, pp. 43–88.

Baumrind, D., 'Current Patterns of Parental Authority', *Developmental Psychology Monographs*, 4, 1, pt 2, 1971.

Beckman, P.J., 'Influence of Selected Child Characteristics on Stress in Families of Handicapped Infants', *American Journal of Mental Deficiency*, 88, 1983, pp. 150–6.

Bee, H., *The Developing Child*, Harper Collins, New York, 1992.

Bell, J., 'Assimilation in NSW', in *Aborigines Now: New Perspectives in the Study of Aboriginal Communities*, ed, M. Reay, Angus & Robertson, London, 1964.

Belsky, J., 'Child Maltreatment: An Ecological Integration', *American Psychologist*, 35, 4, 1980, pp. 320–35.

Belsky, J., 'Two Waves of Day-care Research: Developmental Effects and Conditions of Quality', in *The Child and Day-care Setting*, ed, R. Ainslie, Praeger, New York, 1984, pp. 1–34.

Belsky, J., 'Parental and Nonparental Child Care and Children's Socioemotional Development: A Decade in Review', *Journal of Marriage and the Family*, 52, 1990, pp. 885–903.

Belsky, J., 'Etiology of Child Maltreatment: A Developmental–ecological Analysis', *Psychological Bulletin*, 114, 1993, pp. 413–34.

Belsky, J., 'Developmental Risks (still) Associated with Early Child Care', *Journal of Child Psychology and Psychiatry*, 42, 2001, pp. 845–59.

Belsky, J. & Rovine, M.J., 'Nonmaternal Care in the First Year of Life and the Security of Infant–parent Attachment', *Child Development*, 59, 1988, pp. 157–67.

Belsky, J. & Steinberg, L., 'The Effects of Day Care: A Critical Review', *Child Development*, 49, 1978, pp. 929–49.

Bengston, V.L., 'Beyond the Nuclear Family: The Increasing Importance of Multigenerational Bonds', *Journal of Marriage and the Family*, 63, 2001, pp. 1–16.

Bennett, D. & Rowe, L., *What to Do When Your Children Turn Into Teenagers*, Doubleday, Sydney, 2003.

Benson, B.A., Gross, A.M., Messer, S.C., Kellum, G. & Passmore, L.A., 'Social Support Networks among Families of Children with Craniofacial Anomalies', *Health Psychology*, 10, 1991, pp. 252–8.

Berrueta-Clement, J.R., Schweinhart, L.J., Barnett, W.S., Epstein, A.S. & Weikart, D.P., 'Changed Lives: The Effects of the Perry Preschool Program on Youths through Age 19', in *Monographs of the High/Scope Educational Research Foundation*, 8, 1984.

Bigby, C. & Ozanne, E., 'Shifts in the Model of Service Delivery in Intellectual Disability in Victoria', *Journal of Intellectual & Developmental Disability*, 26, 2001, pp. 177–90.

Birenbaum, A., 'Poverty, Welfare Reform, and Disproportionate Rates of Disability Among Children', *Mental Retardation*, 40, 2002, pp. 212–18.

Birrell, B., Dibden, J. & Wainer, J., *Regional Victoria: Why the Bush is Hurting*, Centre for Population and Urban Research, Monash University, Melbourne, 2000.

Birrell, B. & Rapson, V., 'Poor Families, Poor Children: Who Cares for the Next Generation?', *People and Place*, 5, 3, 1997, pp. 44–53.

Birrell, B., Rapson, V. & Hourigan, C., 'The Origin of Home-Parent Connections in Metropolitan and Regional Australia', *Family Matters*, 62, 2002, pp. 11–17.

Birrell, R., 'Ethnic Concentrations: The Vietnamese Experience', *People and Place*, 1, 1993, pp. 26–32.

Biskup, P., *Not Slaves, Not Citizens*, University of Queensland Press, Brisbane, 1973.

Bittles, A.H., Petterson, B.A., Sullivan, S.G., Hussain, R., Glasson, E.J. & Montgomery, P.D., 'The Influence of Intellectual Disability on Life Expectancy', *Journal of Gerontology: Series A: Biological Sciences and Medical Sciences*, 57A, M470–M472, 2002.

Bittman, M., Hoffman, S. & Thompson, D., *Men's Uptake of Family Friendly Employment Provisions*, Social Policy Research Centre, University of New South Wales, Sydney, 2002.

Bittman, M. & Pixley, J., *The Double Life of the Family: Myth, Hope and Experience*, Allen & Unwin, Sydney, 1997.

Bonnes, M. & Secchaiaroli, G., *Environmental Psychology*, Sage, London, 1995.

Bornstein, M.H., 'Parenting Infants', in *Handbook of Parenting*, vol. 1, ed, M.H. Bornstein, Lawrence Erlbaum, Mahwah, NJ, 2002, pp. 3–43.

Boss, P., Edwards, S. & Pitman, S., *Profile of Young Australians: Facts, Figures and Issues*, Churchill Livingstone, Melbourne, 1995.

Bottomley, G., ed, *From Another Place: Migration and the Politics of Culture*, Cambridge University Press, Cambridge, 1992.

Bower, A. & Hayes, A., 'Mothering in Families With and Without a Child with a Disability', *International Journal of Disability, Development and Education*, 45, 1998, pp. 313–22.

Bowes, J.M., 'Parents' Response to Parent Education and Support Programs: A Review of Selected Programs in the USA', report to the Creswick Foundation, Macquarie University, unpublished report, 2000.

Bowes, J.M., 'Parents' Response to Parent Education and Support Programs', *Newsletter of the National Child Protection Clearinghouse*, 8, 2001, pp. 12–21.

Bowes, J.M, 'Recommendations for Future Research: A Family Researcher's Perspective', in *International Research on Work and Family*, ed, S.A.Y. Poelman, Lawrence Erlbaum, Mahwah, NJ, 2003.

Bowes, J.M., Chen, M-J., Li, Q.S. & Li, Y., 'Reasoning and Negotiation About Child Responsibility in Urban Chinese Families: Reports from Mothers, Fathers and Children', *International Journal of Behavioral Development*, 28, 2004, pp. 48–58.

Bowes, J.M., Flanagan, C.A. & Taylor, A.J., 'Adolescents' Ideas About Individual and Social Responsibility in Relation to Children's Household Work: Some International Comparisons', *International Journal of Behavioral Development*, 25, 2001, pp. 60–8.

Bowes, J.M. & Goodnow, J.J., 'Work for Home, School or Labor Force: The Nature and Sources of Children's Understanding', *Psychological Bulletin*, 119, 1996, pp. 300–21.

Bowes, J.M., Wise, S., Harrison, L., Sanson, A., Ungerer, J. Watson, J. & Simpson, T., 'Continuity of Care in the Early Years? Multiple and Changeable Childcare in Australia', *Family Matters*, 64, 2003, pp. 30–5.

Bowlby, J., *Maternal Care and Mental Health*, World Health Organization, London, 1951.

Bowlby, J., *Attachment and Loss*, 3 vols, Basic Books, New York, 1969–80.

Bowman, D. & Virtue, M., *Public Policy, Private Lives*, Australian Institute of Intellectual Disability, Canberra, 1993.

Brady, M., *Heavy Metal*, Aboriginal Studies Press, Canberra, 1992.

Bramston, P. & Mioche, C., 'Disability and Stress: A Study in Perspective', *Journal of Intellectual & Developmental Disability*, 26, 2001, pp. 233–42.

Brennan, D., *The Politics of Australian Child Care: From Philanthropy to Feminism*, Cambridge University Press, Cambridge, 1994.

Brennan, D. & Cass, B., 'The Communitarian Imaginery: Deconstructing the Concept of "Community" in Australia's Welfare Reform Debate', paper presented at the National Social Policy Conference, Competing Visions, University of New South Wales, Sydney, June 2003, <www.sprc.unsw.edu.au/nspc2001/index.htm>, accessed 5 June 2003.

Broberg, A.G., Wessels, H., Lamb, M.E. & Hwang, C.P., 'Effects of Child Care on the Development of Cognitive Abilities in 8-year-olds: A Longitudinal Study', *Developmental Psychology*, 33, 1997, pp. 62–9.

Bronfenbrenner, U., *The Ecology of Human Development*, Harvard University Press, Cambridge, MA, 1979.

Bronfenbrenner, U., 'Recent Advances in the Research on Human Development', in *Development as Action in Context*, eds, R.K. Silbereisen, K. Eyforth & G. Rudinger, Springer-Verlag, Heidelberg, Germany, 1986, pp. 287–9.

Bronfenbrenner, U., 'Principles for the Healthy Growth and Development of Children', in *Marriage and Family in a Changing Society*, ed, J.M. Henslin, The Free Press, New York, 1989.

Bronfenbrenner, U., 'The Biological Model from a Life Course Perspective: Reflections of a Participant Observer', in *Examining Lives in Context*, eds, P. Moen, G.H. Elder Jr & K. Lüscher, American Psychological Association, Washington, DC, 1995, pp. 599–618.

Bronfenbrenner, U., 'Developmental Ecology Through Space and Time', in *Examining Lives in Context*, eds, P. Moen, G.H. Elder Jr & K. Lüscher, American Psychological Association, Washington, DC, 1995, pp. 619–48.

Brooks-Gunn, J., 'Strategies for Altering the Outcomes of Poor Children and Their Families', in *Escape from Poverty: What Makes a Difference for Children?*, ed, P.L. Chase-Lansdale & J. Brooks-Gunn, Cambridge University Press, Cambridge, 1995, pp. 153–202.

Brooks-Gunn, J., 'Children in Families in Communities: Risk and Intervention in the Bronfenbrenner Tradition', in *Examining Lives in Context*, eds, P. Moen, G.H. Elder Jr & K. Lüscher, American Psychological Association, Washington, DC, 1995, pp. 467–519.

Brooks-Gunn, J., 'Do You Believe in Magic?' What We Can Expect from Early Childhood Intervention Programs', *Social Policy Report of the Society for Research in Child Development*, 17, 2003, pp. 3–14.

Brooks-Gunn, J., Berlin, L.J. & Fuligini, A.S., 'Early Childhood Intervention Programs: What About the Family?', in *Handbook of Early Childhood Intervention* (2nd edn), eds, J.P. Shonkoff & S.J. Meisels, Cambridge University Press, Cambridge, 2000, pp. 549–88.

Brown, B., 'Peer Groups and Peer Cultures', in *At the Threshold: The Developing Adolescent*, eds, S. Feldman & G. Elliot, Harvard University Press, Cambridge, MA, 1990, pp. 171–96.

Buchanan, J., Considine, G., Bretherton, T. & van Wanrooy, B., 'Hours of Work in Australia: Recent Trends and Challenges for Policy', in *Proceedings of the Work, Health and Families Forum*, Australian National University, Canberra, 2003, <http://www-nceph.anu.edu.au/Health_For_Life/publications>, accessed 5 May 2004.

Buchanan, J. & Thornwaite, L., *Paid Work and Parenting: Charting a New Course for Australian Families*, Report prepared for the Chifley Foundation, University of Sydney, Sydney, 2001.

Bullock, R., Little, M. & Millham, S., *Going Home: The Return of Children Separated from their Families*, Dartmouth, Aldershot, 1993.

Burns, A. & Goodnow, J.J., *Children and Families in Australia*, Allen & Unwin, Sydney, 1985.

Burns, A. & Scott, C., *Mother-headed Families and Why They have Increased*, Lawrence Erlbaum, Hillsdale, NJ, 1994.

Bush, D. & Simmons, R., 'Gender and Coping with the Entry into Early Adolescence', in *Gender and Stress*, eds, R. Barnett, L. Beiner & G. Baruch, Macmillan, New York, 1987, pp. 185–217.

Bussey, K., 'The First Socialization', in *Australian Women: New Feminist Perspectives*, eds, N. Grieve & A. Burns, Oxford University Press, Melbourne, 1986, pp. 90–104.

Bussey, K. & Bandura, A., 'Influence of Gender Constancy and Social Power on Sex-linked Modeling', *Journal of Personality and Social Psychology*, 47, 1984, pp. 1292–302.

Bussey, K. & Bandura, A., 'Self-regulatory Mechanisms Governing Gender Development', *Child Development*, 63, 1992, pp. 1236–50.

Buti, A., 'Unfinished Business: The Australian Stolen Generations', *Murdoch University Electronic Journal of Law*, 7, 4, 2000, <http://www.murdoch.edu/elaw/>, accessed 19 November 2003.

Button, S., Pianta, R.C. & Marvin, R.S., 'Partner Support and Maternal Stress in Families Raising Children with Cerebral Palsy', *Journal of Developmental and Physical Disabilities*, 13, 2001, pp. 61–81.

Byrne, E. & Cunningham, C., 'The Effects of Mentally Handicapped Children on Families—A Conceptual Review', *Journal of Child Psychology and Psychiatry*, 26, 6, 1984, pp. 847–64.

Cairns, R.B. & Cairns, B.D., 'Risks and Lifelines in Adolescence', paper presented at the Biennial Meeting of the Society for Research in Child Development, Kansas City, 1989.

Cairns, R.B. & Cairns, B.D., *Lifelines and Risks: Pathways of Youth in Our Time*, Cambridge University Press, New York, 1994.

Cairns, R.B. & Cairns, B.D., 'Social Ecology Over Time and Space', in *Examining Lives in Context*, eds, P. Moen, G.H. Elder Jr & K. Lüscher, American Psychological Association, Washington, DC, 1995, pp. 397–421.

Cant, R., *Interagency Schools Community Centres Pilot Project Evaluation Report*, Department of Education and Training: Social Systems and Evaluations, 1997.

Carr, J., 'Long-term Outcomes for People with Down's Syndrome', *Journal of Child Psychology and Psychiatry*, 35, 3, 1994, pp. 425–39.

Carrington, V., 'The Interethnic Family in 1990s Australia', paper presented at the Australian Family Research Conference, Brisbane, 1996.

Cashmore, J., 'Children: Non-contractual Persons?', in *The New Contractualism?*, eds, G. Davis, B. Sullivan & A. Yeatman, Macmillan, Melbourne, 1997.

Cashmore, J., 'What Can We Learn from the US Experience on Permanency Planning?', *Australian Journal of Family Law*, 15, 2001, pp. 215–29.

Cashmore, J., 'Facilitating the Participation of Children and Young People in Care', *Child Abuse & Neglect*, 26, 8, 2002, pp. 837–47.

Cashmore, J. & de Haas, N., *Legal and Social Aspects of the Physical Punishment of Children*, Commonwealth Department of Human Services and Health, Canberra, 1995.

Cashmore, J. & Paxman, M., *Wards Leaving Care: A Longitudinal Study*, NSW Department of Community Services, Sydney, 1996.

Cashmore, J. & Paxman, M., 'Meeting the Needs of Children in Care: How Can We Do Better? The "Attachment" Needs of Young People Leaving Care', presentation at Australian Institute of Family Studies Conference, Melbourne, February 2002.

Caughy, M.O., DiPietro, J. & Strobino, M., 'Day-care Participation as a Protective Factor in the Cognitive Development of Low-income Children', *Child Development*, 65, 1994, pp. 457–71.

Chao, R.K. & Willms, J.D., 'The Effects of Parenting Practices on Children's Outcomes', in *Vulnerable Children*, ed, J.D. Willms, University of Alberta Press, Alberta, 2002, pp. 149–65.

Chase-Lansdale, P.L. & Vinovskis, M.A., 'Whose Responsibility? An Historical Analysis of the Changing Roles of Mothers, Fathers, and Society', in *Escape from Poverty: What Makes a Difference for Children?*, eds, P.L. Chase-Lansdale & J. Brooks-Gunn, Cambridge University Press, Cambridge, 1995, pp. 11–37.

Cherkes-Julkowski, M. & Gertner, N., *Spontaneous Cognitive Processes in Handicapped Children*, Springer-Verlag, New York, 1989.

Cherlin, A.J., 'Policy Issues in Child Care', in *Escape from Poverty: What Makes a Difference for Children?*, eds, P.L. Chase-Lansdale & J. Brooks-Gunn, Cambridge University Press, Cambridge, 1995, pp. 121–37.

Chodorow, N., 'Family Structure and Feminine Personality', in *Women, Culture and Society*, eds, M. Rosaldo & L. Lamphere, Stanford University Press, Palo Alto, CA, 1974, pp. 43–66.

Cicchetti, D. & Carlson, V., eds, *Child Maltreatment: Theory and Research on the Causes and Consequences of Child Abuse and Neglect*, Cambridge University Press, New York, 1989.

Cicchetti, D., 'Child Maltreatment: Implications for Developmental Theory and Research', *Human Development*, 39, 1996, pp. 18–39.

Cicchetti, D., Toth, S.L. & Maughan, A., 'An Ecological-Transactional Model of Child Maltreatment', in *Handbook of Developmental Psychopathology* (2nd edn), eds, A.J. Sameroff & M. Lewis, Kluwer Academic Publishers, Dordrecht, Netherlands, 2000, pp. 689–722.

Clark, M., *The Great Divide: The Construction of Gender in the Primary School*, Curriculum Development Centre, Canberra, 1989.

Clarke, A.B.D. & Clarke, A.M., 'The Historical Context', in *New Approaches to Down Syndrome*, eds, B. Stratford & P. Gunn, Cassell, London, 1996, pp. 12–22.

Clarke, E. & Hanisee, J., 'Intellectual and Adaptive Performance of Asian Children in Adoptive American Settings', *Developmental Psychology*, 18, 1982, pp. 595–9.

Clark-Stewart, K.A., Gruber, C.P. & Fitzgerald, L.M., *Children at Home and in Day Care*, Lawrence Erlbaum, Hillsdale, NJ, 1994.

Coady, M.M., 'Reflections on Children's Rights', in *Citizen Child: Australian Laws and Children's Rights*, ed, K. Funder, Australian Institute of Family Studies, Melbourne, 1996.

Coates, J., *Woman Talk: Conversation Between Women Friends*, Blackwell, Oxford, 1996.

Cochran, M., 'A Comparison of Group Day Care and Family Childrearing Patterns in Sweden', *Child Development*, 48, 1977, pp. 702–7.

Cochran, M. & Gunnarsson, L., 'A Follow-up Study of Group Child Care and Family-based Childrearing Patterns', *Journal of Marriage and the Family*, 47, 1985, pp. 297–309.

Cochran, M. & Niego, S., 'Parenting and Social Networks', in *Handbook of Parenting*, ed, M.H. Bornstein, Lawrence Erlbaum, Mahwah, NJ, 1995, pp. 393–418.

Cohen, R., 'Eighty-seven and Still Going Strong', *Bernard van Leer Foundation Newsletter*, 87, October 1997.

Cole, M., 'The Supra-individual Envelope of Development: Activity and Practice, Situation and Context', in *New Directions for Child Development*, no. 67, eds, J.J. Goodnow, P.J. Miller & F. Kessel, Jossey-Bass, San Francisco, 1995, pp. 105–18.

Coleman, J.S., 'Social Capital in the Creation of Human Capital', *American Journal of Sociology*, 94, 1988, pp. 94–120.

Commonwealth Department of Education, Science and Training, *Higher Education: Report for 2003 to 2005 Triennium*, Commonwealth Government Publishing, Canberra, 2003.

Commonwealth Parliamentary Debates, House of Representatives, vol. 81, 10 October 1972.

Community Services Commission, *Annual Report 1996–97*, Sydney, 1997.

Cook, C. & Willms, J.D., 'Balancing Work and Family Life', in *Vulnerable Children*, ed, J.D. Willms, University of Alberta Press, Alberta, 2002, pp. 183–98.

Cooke, P. & Standen, P.J., 'Abuse and Disabled Children: Hidden Need...?', *Child Abuse Review*, 11, 2002, pp. 1–18.

Cooley, C.H., *Human Nature and the Social Order*, Scribners, New York, 1902.

Coon, H., Carey, G. & Fulker, D.W., 'Community Influences on Cognitive Ability', *Intelligence*, 16, 2, 1992, pp. 169–88.

Coulton, C.J., Korbin, J.E., Su, M. & Chow, J., 'Community Level Factors and Child Maltreatment Rates', *Child Development*, 66, 1995, pp. 1262–76.

Council of Social Services of New South Wales (NCOSS), 'The Issues Paper', in *Rural Communities Looking Ahead: Papers, Abstracts and Notes from the New South Wales Rural Social Policy Conference*, Dubbo, 1995, pp. 1–8.

Cowan, P.A., Cowan, C.P. & Schulz, M.S., 'Thinking about Risk and Resilience in Families', in *Stress, Coping and Resiliency in Children and Families*, eds, E.M. Hetherington & E.A. Blechman, Lawrence Erlbaum, Mahwah, NJ, 1996, pp. 1–38.

Cox, E., *A Truly Civil Society: 1995 Boyer Lectures*, ABC Books, Sydney, 1995.

Craig, L., 'Caring Differently: A Time Use Analysis of the Type and Social Context of Child Care Performed by Fathers and Mothers', Discussion Paper No. 116, Social Policy Research Centre, University of New South Wales, Sydney, 2002.

Crombie, M., Gunn, P. & Hayes, A., 'A Longitudinal Study of Two Cohorts of Children with Down Syndrome', in *Adolescents with Down Syndrome: International Perspectives on Research and Programme Development*, ed, C. Denholm, University of Victoria, Victoria, BC, 1991, pp. 3–13.

Crockenberg, S.C., 'Rescuing the Baby from the Bathwater: How Gender and Temperament (may) Influence how Child Care Affects Child Development', *Child Development*, 74, 2003, pp. 1034–8.

Croker, A.C., 'Introduction: The Happiness in All Our Lives', *American Journal on Mental Retardation*, 105, 2002, pp. 319–25.

Crouter, A.C., 'Mothers and Fathers at Work: Implications for Families and Children', paper presented at the Johann Jacobs Workshop on Families and Development, Zurich, October 2003.

Crouter, A.C., MacDermid, S.M., McHale, S.M. & Perry-Jenkins, M., 'Parental Monitoring and Perceptions of Children's School Performance and Conduct in Dual- and Single-earner Families', *Developmental Psychology*, 26, 4, 1990, pp. 649–57.

Cummings, B., *Take This Child*, Aboriginal Studies Centre, Canberra, 1990.

Cummings, E.M. & Davies, P., *Children and Marital Conflict: The Impact of Family Dispute and Resolution*, The Guilford Press, New York, 1994.

Cummins, R., 'The Subjective Well-being of People Caring for a Family Member with a Severe Disability at Home: A Review', *Journal of Intellectual & Developmental Disability*, 26, 2001, pp. 83–100.

Cunningham, C. & Glenn, S., 'Parent Involvement and Early Intervention', in *Current Approaches to Down's Syndrome*, eds, D. Lane & B. Stratford, Cassell, London, 1985, pp. 521–9.

Cuskelly, M., 'Adjustment of Siblings of Children with a Disability: Methodological Issues', *International Journal for the Advancement of Counselling*, 21, 1999, pp. 111–24.

Cuskelly, M., Chant, D. & Hayes, A., 'Behaviour Problems in Siblings of Children with Down Syndrome: Associations with Family Responsibilities and Parental Stress', *International Journal of Disability, Development and Education*, 45, 1998, pp. 295–311.

Cuskelly, M. & de Jong, I., 'Self-concept in Children with Down Syndrome', *Down Syndrome Research and Practice*, 4, 1996, pp. 59–64.

Cuskelly, M. & Gunn, P., 'Sibling Relationships of Children with Down Syndrome: Perspectives of Mothers, Fathers and Siblings', *American Journal on Mental Retardation*, 108, 2003, pp. 234–44.

Cuskelly, M., Pulman, L. & Hayes, A., 'Parenting and Employment Decisions of Parents with a Preschool Child with a Disability', *Journal of Intellectual & Developmental Disability*, 23, 1998, pp. 319–33.

Daly, E.A., *Implications of Development in Telecommunications for Indigenous People in Remote and Rural Australia*, Discussion Paper No. 219, Centre for Aboriginal Economic Policy Research, Australian National University, Canberra, 2001.

D'Andrade, R.G. & Strauss, C., eds, *Human Motivation and Cultural Models*, Cambridge University Press, New York, 1992.

Daro, D., *Confronting Child Abuse: Research for Effective Program Design*, The Free Press, New York, 1988.

Davidson-Arad, B., Englechin-Segal, D. & Wozner, Y., 'Short-term Follow-up of Children at Risk: Comparison of the Quality of Life of Children Removed from Home and Children Remaining at Home', *Child Abuse & Neglect*, 27, 2003, pp. 733–50.

Davies, B., 'The Discursive Production of the Male/Female Dualism in School Settings', *Oxford Review of Education*, 15, 1989, pp. 229–42.

Davies, P.T., Harold, G.T., Goeke-Morey, M.C. & Cummings, E.M., Child Emotional Security and Interparental Conflict, *Monographs of the Society for Research in Child Development*, 67, 3, 2002, serial no. 270.

Deater-Deckard, K. & Dunn, J., 'Multiple Risks and Adjustments of Young Children Growing Up in Different Family Settings', in *Coping with Divorce, Single Parenthood and Remarriage: A Risk and Resiliency Perspective*, ed, E.M. Hetherington, Lawrence Erlbaum, Mahwah, NJ, 1999, pp. 47–64.

Deater-Deckard, K., Pinkerton, R. & Scarr, S., 'Child Care Quality and Children's Behavioral Adjustment: A Four-year Longitudinal Study', *Journal of Child Psychology and Psychiatry*, 37, 1996, pp. 937–48.

Delfabbro, P.H., Barber, J.G. & Cooper, L.L, 'Placement Disruption and Dislocation in South Australian Substitute Care', *Children Australia*, 25, 2, 2000, pp. 16–20.

Delfabbro, P.H., Barber, J.G. & Cooper, L.L., 'Predictors of Short-term Reunification in South Australian Substitute Care', *Child Welfare*, 82, 2002, pp. 27–51.

de Lissa, L., *Talks Given at the Golden Jubilee of the Kindergarten Union of South Australia*, Adelaide, Kindergarten Union of South Australia, 1955.

Department of Health, *Child Protection: Messages from Research*, HMSO, London, 1995.

Department of Health and Family Services, *The Development of a National Planning Framework for Child Care*, Canberra, 1996.

Department of Health and Family Services, *Children's Services: Statistical Report*, Canberra, 1997.

de Vaus, D., 'Understanding Family Change', *Family Matters*, 62, 2002, pp. 52–5.

de Vaus, D., Qu, L. & Weston, R., 'Changing Patterns of Partnering', *Family Matters*, 64, 2003, pp. 10–15.

de Vaus, D. & Wolcott, I., eds, *Australian Family Profiles: Social and Demographic Patterns*, Australian Institute of Family Studies, Melbourne, 1997.

De Witt, D.J., Offord, D.R. & Brown, K., *The Relationship Between Geographic Relocation and Childhood Problem Behaviour*, Applied Research Branch Strategic Policy Human Resources Development, Quebec, 1998, <http://www.hrdc.rhc.go.ca/arb/publications/research/abw-98-17e.html>, accessed 13 November 2001.

Dingwall, R., Eekelaar, J. & Murray, T., *The Protection of Children: State Intervention and Family Life* (2nd edn), Avebury, Aldershot, 1995.

Dodson, M., 'My People and Place: Why Does Place Matter?', Keynote Address, People, Places, Partnerships Conference, University of New South Wales, Sydney, April 2003.

Donovan, A., 'Family Stress and Ways of Coping with Adolescents Who Have Handicaps', *American Journal on Mental Deficiency*, 92, 6, 1988, pp. 502–9.

Dowse, S., 'The Women's Movement's Fandango with the State: The Movement's Role in Public Policy Since 1972', in *Women, Social Welfare and the State* (2nd edn), eds, C.V. Baldock & B. Cass, Allen & Unwin, Sydney, 1988, pp. 205–26.

Dubowitz, H., Black, M., Starr, R.H. & Zuravin, S., 'A Conceptual Definition of Child Neglect', *Criminal Justice and Behavior*, 20, 1993, pp. 8–26.

Duchesne, S., *Parental Beliefs and Behaviours in Relation to Schooling*, unpublished PhD thesis, Macquarie University, 1996.

Duncan, G.J., Brooks-Gunn, J. & Klebanov, P.K., 'Economic Deprivation and Early Childhood Development', *Child Development*, 65, 1994, pp. 296–318.

Dunlop, R., 'Family Processes: Towards a Theoretical Framework', in *Images of Australian Families*, ed, K. Funder, Longman Cheshire, Melbourne, 1991, pp. 122–35.

Dunn, J., *The Beginnings of Social Understanding*, Harvard University Press, Cambridge, MA, 1988.

Dunn, J., *Young Children's Close Relationships: Beyond Attachment*, Sage, London, 1993.

Dunn, J., Bretherton, I. & Munn, P., 'Conversations about Feeling States Between Mothers and their Young Children', *Developmental Psychology*, 23, 1986, pp. 132–9.

Dunst, C., Trivette, C. & Deal, A., *Supporting and Strengthening Families: Methods, Strategies and Practices*, Brookline Books, Cambridge, MA, 1994.

Durkin, K., *Developmental Social Psychology*, Blackwell, Oxford, 1995.

Durlak, J.A., 'Common Risk and Protective Factors in Successful Prevention Programs', *American Journal of Orthopsychiatry*, 68, 1998, pp. 512–20.

Durrant, J.E., 'Trends in Youth Crime and Well-being Since the Abolition of Corporal Punishment in Sweden', *Youth and Society*, 31, 4, 2000, pp. 437–55.

Durrant, J.E. & Olsen, G.M. 'Parenting and Public Policy: Contextualising the Swedish Corporal Punishment Ban', *Journal of Social Welfare and Family Law*, 19, 4, 1997, pp. 443–61.

Economic Planning and Advisory Commission, Child Care Task Force, *Future Child Care Provision in Australia: Child Care Task Force Interim Report*, Australian Government Publishing Service, Canberra, 1996a.

Economic Planning and Advisory Commission, Child Care Task Force, *Future Child Care Provision in Australia: Final Report*, Australian Government Publishing Service, Canberra, 1996b.

Eddy, G., ed, *Insite*, 13, The National Dissemination Program of the Family Action Centre, 1997.

Eden-Piercy, G., Blacher, J. & Eyman, R., 'Exploring Parents' Reactions to their Young Child with Severe Handicaps', *Mental Retardation*, 24, 5, 1986, pp. 285–91.

Egeland, B., Yates, T., Appleyard, K. & van Dulmen, M., 'The Long-term Consequences of Maltreatment in the Early Years: A Developmental Pathway Model to Antisocial Behavior', *Children's Services: Social Policy, Research, & Practice*, 5, 4, 2002, pp. 249–60.

Einam, M. & Cuskelly, M., 'Paid Employment of Mothers and Fathers of an Adult Child with Multiple Disabilities', *Journal of Intellectual Disability Research*, 46, 2002, pp. 158–67.

Eisenstein, H., *Contemporary Feminist Thought*, Allen & Unwin, Sydney, 1984.

Emerson, E., 'Mothers of Children and Adolescents with Intellectual Disability: Social and Economic Situation, Mental Health Status, and the Self-assessed Social and Psychological Impact of the Child's Difficulties', *Journal of Intellectual Disability Research*, 47, 2003, pp. 385–99.

Erikson, E., *Childhood and Society*, Norton, New York, 1963.

Essex, E.L., Seltzer, M.M. & Krauss, M.W., 'Differences in Coping Effectiveness and Well-being Among Aging Mothers and Fathers of Adults with Mental Retardation', *American Journal on Mental Retardation*, 104, 1999, pp. 545–63.

Fabes, R.A., Hanish, L.D. & Martin, C.L., 'Children at Play: The Role of Peers in Understanding the Effects of Child Care', *Child Development*, 74, 2003, pp. 1039–43.

Family and Community Services, *1999 Census of Child Care Services: Summary Booklet*, 2000.

Family Resource Coalition, *Family Support Programs and the Prevention of Child Abuse*, Family Resource Coalition, Chicago, IL, 1995.

Fanshel, D. & Shinn, F.B., *Children in Foster Care: A Longitudinal Study*, Columbia University Press, New York, 1978.

Farber, B. & Ryckman, D.B., 'Effects of Severely Mentally Retarded Children on Family Relationships', *Mental Retardation*, 2, 1965, pp. 1–17.

Farran, D.C., 'Another Decade of Intervention for Children who are Low Income or Disabled: What do we Know Now?', in *Handbook of Early Childhood Intervention* (2nd edn), eds, J.P. Shonkoff & S.J. Meisels, Cambridge University Press, Cambridge, 2000, pp. 510–48.

Fegan, M., 'CONTACT: Facilitating Adult–child Interactions in the Australian Context', paper presented at the China–Asia–Pacific Conference, Beijing, China, 1995.

Ferguson, A., 'The Industries Set for Success', *Business Review Weekly*, 25 July 1995, p. 50.

Fergusson, D.M., Horwood, L.J. & Lynskey, M.T., 'A Longitudinal Study of Early Childhood Education and Subsequent Academic Achievement', *Australian Psychologist*, July 1994, pp. 110–15.

Fields, B.A., 'Children on the Move: The Social and Educational Effects of Family Mobility', *Children Australia*, 22, 3, 1997, pp. 4–9.

Fisman, S. & Wolf, L., 'The Handicapped Child: Psychological Effects of Parental, Marital and Sibling Relationships', *Psychiatric Clinics of North America*, 14, 1991, pp. 199–217.

Fivush, R., 'Exploring Sex Differences in the Emotional Content of Mother–child Conversations about the Past', *Sex Roles*, 20, 1989, pp. 675–91.

Flanagan, C., 'Families and Schools in Hard Times', in *New Directions for Child Development*, no. 46, eds, V.C. McLoyd & C.A. Flanagan, Jossey-Bass, San Francisco, 1990, pp. 7–26.

Flynt, S. & Wood, T., 'Stress and Coping of Mothers of Children with Moderate Mental Retardation', *American Journal of Mental Deficiency*, 94, 3, 1989, pp. 278–83.

Fox Harding, L., *Perspectives in Child Care Policy*, Longman, London, 1991.

Franks, A., *Indigenous Services in the Northern Rivers Region of NSW*, NSW Health, Sydney, 2001.

Fraser, A., 'Is Making Money out of Childcare as Easy as ABC?', *Weekend Australian*, 12–13 October 2003, p. 32.

Frodi, A.M. & Lamb, M.E., 'Child Abusers' Responses to Infant Smiles and Cries', *Child Development*, 51, 1980, pp. 238–41.

Fujuira, G.T., 'Demography of Family Households', *American Journal on Mental Retardation*, 104, 1998, pp. 545–63.

Fullwood, D. & Cronin, P., *Facing the Crowd: Managing Other People's Insensitivities to Your Disabled Child*, Royal Victorian Institute for the Blind, Melbourne, 1986.

Funder, K., ed, *Images of Australian Families*, Longman Cheshire, Melbourne, 1991.

Furstenberg, F.F., 'Social Capital and the Role of Fathers in the Family', in *Men in Families*, eds, A. Booth & A.C. Crouter, Lawrence Erlbaum, Mahwah, NJ, 1998, pp. 295–301.

Galambos, N., Almeida, D. & Petersen, A., 'Masculinity, Femininity and Sex Role Attitudes in Early Adolescence: Exploring Gender Intensification', *Child Development*, 51, 1990, pp. 1905–14.

Gallagher, J.J. & Bristol, M., 'Families of Young Handicapped Children', in *Handbook of Special Education: Research and Practice: Low Incidence Conditions*, eds, M.C. Wang, M.C. Reynolds & H.J. Walberg, Pergamon, Oxford, 1989, pp. 295–317.

Gallimore, R.G., Bernheimer, L.P. & Weisner, T.S., 'Family Life is More Than Managing a Crisis: Broadening the Agenda of Research on Families Adapting to Childhood

Disability', in *Developmental Perspectives on Children with High Incidence Disabilities*, eds, R. Gallimore, L.P., Bernheimer, D. MacMillan, D. Spence & S. Vaughn, Lawrence Erlbaum, Mahwah, NJ, 1999, pp. 40–80.

Gallimore, R.G., Coots, J.J., Weisner, T.S., Garnier, H. & Guthrie, D., 'Family Responses to Children with Early Developmental Delays II: Accommodation Intensity and Activity in Early and Middle-childhood', *American Journal on Mental Retardation*, 101, 1996, pp. 215–32.

Garbarino, J., *Children and Families in the Social Environment*, Aldine de Gruyter, New York, 1992.

Garbarino, J., 'Growing up in a Socially Toxic Environment: Life for Children and Families in the 1990s', in *The Individual, the Family, and Social Good*, ed, G.B. Melton, University of Nebraska Press, Lincoln, NA, 1995, pp. 1–19.

Garbarino, J., *Raising Children in a Socially Toxic Environment*, Jossey-Bass, San Francisco, 1995.

Garbarino, J. & Abramowitz, R.H., 'The Family as a Social System', in *Children and Families in the Social Environment*, ed, J. Garbarino, Aldine de Gruyter, New York, 1992, pp. 71–98.

Garbarino, J. & Crouter, A., 'Defining the Community Context for Parent–child Relations: The Correlates of Child Maltreatment', *Child Development*, 49, 1978, pp. 604–16.

Garbarino, J. & Kostelny, K., 'Neighborhood-based Programs', in *Protecting Children from Abuse and Neglect: Foundations for a New National Strategy*, eds, G.B. Melton & F.D. Barry, The Guilford Press, New York, 1994, pp. 304–52.

Garbarino, J. & Kostelny, K., 'Parenting and Public Policy', in *Handbook of Parenting*, vol. 3, ed, M.H. Bornstein, Lawrence Erlbaum, Mahwah, NJ, 1995, pp. 419–36.

Garbarino, J. & Sherman, D., 'High Risk Neighbourhoods and High Risk Families: The Human Ecology of Child Maltreatment', *Child Development*, 51, 1980, pp. 188–98.

Garmezy, N., 'Resilience and Vulnerability to Adverse Developmental Outcomes Associated with Poverty', *American Behavioral Scientist*, 34, 1991, pp. 416–30.

Garmezy, N., 'Children in Poverty: Resilience Despite Risk', *Psychiatry*, 56, 1993, pp. 127–36.

Garnett, L., *Leaving Care and After*, National Children's Bureau, London, 1992.

Gath, A. & Gumley, D., 'Family Background of Children with Down's Syndrome and of Children with a Similar Degree of Mental Retardation', *British Journal of Psychiatry*, 149, 1986, pp. 161–71.

Gifford, J., *Child Care Funding Re-assessed: Operational Subsidies, Fee Relief and Taxation Measures*, Australian Early Childhood Association and National Association of Community Based Children's Services, Canberra, 1992.

Giles, H., Coupland, N. & Coupland, J., 'Accommodation Theory: Communication, Context and Consequence', in *Contexts of Accommodation*, eds, H. Giles, N. Coupland & J. Coupland, Cambridge University Press, Cambridge, 1991, pp. 1–68.

Gilley, T. & Taylor, J., *Unequal Lives? Low Income and the Life Chances of Three Year Olds*, Brotherhood of St Laurence, Melbourne, 1995.

Gillham, B., Tanner, G., Cheyne, B., Freeman, I., Rooney, M. & Lambie, A., 'Unemployment Rates, Single Parent Density, and Indices of Child Poverty: Their Relationship to Different Categories of Child Abuse and Neglect', *Child Abuse & Neglect*, 22, 1988, pp. 79–90.

Gittins, D., *The Family Question* (2nd edn), Macmillan, London, 1993.

Glaser, D., 'Child Abuse and Neglect and the Brain—A Review', *Journal of Child Psychology and Psychiatry*, 41, 2000, pp. 97–116.

Goddard, C., *Child Abuse and Child Protection*, Churchill Livingstone, Melbourne, 1996.

Goelman, H. & Pence, A.R., 'Effects of Child Care, Family and Individual Characteristics on Children's Language Development: The Victoria Day Care Research Project', in *Quality in Child Care: What Does Research Tell Us?*, ed, D.A. Phillips, National Association for the Education of Young Children, Washington, DC, 1987, pp. 89–104.

Goffman, E., *Stigma*, Penguin, Harmondsworth, 1963.

Golombok, S. & Fivush, R., *Gender Development*, Cambridge University Press, Cambridge, 1994.

Gomby, D.S., Larner, M.B., Stevenson, C.S., Lewitt, E.M. & Behrman, R.E., 'Long-term Outcomes of Early Childhood Programs: Analysis and Recommendations', *The Future of Children*, 5, 1995, pp. 6–24.

Goodfellow, J., 'Multicare Arrangement Patchworks: The Multiple Use of Formal and Informal Childcare in NSW', report prepared for the Office of Childcare, NSW Department of Community Services, Sydney, 1999.

Goodfellow, J., 'Grandparents as Regular Child Care Providers: Unrecognised, Under-valued and Under-resourced', *Australian Journal of Early Childhood*, 28, 2003, pp. 7–17.

Goodnow, J.J., 'Acceptable Disagreement Across Generations', in *Beliefs About Parenting*, ed, J.G. Smetana, Jossey-Bass, San Francisco, 1995, pp. 51–64.

Goodnow, J.J., 'From Household Practices to Parents' Ideas about Work and Interpersonal Relationships', in *Parents' Cultural Belief Systems*, eds, S. Harkness & C. Super, The Guilford Press, New York, 1996, pp. 313–44.

Goodnow, J.J., 'Differentiating Among Social Contexts: By Spatial Features, Forms of Participation, and Social Contracts', in *Examining Lives in Context*, eds, P. Moen, G.H. Elder Jr & K. Lüscher, American Psychological Association, Washington, DC, 1995, pp. 269–301.

Goodnow, J.J., 'Meeting the Needs of Children, Families and Communities', in *Shaping the Future for Young Children, Their Families and Communities*, Centenary Conference Monograph, eds, A. Fleet & A. Hayes, Institute of Early Childhood, Macquarie University, Sydney, 1997, pp. 13–26.

Goodnow, J.J., 'Parenting and the "Transmission" and "Internalization" of Values: From Social–cultural Perspectives to Within-family Analyses', in *Parenting Strategies and Children's Internalization of Values: A Handbook of Theoretical and Research Proposals*, eds, J. Grusec & L. Kuczynski, Wiley, New York, 1997, pp. 333–61.

Goodnow, J.J., 'Contexts, Diversity, Pathways: Linking and Extending', in *Hills of Gold: Rethinking Diversity and Contexts as Resources for Children's Developmental Pathways*, eds, C.R. Cooper, G. Coll, T. Bartko, H. Davis & C. Chatman, Lawrence Erlbaum, Mahwah, NJ, in press.

Goodnow, J.J. & Bowes, J.M., *Men, Women and Household Work*, Oxford University Press, Melbourne, 1994.

Gottlieb, B., *The Family in the Western World from the Black Death to the Industrial Age*, Oxford University Press, Oxford, 1993.

Gough, D., 'Defining the Problem', *Child Abuse & Neglect*, 20, 1996, pp. 993–1002.

Gray, D.E., 'Ten Years On: A Longitudinal Study of Families of Children with Autism', *Journal of Intellectual & Developmental Disability*, 27, 2000, pp. 215–22.

Greenberg, J.S., Seltzer, M.M., Krauss, M.W. & Kim, H.W., 'The Differential Effects of Social Support on the Psychological Well-being of Aging Mothers of Adults with Mental Illness or Mental Retardation', *Family Relations*, 46, 1997, pp. 383–94.

Greenwood, P.W., Model, K.E., Rydell, C.P. & Chiesa, J., *Diverting Children From a Life of Crime: Measuring Costs and Benefits*, RAND Corporation, Santa Monica, CA, 1996.

Gregory, R.G. & Hunter, B, *The Macro Economy and the Growth of Ghettos and Urban Poverty in Australia*, ANU Discussion Paper No. 325, Centre for Economic Policy Research, Canberra, 1995.

Griffiths, D.L. & Unger, D.G., 'Views about Planning for the Future among Parents and Siblings of Adults with Mental Retardation', *Family Relations*, 43, 1994, pp. 1–8.

Groce, N.E., *Everybody Here Spoke Sign Language: Hereditary Deafness on Martha's Vineyard*, Harvard University Press, Cambridge, MA, 1985.

Hagekull, B. & Bohlin, G., 'Quality of Care and Problem Behaviors in Early Childhood', paper presented at the Biennial Meeting of the Society for Research in Child Development, New Orleans, LA, 1993.

Hagekull, B. & Bohlin, G., 'Child Care Quality, Family and Child Characteristics and Socioemotional Development', *Early Childhood Research Quarterly*, 10, 1995, pp. 505–26.

Hallidie-Smith, K.A., 'The Heart', in *New Approaches to Down Syndrome*, eds, B. Stratford & P. Gunn, Cassell, London, 1996, pp. 85–99.

Hand, K. & Lewis, V., 'Fathers' Views on Family Life and Paid Work', *Family Matters*, 61, 2002, pp. 26–9.

Hanson, M. & Hanline, M., 'Parenting a Child with a Disability: A Longitudinal Study of Parental Stress and Adaptation', *Journal of Early Intervention*, 14, 3, 1990, pp. 234–48.

Hardiment, C, *Dream Babies*, Oxford University Press, Oxford, 1984.

Harding, A. & Szukalska, A., 'A Portrait of Child Poverty in Australia in 1995–1996', paper presented at the Australian Institute of Family Studies Conference, Melbourne, November 1998.

Harkness, S. & Super, C., eds, *Parents' Cultural Belief Systems*, The Guilford Press, New York, 1996.

Harkness, S., Super, C.M., Keefer, C.H., Raghavan, C.S. & Kipp, E.K., 'Ask the Doctor: The Negotiation of Cultural Models in American Parent–Pediatrician Discourse', in *Parents' Cultural Belief Systems*, eds, S. Harkness & C.M. Super, The Guilford Press, New York, 1996, pp. 289–310.

Harris, J., 'Where is the Child's Environment? A Group Socialisation Theory of Development', *Psychological Review*, 102, 1995, pp. 458–80.

Harrison, A.O., Wilson, M.N., Pine, C.J., Chan, S.Q. & Buriel, R., 'Family Ecologies of Ethnic Minority Children', *Child Development*, 61, 1990, pp. 347–62.

Harrison, L.J. & Ungerer, J.A., 'The Sydney Family Development Project: Family and Child Care Predictors at Age Six', paper presented in the symposium, Longitudinal Studies of Early Childhood in Australia, J. Bowes (Chair), at the Australian Association for Research in Education Conference, Brisbane, December 2002.

Harrison, R., *The Sydney Kindergarten Teachers' College, 1897–1981*, Sydney Kindergarten Teachers' College Graduates Association, Sydney, 1985.

Hartley, R., ed, *Families and Cultural Diversity in Australia*, Australian Institute of Family Studies, Melbourne, 1995.

Hartley, R., 'Families, Values and Change: Setting the Scene', in *Families and Cultural Diversity in Australia*, ed, R. Hartley, Allen & Unwin, Sydney, 1995, pp. 1–24.

Hastings, R.P. & Taunt, H.M., 'Positive Perception in Families of Children with Developmental Disabilities', *American Journal on Mental Retardation*, 107, 2002, pp. 116–27.

Hayes, A., 'Developmental Psychology, Education and the Need to Move Beyond Typological Thinking', *Australian Journal of Education*, 34, 1990, pp. 235–41.

Hayes, A., 'Families and Disabilities: Another Facet of Inclusion', in *Educating Children with Special Needs*, eds, A. Ashman & J. Elkins, Prentice Hall, New York, 1998, pp. 39–66.

Hayes, A. & Gunn, P., 'Developmental Assumptions about Down Syndrome and the Myth of Uniformity', in *Adolescents with Down Syndrome: International Perspectives on Research and Programme Development*, eds, C. Denholm & J. Ward, University of Victoria, Victoria, BC, 1990, pp. 73–80.

Hayes, C.D., Palmer, J.L. & Zaslow, M.J., *Who Cares for America's Children? Child Care Policy for the 1990s*, National Academy Press, Washington, DC, 1990.

Hedov, G., Anneren, G. & Wikblad, K., 'Swedish Parents of Children with Down's Syndrome', *Scandinavian Journal of Caring Sciences*, 16, 2002, pp. 424 30.

Heiman, T., 'Friendship Quality Among Children in Three Educational Settings', *Journal of Intellectual & Developmental Disability*, 25, 2000, pp. 1–12.

Helburn, S., ed, *Cost, Quality and Child Outcomes in Child Care Centers*, University of Colorado, Denver, CO, 1995.

Hernandez, D.J., 'Child Development and the Social Demography of Childhood', *Child Development*, 68, 1, 1997, pp. 149–69.

Herrara, C. & Dunn, J., 'Early Experiences with Family Conflict: Implications for Arguments with a Close Friend', *Development Psychology*, 33, 5, 1997, pp. 869–81.

Herron, J., Minister for Aboriginal and Torres Strait Islander Affairs, 'Bringing Them Home—Commonwealth Initiatives', media release, Canberra, 26 August 1999.

Hetherington, E.M., 'Stress and Coping in Children and Families', in *Children in Families Under Stress*, eds, A. Doyle, D. Gold & D. Moscowitz, Jossey-Bass, San Francisco, 1984, pp. 7–33.

Hetherington, E.M. & Stanley-Hagan, M., 'Parenting in Divorced and Remarried Families', in *Handbook of Parenting, Vol. 3, Being and Becoming a Parent*, ed, M.H. Bornstein, Lawrence Erlbaum, Mahwah, NJ, 2002, pp. 287–315.

Hirschfield, L.A., *Race in the Making: The Child's Construction of Human Kinds*, MIT Press, Cambridge, MA, 1996.

Historical Records of Australia, Additional Instructions to Governor Bligh, 20.11.1805, HRA Series I, Vol VI, Government Printer, Sydney, 1915, pp. 18–19.

Hoffman, M.L., 'Conscience, Personality, and Socialization Techniques', *Human Development*, 13, 1970, pp. 90–126.

Hojet, M., 'Can Affectional Ties be Purchased? Comments on Working Mothers and Their Families', *Journal of Social Behavior and Personality*, 5, 1990, pp. 493–502.

Horin, A., 'When Making Money is Child's Play', *Sydney Morning Herald*, 4 October 2003; *Age*, 4 September 2003.

Horn, M., 'Families and Homelessness: Prospects and Policies for the 21st Century', paper presented at the Fifth Australian Family Research Conference, Brisbane, 1996.

Hornby, G. & Seligman, M., 'Disability and the Family: Current Status and Future Developments', *Counselling Psychology Quarterly*, 4, 1991, pp. 267–71.

Hornosty, J., 'Wife Abuse in Rural Regions: Structural Problems in Leaving Abusive Relationships—A Case Study in Canada', in *With a Rural Focus: An Edited and Refereed Collection of Papers with a Rural Focus presented to the Annual Conference of the Australian Sociological Association Inc.*, ed, F. Vanclay, Deakin University, 1994, pp. 21–34.

Horwitz, W.A. & Kazak, A.E., 'Family Adaptation to Childhood Cancer: Sibling and Family Systems Variables', *Journal of Clinical Child Psychology*, 19, 1990, pp. 221–8.

Howard, J., *Hansard*, Commonwealth of Australia: House of Representatives, Statement on the Motion of Reconciliation, 26 August 1999.

Howes, C., 'Relations Between Early Child Care and Schooling', *Developmental Psychology*, 24, 1988, pp. 53–7.

Howes, C., 'Can the Age of Entry into Child Care and the Quality of Child Care Predict Adjustment in Kindergarten?', *Developmental Psychology*, 26, 1990, pp. 292–303.

Howes, C., 'The Earliest Friendships', in *The Company they Keep*, eds, W.M. Bukowski, A.F. Newcomb & W.W. Hartup, Cambridge University Press, New York, 1996, pp. 66–86.

Howes, C., Rodning, C., Galluzzo, D.C. & Myers, L., 'Attachment and Child Care: Relationships with Mother and Caregiver', *Early Childhood Research Quarterly*, 3, 1988, pp. 403–16.

Hubbard, J. & Coie, J., 'Emotional Correlates of Social Competence in Children's Peer Relationships', *Merril-Palmer Quarterly*, 40, 1994, pp. 1–20.

Hughes, D. & Chen, L., When and What Parents Tell Their Children About Race: An Examination of Race-related Socialization in African-American Families, *Applied Development Sciences*, 1, 1997, pp. 200–14.

Hughes, C., Rodi, M.S. Lorden, S.W., Pitkin, S.E., Derere, K.R., Hwang, B. & Cai, X., 'Social Interactions of High School Students with Mental Retardation and Their General Education Peers', *American Journal on Mental Retardation*, 104, 1999, pp. 533–44.

Hughes, R., Fleet, A. & Nicholls, J., 'Both-Ways Learning: The Development of an Indigenous Bachelor of Teaching', *Change: Transformations in Education*, 6, 2003, pp. 67–74.

Hugo, G., 'Australia's Future Population: Where will they Live?', in *Australia's Population Challenge*, eds, S. Vizard, H.J. Martin & T. Watts, Penguin Books, Victoria, 2003.

Human Rights and Equal Opportunity Commission (HREOC), *Bringing Them Home*, HREOC, Sydney, 1997.

Hunter, B. & Gray, M., 'Family and Social Factors Underlying the Labour Force Status of Indigenous Australians', *Family Matters*, 62, 2002, pp. 18–25.

Huston, C., 'From Research to Policy: Choosing Questions and Interpreting the Answers', in *Science for Society: Informing Policy and Practice Through Research in Developmental Psychology, New Directions for Child and Adolescent Development*, no. 98, eds, A. Higgins-D'Alesssandro & K.R.B. Jankowski, 2002, pp. 29–41.

Hyde, J., Fennema, E., Ryan, M. & Frost, L., 'Gender Comparisons of Mathematics Attitudes and Achievement: A Meta-analysis', *Psychology of Women Quarterly*, 14, 1990, pp. 299–324.

Hyde, J. & Linn, M., 'Sex Differences in Verbal Ability: A Meta-analysis', *Psychological Bulletin*, 104, 1988, pp. 53–69.

Institute for Research on Poverty, 'Two Generation Programs: A Roadmap to National Evaluations', *Focus*, 19, 1997, pp. 28–33.

Isolated Children's Parents' Association, 'Isolated Children's Parents' Association Submission to the National Inquiry into Rural and Remote Education', 1999 <http://www.icpa.com.au>, accessed 19 September 2003.

Ife, J., *The Place of Human Rights in Community*, Keynote Address, People, Places, Partnerships Conference, University of New South Wales, Sydney, April 2003.

Jack, G., 'Ecological Influences on Parenting and Child Development', *British Journal of Social Work*, 30, 2000, pp. 703–20.

Jackson, A., 'ABC Learning Acquisition Alert', *Sydney Morning Herald*, 15 September 2003.

Jaffe, P., Wolfe, D. & Wilson, S., *Children of Battered Women*, Sage, Newbury Park, CA, 1990.

Jenkins, J.M., Rasbash, J. & O'Connor, T.G., 'The Role of Shared Family Context in Differential Parenting', *Developmental Psychology*, 39, 2003, pp. 99–113.

Jeremy, J., 'Australia: Generating a Sense of Community', *Bernard van Leer Foundation Newsletter*, 78, 4, 1995, pp. 5–6.

Jobling, A. & Cuskelly, M., 'Life Styles of Adults with Down Syndrome Living at Home', in *Down Syndrome Across the Life Span*, eds, M. Cuskelly, A. Jobling & S. Buckley, Whurr Publishers, London, 2002, pp. 109–20.

Johnson, H. McB., 'My Right to Life', *Weekend Australian Magazine*, 3–4 May, 2003, p. 21.

Kahn, J. & Kamerman, S.B., *Beyond Child Poverty: The Social Exclusion of Children*, Institute for Child and Family Policy, Columbia University, New York, 2003.

Kamerman, S.B., 'Child Care Policies and Programs: An International Overview', *Journal of Social Issues*, 47, 1991, pp. 179–90.

Kamien, M., *The Dark People of Bourke*, Australian Institute of Aboriginal Studies, Canberra, 1978.

Kaufman, J. & Zigler, E., 'The Prevention of Child Maltreatment: Programming, Research and Policy', in *Prevention of Child Maltreatment: Developmental and Ecological Perspectives*, eds, D.J. Willis, E.W Holden & M. Rosenberg, Wiley, New York, 1992, pp. 269–95.

Kattan, R., 'What Counts in the Quality of Life Education', paper presented at the People, Places, Partnerships Conference, University of New South Wales, Sydney, April 2003.

Kazdin, A.E., 'Conduct Disorder Across the Life-span', in *Developmental Psychopathology: Perspectives on Adjustment, Risk and Disorder*, eds, S.S. Luthar, J.A. Burack, D. Cicchetti & J.R. Weisz, Cambridge University Press, Cambridge, 1997, pp. 248–72.

Keating, D.P. & Hertzman, C., *Developmental Health and the Wealth of Nations*, The Guilford Press, New York, 1999.

Kendall-Tackett, K., Williams, L. & Finkelhor, D., 'Impact of Sexual Abuse on Children', *Psychological Bulletin*, 113, 1993, pp. 164–80.

Kidd, R., 'You Can Trust Me, I'm With the Government', paper presented at One Family, Many Histories Conference, September 1994, Brisbane.

Kilmartin, C., 'Working Mothers Throughout the Decade', *Family Matters*, 26, 1990.

Kingwill, S., 'Isolation: A Key Factor which Affects Australian Families and Their Children: Implications of CONTACT Inc. Initiatives for Commonwealth Policies and Priorities in Education and Child Support', Submission to Employment, Education and Training Reference Committee, Canberra, 1995.

Kitzman, H., Olds, D.L., Henderson, C.R., Tatelbaum, R., McConnochie, K.M., Sidora, K., Luckey, D.W., Shaver, D., Engelhardt, K., James, D. & Barnard, K., 'Effect of Prenatal and Infancy Home Visitation by Nurses on Pregnancy Outcomes, Childhood Injuries, and Repeated Childbearing', *Journal of the American Medical Association*, 278, 1997, pp. 644–52.

Kohen, D.E., Brooks-Gunn, J., Leventhall, E.T. & Hertzman, C., 'Neighbourhood Income and Physical and Social Disorder in Canada: Associations with Young Children's Competencies', *Child Development*, 73, 2002, pp. 184–6.

Kohlberg, L., 'A Cognitive-developmental Analysis of Children's Sex-role Concepts and Attitudes', in *The Development of Sex Differences*, ed, E. Maccoby, Stanford University Press, Stanford, CA, 1966, pp. 82–173.

Kolar, V. & Soriano, G., *Parenting in Australian Families*, Australian Institute of Family Studies, Melbourne, 2001.

Korbin, J., 'Cross-cultural Perspectives and Research Directions for the 21st Century', *Child Abuse & Neglect*, 15, Supplement 1, 1991, pp. 66–77.

Krauss, M.W., Seltzer, M.M., Gordon, R. & Friedman, D.H., 'Binding Ties: The Roles of Adult Siblings of Persons with Mental Retardation', *Mental Retardation*, 96, 1996, pp. 83–93.

Kutena, Z., *Identified Needs of Remote and Isolated Aboriginal Children, Families and Communities in New South Wales: An Overview*, CONTACT Incorporated, Sydney, 1995.

Ladd, G., 'Peer Relationships and Social Competence During Early and Middle Childhood', *Annual Review of Psychology*, 50, 1999, pp. 333–59.

Lahti, J., 'A Follow-up Study of Foster Children in Permanent Placements', *Social Service Review*, 56, 1982, pp. 556–71.

Lamb, M.E., 'Infant Care and Practices and the Application of Knowledge', in *Applied Developmental Psychology*, eds, C.B. Fisher & R.M. Lerner, McGraw-Hill, New York, 1994, pp. 23–45.

Lamb, M.E., 'Fathers and Child Development: An Introductory Overview and Guide', in *The Role of the Father in Child Development*, ed, M.E. Lamb, John Wiley & Sons, New York, 1997, pp. 1–18.

Lamb, M.E., 'Nonparental Child Care: Context, Quality and Correlates', in *Handbook of Child Psychology, Vol. 4: Child Psychology in Practice* (5th edn), eds, W. Damon, I.E. Sigel & K.A. Renninger, Wiley, New York, 1998, pp. 73–134.

Lamb, M.E. & Sternberg, K.L., 'Sociocultural Perspectives on Nonmaternal Child Care', in *Child Care in Context: Cross-cultural Perspectives*, eds, M.E. Lamb, K.L. Sternberg, C.P. Hwang & A.G. Broberg, Lawrence Erlbaum, Hillsdale, NJ, 1992.

Lamb, M.E., Sternberg, K.L. & Prodromidis, M., 'Nonmaternal Care and the Security of Infant–mother Attachment: A Reanalysis of the Data', *Infant Behavior and Development*, 15, 1992, pp. 71–83.

Larner, M., 'Local Residential Mobility and its Effects on Social Networks: A Cross-cultural Comparison', in *Extending Families: The Social Networks of Parents and their Children*, eds, M. Larner & D. Hendersen Jr, Cambridge University Press, Cambridge, 1990, pp. 205–29.

Laszloffy, T.A., 'Rethinking Family Development Theory: Teaching with the Systemic Family Development (SFD) Model', *Family Relations*, 51, 2002, pp. 206–14.

Lave, J. & Wenger, E., *Situated Learning: Legitimate Peripheral Participation*, Cambridge University Press, Cambridge, 1999.

Laverty, J., 'The Experience of Grandparents Providing Regular Child Care for their Grandchildren', unpublished MEd (Hons) thesis, University of Western Sydney, 2003.

Lerner, M., Gunnarsson, L., Cochran, M. & Haggund, S., 'The Peer Relations of Children Reared in Child Care Centers or Home Settings: A Longitudinal Analysis', paper presented to the Biennial Meeting of the Society for Research in Child Development, Kansas City, MO, 1989.

Levy, G. & Carter, D., 'Gender Schema, Gender Constancy and Gender Role Knowledge', *Developmental Review*, 25, 1989, pp. 444–9.

Linville, P.W., Salovey, P. & Fischer, G.W., 'Stereotyping and Perceived Distributions of Social Characteristics: An Application of Ingroup–outgroup Perception', in *Prejudice, Discrimination, and Racism*, eds, J.F. Davidio & S.L. Gaertner, Academic Press, San Diego, CA, 1986, pp. 165–208.

Liossis-Vernados, C., 'Dual Working Parents and Their Families', unpublished PhD thesis, University of Queensland, 1997.

Little, L., 'Differences in Stress and Coping for Mothers and Fathers of Children with Asperger's Syndrome and Nonverbal Learning Disorders', *Pediatric Nursing*, 28, 2002, pp. 565–70.

Loane, S., *Who Cares?*, Reed Books, Kew, Victoria, 1996.

Love, J.M., Harrison, L., Sagi-Schwartz, A., van Ijzendoorn, M.H., Ross, C., Ungerer, J.A., Raikes, H., Brady-Smith, C., Boller, K., Brooks-Gunn, J., Constantine, J., Kisker, E.E., Paulsell, D. & Chazan-Cohen, R., 'Child Care Quality Matters: How Conclusions May Vary with Context', *Child Development*, 74, 2003, pp. 1021–33.

Lustig, D.C., Family Coping in Families with a Child with a Disability', *Education and Training in Mental Retardation and Developmental Disabilities*, 37, 2002, pp. 14–22.

Maas, F., 'Child Care Needs of Working Families in the 1990s', *Family Matters*, 26, 1990, pp. 59–63.

Maccoby, E., 'The Two Sexes and their Social Systems', in *Examining Lives in Context: Perspectives on the Ecology of Human Development*, eds, P. Moen, G. Elder Jr & K. Lüscher, American Psychological Association, Washington, DC, 1995, pp. 347–64.

Maccoby, E., 'Gender and Relationships: A Developmental Account', *American Psychologist*, 45, 1990, pp. 513–20.

Maccoby, E. & Jacklin, C., *The Psychology of Sex Differences*, Stanford University Press, Stanford, CA, 1974.

Mackay, H., *Reinventing Australia: The Mind and Mood of Australia in the 90s*, Angus & Robertson, Sydney, 1993.

McCain, M. & Mustard, J.F., *Reversing the Real Brain Drain: Early Years Study, Final Report*, 1999, <http://www.childsoc.gove.on.ca>, accessed 2 March 1999.

McCartney, K., 'Effect of Quality Care Environment on Children's Language Development', *Developmental Psychology*, 20, 1984, pp. 244–60.

McCartney, K., 'The Family-child Care Mesosystem', paper presented at the Johann Jacobs Foundation Workshop on Families and Development, Zurich, October 2003.

McCaughey, W., 'Day Care—Liberating Who for What?', *Dissent*, 28, Winter 1972, pp. 3–8.

McDonald, P., 'Families and Welfare Services', in *Australia's Welfare 1997*, eds, H. Moyle & D. Gibson, Australian Institute of Health and Welfare, Canberra, 1997, pp. 55–95.

McDonald, P., 'Low Fertility in Australia: Evidence, Causes and Policy Responses, *People and Place*, 8, 2000, pp. 6–21.

McGurk, H., Caplan, M., Hennessy, E. & Moss, P., 'Controversy, Theory and Social Context in Contemporary Child Care Research', *Journal of Child Psychology and Psychiatry*, 34, 1993, pp. 3–23.

McKim, M.K., Stuart, B. & O'Connor, D.L., 'Infant Care: Evaluation of Pre-care Differences Hypotheses', *Early Education and Development*, 7, 1996, pp. 107–19.

McLaren, P., *Life in Schools*, Longman, White Plains, NY, 1989.

McLellan, J., 'Access to Education', in *Rural Communities Looking Ahead: Papers, Abstracts and Notes from the New South Wales Rural Social Policy Conference*, ed, Council of Social Service of New South Wales (NCOSS), Dubbo, 1995.

McLoyd, V.C. & Flanagan, C.A., eds, *New Directions for Child Development*, no. 46, Jossey-Bass, San Francisco, 1990.

McNaughton, S., *Patterns of Emergent Literacy*, Oxford University Press, Auckland, 1995.

Malinkovsky-Rummell, R. & Hansen, D., 'Long-term Consequences of Childhood Physical Abuse', *Psychological Bulletin*, 114, 1994, pp. 68–79.

Manne, R., 'The Stolen Generation', *Quadrant*, January/February 1998, pp. 53–63.

Markus, A., *Governing Savages*, Allen & Unwin, Sydney, 1990.

Martin, J.I., *The Migrant Presence*, Allen & Unwin, Sydney, 1979.

Mathematica Policy Research Inc., 'Making a Difference in the Lives of Infants and Toddlers and Their Families: The Impacts of Early Head Start', 2002, <http://www.acf.dhhs.gov/programs/core/ongoing/research/ehs>, accessed 24 July 2003.

Mattingley, C. & Hampton, K., *Survival in Our Own Land*, Hodder & Stoughton, Sydney, 1992.

Meadows, S., *Parenting Behaviour and Children's Cognitive Development*, Psychology Press, Hove, 1996.

Mekertichian, L.K. & Bowes, J.M., 'Does Parenting Matter? The Challenge of the Behaviour Geneticists', *Journal of Family Studies*, 2, 1996, pp. 131–45.

Melhuish, E.C. & Moss, P., 'Child Care in the United Kingdom in Historical Perspective', in *Child Care in Context: Cross-cultural Perspectives*, eds, M.E. Lamb, K.J. Sternberg, C.P. Hwang & A.G. Broberg, Lawrence Erlbaum, Hillsdale, NJ, 1992, pp. 157–83.

Melton, G.B., 'Chronic Neglect of Family Violence: More than a Decade of Reports to Guide US Policy', *Child Abuse & Neglect*, 26, 2002, pp. 569–86.

Mercer, J., *Labelling the Mentally Retarded*, University of California Press, Berkeley, 1973.

Meyer-Probst, B., Rosler, H.D. & Teichmann, H., 'Biological and Psychosocial Risk Factors and Development During Childhood', in *Human Development: An Interactional Perspective*, eds, D. Magnusson & V.L. Allen, Academic Press, New York, 1983, pp. 225–46.

Miller, N.B., Cowan, P.A., Cowan, C.P., Hetherington, E.M. & Clingempeel, G., 'Externalising in Preschoolers and Early Adolescents: A Cross-study Replication of a Family Model', *Developmental Psychology*, 29, 1993, pp. 3–18.

Miller, P.J. & Goodnow, J.J., 'Cultural Practices: Toward an Integration of Culture and Development', in *New Directions for Child Development*, no. 67, eds, J.J. Goodnow, P.J. Miller & F. Kessel, Jossey-Bass, San Francisco, 1995, pp. 5–16.

Miller, P.J., Hengst, J.A. & Wang, S., 'Ethnographic Methods: Applications from Developmental Cultural Psychology', in *Qualitative Research in Psychology: Expanding Perspectives in*

Methodology and Design, eds, P.M. Camic, J.E. Rhodes & L. Yardley, American Psychological Association, Washington, DC, 2003, pp. 219–41.

Milligan, S. & Thomson, K., *Listening to Girls*, Australian Education Council, Canberra, 1991.

Millward, C., 'Intergenerational Family Support', *Family Matters*, 39, 1994, pp. 10–13.

Millward, C., 'Work Rich, Family Poor? Non-standard Working Hours and Family Life', *Family Matters*, 61, 2002, pp. 40–7.

Minty, B., 'A Review of the Effects of Living Long-term in Substitute Care in the Context of a Discussion of Outcome Criteria', *Social Work & Social Sciences Review*, 8, 2000, pp. 169–93.

Minuchin, S., *Family Therapy Technique*, Cambridge University Press, Cambridge, 1981.

Monsour, M., Harris, B. & Kurzweil, N., 'Challenges Confronting Cross Sex Friendships: "Much Ado About Nothing"', *Sex Roles*, 31, 1994, pp. 55–77.

Morgan, S., *My Place*, Fremantle Arts Centre Press, Fremantle, 1987.

Moss, P. & Melhuish, E., *Maternal Employment and Child Care in the First Three Years After Birth*, Report prepared for the Department of Health and Social Security, London, 1988.

Muirhead, S., 'An Appreciative Inquiry About Adults with Down Syndrome', in *Down Syndrome Across the Life Span*, eds, M. Cuskelly, A. Jobling & S. Buckley, Whurr Publishers, London, 2002, pp. 149–58.

Mrug, S. & Wallander, J.L., 'Self-concept of Young People with Physical Disabilities: Does Integration Play a Role?', *International Journal of Disability, Development and Education*, 49, 2002, pp. 267–80.

Murray, N., 'Listening to the Silent Minority', *Community Care*, 20, 1992, pp. 12–13.

Najman, J.M., Behrens, B.C., Andersen, M., Bor, W., O'Callaghan, M. & Williams, G.M., 'Impact of Family Type and Family Quality on Child Behavior Problems: A Longitudinal Study', *Journal of American Academic Child Adolescent Psychiatry*, 36, 1997, pp. 1357–65.

Nakamura, M., 'Acceptance or Refusal of Disability in a Tolerant Society: Reexamination of the History of People with Disabilities in America', *Japanese Journal of Special Education*, 39, 2002, pp. 15–29.

National Association of Community Based Children's Services (NACBCS), *Care Versus Quality—The Results of a National Survey of Community Owned Children's Services*, NACBCS, Melbourne, 1997.

National Board of Employment, Education and Training Higher Education Council, *Equality, Diversity and Excellence*, Australian Government Publishing Service, Canberra, 1996.

National Institute of Child Health and Human Development Early Child Care Research Network, 'Child Care and Child Development: The NICHD Study of Early Child Care', in *Developmental Follow-up: Concepts, Domains, and Methods*, eds, S.L. Friedman & H.C. Haywood, Academic Press, San Diego, CA, 1994, pp. 377–96.

National Institute of Child Health and Human Development Early Child Care Research Network, 'Characteristics of Infant Childcare: Factors Contributing to Positive Caregiving', *Early Childhood Research Quarterly*, 11, 1996, pp. 267–306.

National Institute of Child Health and Human Development Early Child Care Research Network, 'The Effects of Infant Child Care on Infant–Mother Attachment Security: Results of the NICHD Study of Early Child Care', *Child Development*, 68, 1997, pp. 860–79.

National Institute of Child Health and Human Development Early Child Care Research Network, 'Childcare and Mother–child Interaction in the First 3 years of Life', *Developmental Psychology*, 35, 1999, pp. 1399–413.

National Institute of Child Health and Human Development Early Child Care Research Network, 'Child Care and Child Development, Childcare and Family Predictors of Preschool Attachment and Stability from Infancy, *Developmental Psychology*, 37, 2001, pp. 847–62.

National Institute of Child Health and Human Development Early Child Care Research Network, 'Child-care Structure Process Outcome: Direct and Indirect Effects of Child Care Quality on Young Children's Development', *Psychological Science*, 13, 2002, pp. 199–206.

National Institute of Child Health and Human Development Early Child Care Research Network, 'Does Quality of Child Care Affect Child Outcomes at Age 4½?', *Developmental Psychology*, 39, 2003, pp. 451–69.

Neilsen-Hewett, C.M., 'Children's Peer Relations and School Adjustment: Looking Beyond the Classroom Walls', unpublished PhD thesis, Macquarie University, 2001.

Newcomb, M.D. & Felix-Ortiz, M., 'Multiple Protective and Risk Factors for Drug Use and Abuse: Cross-sectional and Prospective Findings', *Journal of Personality and Social Psychology*, 63, 1992, pp. 280–96.

Newton, P. & Bell, M., 'Mobility and Change: Australia in the 1990s', in *Population Shift: Mobility and Change in Australia*, eds, P. Newton & M. Bell, Australian Government Publishing Service, Canberra, 1996, pp. 1–17.

Nguyen, V. & Ho, M., 'Vietnamese–Australian Families', in *Families and Cultural Diversity in Australia*, ed, R. Hartley, Australian Institute of Family Studies, Melbourne, 1995, pp. 216–40.

Norton, J., 'Deconstructing the Fear of Femininity', *Feminism and Psychology*, 7, 1997, pp. 441–7.

Nowicki, E.A. & Sandieson, R., 'A Meta-analysis of School-age Children's Attitudes Towards Persons with Physical and Intellectual Disabilities', *International Journal of Disability, Development and Education*, 49, 2002, pp. 241–65.

NSW Child Death Review Team, *Second Annual Report 1996–1997*, Sydney, 1998.

NSW Child Protection Council, *Interagency Guidelines for Child Protection Intervention*, 1997.

NSW Children's Commission, Green Paper, NSW Government, Sydney, 1997.

NSW Parliament, *Report of the NSW Aboriginal Children's Research Project to the Select Committee of the Legislative Assembly upon Aborigines*, NSW Government Printer, Sydney, 1981.

Oakley, A., 'Women and Children First and Last: Parallels and Differences Between Children's and Women's Studies', in *Children's Childhoods: Observed and Experienced*, ed, B. Mayall, Falmer Press, London, 1994, pp. 13–32.

O'Brien, M., Alldred, P. & Jones, D., 'Children's Constructions of Family and Kinship', in *Children in Families: Research and Policy*, eds, J. Brannen & M. O'Brien, Falmer Press, London, 1996.

O'Brien, P., 'Are We Helping Them Home?', a paper on the surveys of progress in the implementation of the *Bringing Them Home* Recommendations, Responses by the Government and Opposition Main Committee Room, Parliament House, Canberra, 13 November 2002.

Ochiltree, G., *Effects of Child Care on Young Children: Forty Years of Research*, AIFS Early Childhood Study, paper no. 5, Australian Institute of Family Studies, Melbourne, 1994.

Ochiltree, G. & Edgar, D., *Today's Child Care, Tomorrow's Children!*, AIFS Early Childhood Study, paper no. 7, Australian Institute of Family Studies, Melbourne, 1995.

O'Connor, I., *Our Homeless Children: Their Experiences*, Report to the National Inquiry into Homeless Children by the Equal Rights and Equal Opportunity Commission, Sydney, 1989.

O'Connor, T.G., Rutter, M., Beckett, C., Keaveney, L., Kreppner, J.M. & the English and Romanian Adoptees Study Team, 'The Effects of Global Severe Privation on Cognitive Competence; Extension and Longitudinal Follow-up', *Child Development*, 71, 2000, pp. 376–90.

Olds, D.L., Eckenrode, J., Henderson, C.R., Kitzman, H., Powers, J., Cole, R., Sidora, K., Morris, P., Petitt, L.M. & Luckey, D., 'Long-term Effects of Home Visitation on Maternal Life Course and Child Abuse and Neglect', *Journal of the American Medical Association*, 278, 1997, pp. 637–43.

Olson, D.H., 'Circumplex Model of Marital and Family Systems: Assessing Family Functioning', in *Normal Family Processes*, ed, F. Walsh, The Guilford Press, New York, 1993.

Olsson, M.B. & Hwang, C.P., 'Depression in Mothers and Fathers of Children with Intellectual Disability', *Journal of Intellectual Disability Research*, 45, 2001, pp. 535–43.

Osborn, A.F., Butler, N.R. & Morris, A.C., *The Social Life of Britain's Five-year-olds*, Routledge & Kegan Paul, London, 1984.

Osofsky, J.D. & Thompson, M.D., 'Adaptive and Maladaptive Parenting: Perspectives on Risk and Protective Factors', in *Handbook of Early Childhood Intervention* (2nd edn), eds, J.P. Shonkoff & S.J. Meisels, Cambridge University Press, Cambridge, 2000, pp. 54–75.

Owen, M., 'Children's Pedestrian Risk and Opportunity in a Disadvantaged Community', unpublished PhD Thesis, Macquarie University, Sydney, 2001.

Parens, E. & Ach, A., 'Disability Rights Critique of Parental Genetic Testing: Reflections and Recommendations', *Mental Retardation and Developmental Disabilities Research Reviews*, 9, 2003, pp. 40–7.

Park, J., Turnbull, A.P. & Turnbull, H.R. III., 'Impact of Poverty on Quality of Life in Families of Children with Disabilities', *Exceptional Children*, 68, 2002, pp. 151–71.

Parke, R.D., 'Fathers and Families', in *Handbook of Parenting*, vol. 3, ed, M.H. Bornstein, Lawrence Erlbaum, Mahwah, NJ, 1995, pp. 27–63.

Parke, R.D. & Buriel, R., 'Socialization in the Family: Ethnic and Ecological Perspectives', in *Handbook of Child Psychology*, ed, N. Eisenberg, Wiley, New York, 1997, pp. 463–552.

Parliament of the Commonwealth of Australia, *Boys: Getting it Right: Report on the Inquiry into the Education of Boys*, Australian Government Publishing Service, Canberra, 2002.

Patterson, C., 'Children of Lesbian and Gay Parents', *Child Development*, 63, 1992, pp. 1025–42.

Patterson, J.M., 'Chronic Illness in Children and the Impact on Families', in *Chronic Illness and Disability*, eds, C.S. Chilman, E.W. Nunally & F.M. Cox, Sage, London, 1988, pp. 69–107.

Perry, D. & Bussey, K., 'The Social Learning Theory of Sex Difference: Imitation is Alive and Well', *Journal of Personality and Psychology*, 37, 1979, pp. 1699–712.

Pettitt, F. & Wangmann, J., 'Children's Services in Other Countries', *Interim Report: Commissioned Studies*, Australian Government Publishing Service, Canberra 1996, pp. 153–74.

Pettitt, F. & Wangmann, J., 'Children's Services in Other Countries', unpublished paper prepared for Economic Planning and Advisory Council Child Care Task Force, 1996.

Phillips, D. & Howes, C., 'Indicators of Quality in Child Care: Review of Research', in *Quality in Child Care: What Does Research Tell Us?*, ed, D. Phillips, National Association for the Education of Young Children, Washington, DC, 1987.

Phillips, D.A., McCartney, K. & Scarr, S., 'Child Care Quality and Children's Social Development', *Developmental Psychology*, 23, 1987, pp. 537–43.

Pittman, J., 'Early Childhood Report', paper presented at the Isolated Children's Parents' Association 30th Annual Conference, Adelaide, <http://www.abc.net.au/rural/ICPA2001/ECE.htm11>, accessed 11 June 2003.

Plomin, D. & Daniels, D., 'Why are Children in the Same Family So Different from One Another?', *Behavioural and Brain Sciences*, 10, 1987, pp. 1–16.

Pocock, B., *The Work/Life Collision*, Federation Press, Annandale, 2003.

Power, D., 'Deaf and Hard of Hearing Students', in *Educating Children with Special Needs*, eds, A. Ashman & J. Elkins, Prentice Hall, New York, 1998, pp. 345–81.

Powers, L., 'Disability and Grief: From Tragedy to Challenge', in *Families, Disability, and Empowerment: Active Coping Skills and Strategies for Family Interventions*, eds, G. Singer & L. Powers, Paul H. Brookes, Baltimore, 1993, pp. 119–49.

Preston, N. & Symes, C., *Schools and Classrooms: A Cultural Studies Analysis of Education*, Longman, Melbourne, 1997.

Press, F. & Hayes, A., *OECD Thematic Review of Early Childhood Education and Care Policy*, Australian Background Report prepared for the Commonwealth Government of Australia, 2000.

Price, C., 'Ethnic Intermixture in Australia', *People and Place*, 2, 1993, pp. 8–10.

Provence, S. & Lipton, R., *Infants in Institutions*, International Universities Press, New York, 1962.

Pryer, J. & Rodgers, B., *Children in Changing Families: Life After Parental Separation*, Academy of the Social Sciences in Australia, 2002.

Putnam, F.W., 'Ten-year Research Update Review: Child Sexual Abuse', *Journal of the American Academy of Child & Adolescent Psychiatry*, 42, 2003, pp. 269–78.

Queensland Government, '*Disability:A Queensland Profile*', Queensland Government, Brisbane, 1999.

Quint, J.C., Bos, J.M. & Polit, D.F., New Chance: Final report on a Comprehensive Program for Young Mothers in Poverty and Their Children, Manpower Demonstration Research Corporation, <http://www.mdrc.psiweb.com/Reports/>, accessed 21 March 2000.

Racine, Y. & Boyle, M.H., 'Family Functioning and Children's Behaviour Problems', in *Vulnerable Children*, ed, J.D. Willms, University of Alberta Press, Alberta, 2002, pp. 199–209.

Radke-Yarrow, M., Richters, J. & Wilson, W.E., 'Child Development in a Network of Relationships', in *Relationships Within Families: Mutual Influences*, eds, R.A. Hinde & J. Stevenson-Hinde, Clarendon, Oxford, 1988.

Reiss, F., 'Genetic Influence on Family Systems: Implications for Development', *Journal of Marriage and the Family*, 57, 1995, pp. 543–60.

Reynolds, A. & Temple, J., 'Extended Early Childhood Intervention and School Achievement: Age Thirteen Findings from the Chicago Longitudinal Study', *Child Development*, 69, 1998, pp. 231–46.

Rice, A. & Press, F., *Early Childhood Education in New South Wales: A Comparative Report*, report for the NSW Department of Education and Training commissioned by the Strategic Research Directorate, 2003.

Richters, J.E. & Zahn-Waxler, C., 'The Infant Day Care Controversy: Current Status and Future Directions', *Early Childhood Research Quarterly*, 3, 1988, pp. 319–36.

Rigby, K., 'Psychosocial Functioning in Families of Australian Adolescent School Children Involved in Bully/Victim Problems', *Journal of Family Therapy*, 16, 1994, pp. 173–87.

Roach, M.A., Orsmond, G.I. & Barratt, M.S., 'Mothers and Fathers of Children with Down Syndrome: Parental Stress and Involvement in Childcare', *American Journal on Mental Retardation*, 104, 1999, pp. 422–36.

Robins, L. & Rutter, M., eds, *Straight and Devious Pathways from Childhood to Adulthood*, Cambridge University Press, Cambridge, 1990.

Roggmann, L.A., Langlois, J.H., Hubbs-Tait, L. & Reiser-Danner, L.A., 'Infant Day-Care Attachment and the "File Drawer Problem"', *Child Development*, 65, 1994, pp. 1429–43.

Rogoff, B., *Apprenticeship in Thinking: Cognitive Development in a Social Context*, Oxford University Press, New York, 1990.

Rogoff, B., *The Cultural Nature of Human Development*, Oxford University Press, New York, 2003.

Rose, S.J. & Meezan, W., 'Defining Child Neglect: Evolution, Influences and Issues', *Social Service Review*, 67, 1997, pp. 279–93.

Rosen, M., Clark, G. & Kivitz, M., *The History of Mental Retardation: Collected Papers*, vols. 1 & 2, University Park Press, Baltimore, 1976.

Rossi, A.S., 'Contemporary Dialogue on Civil Society and Social Responsibility', in *Caring and Doing for Others: Social Responsibility in the Domains of Family, Work and Community*, ed, A.S. Rossi, University of Chicago Press, Chicago, 2001, pp. 3–72.

Roupp, R., Travers, J., Glantz, F. & Coelen, C., *Children at the Centre: Final Report of the National Day Care Study*, Abt Associates, Cambridge, MA, 1979.

Rowland, D.T., 'Family Diversity and the Life Cycle', *Journal of Comparative Family Studies*, 12, 1991, pp. 1–14.

Rowley, C., *The Destruction of Aboriginal Society*, Penguin, Ringwood, 1970.

Royal Commission into the New South Wales Police Service, *Final Report vol. V: The Paedophile Inquiry*, 1997.

Ruopp, R., Travers, J., Glantz, F. & Coelen, C., *Children at the Center: Final Report of the National Day Care Study*, Abt Associates, Cambridge, MA, 1979.

Russell, A., 'Individual and Family Factors Contributing to Mothers' and Fathers' Positive Parenting', *International Journal of Behavioral Development*, 21, 1, 1997, pp. 111–32.

Russell, G., 'Sharing the Pleasures and Pain of Family Life', *Family Matters*, 37, 1994, pp. 13–19.

Russell, G. & Bowman, L., *Work and Family: Current Thinking, Research and Practice*, report prepared for the Department of Family and Community Services, Canberra, 2000.

Russell, P., 'Handicapped Children', in *Childcare Research, Policy and Practice*, ed, B. Kahan, Hodder & Stoughton, London, 1989.

Rutter, M., *Maternal Deprivation Re-assessed*, Penguin, New York, 1981.

Rutter, M., 'Resilience in the Face of Adversity: Protective Factors and Resistance to Psychiatric Disorder', *British Journal of Psychiatry*, 147, 1985, pp. 598–611.

Rutter, M., 'Psychosocial Resilience and Protective Mechanisms', *American Journal of Orthopsychiatry*, 57, 1987, pp. 316–31.

Rutter, M., 'Resilience Reconsidered: Conceptual Considerations, Empirical Findings, and Policy Considerations', in *Handbook of Early Childhood Intervention*, eds, J.A. Shonkoff & S.J. Meisels, Cambridge University Press, Cambridge, 2000, pp. 651–82.

Salisbury, C., 'Stressors of Parents with Young Handicapped and Nonhandicapped Children', *Journal of the Division of Early Childhood*, 11, 2, 1987, pp. 154–60.

Salmelainen, P., 'Child Neglect: Its Causes and its Role in Delinquency', *Crime and Justice Bulletin*, 33, 1996.

Sameroff, A. & Seifer, R., 'Familial Risk and Child Competence', *Child Development*, 54, 1983, pp. 1254–68.

Sanders, M.R. & Markie-Dadds, C., 'Triple P: A Multilevel Family Intervention Program for Children with Disruptive Behavior Disorders', in *Early Intervention and Prevention: Mental Health Applications of Clinical Psychology*, eds, P. Cotton & H. Jackson, Australian Psychological Society, Melbourne, 1996, pp. 59–85.

Sanson, A., *Introducing the Longitudinal Study of Australian Children*, Australian Institute of Family Studies, Melbourne, 2002.

Sawyer, M., 'Child and Adolescent Mental Health Issues: Future Directions', in *Investing in Our Children: Developing a Research Agenda*, ed, M. Prior, Academy of the Social Sciences in Australia, Canberra, 2002, pp. 83–94.

Sawyer, M. & Groves, A., *Working from the Inside: Twenty Years of the Office of the Status of Women*, Australian Government Publishing Service, Canberra, 1994.

Scarr, S., *Mother Care / Other Care*, Basic Books, New York, 1984.

Scarr, S. & Eisenberg, M., 'Child Care Research: Issues, Perspectives, and Results', *Annual Review of Psychology*, 44, 1993, pp. 613–44.

Schweinhart, L.J., Barnes, H.V. & Weikart, D.P., *Significant Benefits: The High/Scope Perry Preschool Study through Age 27*, High/Scope Press, Ypsilant, MI, 1993.

Schweinhart, L.J. & Weikart, D.P., 'A Summary of Significant Benefits: The High/Scope Perry Pre-school Study through Age 27', in *Start Right: The Importance of Early Learning*, ed, C. Ball, Royal Society for the Encouragement of Arts, Manufacture & Commerce, London, 1994, pp. 97–102.

Scott, D., 'A Vision for Family Services: Support and Prevention that Works for Families at Risk', Keynote Presentation at Forum, A Vision for Family Services and Prevention that Works for Families at Risk, Sydney, 30 April 2003a.

Scott, D., 'Opening Comments', Presented at CAFWAA Symposium, When Care is Not Enough, Canberra, 17 September 2003b.

Scott, D., Brady, S. & Glynn, P., 'New Mothers Groups as a Social Network Intervention: Consumer and Maternal Child Health Nurse Perspectives', *Australian Journal of Advanced Nursing*, 18, 4, 2001, pp. 23–9.

Scott, S., Knapp, M., Henderson, J. & Maughan, B., 'Financial Cost of Social Exclusion: Follow Up Study of Antisocial Children into Adulthood', *British Medical Journal*, 323, 2001, pp. 1–5.

Scott, D. & Swain, S., '*Confronting Cruelty: Historical Perspectives on Child Protection in Australia*', Melbourne University Press, Melbourne, 2002, p. xii.

Seagrim, G. & London, R., *Furnishing the Mind: A Comparative Study of Cognitive Development in Central Australian Aborigines*, Academic Press, Sydney, 1980.

Seligman, M. & Darling, R.B., *Ordinary Families, Special Children*, The Guilford Press, New York, 1989.

Serbin, L., Powlishta, K. & Gulko, J., 'The Development of Sex Typing in Middle Childhood', *Monographs of the Society of Research in Child Development*, 58, 2, 1993, serial no. 232.

Shapiro, J., 'Stress, Depression and Support Group Participation in Mothers of Developmentally Delayed Children', *Family Relations*, 38, 1989, pp. 169–73.

Shaver, S. & Tudball, J., *Literature Review on Factors Contributing to Community Capabilities: Final Report*, report for the Department of Family and Community, Social Policy Research Centre, University of New South Wales, Sydney, 2001.

Shaw, D.S., Gilliom, M., Ingoldsby, E.M. & Nagus, D.S., 'Trajectories Heading to School-age Conduct Problems', *Developmental Psychology*, 39, 2003, pp. 189–200.

Shepperdson, B., 'Changes in the Characteristics of Families with Down's Syndrome Children', *Journal of Epidemiology and Community Health*, 39, 1985, pp. 320–4.

Sherrod, L., 'The Role of Psychological Research in Setting a Policy Agenda for Children and Families', in 'Science for Society: Informing Policy and Practice Through Research in Developmental Psychology', A. Higgins-D'Alesssandro & K.R.B. Jankowski, eds, *New Directions for Child and Adolescent Development*, no. 98, 2002, pp. 85–94.

Shin, J.Y., 'Social Support for Families of Children with Mental Retardation: Comparison Between Korea and the United States', *Mental Retardation*, 40, 2002, pp. 103–18.

Shonkoff, J. & Phillips, D., *From Neurons to Neighbourhoods: The Science of Early Childhood Development*, National Academy Press, Washington, 2001.

Shore, R., *Rethinking the Brain: New Insights into Early Development*, Families and Work Institute, New York, 1997.

Siegal, M., 'Are Sons and Daughters Treated More Differently by Fathers than by Mothers?', *Developmental Review*, 7, 1987, pp. 183–209.

Signorella, M., Bigler, R. & Liben, L., 'Development Differences in Children's Gender Schemata about Others: A Meta-analytic Review', *Developmental Review*, 13, 1993, pp. 1106–26.

Silbereisen, R.K., Walper, S. & Albrecht, H.T., 'Family Income Loss and Economic Hardship: Antecedents of Adolescents' Problem Behavior', in Economic Stress: Effects on Family Life and Child Development, New Directions for Child Development, no. 46, eds, V.C. McLoyd & C.A. Flanagan, Jossey-Bass, San Francisco, 1990, pp. 27–46.

Silverstein, I., 'Transforming the Debate About Child Care and Maternal Employment', American Psychologist, 46, 1991, pp. 1025–32.

Simeonsson, R.J., McMillen, J.S. & Huntington, G.S., 'Secondary Conditions in Children with Disabilities: Spina Bifida as a Case Example', Mental Retardation and Developmental Disabilities Research Reviews, 8, 2002, pp. 198–205.

Sims, M. & Hutchins, T., 'The Many Faces of Child Care: Roles and Functions', Australian Journal of Early Childhood, 21, 1996, pp. 21–46.

Singer, G., Irvine, L., Irvine, B., Hawkins, N., Hegreness, J. & Jackson, R., 'Helping Families Adapt Positively to Disability: Overcoming Demoralization through Community Supports', in Families, Disability, and Empowerment: Active Coping Skills and Strategies for Family Interventions, eds, G. Singer & L. Powers, Paul H. Brookes, Baltimore, 1993, pp. 67–83.

Singer, G. & Powers, L., 'Contributing to Resilience in Families: An Overview', in Families, Disability and Empowerment: Active Coping Skills and Strategies for Family Interventions, eds, G. Singer & L. Powers, Paul H. Brookes, Baltimore, 1993, pp. 1–25.

Sloat, E. & Willms, J.D., 'A Gradient Approach to the Study of Childhood Vulnerability', in Vulnerable Children, ed, J.D. Willms, University of Alberta Press, Alberta, 2002, pp. 23–44.

Smailes, P.J., 'Socio-economic Change and Rural Morale in South Australia, 1982–1993', Journal of Rural Studies, 13, 1, 1997, pp. 19–42.

Smith, C. & Thornberry, T.P., 'The Relationship Between Childhood Maltreatment and Adolescent Involvement in Delinquency', Criminology, 33, 1995, pp. 451–81.

Smith, P.K. & Drew, L.M., 'Grandparenthood', in Handbook on Parenting: Becoming a Parent (vol. 3), ed, M.H. Bornstein, Lawrence Erlbaum, Mahwah, NJ, 2002, pp. 141–73.

Smith, S., 'Two Generation Programs: A New Intervention Strategy and Directions for Future Research', in Escape from Poverty: What Makes a Difference for Children?, ed, P.L. Chase-Lansdale & J. Brooks-Gunn, Cambridge University Press, Cambridge, 1995, pp. 299–314.

Sontag, J.C., 'Toward a Comprehensive Theoretical Framework for Disability Research: Bronfenbrenner Revisited', Journal of Special Education, 30, 3, 1996, pp. 319–44.

Spearritt, P., 'The Kindergarten Movement: Tradition and Change', in Social Change in Australia: Readings in Sociology, ed, D. Edgar, Cheshire, Melbourne, 1974, pp. 583–96.

Stainton, T. & Besser, H., 'The Positive Impact of Children with an Intellectual Disability on the Family', Journal of Intellectual & Developmental Disability, 23, 1998, pp. 57–70.

St Clair, L. & Osborne, A.F., 'The Ability and Behaviour of Children Who Have Been in Care or Separated from their Parents', Early Childhood Development and Care, Special Issue, 28, 1987.

Steele, J., 'Epidemiology: Incidence, Prevalence and Size of the Down's Syndrome Population', in New Approaches to Down Syndrome, eds, B. Stratford & P. Gunn, Cassell, London, 1996, pp. 46–72.

Steinberg, L.D., Catalano, R. & Dodley, D., 'Economic Antecedents of Child Abuse and Neglect', Child Development, 52, 1981, pp. 975–85.

Steinberg, L.D., Dornbusch, S.M. & Brown, B.B., 'Ethnic Differences in Adolescent Achievement: An Ecological Perspective', American Psychologist, 47, 1992, pp. 723–9.

Steinhauer, P.D., The Least Detrimental Alternative: A Systematic Guide to Case Planning and Decision Making for Children in Care, University of Toronto Press, Toronto, 1991.

Stephens, U., Stengthening Communities Resource Kit, NSW Premier's Department, Sydney, 2001.

Stieler, S., 'Students with Physical Disabilities', in Educating Children with Special Needs, eds, A. Ashman & J. Elkins, Prentice Hall, New York, 1998, pp. 463–519.

Stores, G. & Wiggs, L., *Sleep Disorders in Children and Adolescents with Developmental Disorders*, Mac Keith Press, London, 2001.

Stratford, B., 'In the Beginning', in *New Approaches to Down Syndrome*, eds, B. Stratford & P. Gunn, Cassell, London, 1996, pp. 3–11.

Straus, M.A., Gelles, R.J. & Steinmetz, S.K., *Behind Closed Doors: Violence in the American Family*, Anchor Books, Garden City, NJ, 1980.

Strauss, C., 'Motives and Models', in *Human Motivation and Cultural Models*, eds, R.G. D'Andrade & C. Strauss, Cambridge University Press, New York, 1992, pp. 1–20.

Strazdins, L. & Korda, R.J., 'Around-the-Clock: Parent Work Schedules and Children's Well-being in a 24-hour Economy', in Proceedings of the Work, Health and Families Forum, Canberra, August 2003, <http://www-nceph.anu.edu.au/Health_For_Life/publications>, accessed 5 May 2004.

Sultmann, C.M. & Testro, P., *Directions in Out of Home Care: Challenges and Opportunities*, PeakCare Qld Inc., Paddington, Qld, 2001.

Summers, A., *The End of Equality: Work, Babies and Women's Choices in 21st Century Australia*, Random House, Milson's Point, 2003.

Taanila, A., Syjälä, L., Kokkonen, J. & Järvelin, M.R., 'Coping of Parents with Physically and/or Mentally Disabled Children', *Child: Care, Health & Development* 28, 2002, pp. 73–86.

Tajfel, H., *Human Groups and Social Categories*, Cambridge University Press, Cambridge, 1981.

Tannen, D., 'Gender Differences in Topical Coherence: Creating Involvement in Best Friend's Talk', *Discourse Processes*, 13, 1990a, pp. 73–90.

Tannen, D., *You Just Don't Understand: Men and Women in Conversation*, Morrow, New York, 1990b.

Taussig, H.N., Clyman, R.B. & Landsverk, J., 'Children Who Return Home from Foster Care: A 6-Year Prospective Study of Behavioural Health Outcomes in Adolescence', *Pediatrics*, 108, 2001, pp. 1–7.

Taylor, A. & Birrell, B., 'Communities on the Metropolitan Periphery: The Sunshine Coast and Cranbourne Compared', paper presented at the People, Places, Partnerships Conference, University of New South Wales, Sydney, April 2003.

Taylor, J. & Fraser, A., 'Rich and Poor: Life Chances of Children in Australia', paper presented at the 8th Australian Institute of Family Studies Conference, Melbourne, April 2003.

Taylor, J. & Fraser, A., 'Eleven Plus: Life Chances and Family Income', Brotherhood of St Laurence, <http://www.bsl.org.au/pdfs/11plus.pdf>, accessed 29 August 2003.

Teghtsoonian, K., 'Neo-conservative Ideology and Opposition to Federal Regulation of Child Care Services in the United States and Canada', *Canadian Journal of Political Science*, 26, 1993, pp. 97–121.

Thoburn, J., Lewis, A. & Shemmings, D., *Paternalism or Partnership: Family Involvement in the Child Protection Process*, HMSO, London, 1995.

Thomas, D., *The Social Psychology of Childhood Disability*, Methuen, London, 1978.

Thorne, B., *Gender Play: Girls and Boys in School*, Open University Press, Buckingham, 1993.

Thornton, M.C., Chatters, L.M., Taylor, R.J. & Allen, W.R., 'Sociodemographic and Environmental Correlates of Racial Socialization by Black Parents', *Child Development*, 61, 1990, pp. 401–9.

Tizard, B., *Adoption: A Second Chance*, Open Books, London, 1977.

Tolstoy, L., *Anna Karenina*, trans. A. & L. Maude, Penguin Books, Harmondsworth, 1954 (first published 1875).

Tomison, A., 'Child Maltreatment and Substance Abuse', *National Child Protection Clearing House Discussion Paper No. 2*, Australian Institute of Family Studies, Melbourne, 1996a.

Tomison, A., 'Child Maltreatment and Mental Disorder', *National Child Protection Clearing House Discussion Paper No. 3*, Australian Institute of Family Studies, Melbourne, 1996b.

Tomison, A., 'Exploring Family Violence: Links Between Child Maltreatment and Domestic Violence', *Issues in Child Abuse Prevention*, no. 13, Australian Institute of Family Studies, Melbourne, 2000.

Tomison, M., 'Preventing Child Abuse: Changes to Family Support in the 21st Century', *National Child Protection Clearing House Issues Paper No. 17*, Australian Institute of Family Studies, Melbourne, 2002.

Toohey, M. & Beer, G., 'Is it Worth Working Now? Financial Incentives for Working Mothers Under Australia's New Tax System', paper presented at the 2003 Australian Social Policy Conference, Sydney, July 2003.

Traci, M.A., Seekins, T., Szalda-Petree, A. & Ravesloot, C., 'Assessing Secondary Conditioning Among Adults with Developmental Disabilities: A Preliminary Study', *Mental Retardation*, 40, 2002, pp. 119–31.

Tremblay, R.E., Pagani-Kurtz, L., Masse, L.C., Vitaro, F. & Pihl, R.O., 'A Bimodal Preventive Intervention for Disruptive Kindergarten Boys: Its Impact Through Mid-adolescence', *Journal of Consulting and Clinical Psychology*, 63, 4, 1995, pp. 560–8.

UNICEF, *Official Summary: The State of the World's Children*, UNICEF, New York, 2003.

United States Advisory Board on Child Abuse and Neglect, *Child Abuse and Neglect: Critical First Steps in Response to a National Emergency*, US Government Printing Office, Washington, DC, 1990.

Valsiner, J., 'Two Alternative Epistemological Frameworks in Psychology: The Typological and Variational Modes of Thinking', *Journal of Mind and Behavior*, 5, 1984, pp. 449–70.

Vandell, D.L. & Corasaniti, M.A., 'Child Care and the Family: Complex Contributors to Child Development', in *Child Care and Maternal Employment: A Social Ecology Approach*, ed, K. McCartney, 1990.

Vandell, D.L., Henderson, V.K. & Wilson, K., 'A Follow-up Study of Children in Excellent, Moderate, and Poor Quality Child Care', paper presented at the Biennial Meeting of the Society for Research in Child Development, Baltimore, MD, April 1987.

Vandell, D.L., Henderson, V.K. & Wilson, K., 'A Longitudinal Study of Children with Child Care Experiences of Varying Quality', *Child Development*, 59, 1988, pp. 1286–92.

van Krieken, R., *Children and the State*, Allen & Unwin, Sydney, 1991.

Vardon, S., *Report from the Australian Remote and Isolated Children's and Family Services Mobile Muster*, CONTACT, Birdsville, 1991.

Vaughan, G.M., 'A Social Psychological Model of Ethnic Identity and Development', in *Children's Ethnic Socialization: Pluralism and Development*, eds, J.S. Phinney & M.J. Rotheran, Sage, Newbury Park, CA, 1987, pp. 73–91.

Vig, S. & Kaminer, R., 'Maltreatment and Developmental Disabilities in Children', *Journal of Developmental and Physical Disabilities*, 14, 2002, pp. 371–86.

Vimpani, G., 'How Can We Improve Access to Services for Families with Young Children? The Need for New Models of Interagency Collaboration', paper presented at the Fifth Australian Family Research Conference, Brisbane, 1996.

Vimpani, G., Frederico, M. & Barclay, L., *An Audit of Home Visitor Programs and the Development of an Evaluation Framework*, Report commissioned under the auspices of the National Child Protection Council by the Department of Health and Family Services, 1996.

Vinson, T., *Reports of the Inquiry into the Provision of Public Education in New South Wales*, NSW Teachers Federation and Federation of P & C Associations of NSW, Sydney, 2002.

Vinson, T., Baldry, E. & Hargreaves, J., 'Neighbourhoods, Networks, and Child Abuse', *British Journal of Social Work*, 26, 1996, pp. 523–43.

Vygotsky, L., *Mind in Society: The Development of Higher Psychological Processes*, Harvard University Press, Cambridge, MA, 1978.

Wangmann, J., 'Towards Integration and Quality Assurance in Children's Services', AIFS Early Childhood Study Paper No. 6, Australian Institute of Family Studies, Melbourne, 1995.

Warfield, M.E., 'Employment, Parenting, and Well-being Among Mothers of Children with Disabilities', *Mental Retardation*, 39, 2001, pp. 297–309.

Watamura, S.E., Donzella, B., Alwin, J. & Gunnar, M.R., 'Morning-to-afternoon Increases in Cortisol Concentrations for Infants and Toddlers at Child Care: Age Differences and Behavioural Correlates,' *Child Development*, 74, 2003, pp. 1006–20.

Waterman, A., 'Identity Development from Adolescence to Adulthood', *Developmental Psychology*, 18, 1982, pp. 341–58.

Watson, I., Buchanan, J., Campbell, I. & Briggs, C., *Fragmented Futures: New Challenges in Working Life*, Federation Press, Annandale.

Watson, J., 'Determined to be Self-determined', paper presented at the Frozen Futures Conference, Sydney, November 2002.

Watson, N., 'Well, I Know This is Going to Sound Very Strange to You, But I Don't See Myself as a Disabled Person: Identity and Disability', *Disability and Society*, 17, 2002, pp. 509–27.

Wearne, J., 'Local Government in Rural and Remote Communities', in *Rural Communities Looking Ahead: Papers, Abstracts and Notes from the New South Wales Rural Social Policy Conference*, Dubbo, 1995, pp. 28–31.

Weatherburn, D. & Lind, B., *Social and Economic Stress, Child Neglect and Juvenile Delinquency*, NSW Bureau of Crime Statistics and Research, Sydney, 1997.

Webber, R., 'Life in Step Families: Conceptions and Misconceptions', in *Images of Australian Families*, ed, K. Funder, Longman Cheshire, Melbourne, 1991, pp. 88–101.

Weikart, D.P. & Schweinhart, L.J., 'High/Scope Preschool Program Outcomes', in *Preventing Antisocial Behavior: Interventions from Birth through Adolescence*, eds, J. McCord & R.E. Tremblay, The Guilford Press, New York, 1992, pp. 67–88.

Weinrub, M., Horrath, D.L. & Gringlas, M.B., 'Single Parenthood', in *Handbook of Parenting, Vol. 3, Being and Becoming a Parent*, ed, M.H. Bornstein, Lawrence Erlbaum, Mahwah, NJ, 2002, pp. 109–40.

Wellesley, B., 'Connecting with Good Beginnings', *Every Child*, 8, 2002, pp. 10–11.

Wenger, E., *Communities of Practice: Learning Meaning and Identity*, New York, Cambridge University Press, 1998.

Werner, E.E., 'Risk, Resilience and Recovery: Perspectives from the Kauai Longitudinal Study', *Developmental Psychopathology*, 5, 1993, pp. 503–15.

Werner, E.E. & Smith, R.S., *Kauai's Children Come of Age*, University of Hawaii Press, Honolulu, HI, 1977.

Werner, E.E. & Smith, R.S., *Vulnerable but Invincible*, Wiley, New York, 1982.

Werner, E.E. & Smith, R.S., *Vulnerable but Invincible: A Longitudinal Study of Resilient Children and Youth*, Adams-Bannister-Cox, New York, 1989.

Werner, E.E. & Smith, R.S., *Overcoming the Odds: High Risk Children from Birth to Adulthood*, Cornell University Press, Ithaca, NY, 1992.

Wessels, H., Lamb, M.E. & Hwang, C.P., 'Cause and Causality in Daycare Research: An Investigation of Group Differences in Swedish Child Care', *European Journal of Psychology of Education*, XI, 1996, pp. 231–45.

Weston, R., Qu, L. & Soriano, G., 'Implications of Men's Extended Work Hours', *Family Matters*, 61, 2002, pp. 18–25.

Whipple, E.E. & Webster-Stratton, C., 'The Role of Parental Stress in Physically Abusive Families', *Child Abuse & Neglect*, 15, 1991, pp. 279–91.

Whitebrook, M., Howes, C. & Phillips, D., *Who Cares? Child Care Teachers and the Quality of Care in America*, final report of the National Child Care Staffing Study, Child Care Employee Project, Oaklands, CA, 1990.

Wicker, A.W., *An Introduction to Ecological Psychology*, Cambridge University Press, Cambridge, 1979.

Wilkinson, J.E., Kelly, B. & Stephen, C., 'A Participatory Methodology for the Evaluation of Innovation in the Context of the Integrated Pre-school Services', *Early Child Development and Care*, 108, 1995, pp. 35–49.

Wolfe, D.A., 'Child-abusive Parents: An Empirical Review and Analysis', *Psychological Bulletin*, 97, 1985, pp. 462–82.

Wong, L.Y. &. Paulozzi, L.J., *International Classifications of Functioning, Disability and Health*, WHO, Geneva, 2001.

Wylie, C., Thompson, J. & Hendricks, A.K., *Competent Children at 5: Families and Early Education*, NZCER, Wellington, 1997.

Zigler, E. & Hall, N., *Child Development and Social Policy*, McGraw-Hill, New York, 2000.

Zigler, E. & Styfco, S.J., 'Using Research and Theory to Justify and Inform Head Start Expansion', *Social Policy Report*, vol. vii, no. 2, Society for Research in Child Development, Washington, 1993.

Zimmerman, M.A. & Arunkumar, R., 'Resiliency Research: Implications for Schools and Policy', *Social Policy Report*, VIII, no. 4, Society for Research in Child Development, Ann Arbor, MI, 1994.

Index